CP 2204

D1346527

Paper Bullets

Paper Bullets

Print and Kingship under Charles II

Harold Weber

THE UNIVERSITY PRESS OF KENTUCKY

Copyright © 1996 by The University Press of Kentucky

Scholarly publisher for the Commonwealth,
serving Bellarmine College, Berea College, Centre
College of Kentucky, Eastern Kentucky University,
The Filson Club, Georgetown College, Kentucky
Historical Society, Kentucky State University,
Morehead State University, Murray State University,
Northern Kentucky University, Transylvania University,
University of Kentucky, University of Louisville,
and Western Kentucky University

Editorial and Sales Offices: The University Press of Kentucky
663 South Limestone Street, Lexington, Kentucky 40508-4008

Library of Congress Cataloging-in-Publication Data

Weber, Harold.
    Paper bullets : print and kingship under Charles II / Harold
Weber.
        p.   cm.
    Includes bibliographical references and index.
    ISBN 0-8131-1929-4 (alk. paper)
    1. Great Britain—History—Charles II, 1660-1685—Historiography.
2. Journalism—Political aspects—Great Britain—History—17th
century. 3. English literature—Early modern, 1500-1700—History
and criticism. 4. Printing—Political aspects—Great Britain—
History—17th century. 5. Politics and literature—Great Britain
—History—17th century. 6. Charles II, King of England, 1630-1685
—In literature. 7. Censorship—Great Britain—History—17th
century. 8. Monarchy—Great Britain—History—17th century.
9. Kings and rulers in literature. I. Title.
DA445.W43   1996
941.06'6—dc20   95-14184

This book is printed on acid-free recycled paper meeting the requirements of the
American National Standard for Permanence of Paper for Printed Library Materials.

Contents

Illustrations

Acknowledgments

It is a great pleasure to thank Elizabeth A. Meese and David Lee Miller, who were there for the long haul on this one. Over the many years when this book was being conceived, written, and revised, they have proven themselves to be demanding readers, wise counselors, and patient friends: Aces of Cups both. Brean Hammond, Gerald M. MacLean, and Ellen Rosenman provided helpful and suggestive criticisms of the manuscript in its final stages. I began this book while a member of a study group at the University of Alabama, and I'd like to thank the individuals who made the group so important in the initial stages of this project: Lynne Adrian, Rhoda Johnson, Steve Karatheodoris, Francesca Kazan, Elizabeth A. Meese, Sharon O'Dair, and Alice Parker. Colleagues in the English department have been supportive throughout—particularly Pat Hermann, who first alerted me to the importance of Alfred and his burnt cakes; Joe Hornsby, who weighed in with sound advice about medieval law; and Sharon O'Dair, whose sophistication about matters of class, rank, and hierarchy saved me from many an embarrassing error. Richard Lachmann, a colleague for only a week while attending a symposium at the University of Alabama, nonetheless provided a helpful reading of the chapter on the king's touch.

Claudia Johnson was chair of the Department of English during the book's composition. Her ferocious commitment to research, administrative expertise, and political sophistication allowed me to complete the book in a timely fashion. Many thanks to Virginia Blum and Ellen Rosenman for first introducing me to the University Press of Kentucky. Research for the project was carried out at the British Library and William Andrews Clark Memorial Library; staffs at both were friendly, helpful, and knowledgeable. Matthew Miller and Lisa Broome have been excellent research assistants.

The first chapter is a revised and expanded version of an essay that originally appeared in *Studies in Philology* 85 (1988): 489-509, while pieces of chapter 3 first appeared in *Criticism* 32 (1990): 193-221, and *Cultural Readings of Restoration and Eighteenth-Century English Theater*, ed. J. Douglas Canfield and Deborah C. Payne (Athens: University of Georgia Press, 1995). I am obliged to them for permission to republish this material here. All photographs have been reproduced by permission of the British Library.

The University of Alabama has been particularly generous with funds that allowed me to pursue my research. Grants from the Research Grants Committee for the summers of 1986-1988 and 1990, as well as a Cecil and Ernest Williams Faculty Enhancement Award for 1991-1992, provided necessary support for travel and research.

Finally, since most of this book was written during my peripatetic summers, sabbaticals, and leaves, I want to end by thanking those friends who shared with me their homes and geographies, providing comfortable spaces where I was able to work productively and happily: Ross and Brenda in Poplar Point, Manitoba; Sally and Jeffrey in Kuau and Haiku, Maui; Chase and Russell in Keene, New York; Francesca in Richmond, Surrey; and Maire in Kensal Rise, London.

Introduction

For all the variety, even tumultuousness of his life—the years in exile, the execution of his father, the battle of and escape from Worcester, the innumerable mistresses, the twenty-five years of rule—Charles's Restoration remains the most dramatic event in his biography, the incandescent moment that defines his uniqueness as an English monarch. Whether we restrict his return to simply the instant described by Pepys, when Charles first touched English soil as its "legitimate" sovereign, or extend it to include his triumphant progress to and eventual entrance into London, these three accounts of that "moment" of return suggest its genuine complexity, the weight of history on an event celebrated as history even as it occurred:

> . . . and so got on shore when the King did, who was received by Generall Monke with all imaginable love and respect at his entrance upon the land at Dover. Infinite the Croud of people and the gallantry of the Horsmen, Citizens, and Noblemen of all sorts.
>
> The Mayor of the town came and gave him his white staffe, the badge of his place, which the King did give him again. The Mayor also presented him from the town a very rich Bible, which he took and said it was the thing that he loved above all things in the world. . . .
>
> The Shouting and joy expressed by all is past imagination.[1]

From *Canterbury* he came, on *Monday*, to *Rochester*, where the people had hung up, over the midst of the streets, as he rode, many beautifull Garlands, curiously made up with costly scarfs and ribbens, decked with spoons and bodkins of silver, and small plate of several sorts; and some with gold chains, in like sort as at *Canterbury*; each striving to outdoe other in all expressions of joy. . . . on which spacious plain [the farther side of *Black-heath*] he found divers great and eminent Troops of Horse, in a most splendid and glorious equipage; and a kind of rurall Triumph,

exprest by the Country swains, in a Morrice-dance with the old Musique
of Taber and Pipe; which was performed with all agility and cheerfulness
imaginable.[2]

This day came in his Majestie *Charles* the 2d to London after a sad, &
long Exile, and Calamitous Suffering both of the King & Church: being
17 yeares. . . . I stood in the strand, & beheld it, & blessed God: And all
this without one drop of bloud, & by that very army, which rebell'd
against him: but it was the Lords doing, *et mirabile in oculis nostris*: for
such a Restauration was never seene in the mention of any history,
antient or modern, since the returne of the *Babylonian* Captivity, nor so
joyfull a day, & so bright, ever seene in this nation: this hapning when
to expect or effect it, was past all humane policy.[3]

Pepys's diary entry for that day attests to the vertiginous nervous
excitement of this unlooked-for and, to Charles's supporters, miraculous
occurrence, not only the enormity of his Restoration, but the sheer
wonder of it, its inexplicable mystery to those who had so long anticipated his return. The "infinite" crowds, the "Shouting and joy . . . past
imagination," reflect some of this astonishment, the noise, joy, and
frenzy providing an inarticulate version of Evelyn's moving reflections
four days later. In Evelyn's account this consciousness of the unexplain-
able shapes itself against the turbulence of "brandish[ed] swords," "unexpressable joy," "wayes straw'd with flowers," "bells ringing,"
"Trumpets, Musick, & myriads of people flocking the streetes." Both
observers, two of the finest diarists in the language, marvel at a moment
that they insist cannot be interpreted; the Restoration transcends linguistic apprehension, so miraculous that it cannot be captured by
language; its nature is "past imagination," "past all humane policy,"
"unexpressable."

Yet all three descriptions reveal as well just how firmly the iconic
splendor of Stuart court pageantry gave formal expression to this chaotic
emotional intensity. All three accounts are structured around the careful
juxtaposition between the unbridled excitement of the celebrating
masses and the elaborate processions and gallant rituals that visibly
manifest the return of measure and harmony. The potentially disruptive
enthusiasm that has driven the nation for twenty years can now be
contained, made productive by a king whose person represents a spiritual
power previously absent from the kingdom. In surrendering his staff, the
mayor acknowledges the now potent authority of the fourteen-year exile
and wanderer; in presenting a Bible he both confirms the returning

king's status as God's anointed on earth and also asserts his hope that God's word will guide Charles's reign. Charles's pious, formulaic response emphasizes the theatrical nature of this exchange, the way in which the dramatic spectacle creates a quiet, ordered space within the tumult, a focal point for the otherwise unruly energies of the day.

Charles here dramatizes his own kingship, representing it in a theatrical ceremony whose gestures were choreographed a century before by Elizabeth. Her official passage through London on 14 January 1559, the day before her coronation, was deliberately presented as a dramatic event in its own right, not simply as an introduction to her coronation. Her progress that day, as she beheld her subjects from a golden litter, was periodically interrupted by sundry entertainments and pageant devices. At the Little Conduit in Cheapside, two figures, Time and his daughter Truth, approached the queen and presented her with an English Bible: "as soone as she had received the booke, [she] kyssed it, and with both her handes held up the same, and so laid it upon her brest, with great thankes to the citie therfore."[4] Like Elizabeth before, Charles affirms that he will be guided by Truth and her Word, the theatrical moment a dramatic representation of his monarchical power and responsibility.

Charles's reiteration of Elizabeth's dramatic text reveals the extent to which he inherited upon his return a sophisticated court art that through acts of theatrical self-presentation, particularly civic pageantry and court masque, projected an idealized courtly mythology. Certainly the passage in *Englands Joy* reveals how that pageantry attempted to encompass the entire kingdom, providing a ritualistic way to embrace both high—"great and eminent Troops of Horse, in a most splendid and glorious equipage"—and low—"a kind of rurall Triumph, exprest by the Country swains, in a Morrice-dance with the old Musique of Taber and Pipe"—city and country, new and old. The attention paid here to the traditional festive culture disdained by Puritan authorities reveals as well some of the social values involved in the struggle between king and Parliament, and the way in which Charles's return seemed to assure that culture's triumph.[5]

These elaborate and self-conscious ceremonies display an immense social and cultural power, which Charles attempted to exploit, according to Paula R. Backscheider, by transforming London into a "national theater" that could help both secure his throne and affirm his interpretation of monarchy.[6] Yet in fashioning and maintaining Charles's restored royal identity, these public spectacles are no more important than their description in *Englands Joy*, the printed representation as politically significant as the splendid and costly celebrations themselves. *Englands Joy* must be considered apart from the diary entries of Pepys and Evelyn, its publication following the king's return marking it as a significantly different type of text. The diary entries of Pepys and Evelyn represent private expressions of individual belief, their many evasions and mystifications—the pretense of universal joy, of a bloodless transfer of authority, of the miraculousness of a historical incident without precedent or explanation—indicative of their desire to vindicate their own faith in Charles by removing the Restoration from the realm of mundane and sordid politics, individual greed, ambition, and fear. Their rhetoric attempts to cheat time by marginalizing the important changes that had taken place in England during the twenty years since 1640; they wish to celebrate the fact of Charles's Restoration while at the same time ignoring its historical implications, transforming Charles's return from a historical to a mythical event, from a contingent reality dependent on accident and force to the inevitable assumption of a timeless identity and right.

   Englands Joy, to be sure, participates in these same obfuscations, but it does so not simply out of the desire to justify personal beliefs and political commitments—though for the anonymous author that may very well have conditioned the writing and publication of such a work—but in order to help or convince or seduce others to share in those beliefs and commitments. As a printed text, published through a commercial London press in the months following Charles's return, *Englands Joy* and texts like it become, as Buchanan Sharp insists, "evidence of attempts to shape popular opinion on issues rather than as genuine expressions of that opinion."[7] Sharp's emphasis on "genuine expressions" should not blind us to the recognition that persuasive rhetoric might be as "genuine" as private, or that the rhetoric of private meditation is as fully mediated as that of public celebration. Yet unlike the private writing of Pepys and Evelyn, the public status of *Englands Joy* allows it to constitute the very triumph it ostensibly only describes; like the theatrical event that it represents, the printed text is performative, creating history in the very act of simply narrating it.

This relationship between print and history, which today we take for granted, was hardly twenty years old when Charles returned to claim his throne. The Restoration generated a quantity of publication, a sheer mass of print, equaled by only two or three other events during the seventeenth century: the Civil War, Exclusion Crisis, and Glorious Revolution were defined as well by their participation in a print culture that had not existed before 1641.[8] Indeed, these events mark the first time in England when history cannot be understood, or even imagined, apart from the printed word: they might very well have not occurred and certainly would have assumed very different forms had there existed no print industry in England. This book examines the relationship between this print culture and the kingship of Charles II, between the intersecting historical evolutions of an ancient political institution and a young commercial industry. The transformation of the English monarchy during the seventeenth century was not simply played out against a backdrop of changes in the production, marketing, and consumption of printed matter, but was itself part of these very changes. My book takes its shape from these two related processes of historical and cultural change.

The monarchy, of course, had from the start played an important role in fashioning the print trade in England: as early as 1538—not fifty years after the establishment of the first press in the country—a proclamation of Henry VIII formalized government control over all printing. During the course of the next century, successive monarchs regulated the industry in ways that shaped the administration and nature of both commercial printing and state power. Such regulation, predicated since 1557 on an alliance between the crown, ecclesiastical officials, and the Stationers' Company, had never achieved complete control over the press: both Puritans and Catholics maintained secret minority presses, and during the first decades of the seventeenth century, more than half the books published appear to have evaded the official licensing system.[9] A long list of proclamations issued by every monarch from Henry VIII to Charles I attests to royal frustration with the "itching in the tongues and pennes of most men" (James I, 1610), the "erroneous opinions . . . sown and spread by blasphemous and pestiferous books" (Henry VIII, 1530).[10] For all of its grumbling, however, the crown remained master of the press, severely limiting both the growth of the industry and the dissemination of its products.

The extent of the government's success may be measured by what resulted from Parliament's abolition on 5 July 1641 of the Court of Star Chamber, which effectively ended the crown's ability to censor the press. David Cressy has computed that England underwent an almost tenfold expansion of print after 1640, an average of three hundred thousand volumes a year published during the period 1576–1640 becoming two million or more between 1640 and 1660.[11] In 1640 George

Thomason purchased twenty-two books or pamphlets dealing with political matters; during the crisis year of 1642 he collected 1,966, and for the entire period 1640–1661 he assembled nearly fifteen thousand pamphlets. The first newspaper dealing with domestic English news went on sale in November 1641; by the first week of 1644, Londoners could choose from a dozen English newspapers. Thomason collected 4 news-sheets in 1641, 167 in 1642, and 722 in 1645, eventually acquiring more than seven thousand by 1661.[12] Such numbers can be contrasted to H.S. Bennett's survey of the titles in the *Short-Title Catalogue*, where an increase from 46 in 1500, to 259 in 1600, to 577 in 1640 reveals the steady, plodding growth of an industry granted an illusory stability by a monarchy concerned to regulate everything from the number of master printers to the number of presses they might own and the number of apprentices they might employ.[13]

Such figures are astonishing, the scale of the increases only the crudest indication of the revolutionary character of the new relationship between not just monarchical but all political authority and the printed word. Prior to the assumption of power by the Stuarts, writing on topical political events was essentially unknown in England. The official government newsletter rarely referred to current domestic political matters; newspapers normally reported only on foreign affairs; panegyric and heroic poetry conventionally eschewed sustained attention to contemporary history; verse satire tended toward the typical rather than the topical; the writing of history focused primarily on the past.[14] The unprecedented intervention of the press into the growing conflict between king and Parliament in 1641 proved instrumental in the creation of contemporary history, a discursive field within which political authority had now necessarily to act.[15] After 1641 London's print industry could no longer simply be "silenced," the historical present ignored, banished, or disregarded; competing accounts of current political events became a necessary condition for the achievement and maintenance of power. Roger L'Estrange, the chief censor during most of Charles II's reign, suggests his unwilling recognition of this fact when he introduced the first issue of his official newspaper, *The Intelligencer* (31 August 1663), by announcing his disdain for such a task: "A *Publick Mercury* should never have *My Vote*; because I think it makes the *Multitude* too *Familiar* with the *Actions*, and *Counsels* of their *Superiors*." He publishes, however, because he must "*Redeem* the *Vulgar* from their *former Mistakes*, and *Delusions*. . . . the *Common People* . . . are much more Capable of being *tuned*, and *wrought upon*, by convenient *Hints*, and *Touches*, in the *Shape*, and *Ayre* of a *Pamphlet*, than by the *strongest Reasons*, and *best Notions imaginable*."[16] The Parliament and lord protector, as well as Charles II, would all labor with varying degrees of success to "master" the press, but after 1641 such attempts inevitably depended on the press itself; competing versions of contemporary history "in the *Shape*, and *Ayre* of a *Pamphlet*" became the very ground of political debate.

Understandings of history itself changed significantly during the seventeenth century, to some extent as a result of this inclusion of the present in the historiographic imagination. Providential interpretations of history increasingly came under attack by "rational" attempts to discover causality in matters of state and governmental relations.[17] Providential history, of course, did not lose its explanatory power all at once during the seventeenth century, but it became only one among competing historical models. Richard Ollard, in fact, in his study of the two Charleses, has suggested that changing conceptions of history distinguish father from son, Charles I convinced that the slow unfolding of God's judgment defined history, Charles II that it was a secular and rational process.[18]

Another historian, Gordon Wood, argues that the conspiratorial fears that characterize Restoration politics, the many plots and intrigues that litter Charles's reign, indicate the presence not only of new conceptions of history but of a new type of politics: "the conspiratorial interpretations of the Augustan Age flowed from the expansion and increasing complexity of the political world. . . . Relationships between superiors and subordinates, rulers and ruled, formerly taken for granted, now became disturbingly problematical."[19] Wood's sense of the "expansion" of Restoration politics seems to me crucial, for both a cause and consequence of the press's involvement in the formulation and interpretation of contemporary history was the creation of a new and literate public determined to participate in political decisions.

The extraordinary increases in publication during the early 1640s only make sense in the context of a substantial audience interested in, and prepared to buy, the new products of an aggressive print industry. Although literacy remains a difficult skill to measure at three centuries remove, current scholarship—linking literacy to the ability to sign one's name—suggests that the first three-quarters of the seventeenth century saw a substantial and unprecedented rise in the ability to read and write in England. According to Lawrence Stone, the literacy rate for adult males in England and Wales had perhaps doubled between 1600 and

1675, from 25 to 45 percent.[20] Though women certainly lagged behind men, David Cressy estimates that they made rapid progress during the last three decades of the seventeenth century: while women "were almost universally unable to write their own names" during the sixteenth and early seventeenth centuries, 22 percent could sign in the 1670s, 36 percent in the 1680s, and 48 percent during the 1690s.[21] In *Before Novels: The Cultural Contexts of Eighteenth-Century English Fiction*, J. Paul Hunter presents an impressive summarization and interpretation of contemporary research into English literacy; he concludes that "the steepest acceleration in literacy occurred early on in the seventeenth century," characterizing the years between James I and Charles II as "the linguistic divide."[22]

Moreover, these gains in literacy occurred in portions of the population below the top rank. Cressy estimates that by 1630 almost all gentlemen could read, thus implying that the middling ranks of society and women enjoyed the greatest increases in literacy between 1630 and 1675.[23] During the mid-seventeenth century the print trade produced a greater number of titles and volumes for a readership expanding both in size and social range, particularly in London, which possessed a literate public proportionally far greater than the rest of the kingdom. Peter Burke notes that in an early seventeenth-century sample, 76 percent of the craftsmen and shopkeepers in the city could sign their name, while Valerie Pearl suggests that seventeenth-century London possessed more grammar and private schools than would exist again before the twentieth century, more bookshops per capita than exist today.[24] The shift from an oral to a literate culture that had begun even before the sixteenth century accelerated rapidly during the seventeenth century, the political, social, and economic worlds of Restoration England increasingly dominated by the printed word, which became essential to the transmission of ideas and values, the figuration of authority and power.

By 1660, of course, the printing press had not transformed England from an oral to a print culture. Oral traditions proved exceedingly durable, the vitality of seventeenth-century England perhaps contributable to a dynamic interaction between the two cultures, "a constant feeding from the one to the other."[25] In mid-century England, elegantly produced and very expensive examples of the book arts jostled in the marketplace with the cheap ballads and chapbooks of hawkers and pedlars and the manuscripts of writers who either saw no need to commit themselves to publication, or because of government censorship were afraid to do so.[26] Hybrid forms could result from the interplay between the two worlds, the printed sermon, for example, which made the pulpit even more influential in the forming of opinion, the printed ballad, which reached both literate and illiterate audiences, or, in the political realm, popular demonstrations that depended equally on both mass gatherings in the streets and the collection of petitions to make their point.[27] Insisting on an absolute and unnatural distinction between the oral and the written does considerable violence to English culture in the seventeenth century; so rich and productive is the rapport between these two that at times I will go beyond my primary concern with print and consider as well the circulation of manuscripts, the role of the coffeehouse in the dissemination of published and unpublished literature, the political and cultural significance of trials, demonstrations, progresses, and court rituals. Though I maintain that print was integral to the processes that generated royal authority, I nonetheless recognize the important part played by other media in generating and diffusing the royal identity. The image building of Charles's government was conducted through a variety of forms that included both the oral and the performative. Print must be situated within a wider range of aesthetic, social, and cultural practices that Charles employed to enforce his vision of monarchy.

The "leveling tendency" of print, which, according to Gerald MacLean, was recognized and often deplored during the seventeenth century,[28] along with the vigorous engagement between the print trade and an older oral culture, helped to create a new political consciousness in the nation, a popular political culture formed by a concerned and active citizenry of an unprecedented size and awareness.[29] English monarchs, of course, had always regarded matters of state as part of their personal prerogative; the monarch was the state, jealously resisting even the intrusion of Parliament into royal affairs. The creation of a public determined to participate in the political world did not happen in an instant; we probably cannot even point with certainty to an originary moment. Jurgen Habermas argues that in Great Britain the turn of the eighteenth century marks the creation of "a public sphere that functioned in the political realm"; Buchanan Sharp suggests that "an upsurge in both the expression and the prosecution of seditious words" during the period 1640–1660 defines those years as a "turning point in the political education of large segments of the English population"; and Franco Moretti has declared that Elizabethan and Jacobean tragedy, in fact, provided a decisive influence in constituting a public "that for the first time in history assumed the right to bring a king to justice."[30]

There can be no single historical moment when an abstract entity such as "the public" takes concrete form. But if we imagine some type of progression from Moretti's spectator public—situated within a theater in which "all the world's a stage"—to what Habermas describes as "the public sphere in the world of letters," the print industry will have played a crucial role in its development and enlargement.[31] In trying to describe the reading public that so enthusiastically welcomed the novel, J. Paul Hunter has posited a late seventeenth-century audience of "ambitious, aspiring, mobile, and increasingly urban young people, both men and women," a "distinctive youth culture [that] was beginning to have an effect on the marketplace, including the intellectual marketplace and the world of booksellers and print."[32]

This public had a significant effect not only on the intellectual but on the political marketplace; concerned not simply with new forms of reading, but new forms of politics, they confronted Charles almost from the moment of his return with a "public opinion" that existed for no previous monarch.[33] Valerie Pearl has shown how the precinct and ward in seventeenth-century London provided not only a high degree of citizen participation in matters of local government and administration, but "an arena for public opinion—a platform from which popular views could be put before the Court of the Lord Mayor and Aldermen."[34] And recently Tim Harris, in his study of the London crowd, has argued that ordinary people, "the middling sort" that would include shopkeepers, tradesmen, and craftsmen, "had a more important political role than is normally conceded. . . . they were capable of coordinating direct political action themselves; and [displayed] a high degree of political awareness . . . even amongst quite lowly groups."[35] During the Exclusion Crisis the establishment of the first political parties gave concrete form to this new politics, which, along with the new reading public, defines the uniqueness of Charles's reign, the special responsibilities, dangers, and opportunities that he faced as a monarch whose royal identity was to a great extent constituted in print, embodied in the mass of political and literary material generated during his reign.

To a large degree the evolution of this civic sphere of print, parties, and public corresponds to and plays a part in what Franco Moretti has called "the deconsecration of sovereignty." There can be little doubt that the Civil War years and execution of Charles I signal an alteration in conceptions of the monarchy, its sacred and divine character questioned by the radical politics of mid-century England. "This Bloody Stroke being struck upon the Royal Neck . . . it seemed rather to fall upon the People than the King; for as soon as it fell upon his Neck, the People cryed out." This contemporary reaction to the regicide suggests a unity between people and monarch, country and king, that seemed even at the time to be irrevocably sundered at that moment when Charles's head was separated from his body: "we lost our king, / And in Him lost our selves."[36]

Charles II returns to a throne no longer buttressed quite so firmly by divinely sanctioned hierarchies or transcendent providential design. Even as staunch a supporter of the king as Pepys, at the very moment he describes the king's triumphant landing, registers the complexity of his attitudes to the royal body and what it represents: "About noon (though the Brigantine that Beale made was there ready to carry him [the king]), yet he would go in my Lord's barge with the two Dukes; . . . I went, and Mr. Mansell and one of the King's footmen, with a dog that the King loved (which shit in the boat, which made us laugh and me think that a King and all that belong to him are but just as others are)."[37] Pepys's ability, even in the midst of his breathless excitement, to assert the equality of monarch and subject suggests his ambivalent perceptions of the divine monarchy that Charles returned to claim. This unexpected movement from excrement to kingship calls into question the hierarchical structures that the day's festivities and rituals affirm.

Yet like the popular oral culture of which it was a part, the divine kingship proved surprisingly durable, surviving even the execution of Charles I, whose invocation as the royal martyr in *Eikon Basilike* reinvigorated the divine magic of monarchy. Christopher Hill cautions that we "must never forget the strength of monarchy's appeal to ordinary people, which is one of the most difficult things for us to grasp about the collapse of the English republic."[38] But even Hill's warning suffers from a condescension that suggests a failure to appreciate the depths of the English need for a sacred figure to animate the structures of society and embody a unitary polity untouched by the momentous dislocations of Civil War and protectorate; Pepys and Evelyn were far from "ordinary people," and their responses to Charles's Restoration demonstrate that the offer of a crown to Cromwell was not a political freak or aberration. Many in England preferred to believe in a world that had been lost; indeed, few would have shared the twentieth-century historian's comfortable certainty that a world had been lost at all.

The sacred authority of the throne, in fact, rarely passed from monarch to monarch without a struggle; successive kings and queens had always to refashion the royal ideology in their own particular image, corresponding to the novel historical and personal circumstances of their assumption of power. Recent scholarship, for example, has recognized the particular difficulties confronting Elizabeth, a woman attempting to locate her majesty within patriarchal structures of authority.[39] The problems confronting Charles as he endeavored to fabricate his royal identity were certainly unique, but they did not prevent him from manipulating the signs and symbols of sacred authority employed by his forebears.

What distinguishes Charles's reign from those of his predecessors is not, therefore, the need to rejuvenate an "older" language of sanctified kingship—which would not have appeared "older" to the king or most of his contemporaries, and which each monarch had necessarily to make his or her own—but the new means at hand to exploit its tropes. Charles attempted to fashion his own semiotics of power by utilizing and manipulating the transformations in the political realm that had turned his world upside down. The press that had helped bring down his father could be turned on his enemies, its power to subvert royal authority converted into a support and bulwark. The resources of a newly powerful print industry became essential to the "manipulated monarchy" that Christopher Hill sees as one consequence of the Civil War.[40] Indeed, the versatile and plastic nature of print culture is exemplified during this period of its burgeoning power, for in the last half of the seventeenth century, it proved integral to the survival and transmission of both royalist and nonconformist culture.[41] In the words of Richard Kroll, "the printing trope is pandemic, serving both the language of hegemony and of dissent."[42]

The "deconsecration of sovereignty," therefore, should not be understood to imply the inevitable progressive decay of royal power, nor should the crystallization of a public sphere lead us naively to assume the eventual triumph of reason and "democratization." Charles does fall, as it were, into print; he becomes a subject of and subject to its power. But that power, as Richard Helgerson explains, could be employed by competing and even contradictory ideologies:

> Within a generation of his [James I's] death his son was overthrown by a revolution enabled by print and by the power it gave readers to interpret the authoritative texts of their culture. . . . But in the after-

math of that overthrow a new possibility emerged, one enabled by the continuing force of the iconic and the theatrical and by the continuing class interests that had been served by those modes. Print could at last be made the medium for a posthumous royal performance whose power, in threatening its readers' self-possession, threatened the new revolutionary regime's possession of England. These opposed sets of possibilities and interests . . . emerged in part at least as a consequence of the technological innovation of print.[43]

In one of James I's favorite images, the monarch takes his being and power from his domination of the stage, where he rules as the unknowable focus of all eyes.[44] Charles II, his father executed upon that "Tragick Scaffold," the first decade of his reign spent in humiliating exile, finds himself plucked from that stage, reduced to an object in the promiscuous and infinitely reproducible field of print. This translation from stage to page may represent a loss of royal power, the particular weakness and vulnerability of Charles's kingship. At the same time, however, new strategies of control become available to the monarchy as it exploits the power of the printed word to constitute the subjectivity of its citizens. If, as many scholars now believe, the modern state dominates the individual through the supplementary relationship between signs and violence, exerting its authority most effectively through discursive formulations that govern or direct the employment of force, Charles found himself in a position to take advantage of a print industry instrumental to the creation of this new dispensation of power.[45]

I am positing a singularly fluid realm of discourse and power during Charles's reign, generated by the instability of the restored monarchy, dynamism of an expanding print industry, and immaturity of protocols for dealing with the new and unprecedented demands of politics and interpretation. In attending to some of the forces at work in shaping Charles's monarchical identity, and specifically the way in which printed texts functioned as both author and effect of this process, I will follow models of power relations formulated by Carolyn Porter and Theodore B. Leinwand, in which "cultural conversation" and "negotiation and exchange" characterize the reproduction and transformation of cultural forms. The confrontation between those determined to put an end to the social and political experiments of the Interregnum by restoring the monarchy and those attempting to refashion or even dismantle the locus of royal authority did not during Charles's reign end in victory for either side; as Leinwand insists, the proper terms for describing such an encounter are "compromise, negotiation, exchange, accommodation, give and take."[46]

Such a process particularly distinguishes Restoration England, a "traumatized" society, according to Paula R. Backscheider, in which "the negotiation of a stabilizing ideology . . . [and] the processes of refinement, competition, and selection and rejection of symbols and myths" was visible from the moment of Charles's return.[47] The implementation of the Restoration settlement inevitably revealed the unresolved tensions that had divided the nation during its mid-century upheavals, and created new conflicts as well. Venner's rebellion of January 1661 and the mass arrests and widespread searches that aborted a Yorkshire rising in October 1663 are only the most obvious manifestations of the struggles for power occasioned by the king's reassumption of a throne that had been for over a decade not only unoccupied but abolished. Though the first was easily put down and the second stifled, they point to the resistance that Charles confronted as his new government began to establish itself and test the limits of its power.

Yet the difficulties that beset the articulation and evolution of Charles's royal authority reveal themselves most powerfully not in these exceptional and melodramatic moments but in the mundane stresses and strains, frustrations and resentments that accompanied the material workings out of the Restoration settlement, as the pious sentiments and rhetorical flourishes of the Declaration of Breda were transformed into specific policies and concrete actions. Charles, for instance, was bitterly disappointed by the first election of London MPs early in 1661, while for its part the city quickly displayed its unhappiness with the Excise and Heath taxes as well as the king's penchant for demanding large loans. And such political and economic tensions were only exacerbated by the doubts about Charles's religion raised by his decision to marry a Catholic and insistence—contained in his Christmas message of 1662—on a religious toleration that included Catholics. The press brokered the untidy, rancorous, and often violent dialogue that accompanied these processes of "settlement, adjustment, even alteration";[48] employed by royalist and parliamentarian, Tory and Whig, Catholic and radical sectarian alike, the press became an essential component of political authority, the printed word both a significant source and manifestation of power.

The body of the king represents a circumscribed yet important field wherein this complex cultural conversation, and the conjunction between the powers of monarchy and print, can be surveyed. Before the execution of Charles I, that mortal but divine human form, acting as a sacred emblem of the body of the kingdom, had symbolized the seamless relationship between sovereign and subject.[49] In exacting justice on the monarch's body, Parliament determined to sunder that sacrosanct relationship, the emphasis on paternity and posterity in "An Act for the abolishing the kingly office in England and Ireland" revealing how the body of Charles II became from the very first the focus of conflicting ideologies:

> his [Charles I's] issue and posterity, and all other pretending title under him, are become incapable of said crowns, or of being king or queen of the said kingdom or dominions. . . . all the people of England and Ireland . . . are discharged of all fealty, homage and allegiance which is or shall be pretended to be due unto any of the issue and posterity of the said late king, or any claiming under him; and that Charles Stuart, eldest son, and James called Duke of York, second son . . . are and be disabled to hold or enjoy the said Crown of England and Ireland.[50]

Charles, of course, dated his reign from the death of his father in 1649, rewriting history to confirm this fact after he assumed the throne in 1660. This parliamentary act attempts as well to rewrite history, in this case by desacramentalizing the royal body, emptying it of its divine significance, rendering it "incapable" of transmitting the sacred meaning attributed to it by medieval judicature and theology.[51] Both king and Parliament attempt to legitimate themselves by generating competing "fictions" of power that depend on the intricate relationship between the body royal and political authority.

In chapters 1 through 3, I examine three different narratives concerning the king's body, three fictions developed in print that attempt to place that body in history. In chapter 1, I consider accounts of Charles's escape from Worcester, all structured by romance conventions governing the figure of the disguised king. Peter Burke, in *Popular Culture in Early Modern Europe*, identifies the incognito ruler as a staple of popular belief throughout Europe, one of the recurrent images that represent the king as a folk hero.[52] In England the well-known story of "Alfred and the Cakes," though first appearing in print during the sixteenth century, probably predates the twelfth century.[53] Legends of Richard I and Robin Hood participate in this archetype, as do the dramatic adaptations employed by Shakespeare in *Measure for Measure* and John Marston in *The Malcontent*. In the case of Charles's abortive invasion of England in 1651, life was to imitate art when Charles successfully disguised himself for six weeks before taking ship to France. His triumphant return in 1660 produced many accounts of his escape, which, particularly in the image of the royal oak, became an important part of his personal iconography of power. Shrewdly exploiting the literary formulas of the popular folk legend, these accounts celebrate the victory of a majesty denied and threatened by an illegitimate government but protected by divine Providence; the true king cannot be hidden from the eye of God. Yet the attempt to weld biography to romance reveals certain divisions between the king and the country he would rule; the evasions and obfuscations of the escape narratives suggest the fragility of Charles's restored power, the complicated acts of forgetting required of both the new king and his subjects. The restoration of legitimacy is not simply a legal matter, and accounts of Charles's escape from Worcester demonstrate some of the necessary fabrications that accompanied his transformation from penniless exile to exalted monarch.

The escape narratives employ a popular romance model in which the royal body appears shorn of all the awful trappings of majesty. In chapter 2, I consider a contrasting image of the king's body, analyzing accounts of the royal ability to heal scrofula, the "King's Evil." Though the "touch" also began in popular legends that circulated before the twelfth century, attaching themselves in this case to Edward the Confessor, by the time of Edward I the royal touch had become a part of official Plantagenet ritual and bureaucracy, a public demonstration of the divine powers inherent in the sacred body of majesty. By the mid-seventeenth century the healing ceremony had assumed a definite form and office, included in the *Book of Common Prayer* and performed at regular intervals. Though Charles II had continued to heal during his years in exile—to demonstrate that the loss of his throne had not compromised his majesty—after his Restoration the touch became an even more important part of his self-presentation, unprecedented numbers healed in elaborate public ceremonies. The enlargement of these public rites was accompanied by a literature concerned with the medical status of the royal miracle. During the seventeenth century the royal touch became an object of scientific inquiry, the truth of its miraculous nature confirmed by the published accounts of royal physicians and surgeons. Subjected, however, to the scrutiny of a medical community that over the course of a century determined to assert its own power, the royal touch was eventually denied by those who had at first upheld it, its sacred mystery undermined by the printed word that had originally been pressed into its service.

Chapters 1 and 2 concern themselves with Charles's own manipulation of his body, his government's attempt to reinvigorate traditional symbols and icons of divine majesty. In chapter 3, I consider how the royal body and a specific image embodying its erotic potency became instead the focus for doubts, anxieties, and questions about Charles's political power. The idea of the father king, *pater patriae*, possessed classical roots, though in England it possessed particular resonance because of its connection to a patriarchal theory of government that depended on a series of correspondences between god, king, and father. Larry Carver has suggested that while belief in this mystical conception of kingship may have waned before the years of Civil War, it became even more important after the execution of Charles I, when "guilt became transformed into sympathy for the father who, phoenix-like, had returned in the son."[54] The most famous image of the powerful and fertile father king opens Dryden's *Absalom and Achitophel*, but the context for Dryden's cynical use of Charles's promiscuous sexuality had been previously established by satires in which representations of the king's sexual irresponsibility undermined his political majesty:

> Yea princes, sirs, are gods, as they're above,
> Though as men in a mortal sphere they move.
> As gods, 'tis sacrilegious to present
> Them in such shapes as may bespeak contempt.[55]

These lines from "The Answer of Mr. Waller's Painter to his Many New Advisers" (1667) register concern over a literature that had usurped the king's body for its own political purposes, transforming Charles's notorious heterosexual promiscuity into "sacrilegious" representations of monarchical sterility, impotence, and effeminacy. This anonymous poem attempts to control civic speech, insisting that respect for the king's mystical body must condition public apprehensions of the king's mortal body. Here a divine law dictates limits to public appropriations of the royal identity; the author of this poem claims that only certain "shapes" of majesty possess cultural legitimacy. In its fear of the shapes that may degrade royal majesty, "An Answer" thus expresses dismay at the failure of authorities to regulate the cultural productions that figure monarchical power, acknowledges the increasing influence and independence of a print trade that oppositional forces had already begun to exploit, and suggests the ways in which depictions of Charles's royal phallus participated in a political struggle over the nature of monarchical power and responsibility.

These first three chapters attend to the literary dimension of political life, the narrative structures used by government and opposition to create coherent and plausible accounts of contemporary history. In fixing on the literary use of signs and symbols of royal power that possess a history prior to their appearance in print, I want to demonstrate the transformations occasioned in political rhetoric and royal identity by the printed word, examining the changes wrought in traditional images of monarchical power and authority when they became objects of industrial reproduction. To achieve this goal I move after the third chapter from narrative structures to institutional relations, from the ideology of literary products to the cultural economy of literary production. In chapters 4 and 5, I turn from matters of representation to the source of the material production of these images, the press industry itself. The constructions of kingship that occupy my first three chapters are replaced by an attention to the ways in which royal authority constructed the print industry and those individuals, particularly the reading public and the author, who attempted to appropriate its cultural powers.

In chapter 4, I consider the relationship between that industry and the monarchy, the convoluted history of royal censorship that Charles inherited and attempted to use against a print trade that had played such an important role in the overthrow and death of his father. When Andrew Marvell wrote that "Lead, when moulded into Bullets, is not so mortal as when founded into Letters,"[56] he stated a truth recognized by many after the crises and convulsions of midcentury. What weapons did Charles possess in his struggle to control an industry whose printed words had become as dangerous as bullets? After his return how did he attempt to impress his own image on the print trade and make it reproduce that image within the kingdom?

To a large extent, royal attempts at censorship depended on regulating the economics of printing, the specific trade practices that governed relations between writers and publishers, printers, and booksellers. Yet restricting the dissemination of print involved not just the industry itself, but its audience. In 1570, for instance, Elizabeth complains about the power of print to disrupt established hierarchy, the "divers monstrous absurdities" that "engender in the heads of the simple

ignorant multitude a misliking or murmuring against the quiet government of the realm."[57] The legal language of Tudor and Stuart censorship
constructed not just the print industry, but a public, "a simple ignorant
multitude" unfit to participate in written culture.

In chapter 5, I examine a particular episode in Charles's legal
engagement with the press and that "multitude," the trial and execution
in 1681 of Stephen College, "the Protestant Joiner." Provocateur,
inventor of the "Protestant flail," and Whig propagandist, College may
also lay claim to being the first modern political cartoonist.[58] During
the Popish Plot and Exclusion Crisis of 1678–1681, College authored a
series of poems and accompanying prints that attacked the king as well
as the duke of York. In "A Raree Show," printed in the critical months
before Parliament was to meet in Oxford, College parodies the famous
illustration on the title page of Hobbes's *Leviathan* in order to present
Charles as a frightening tyrant determined to impose popery and absolute rule on a nation that must defend itself by treating Charles II as an
image of Charles I: "Like Father, Like Son."[59] At the same time College
succeeds in drawing Charles as a figure of burlesque, a lecherous,
religious hypocrite who carries a peep show on his back and finds himself
fallen into the mire outside of Oxford. Indicted shortly after the dissolution of the Oxford Parliament, College was accused of plotting to
kidnap the king at Oxford.

College's trial and execution vividly reveal the importance attributed to his publications by the government; College the propagandist seemed far more threatening than College the conspirator, his
execution intimately tied to issues involving access to the press, social
hierarchy and print culture, authorial identity and responsibility.
George Monck, created duke of Albemarle for his services as architect
of the Restoration, reflects the sentiments of the monarchy he brought
into power when he bluntly asserts that "the poorer and meaner people
. . . have no interest in the common-weal, but the use of breath."[60]
College's brief fifteen minutes of fame suggest that for such a government his treason lay not in the alleged plot to seize the king's person,
but in his attempt to appropriate the cultural authority of the press and
by doing so participate in a political process in which he had, according
to the government, no rights.

James I and Charles I increasingly depended on print to structure and
dominate that political process, though, as Richard Helgerson has
argued, this reliance on the printed word was to have unanticipated

consequences: "Though James may have found in the fixity of print a counterpart of his absolutist conception of kingship, in becoming an author he sacrificed the mystery of power so effectively preserved through performance by the medieval church, by Shakespeare, and by Queen Elizabeth. . . . He thus contributed to the movement that a generation later led a nation of readers to try governing themselves without a king. Print had, at least for a moment, made readers kings indeed."[61] That "moment," Charles II's bitter patrimony, irrevocably shaped his kingship, fixing it within the confines and limits, as well as the possibilities, of the printed word. Like no monarch before him, Charles was forced from the very beginning of his reign to generate his royal identity through the commercial press, control of the production and distribution of the printed word essential to the realization of his monarchical ambitions and authority. The years during which Charles II ruled define a crux in the relationship between print and power, a historical "moment" when a monarchy forced to restore and redefine its own identity could do so only through an industry that had in midcentury assumed a political identity of its own. Charles's history as king cannot be separated from the printed texts that record and fabricate it, the power that had helped destroy his father having become a requisite component of political authority.

This transformation in political power, and its consequences, could not be anticipated by those participating in the Restoration settlement, for Charles's brief reign marks but a moment in the evolution of this new articulation of political authority. Abraham Cowley, for instance, reveals the powerful nostalgia that shaped so many celebrations of Charles's return:

> All *England* but one *Bonefire* seems to be,
> One *Aetna* shooting *flames* into the *Sea*,
> The *Starry Worlds* which shine to us afar,
> Take *ours* at this time for a *Star*.
> With *Wine* all *rooms*, with *Wine* the *Conduits* flow;
> And *We*, the *Priests* of a *Poetick* rage,
> Wonder that in this *Golden Age*
> The *Rivers* too should not do so.[62]

Cowley's Pindaric ode participates in the pompous self-glorification of Stuart art, appropriating the potent tools wielded by the "Priests" of a Stuart monarchy that since the early years of the seventeenth century had refined aesthetic representations of their power. Here Cowley cleverly seizes on the bonfires that anticipated and greeted the king's return as a way to legitimate Charles's rule, translating the popular rite into an aesthetic codification of the national will. Cowley uses these bonfires to sustain his image of the theological relationship between poet and king, the poetic word and royal authority. The poet as priest uses the Word to figure forth the divine nature of the monarch's royal identity.

The events of 1640–1660, however, suggest the anachronistic nature of such a theological vocabulary; a *"Golden Age"* in which the idealized praise of aristocratic power and royal values could dominate the linguistic field had been compromised not only by the Civil War, execution of a king, and increasing power of Parliament, but by the print industry itself. The revolutionary powers of mechanical reproduction, the vast increase in publication that had occurred during the seventeenth century, the transformations in the production and marketing of literature had all recreated, as Alexander Pope complained almost three-quarters of a century after Cowley's ode, the punishment visited by God on a sinful people: "(after providence had permitted the Invention of Printing as a scourge for the Sins of the learned) Paper also became so cheap, and printers so numerous, that a deluge of authors cover'd the land."[63] Cowley's secondhand rhetoric fails to recognize— and indeed resolutely obscures—a new dispensation in which the sacred symbols of royal authority that he celebrates were being removed from the temples to a new geography mapped by the cartographers of the press. Henceforth the precincts of power would be described and inhabited not by the elite *"Priests* of a *Poetick* rage" but by a despised and multitudinous "Grub-street race."

Part One

Representations of the King

1. Restoration and Escape: The Incognito King and Providential History

The following references to Charles's 1651 escape from Worcester—the first the opening stanza from the ballad "The Royall Oak," probably published in 1660 upon Charles's return to England, the second adorning the very first triumphal arch that greeted Charles in his passage through London prior to his coronation in 1661 and described by John Ogilby in his book commemorating that great event, *The Entertainment of His Most Excellent Majestie Charles II, In His Passage through the City of London To His Coronation*—reveal the extraordinary utility of the king's six weeks in hiding, the diverse ideological purposes it would serve, as well as the wide range of its appeal to the nation:

> Come friends and unto me draw near
> A sorrowfull dity you shall hear,
> You that deny your lawfull Prince
> Let Conscience now your faults convince,
> And now in love and not in fear,
> Now let his presence be your joy,
> *whom God in mercy would not destroy.*[1]

> "Behind the said Figure of Charles the Second, in a large Table
> "is deciphered the Royal Oak bearing Crowns, and Scepters,
> "instead of Acorns; amongst the Leaves, in a Label,
> MIRATUR QVE NOVAS FRONDES ET NON SUA POMA.
> ————"Leaves unknown,
> "Admiring, and strange Apples not her Own.
> "As designing its Reward for the Shelter afforded His Majesty after the
> "Fight at Worcester: an expression of Virgil's, speaking of the
> "Advancement of Fruits by the Art of Graffing.

> "On the Royal Oak in a Label,
> Robur Britannicum.

In allusion to His Majestie's Royal *Navy*, those Floating Garrisons made of Oak. For *Themistocles* ha's observ'd, that *Whosoever desires a secure Dominion by Land, must first get the Dominion of the Sea.*[2]

The simple form and ostentatiously vernacular diction of the broadside-ballad, with its initial evocation of a circle of "friends" listening to a homespun "dity," suggest its consumption by a popular audience transfixed by what the ballad eagerly describes in its subtitle as "The wonderfull travells, miraculous escapes, strange accidents of his sacred Majesty King *Charles* the Second." Contemplating the new king's "presence" must unite the kingdom in admiration for the "mercy" of God, which enfolds not only Charles but those individuals granted the opportunity to repent their denial of the "lawfull Prince" and cleanse their guilty "Conscience." The repetitive emphasis on "now" in lines 4, 5, and 6 points to the gulf between past sorrow and present felicity that can alone give meaning to the "sorrowfull" history of Charles's trials. A merciful God has in Charles's Restoration, his second coming, redeemed both a prince's sorrows and a kingdom's sins.

A year later, the homely accents of the broadside-ballad have been replaced by the pomp and circumstance of a triumphant procession, "a sorrowfull dity" emphasizing Charles's humanity and Christ-like suffering transformed into a learned, emblematic representation of Charles's heroic strength and the puissant power of the nation. Here the oak that sheltered Charles for a day near the beginning of his escape becomes a symbol not simply for his successful flight and ultimate triumph but of his sacred identification with the nation he now governs, the agriculture that sustains and nourishes it, the navy that defends it. These "Floating Garrisons made of Oak" display little of the Christian meekness so essential to the ballad; they suggest, rather, the newly roused nation's militant desire to establish "dominion" over others, the immense power of an England reinvigorated by the return of its rightful monarch.

There can be little doubt that the difference between Charles's triumphant return in 1660 and his reception in 1651—when invasion and not invitation secured his entry into the kingdom, defeat not success the result, six weeks of dangerous hiding and disguise his "sorrowfull" fate rather than public rites confirming his royal identity and authority—made a significant impression on those who supported the restored monarchy. For Charles himself the juxtaposition between ignominious memory and present felicity must have been overwhelming. According to Pepys's diary, during the trip from Scheveningen to Dover the king dwelt, apparently at length, on the escape: Pepys, at least, spends almost two pages delineating the "difficulties that [Charles] had passed through."[3] Shortly after his triumphant return on 25 May, more than half a dozen prose accounts of the escape appeared, all promising to provide, as the title of one anonymous history states, *An Exact Narrative and Relation Of His Most Sacred Majesties Escape from Worcester on the third of September, 1651. Till his Arrivall at Paris.*[4] Yet interest in the adventure did not pass with the first flush of Charles's return: some of the initial accounts were reprinted, while new versions appeared throughout the king's lifetime, one published as late as 1688.[5] Charles apparently delighted and bored listeners for years with the tale and in 1680 he even took pains to commit the escape to paper; two sessions with Pepys at Newmarket in September of 1680 have left us the king's own account of the entire affair. Pepys's fascination with the tale is evident not just in his diary entry for Charles's passage, but in the care he took to secure other firsthand accounts, which in 1685 he collected and bound.[6] Charles's 1651 adventures survive in a host of printed and manuscript sources, including books, pamphlets, broadside-ballads, histories of England, diary entries, and first-person depositions.

The usefulness for the new government of the escape from Worcester, its appearance in such a variety of literary forms, and its iconographic value in representing the king's majesty, suggest its genuine explanatory authority in seventeenth-century England, as well as its ability to generate profits for those exploiting the king's return. Much of its power, both epistemological and economic, undoubtedly stemmed from its participation in the familiar literary conventions of the disguised king. To some extent there probably existed a simple visceral pleasure in the recognition that life was imitating art. The gratification provided by this correspondence appears not only in the narratives and accounts of the escape, which play constantly with the time-honored conventions of the form, but, as Michael McKeon notes, in the historical participants themselves, who eagerly adopted all the methods of disguise and subterfuge approved by the tradition.[7] Moreover, as presented in popular legend, prose romance, and Elizabethan drama, the incognito ruler clearly possessed positive associations that could be exploited by a king who so convincingly claimed the part. Such a ruler, according to Peter Burke, enjoyed the status of a popular hero, his disguise connected to a praiseworthy desire to ensure justice for, or share in the hardships of, his subjects.[8] The humility evident in the Charles of "The Royall Oak,"

"Our Royall King" who "became a serving-man," whose "miseries . . .
force tears from tender eyes," humanizes an otherwise aloof presence,
engendering an audience's sympathy even while proving the king's
own.

Beyond the emotional power of the model, however, lies the
interpretative authority of the Romantic conception of history that
governs tales of disguised, sleeping, and ultimately resurrected rulers.[9]
The nation had executed Charles's father, consigned Charles to four-
teen years of exile, and suffered at the hands of his invading army; now
it welcomes him as its sovereign ruler. The emphasis in the escape
narratives on the "wonderful travells, miraculous escapes, [and] strange
accidents" experienced by Charles during his disguise becomes a way to
comprehend not just Charles's unusual fate but the nation's disordered
history, to accommodate it to a romantic pattern of ultimate triumph
and resurrection. The role reversal forced on Charles during his escape
dramatizes the license and disorder of those years when England betrayed its monarchical traditions; his return as king signals an end to the
upside-down carnival world that the nation had so long endured. Firmly
grounded in this contrast between disguise and revelation, chaos and its
banishment, the escape narratives engage in a semiotics of history,
reading and interpreting the signs of heavenly Providence to justify
Charles's earthly Restoration.

Like the great odes and civic pageants that heralded his return,
these narratives of Charles's escape take their meaning as celebrations
of Charles's monarchical power and identity; far removed from the
formal traditions of court art, these escape narratives nonetheless insist
on the most grandiose pronouncements of royal omnipotence. In emphasizing the providential nature of Charles's successful flight to France,
these narratives betray little discomfort with the self-glorification of
royal panegyric, little questioning of the premises of monarchical
authority. Charles's escape becomes an image or "type" of his Restoration, the role of Providence in both satisfying the form's desire to
celebrate without question the king's divine favor and genuine right to
the throne. Couched in a popular idiom, however, and disseminated in
a variety of printed forms, the escape narratives must also integrate
aspects of the king unavailable or even alien to the more highly structured court arts. The story they tell and the details they emphasize may
even be at odds with the requirements of literary genres more closely
associated with royal patronage. All escape narratives, in fact, begin
with a battle waged by the king against his own people, while the escape

itself assumes the successful disguise of a majesty that court art defines
as inherent, inescapable, and omnipresent.

In this chapter I will examine how these narratives exhibit that
majesty to Charles's new subjects, grounding his authority in a symbolic
order that preceded his Restoration. My concern with these documents
will be not with their status as "objective" history but with their attempt
to legitimate the identity and authority of the new king. I do not desire
to test their often insistent claims to accuracy but to examine the ways
in which the commercial print industry used them to shape, articulate,
and conceive royal power, creating for Restoration audiences compelling and profitable representations of Charles's royal identity. Presented
as history, they generate literary fables whose purpose was to ease the
anxiety created by the relatively sudden elevation of a despised exile to
a position of the highest authority. These accounts are therefore important because, as Jonathan Goldberg insists, "actual power is invested in
fictions, and fictions are potent."[10] The fictions generated by the escape
narratives thus reveal how royal power and identity were produced in
print after the Interregnum. They reflect how such power could be
reconstituted, demonstrating how the late seventeenth century accom-
modated an elevated tradition of royal panegyric to a new king, recent
parliamentary past, and variety of demotic forms produced by a politically and economically sophisticated print trade.

Like Pepys, Evelyn, and the anonymous author of *Englands Joy*, Sir
Harbottle Grimston, the Speaker of the House of Commons who greeted
Charles upon his majesty's entry into London, insists that the Restora-
tion simply cannot be understood or even expressed:

> The restitution of Your Majesty to the exercise of Your just and most
> indubitable Native Right of Soveraignty, and the deliverance of Your
> people from bondage and slavery, hath been wrought out and brought
> to passe, by a miraculous way of Divine Providence, beyond and above
> the reach and comprehension of our understandings, and therefore to
> be admired, impossible to be expressed.[11]

Again we attend to a moment that resists interpretation, which frus-
trates our ability to comprehend the workings of history. Admiration,
Parliament's tactful Speaker here suggests, defines the only proper
response to such a "miraculous" manifestation of "Divine Providence."
For pro-Stuart propagandists, the anxious and perhaps doubting popu-

lation must be convinced of the truth of such an interpretation of history. Used in such a fashion, Providence becomes not simply the designation for what is "impossible to be expressed"—an emblem of the unknowable rather than an explanation for it—but the very proof of Charles's "indubitable Native Right of Soveraignty." The involute and unknowable mechanism of history may elude our understanding; its meaning remains nonetheless plain, for it makes manifest the intimate relationship between God and his anointed on earth.

In providential readings of history Charles's legitimacy as king finds expression not only in his moment of triumph, the Restoration itself, but in the entire fabric of his life. Providence, in the words of Simon Ford's ΠΑΡΆΛΛΗΛΑ; Or The Loyall Subjects Exultation For the Royall Exiles Restauration (1660), "hath restored [Charles] to his Dominions again, *untouched* in his *Person*, and *untainted* in his *Religion*."[12] Providence comes to govern not just the ultimate public vindication of Charles's right, but all of the difficult years that prepared him for his Restoration, that allowed him to go "*untouched*" and "*untainted*" through the world's great snare. Ford's language refers, not surprisingly, to the doubts about the king's religious sincerity that particularly concerned his new subjects. Ford here must use Providence to disarm questions about Charles raised during the nine years between the abortive invasion and the triumphant return, to persuade a wary population of the king's fitness to rule. The escape from Worcester prefigures the Restoration, an emblem of Charles's twenty years in the wilderness; like the Restoration itself, the escape finds expression as an exemplary moment in Charles's providential pattern of converting loss into triumph, bondage into freedom, danger into safety: "doubtlesse, had the King that day been a *conquerour*, God had been lesse seen in his *victory*, then in his *escape*; lesse seen in the *field* then in the *wood*; It was a more wonderfull Providence for God to secure him *in a defeat*, then to save him *by a Conquest*."[13] For Francis Gregory, in his sermon entitled *David's Returne From His Banishment* (1660), the defeat at Worcester proves Charles's right and God's Providence in a way that a victory could not. In this early use of the Book of Samuel as a source for Charles's iconography, Gregory enunciates a type of "negative Providence" in which Charles's ability to encounter loss and danger reveals his legitimacy. To transform defeat into victory is an act worthy of God and his anointed.

As Gregory so clearly reveals, writers who deal with either Charles's life or escape must assert the efficacy of Providence precisely because the recent tumultuous history of England seems to deny it.

Gregory himself insists, "Now, the result of all is this; when God banisheth a King, he may intend him mercy; and consequently, a Kings banishment can be no Argument that God disowneth him."[14] Without a framework that assumes the subtle and secret workings of God, Charles's "too, too active Age" makes not the slightest bit of sense. The popular *Chronicle of the Kings of England*, for instance, apologizes for devoting so much space to the history of Charles II with its "Intricate Turns and Labyrinths of Fortune," "an Interval of such Wonders, such strange and Capricious Revolutions as are scarce to be parallell'd by any Age or Kingdom."[15] For Sir Richard Bulstrode, in his history of Charles and his father, to "remember the Turns of those Times, I seem rather to dream, than to think the Relation true, of so many surprizing Revolutions, which are scarce credible in this our Age."[16] The twenty years of civil war appear so various and convoluted that Sir Percy Herbert, in his romance *The Princess Cloria* (1653–1661) finds them a perfect pattern upon which to design a fiction: "for what faults soever may appear to rigid Criticisme, nevertheless it cannot be denied, but the Ground-work for a *Romance* was excellent; and the rather, since by no other way almost, could the multiplicity of strange Actions of the Times be exprest, that exceeded all belief, and went beyond every example in the doing."[17]

Without Providence, history remains a puzzle that cannot be solved, a passage of time "strange," "Capricious," "intricate," "surprizing," "scarce credible." Such a history makes Providence necessary; at the same time it becomes the very proof of Providence itself. Such a circular logic suggests at least some of the intellectual and rhetorical shifts demanded by Stuart myth, the locus, such language reveals, of inescapable contradictions.

These forceful assertions of Charles's providential triumph, designed precisely to obscure these contradictions, should not blind us to the difficulty during the Restoration of maintaining providentialist readings of history. Belief in the efficacy of divine Providence was far from unanimous, for many divines stressed the incomprehensibility of Providence, the unequal treatment on earth of the sinful and the virtuous.[18] Doubts about the human ability to comprehend the purpose of God's actions characterize the last half of the seventeenth century. During the sixteenth and early seventeenth centuries, history was defined as a revelation of God's purpose; by the middle of the eighteenth century it had become the delineation of cause and effect operating in a complex natural world. During the years 1640–1750 both explanations exert a considerable and competing power.[19]

At the same time, providentialist interpretations generated very different readings of history, attesting to the contradictory purposes to which providential history could be put. According to Michael McKeon, "the invalidation of 'pretended Providence,' the demonstration that interested readings of providence require the arbitrary inversion of terms, was practiced by all interests even while their own interpretations were tacitly accorded the status of unarguable revelation."[20] Authors of the escape narratives were well aware that what they celebrated as a providential liberation many in the nation regarded as a bondage, a terrible repudiation of Puritan attempts to establish God's kingdom in England.

The narratives of escape do not articulate this tension in any conscious or coherent fashion, but they do reveal it in the contradictions that occasionally disrupt their rhetoric of royal praise. At one moment, for instance, John Dauncey, to reject the government's attempt to claim God as the "patronizer" of its victory at Worcester, derides the belief *"That successe denotes actions to be either just or unjust."* On the very next page, however, he insists that "it was not the justice of their cause, but our own and the Nation's sinnes which caused God to raise up those men as scourges both to Prince and People."[21] Dauncey must deny providential explanations to Charles's enemies to prove that Worcester cannot call into question Charles's right to rule; at the same time, he clearly finds it impossible to assert Charles's right without using the argument he has just exploded. Contradictions so gross suggest not simply the partisanship of the author but the importance of his attempt to legitimize Charles's power. Dauncey is the prisoner of a rhetoric that he simply cannot afford to wholeheartedly accept or reject.

Francis Eglesfield is not quite as unselfconscious as Dauncey, but he too betrays the difficulty of his task. In describing Charles's escape he insists that "the manner of his Majesties escape was in a strict sense not miraculous, yet as near a miracle as almost any thing that is barely possible by natural means." Having drawn this painfully fine distinction, however, he rather quickly muddles it: "he, I say, that shall consider no more but this, will no doubt think himself oblig'd to adore the Divine Providence, which never own'd the Royal Cause more apparently then in this Deliverance."[22] Here the careful qualifications of Eglesfield's first remark become the bold assertions of his second, the "not miraculous" transformed into an obligation to "adore the Divine Providence." Though the doubts and uncertainties about Providence can generate an awkward rhetoric, clearly they also give meaning and point to the very act of asserting divine favor. Only after insisting that "it is no easy matter to understand the voice of God speaking by his Providence" can Francis Gregory assure his auditors that "so far as man can *rationally* become Gods *interpreter*, this voyce of his Providence seems to whisper this language; Namely, *that the King of England is a King in favour with God*; see how God seemes to own him in two Particulars." The "Particular" that most impresses Gregory is Charles's escape from Worcester, which became for many royalists one of the two or three biographical incidents demonstrating the king's special status.[23]

The belief in Providence engendered by the escape governs not only historical understandings of, but individual perceptions of and participation in, the escape. While histories and narratives of the escape inevitably point to the larger scheme of history in order to understand the way in which Charles's flight from Worcester participated in a providential universe, the first-person depositions that Pepys collected understand Providence in a much more local and mundane fashion. What concerns the individual participant is not the grand providential movement of history, but the particular moments when God's will reveals itself to the individual immersed in the trivial details of the escape. For instance, Colonel George Gounter, who helped the king secure shipping from Shoreham to France, assures us near the beginning of his account that "in the relation of miracles, every petty circumstance is materiall and may affoord to the judicious reader matter of good speculation." Gounter goes on to explain that he had been "confyned, upon paine of imprisonment, not to stirre five miles from home." This prohibition ended only a few days before his majesty had sought Gounter's aid: "I thinck it will easily be graunted by any that reades and considers, that this was not without a providence, since that it is apparent that if his friends had come before he had beene licenced to goe abroad, he must needs have beene excused: and if they had come much after, it was possible a new restraint might have come betweene, or his libertie in goeing soe freely up and downe, after his busines ended, more suspected."[24] Here "a providence" expresses itself not in the long flow of historical time, but in the felicitous conjunction of particular days and actions. Only the judicious observer, one "that reades and considers," can see the hand of God in the everyday. Indeed, Father Huddleston, who helped the king to shelter immediately after the battle, sees an "extraordinary instance of God's providence" in a meeting occasioned by the delivery of six new shirts: "Father H. observes very particularly, as [an] extraordinary instance of God's providence in this

[a]faire, the contingency of his first meeting w[ith] Jo. Penderell, occasioned by one Mr. Garrett's comeing the Thursday after the fight out of Warwickshire from Mrs. Morgan, grandmother to little Sir Jo. Preston, with some new linnen for Sir Jo. and some for Father H. himselfe, namely, six new shirts, one whereof he gave to the King and another to my Lord Wilmot."[25] Huddleston's account can only move us to admire the economy of a Providence that arranges an escape for Charles while at the same time providing for him a change of linnen. Seen from a providential perspective, the common and daily coincidences of life become animated with meaning, irrelevant and serendipitous no longer, but an intimate part of the warp and woof of history. And history, imaged both as the narrative of decades and the passage of a single day, asserts a divine will that makes manifest Charles's identity as God's anointed.

The king himself, however, carefully eschews an explicitly providential vocabulary, although his language recognizes the unusualness of the events that shaped his successful escape. Speaking of the day after the battle, when he hid in a wood, he assures us that "one thing is remarkeable enough, that those with whome I have since spoake, of them that joyned with the Horse upon the Heath, did say that it rained little or Nothing with them all the day, but onely in the Wood where I was; this contributeing to my safety."[26] A similar sentiment infuses his account of the voyage to France: "One perticuler more there is observable in Relacion to this our Passage into France, that the Vessell that brought us over had noe sooner Landed me . . . but the Winde turned soe happily for her as to carry her directly for Poole, without its being knowne that she had ever beene upon the Coast of France."[27] Charles recognizes the "perticuler" nature of events that befell him, but doesn't feel the necessity to transform the "remarkable" into the miraculous. As we shall see later, Charles appears not to labor under the same ideological constraints as others writing about or participating in the escape, a freedom attributable perhaps to the private nature of his memoirs, his privileged position as king, or simply his secular understanding of history.

However, the providential nature of that escape in all other accounts empowers not just the king but his people. Charles, of course, passes from the certainty of capture and death to the paradoxical freedom of exile; in the words of An Exact Narrative, "Divine Wisedome and Goodness" conveys him out "of the hands of his blood-thirsty Trayterous Enemies, who thought themselves sure of Him, *That so killing the Heir, the Inheritance might be theirs.*"[28] In A Chronicle of the Kings of

England, on the other hand, the escape symbolizes the eventual liberation of the nation itself: "A Providence indeed not parallel'd in History, and able to have convinced his Rebells, if their rage had not blinded them; but it cheared the minds and hopes of his Subjects, by this Pledge of their deliverance from thraldome, in this marvellous protection of Gods Anointed; (no less than two and fifty persons being privy to his Escape.)"[29] For those celebrating the escape it represents not simply Charles's own liberation from "the hands of his blood-thirsty Traytorous Enemies," but a foreshadowing of the nation's "deliverance from thraldome." In vindicating Charles's right to the throne, the escape inevitably suggests the illegitimacy of those who occupy his place and in doing so enslave the nation. Though many during the late seventeenth century felt that individual lives could hardly enjoy special providential dispensation, the just community and nation could command divine protection. Seen from this providential perspective, Charles emerges not simply as "God's anointed," the legitimate "Heir" dispossessed by "Traytorous Enemies," but as a type of Moses who will lead his people from "bondage and slavery," his sacred identification with the nation both proof of and proven by the special care lavished on him by Providence.

Given the nature of the event, almost all accounts of the king's escape begin with the battle of Worcester itself. This formal and pompous opening of the anonymous *An Exact Narrative* reveals the tragic context that allows those who treat the escape to transform the loss of the battle into a type of victory for Charles:

> Fortune had now twice Counterfeited and double-Gilt the Trophees of Rebellion, and its Brazen Trumpet repeated *Victory*, betrayed or prostituted before at *Dunbar*, & now ravished at *Worcester* by numerous over-powring Force, on that Black and White day *September* the 3d. 1651, in the Dusk of which Fatall Evening, when the ashamed Sun had blush't in his setting, and plunged his Affrighted Head into the depth of Lucklesse *Severn*, and the Night ready to Stain and Spot her guilty Sables with loyal Blood, was attiring her self for the Tragedy.[30]

The king's defeat, of course, could represent a most serious problem, for triumph should crown the conventional image of the warrior king; victory in the field rewards the efforts of Edward III at Crecy, Henry V at Agincourt, and Elizabeth over the Armada. The forces ranged against Charles do not win fairly, however: "Rebellion" triumphs only through betrayal, prostitution, and, at Worcester, only

because they have "ravished" the victory from Charles. Worcester
becomes a rape, where the "numerous overpowering Force" of the rebels
overcomes Charles's valiant but hopelessly outnumbered army. Francis
Eglesfield quite sensibly explains this in his 1661 biography of Charles,
Monarchy Revived: "surrounded with a numerous Army of three-to-one in
an ill-fortified City. Which odds, being consider'd, I presume no rational
man will account it a Miracle for the better cause and lesser number to be
worsted by the greater."[31] Indeed, though a superiority of three-to-one
slightly overstates the case, the parliamentary forces numbered approximately twenty-eight thousand, while about twelve thousand had
marched with Charles from Scotland and arrived at Worcester. Cromwell's superiority in numbers becomes the conventional explanation for
Charles's defeat, though royalist commentators conveniently ignore the
implications of such numbers for the popularity of the Stuart cause.

Faced with such odds, of course, Charles can distinguish himself
in battle, defeat thus providing the occasion for expressions of his martial
prowess: "The King (whose Horse was twice that day shot under Him)
could not be induced to quit the field, untill He saw all the field almost
cleared."[32] Here the anonymous *Englands Triumph* emphasizes the two
details that become the almost obligatory proofs of the king's valor. The
two horses shot from under him—suggesting his great activity and
forwardness in thrusting himself into battle—and his refusal to desert
his army and leave the field become the twin marks of his bravery.
Though Charles's most recent biographer, Ronald Hutton, provides no
reason to question the king's bravery during the battle, the ritualistic
reiteration and inevitable amplification of these two "proofs" in the
escape narratives call into question their status as fact.[33] When Eglesfield insists that His Majesty "was one of the last in the field, and could
hardly be perswaded to outlive that day,"[34] the rhetorical excess, which
assures a reader that this is not a king who basely deserts his army or, by
implication, his nation, subverts the claims to battlefield reportage.

Yet even with such opportunities for representing the heroism of
the king, many of the accounts show a disinclination to dwell on the
battle itself; descriptions of the fighting can be brief and even cursory.
Even when distinguished by Charles's heroism, the battle can occasion
a curious unease:

> whereupon his Majesty in person, and in the head of the Horse, sallied
> out upon him [Cromwell], and that with so much valour and courage,
> that *Cromwell's* own life-guard, and the best of his old souldiers (who

were thought almost invincible) were forc't to retire, 'till seconded by those numerous supply's of fresh souldiers, who served only like the *Turkish Asapi*, to blunt the Royall swords, so that their wearied arms no longer able to hold out, were forced to retreat, and at length (notwith-standing the generous example of his Majesty, who performed things worth wonder) to a disorderly flight; and not withstanding his Majestie's earnest endeavours (in which he had his horse twice shot under him) to bring them again to a rally.[35]

In this passage from John Dauncey's *The History of His Sacred Majesty Charles the II* (1660), one senses a certain awkwardness about dwelling on the king's prowess. All heroic details are removed to parentheses and define his heroism either in terms of his enemies "(who were thought almost invincible)," what is done to him (the shooting of his horses), or with a vagueness that betrays any genuine meaning: "performed things worth wonder."

The true difficulty posed by the battle is not defeat but the lack of an enemy over whom the king can genuinely triumph. Descriptions of the king's heroism must be vague, formulaic, and passive because the army he fights consists of his own people. The ability of Providence to manifest itself in Charles's life depends to some extent, as we have seen, on the identification between Charles and the nation: as a mere indi-vidual Charles suffers like all people from the fickleness of earthly rewards and punishments. As the true king, however, he and his nation secure their just deserts on earth. The battle occasions discomfort precisely because it reveals that Charles and the nation are not one. Division, not defeat, is the burden of the battle, and accounts of it must be circumspect to obfuscate this unpleasant truth. Few descriptions of the field wish to remind Charles's new subjects that just nine years before "many men their lives laid down / To bring their Soveraign to the Crown, / The which was a most glorious sight." The militarist relish displayed here by "The Royall Oak" is exceptional; most accounts are understandably more discreet about the glories of the dead.

After the Restoration heroism in such a context proves awkward unless redirected against a convenient scapegoat like Cromwell. Dauncey, in both of the histories that he published in 1660, emphasizes the king's charge against "Cromwell's own life-guard," almost devising a personal confrontation between Charles and Cromwell: "Cromwell having pass't his Army over *Severn*, he march't directly to the Town on that side, whereupon his Majesty in person, and in the head of the Horse, sallied out upon him."[36] This detail, which I've not found in any other

1651 or 1660 account of the battle, later finds embellishment in the 1670 edition of Sir Richard Baker's *A Chronicle of the Kings of England*: "In the head of one of these Bodies the King himself charged with marvellous gallantry and conduct, and press'd so hard upon *Cromwels* Life-Guard, that the Troop was very much disordered, and the Captain very dangerously wounded."[37]

Charles's valor can be legitimated by directing it against Cromwell, the specific enemy, the individual on whom the sins of the nation now gather. Charles's return generated a great deal of public revulsion against the once lord protector: the old authority would be cast off, excoriated, before the new one could be accepted. England had to purge itself of its own betrayal of the king, and *Englands Triumph* describes the public rites that serve such a purpose. Before the king's return, a jury is impaneled and "*John Bradshaw* and *Oliver Cromwell*, whose Effigies were artificially prepared and brought thither by a Guard of Souldiers, were indicted of High Treason, and murthering of the King, commanded to hold up their bloudy-hands, which for the purpose were besmeared with bloud." The effigies were then tried and convicted, sentenced, dragged to the place of execution, and hung upon two gibbets: "As they hung upon the Gibbets, they were so hack'd and hew'd, so gored and shot through, that in a short time little remained besides *Cromwells* Buffe-coat and Bloudy scarfe, that was worth the burning; yet would not the people be satisfied till they had made a fire between the Gibbets, and burnt all they could get of their garbage or garments."[38] What begins as a spectacle stage-managed by the authorities and army ends, this description insists, as a genuine expression of the nation's outrage and guilt.

The predictable violence of the reaction against Cromwell reveals how convenient a target he made for expressions of Charles's power. By focusing Charles's heroism against Cromwell, chroniclers can not only sanction Charles's violence, but punish the nation's transgressions; Charles fights not against his new kingdom but against the evil that had enslaved it by depriving him of his right. Accounts of the escape, because they present themselves as history, cannot do more than hint at this subtle psychological process; in the fictive world, however, this scapegoating can be completely developed. Sir Percy Herbert's romance *The Princess Cloria* models itself, as we have seen, on contemporary European history. Though the preface tells us not to "look for an exact History, in every particular circumstance," it does insist that "upon due consideration you will finde, a certain methodical coherency between the main Story, and the numerous Transactions that passed, both at home and abroad."[39] In Part IV the youthful and heroic prince Arethusius returns with an army to the kingdom of Lydia that he by birth should rule. His army comes from Myssia, a related and neighboring kingdom, where the rebel leader and general Hercrombrotus has pursued the prince. All this, of course, closely resembles Cromwell's invasion of Scotland and Charles's subsequent invasion of England. Their two armies finally encounter each other at a parody of Worcester, and during the battle, in a series of single, iliadic combats, the two rivals meet:

> No sooner had *Arethusius* espyed *Hercrombrotus*, but with a certain kinde of instinct of hatred, mixed with passion, he gave his horse both spurs and raines in a full and violent career, towards the place where he stood: *Hercrombrotus* quickly finding his meaning by his posture, not expecting any equality in the meeting, the Prince having onely his naked Sword in lieu of a Lance, putting presently his Spear in his Rest, encountered him with no other success then that he brake his staff up to the very handle upon *Arethusius* shield.

On two separate occasions the two draw swords against each other, the rebel Hercrombrotus finally forced to admit that "the young man deserved an Empire for his courage."[40] At such a moment the romance functions as a form of wish fulfillment that the escape narratives can only suggest by their subtle redirection of Charles's valor against Cromwell. Only in the allegorical landscape can complete satisfaction be achieved.

But satisfaction can be achieved in another fashion, even if Worcester must be portrayed as a military defeat. It can be transformed into a triumph not only by Providence, which sees in Charles's adversity the very proof of God's favor, but by a redefinition of the king's courage and heroism. The escape narratives reinterpret heroism, subordinating military success to steadfastness and fortitude. Patience, not military prowess comes to describe Charles's highest virtue, as Thomas Blount emphasizes in his preface to *Boscobel* (1660), the most popular of the escape narratives: "Expect here to read the highest Tyranny and Rebellion that was ever acted by Subjects, and the greatest hardships and persecutions that ever were suffer'd by a King; yet did His Patience exceed His sorrows, and His vertue at last became victorious."[41] Charles "conquers" not as a military victor but, according to Sir Richard Bulstrode, as a patient martyr: "And tho' he was forced away by a Whirlwind of Rebellion, he was restored to his Three Kingdoms with the still Voice of Peace and Mercy; a happy Presage how his Majesty would govern, whose Reign, at least the Beginning of it, shewed sufficiently his meek and generous Temper."[42] The "meek" king of Bulstrode's history, like the "poor Prince" of "The Royall Oak," becomes a type of Christ, celebrated as his people's caring and loving shepherd, who would not sacrifice their lives for his right.

At the moment of the Restoration, the loss of Worcester can be turned to Charles's advantage, for his triumph can now be celebrated not as a military victory over his own people but as a conquest of their hearts. The distinction between the two types of victories lies at the center of Sir Harbottle Grimston's address to the king:

> They conquered bodies, but Your Majesty hath conquered souls; they conquered for the honour and good of themselves, but Your Majesty hath conquered for the honour and good of Your people; they conquered with force, but Your Majesty hath conquered with faith; they conquered with power, but Your Majesty hath conquered with patience. . . . Their triumphs were in narrow streets, but Your Majesties triumphs must be in large hearts; their triumph lasted but for a day, but Your Majesties triumph must last for all Your days, and after that to triumph in Heaven to all Eternity.[43]

Only from such a perspective can Charles's Restoration be celebrated as a triumph that rebukes and transcends a mere military victory. Those who usurped his right triumphed by arms; Charles gains a greater victory through love: "The Souldiery who had hitherto made Clubs trump, resolve now to enthrone the King of Hearts in their affections."[44]

Charles's transformation from the King of Clubs who invaded his own kingdom into the King of Hearts who has now returned in peace and love begins with the loss of the battle and the complicated process of divestiture that it sets in motion: "his majesty is none other than the armed troop that surrounds him, like the discourse of signs that belong to him. . . . The scarred veterans, trumpets, drums, and legions are to the king what the bands, thread, braid, and wig are to the elegant man. They are the king's *costume*, which *designates* his body as a body multiplied in majesty. Majesty is venerable only through it."[45] The loss of majesty, of the king's true form, would begin, according to Louis Marin, when the king must flee the battlefield, disjoining himself from the army that has provided him with the "*costume*" of majesty. Events continue to strip that costume from Charles, flight followed by isolation, danger, and the final necessity for disguise, the assumption of another form and costume entirely:

> And being full of discontents
> Stript off his Princely Ornaments,
> Thus full of troubles and of cares,
> A knife cut off his curled hairs,
> Whereby the hunters he prevents.

"The Royall Oak" presents Charles's metamorphosis as one of pathos and pain, full of "discontents," "troubles," and "cares." The king here loses his body of power, forced to forego the ornaments that mark it as unique, even the hair that conventionally symbolizes male strength.

Yet for all of this, few accounts of the escape can contain their excitement and eagerness as they chart the process that transforms Charles from king to servant. Even after the battle Charles is never entirely alone, of course, never without retainers and other bodies who can multiply his own, serving as the signs of his undimmed majesty. Henry Wilmot—a gentleman of the king's bedchamber at the time of the escape, later earl of Rochester—though separated from the king for a number of days as each attempts a different escape route, is rewarded by almost all escape narratives with the part of the king's faithful servant, honored as "most valiant and stout" by "The Royall Oak," which even devotes a stanza to Wilmot's own comic plight when he "was hid in a fiery kiln of Mault." A type of Sancho Panza, Wilmot acts as a foil to Charles, demonstrating both the inherent dignity of the king and the less than desperate nature of their plight.

In a similar fashion, most escape narratives subsume the pathos of disguise in their relish to describe the conversion of the royal into the common. Most pay careful attention to both *how* Charles disguises himself—cutting his hair, besmearing himself with soot, the proper modes of disguise common to the tradition—and to *what* he uses to disguise himself. Most accounts linger over the various articles of clothing that he dons, the hesitancies that characterize descriptions of the battle having disappeared in a growing fascination with the practical problems of preparing a choice costume:

> Breeches of Green course Cloth and a Doe skin Leather Doublet, . . .
> the Shirt (which in that Countrey Language they call'd an Hurden or
> Noggen Shirt, of Cloath that is made of the coursest of the Hemp,) . . .

and *William Creswells* Shoos; which the King having presently un-
stripped himself of his own Cloaths, did nimbly d'on. His Buffe Coat,
and Linnen Doublet, and a Gray pair of Breeches which he wore before,
he gave into these Brothers Hands, who forthwith buried them under
ground, where they lay five weeks, before they durst take them up again.
The Jewels off his Arm he gave to one of the Lords then departing.[46]

As in the passage above from *An Exact Narrative*, close observation of
the mundane world provides the excitement that drives the escape
narratives forward once the awkward battle has been put to rest. Not
heroic action, but nice detail provides the focus for these tales of a long
and drawn-out escape; waiting and hiding, not dramatic leaps from cruel
fortresses, form the substance of these accounts. Although *The Princess
Cloria* creates an extravagant fantasy out of Arethusius's flight from
Hercrombrotus—which includes, we may be sure, a beautiful damsel—
the appeal of the escape narratives themselves seems to derive from
their ostensibly "realistic" character. They have little in common for
instance, with the story of his fifth escape, which Sir Lewis Dyve
recounted to Evelyn just weeks before Evelyn, in Paris, heard "the newes
of the fatal Battail at *Worcester*": "Sir *Lowes Dives*, . . . entertain'd us
with his wonderfull Escape out of Prison in *White-hall*, the very evening
before he was to have ben put to death, leaping down out of a *jakes* 2
stories high into the *Thames* at high-Water, in the coldest of Winter, &
at night: so as by swiming he got to a boate that attended for him: tho'
he was guarded with six musqueteeres." Such a transparently "literary"
tale moves Evelyn not at all; though he admits that "this Knight was
indeede a valiant Gent," he also accuses him of being "not a little given
to romance, when he spake of himselfe."[47]

For the most part the escape narratives take great care to avoid
the label of "romance," even as they shrewdly manipulate the conventions of the form, at times even adopting particular tales and incidents
from popular legend. Almost every account of the escape, for instance,
includes a foul-tempered kitchen maid who abuses the disguised king for
improperly winding the jack. This tale bears so close a resemblance to
the popular medieval tale of "Alfred and the Cakes," where a shrewish
swineherd's wife rebukes the disguised Alfred for allowing some loaves
of bread to burn, that separating fact from fiction becomes a delicate
task. Insistent on their status as "history," the escape narratives generally
eschew the most dramatic and obvious features of fictive romance,
attending instead to a pronounced interest in practical details that image

the king's metamorphosis primarily in terms of the physical objects that define identity. Like the account in *An Exact Narrative*, Thomas Blount's *Boscobel* emphasizes the act of taking off and putting on, the way in which the king "put off his blue Ribband, Buff-coat, and other Princely ornaments," while borrowing ordinary clothing from the Penderel brothers.[48] Blount's account, more than most, generates a densely textured world of physical sensation in which clothing defines both action and identity. During the king's abortive nighttime attempt to cross the Severn into Wales, "*His Majesty* (as he afterwards pleasantly observed) was in some danger of losing his Guide, but that the rusling of *Richards* calves-skin breeches was the best direction *His Majesty* had to follow him in that dark night."[49]

Yet clothing functions not merely as part of the ordinary, sensible world from which the king must struggle to escape but, for those who help him, as an expression of Charles's genuine royal identity. The objects that belong to him or that he uses become a form of treasure, booty that in *An Exact Narrative* must remain buried for over five weeks. Such marks of the king, even when part of his disguise, attain status as types of holy relics that are fetishized by those who attend his person: "whilst he [Charles] thus sat, his Nose bled; at this accident, Mr. *Hudleston* seemed concerned; but His Majesty said it was usual with him; then taking out of his Pocket an old course Clout which the *Pendrels* had given him instead of a Handkerchief, he received the Blood into it. Mr. *Hudleston* then presented him with a fair Handkerchief, and kept the bloody Clout to himself."[50] This bloody handkerchief, we learn from the notes written by Father Huddleston and sent on to Pepys, was later given by the Father to "one Mr. Brithwayte, who kept it with great [ven]eracion, as a remedy for the King's Evil."[51]

The veneration that Brithwayte feels stems from the king's divinity: as God's anointed, Charles possesses a magical presence, an inherent majesty that inevitably marks his superiority to all other people. The royal identity depends on a spiritual authority and power that invests the mortal body of the individual king; the true king must reveal himself. This becomes a crucial paradox of the escape narratives, for they must portray the successful escape and disguise of a king who cannot truly disguise himself. As Francis Gregory insists:

> Consider how hard a thing it is for a *King* to be *concealed*. Alas! Kings and Princes are *Publique Persons*, more Generally known, especially in a time of *warre*, then other men. 'Tis an easy matter for the *low shrub* to

lie *hid*, but the *tall Oak* will be *visible*; you may pull off the *leaves* of a
Cedar, yet its own heigth will discover what tree it is; so here, there is
that *Grandour*, that *Majesty* in a Prince, that is apt to betray him, even
under a *disguise*. If a *Gentleman* may be known by his *face*, much more
may a *Prince* be known by his *Majesty*.[52]

Though Gregory begins by reminding us of the very practical problem
presented by a "Generally known" public figure, he ends by speaking of an
insubstantial "*Majesty*" that marks the king as surely as a well-known "*Face*."
A king can "betray" himself not because people know what he looks like,
but because his royal identity cannot be hidden or disguised. In Colonel
Gounter's report on his role in the escape, Gounter emphasizes the
difficulty this presents: "In very deede, the King had a hard task, soe to
carrie himselfe in all things that he might be in nothing like himselfe,
majestie beeing soe naturall unto him, that even when he said nothing, did
nothing, his very lookes (if a man observed) were enough to betray him."[53]

As celebrations of the king, as royalist propaganda, the escape
narratives must insist that Charles assumes the throne as the legitimate
king. This necessity, however, asserts a fundamental pressure on the
narratives, which must at once explain how the king successfully disguised himself and at the same time insist on his inability to conceal his
royal nature. The escape narratives achieve this sleight of hand by
balancing dramatic instances of disguise against equally dramatic moments of revelation. In *Englands Triumph*, for instance, the narrative
takes great pleasure in recounting the anecdote that was probably
inspired by the Alfred legend, in which a kitchen maid scolds the king:
"after some other discourse the Jack being down, the Maid desires Him
to wind it up, which He undertakes, but being unskilfull therein, goes
the wrong way about it, and somewhat prejudices it; the Maid herewith
highly incensed, (Cooks being most part of a chollerick disposition,)
vents her passion in scolding tearms, asking Him where He was bred,
and telling him He was the veriest Ignorant fellow she ever saw in her
life." This wonderfully comic tale, however, is immediately followed by
an account of the failure of the king's disguise: "*His Majesty* . . . desires
of the Butler a glasse of wine, who courteously invites Him into the
butlery, where the Butler forces Him to drink two or three Healths; one
to *His Majesty*, and another to His Mother: But at length notwithstand-
ing His disguise, suspected Him to be the King, and thereupon falling
on his Knees he begged *His Majesties* pardon, and assured Him that he
would be faithfull to Him in whatever He should command."[54]

This type of balance, with revelation succeeding disguise, characterizes many of the accounts of the king's flight. In the long *Chronicle of the Kings of England*, Charles's escape occupies but a few pages; nonetheless, within that short compass we find two incidents that demonstrate the power of the king's disguise and two that reveal its inability to conceal the royal identity.[55] We find this type of symmetrical construction even in the first-person depositions that Pepys collected. Thomas Whitgreave, who deals with only the first week of the flight, admits that "when hee [the king] came to the door, with the Pendrells guarding him, he was so habitted, like one of them, that I could not tell which was hee, only I knew all the rest." Following this, however, we find an elaborate moment of ceremony in which the royal presence reveals itself: "his Lordship [Wilmot] said to mee, this gentleman under disguize, whom I have hitherto concealed, is both your maister, mine, and the maister of us all, to whom wee all owe our duty and allegiance; and so, kneeling down, he gave me his hand to kiss, and bidd me arise."[56] This same scene of formal recognition forms an emotional climax in Father Huddleston's account, for it presents the reunion of Wilmot and Charles after a separation in which each tried a different route of escape:

> Mr. Whitgreeve steept a litle before to give his Lordship [Wilmot] notice that his friend [Charles] was coming upstairs. The King was in my Lord's chamber, had his arm over my Lord's shoulder, and kissed him upon his cheek before my Lord was well aware, my Lord's back being towards the door when the King stept in.
>
> There my Lord declared unto them that the person there under that disguise was his maister and theirs, and the maister of us all. They kneeling down, his Majesty honoured them with his hand to kiss, bid them arise, . . .[57]

The alternation of such scenes of disguise and revelation suggests the divided purposes of the escape narratives. We can appreciate this tension particularly when we note that the one account least affected by it is the king's own. The cynical, ironic "Merry Monarch" takes by far the most glee in his ability to move unrecognized through his realm. He does, to be sure, record those moments when his disguise fails and puts him at risk: "I observed that the maister of the vessell looked very much upon me. And as soon as we had supped, calling the Merchant aside, the Maister told him that he had not dealt fairly with him: for though he had given him a very good price for the carrying over that Gentleman, yet he had not been cleare with him, for says he, he is the King, and I very well know him to be soe." Yet no account takes such obvious pleasure in detailing the incidents that demonstrate the irrelevance or nonexistence of his inherent majesty:

> He answered that he did not heere that that Rogue Charles Steward was taken, but some of the others he said were taken, but not Charles Steward. I told him that if that Rogue were taken he deserved to be hanged more then all the rest for bringing in the Scotts. Upon which he said that I spoake like an honnest man, and soe we parted.

> Therefore I told him, Friend, Certainly you have seene me there at Mr. Potters, for I served him a good while, above a yeare. Oh, sayes he, then I remember you a Boy there, and with that was putt off from thinking any more on it but desired that we might drinck a Pott of Beere together.

> I sent downe the maid of the House (who knew me) to enquire what the matter was. Who returning, came up and told me; that there was a Rogue a Trooper come out of Cromwells Army that was telling the people that he had killed me, and that that was my Buffe-Coate which he had then on. Upon which most of the Villiage being Fanatiks, they were ringing the Bells and makeing a Bone-Fyer for joy of it.[58]

The king who forgave the poet Rochester—son and heir to Charles's companion during the escape—for telling him that "his scepter and his prick are of a length" is much in evidence here. As we saw earlier, in his reluctance to claim happy coincidence as divine favor, the king possesses a greater freedom than those who would celebrate him; because of this he reveals how constrained other accounts must be to finesse the realities of his successful disguise. His unrestrained delight in fooling others suggests how careful the escape narratives were not to violate their ideological framework and purposes.

The difficulties involved in the ideological work performed by the escape narratives should not be overlooked in assessing their importance to the new government, even though the essential paradox of disguise narratives, what Stephen Greenblatt has identified as "the apparently fragile and mutable social codes [that] are almost always reinscribed," had always been a part of the deeply conservative romance form.[59] For centuries such legends and fictions had functioned effectively to ground social order and personal worth on lineage and family, in spite of the temporary embarrassment of a necessary disguise. For six weeks Charles remains a prisoner of his disguise, of course, but the eventual resumption of his proper role is never in doubt.

So, at least, all can pretend during the heady weeks and months following his return, when the correlations between romance and history seemed delightfully apropos. At such a time few chose to remember or commemorate in print a rather different convergence between royal biography and romance literature, that moment on 27 April 1646 when King Charles I had cut his hair and beard, dressed as a servant, and slipped out of Oxford with two companions in order to evade the encircling parliamentary armies and deliver himself to the Scots. Neither in 1646 nor 1660 did this romantic adventure excite royalist pens anxious to exploit the friendly ideology of disguise narratives, though both John Cleveland and Henry Vaughan wrote poems that attempted to decipher what Vaughan called "our Hieroglyphic King." As Cleveland recognizes in "The Kings Disguise," true majesty should not attempt to play such a role:

Oh for a State-distinction to arraigne
Charles of high Treason 'gainst my Soveraigne.
What an usurper to his Prince is wont,
Cloyster and shave him, he himself hath don't.[60]

The merest historical accident, we might say, determined why the disguise of the father should have fallen into historical and literary oblivion, while that of the son should have become commemorated in print and celebrated as an intimate part of his royal identity: an execution and a coronation are all the difference between the two. But Vaughan's and Cleveland's sure sense of the danger inherent in the defacement of majesty reminds us just how problematic was the status of a sovereign forced to live out a romantic fantasy of disguise and adventure, a true king inhabiting a popular legend. In his poem Cleveland attempts to wrest meaning from this awkward act of "puzling Pourtraiture," to interpret this "obscure" and unusual "Text Royall." Eventually he pretends to make sense of the "Riddles" presented by a king who has betrayed himself, reminding us that "A Prince most seen, is least: What Scriptures call / The Revelation, is most mysticall" (lines 113–14). But the poem reveals Cleveland's dissatisfaction with the task of writing royal panegyric by way of a popular romance trope, of rationalizing Charles's "dark mysterious dresse."

After the Restoration, of course, when historical circumstance had apparently vindicated the promises of aristocratic ideology, the doubts of Vaughan and Cleveland, as well as Charles I's embarrassing adventures, could be swept aside in the general royalist euphoria. Yet the narrative inconsistencies, obfuscations, and evasions that mark the chronicles of Charles's escape from Worcester suggest their difficulty in accounting for the social and cultural changes wrought by the regicide and Civil War. Over the next century, royal panegyric, even when transposed to more popular literary forms, ceased to provide a convincing model of historical explanation, as Pope so emphatically demonstrates almost eighty years after Charles's Restoration:

> Not with such Majesty, such bold relief,
> The Forms august of King, or conqu'ring Chief,
> E'er swell'd on Marble; as in Verse have shin'd
> (In polish'd Verse) the Manners and the Mind.
> Oh! could I mount on the Maeonian wing,
> Your Arms, your Actions, your Repose to sing![61]

Here Pope "sings" to a Hanover, not a Stuart, employing a discourse of monarchical praise in order to degrade the very ideology such a language should express. "The Forms august," however, have been shorn of their meaning; the "Majesty" that should animate the monarchy has vanished. For Pope and the opposition the panegyrical tradition supplies a form of "polish'd Verse" that can only be used to subvert itself. The "Epistle to Augustus," one of Pope's most wickedly ironic poems, takes its meaning from its implicit denial of what it must explicitly affirm. Satire during the Restoration and early eighteenth century does not simply replace panegyric as a vital form, but adopts for its own ideological purposes the very forms that originally figured and expressed royal power and glory. Pope's use of the lord mayor's Day procession in *The Dunciad*—"(Pomps without guilt, of bloodless swords and maces, / Glad chains, warm furs, broad banners, and broad faces)"—reveals the way in which civic pageantry could be used to ridicule the power that it once represented.

Part of Pope's antipathy to the royal discourse he abuses stems from his conviction that too many poets have betrayed their art in order to curry favor, generating mountains of banal praise to put food on their tables. The chaotic landscape of *The Dunciad* is inhabited by the pathetic and unprincipled poets, critics, publishers, and booksellers who have helped bring "The Smithfield Muses to the ear of

Kings," who no longer recognize the difference between literature and panegyric:

> A *Feather* shooting from another's head,
> Extracts his brain, and Principle is fled,
> Lost is his God, his Country, ev'ry thing;
> And nothing left but Homage to a King![62]

The escape narratives are formed by the related changes that overtook both the monarchy and literary marketplace during the middle of the seventeenth century. They try to take advantage of a new, larger audience even while preserving an older tradition of royal panegyric. And this panegyric itself is being used to celebrate a new king and, because of the tumultuous events of 1640–1660, a new conception of kingship. The escape narratives are situated at the intersection of literary and political changes that inevitably speak through the ostensibly unproblematic discourse of royal panegyric. Those who celebrate Charles's triumph in his escape employ a political language that had been refined for almost a century. But the form to which they adapt it, and the historical moment they express, impress themselves on that language in subtle and uncontrollable ways. Charles employs forms and ceremonies, fictions and representations that had sustained the power of his forebears; adapted, however, to a different marketplace and royal history, these projections of monarchical power suggest the unique and unstable settlement he had achieved, the problematic relation of the new king to his power.

2. The Monarch's Sacred Body: The King's Evil and the Politics of Royal Healing

The excitement that propels the escape narratives betrays a primitive fascination with Charles's body, a naive wonder in finding his royal person amidst a commonplace reality. Normally, of course, that body participates in an awful majesty that protects, dramatizes, and empowers itself through elaborate and costly rituals. The court procedures governing, for instance, the dressing and feeding of the king transform the mortal body—which might have needs or feel pain—into an icon of individual and state power that transcends the merely physical. The pompous rites of majesty possess a very important meaning, for they help define royal identity in terms of its unique assumption of a divine power. The escape narratives at every point respond to the rare and complex moment when majesty relinquishes the tangible manifestations of its imperial self and the royal body consents to inhabit our mundane physical universe.

This unusual royal predicament, despite the danger it necessarily courts, contains genuinely comic possibilities as well, the escape narratives often playing with the humor that results from describing the great through the base. As when dealing with the success of Charles's disguise, however, the narratives take great care not to undermine the royal identity; comedy at the king's expense is normally balanced by a serious demonstration of his majesty. The importance of this symmetry is demonstrated by that moment examined above when Charles's nosebleed becomes an occasion to remind us of his ability to cure the king's evil. Here the narrative transforms the embarrassment of a royal nosebleed into one of the most substantial proofs of Charles's right to the throne, his participation in a healing touch that according to popular belief stretched back to Edward the Confessor.

Few proofs of Charles's legitimacy possessed more resonance than the royal touch, for the miraculous nature of his cures emphasized both the inherent majesty residing in his flesh and the divine favor manifested through him: "The *Royal Hand* is accompanied with God's Hand, he approves it by many Miracles, which exceed the condition of Law and Nature." Here Thomas Allen in his ΧΕΙΡΕΞΟΚΗ *The Excellency or Handy-Work of The Royal Hand* (1665) inverts the procedures of the escape narratives, for he locates in the royal anatomy an undoubted power that can never be disguised; the king's corporeal substance necessarily figures forth divine majesty. The miracles performed by the royal hand transcend nature, just as they give the lie to a corrupt and felonious law: "if an Assassinate or an Usurper (such there have been too late, and God knows what Fates yet attend kingdoms) should dethrone a lawful Prince, he could not . . . acquire this virtue. *Quippe pro Imperio*, though *Cromwel* durst do any thing, and wrought no lesse then Miraculous, for his time, he never so much as offered at this."[1] Power might usurp the place of right in a fallen world, but the true king will nonetheless always be known by his ability to heal. While Allen's reference to Cromwell confesses the lord protector's undoubted might, it degrades such trivial successes by contrasting the merely human to the miraculous and divine: Cromwell may have attempted the "Miraculous, for his time," but Allen confidently assumes the separation of the temporal realm of man from that of God and king.

Allen insists that the king's touch symbolizes the way in which Charles's return reanimated civil structures with divine intent, a symbolism not lost on a new government anxious to demonstrate its legitimacy. Charles, who had touched during his exile in order to maintain and affirm his royal identity, held public ceremonies to heal the king's evil both in Holland prior to his voyage to England and in London shortly after his return.[2] A crude song published to celebrate the Restoration reveals the rather sophisticated and cynical uses to which the touch could be adopted when it converts the martial emphasis of the original tune, "When Cannons are Roaring," into a glorification of Restoration peace, love, and harmony:

> The poorest wretch that hath
>   this Evil, sure
> May have ease from the King,
>   and perfect Cure;
> His Grace is meek and wise,
>   loving and civil,
> And to his enemies
>   doth good for evil.

Yet even as this song elaborates Charles' representation as that Christ-like "King of Hearts," the monarch who wins back his kingdom through love and humility rather than violence, it registers the complicated set of beliefs that governed the apprehension and acceptance of Charles's identity as what the poem labels "our nursing Father":

> Though simple people say,
>   Doctors do as much:
> None but our lawful king
>   can cure with a touch,
> As plainly hath been seen
>   since he returned;
> Many have cured been,
>   which long time have mourned.[3]

In distinguishing between the healing powers of doctor and king, the song clearly means to privilege the latter: "None but our lawful king / can cure with a touch." Indeed, the emphasis on "lawful" implicitly characterizes the government Charles replaces as criminal, the ability to touch "plainly" become the proof of Charles's right to the throne. At the same time, however, these lines acknowledge the controversy that accompanied Charles's return, fixing a political debate within competing medical ideologies: "Doctors do as much." This song translates doubts about the wisdom or justice of the king's return into questions of rival medical belief and practice.

Charles's deployment of the mythology of the king's evil and exploitation of his identity as the royal physician cannot then be understood outside of its seventeenth-century medical context. Charles's use of his royal touch to dramatize his divinity participates in a larger historical debate about the nature of medical knowledge and practice. The song participates in this controversy when it aligns the foolish not with a magical belief in the king's ability to "cure with a touch" but with the qualified medical professional; for this ballad, at least, the worldly-wise identify not with new technologies but with older folk practices. Yet the song doesn't deny that doctors may heal the king's evil, only that they are neither as effective nor spectacular as the king: both the scientific and the magical represent valid forms of treatment. In this refusal to discount either method, the song suggests that in the latter half of the seventeenth century, as many modern medical historians argue, a strict "polarisation between folk and learned medicine simply did not exist. Licensed and unlicensed, educated and unlearned healers shared both theories and therapies among themselves."[4] Though diverse medical practitioners engaged in fierce competition, the medical community was characterized by "the coexistence of forms of medical practice based on rational and magical systems of belief."[5]

Indeed, Charles functioned both as the royal healer and the patron of the Royal Society, many of whose members saw no necessary contradiction between science and magic; Newton assiduously pursued both the mathematical laws and the alchemical truths of the physical universe, seeing in each a manifestation of divine Providence in the natural world.[6] In Restoration England few people would have accepted the almost complete separation of science from religion that characterizes our world. The seventeenth century doesn't participate in a slow and stately "progress" toward rational and scientific knowledge, but reveals instead a raucous and disorderly crush of competing claims to truth.

The arc of the royal touch's evolution and demise reveals the ultimate triumph of one of these "truths," the displacement of the sacred by the professional, which Reverend William Vickers laments in his early eighteenth-century attack on the medical profession: "Physicians, and those depending on them, have in all Places, so bitterly run down Persons and Things exclusive of their own Knowledge and Practice, that People think there's no Balm in Gilead but what's in their Hands."[7] The "Hands" that once represented the monarch and his miraculous powers have become instead an emblem of a grasping medical community that would engross all healing powers unto itself. In a process governed by the distinction between the legitimate practitioner and the quack, doctors succeeded in privileging their own skills at the expense of all others, forging a professional medical class that came to dominate the new "business" of healing. At issue in the treatment of the king's evil was not simply a specific cure but the very ground of what may constitute a proper course of healing, of who may properly prescribe medical treatment, of how a medical practitioner may shape the relationship between doctor and patient.

In this chapter I will examine the interplay between the political and the medical, not only the contest between competing medical and scientific ideologies, but the way in which such ideologies were adapted by and themselves transformed political debate. In this process the press played an important role, for it helped create a public forum in which popular belief jostled with scientific investigation; under the scrutiny of the press, the healing touch provoked interest and wonder as a magical rite, popular legend, and subject of scientific examination. During the seventeenth century, the Stuart conception of kingship became inextricably intertwined with a medical practice that happily acknowledged and celebrated the magical properties of divine majesty. During Charles's reign, however, the king's evil became a source of conflict as both a medical and a political phenomenon; rival healers and rival politicians assailed Charles's monopoly on the royal touch, the highly specific nature of their struggle over the healing power indicative not of a general trend to rational thought but of particular conflicts involving scientific knowledge, medical authority, and political right. By the first half of the eighteenth century, a medical profession that had at first served its political masters became another measure of Stuart defeat, their conception of the royal physician denied by a medical community anxious to enforce its own power over the mysteries of healing.

In this century medical science has identified scrofula or struma—the other common name for the king's evil—as a tubercular infection of the lymph nodes, glands, or bones of the neck. In practice, given the vagaries of medieval medical diagnosis, the king's evil described not a single specific disease but a host of complaints involving particularly the eyes, head, and neck. Thomas Fern, who published A *Perfect Cure for the King's Evil* in 1709, describes the symptomatology of the various maladies encompassed by the term, and in doing so may explain why this disease provided a proof of the sacred character of monarchy: "the Scrofula, of all other Distempers, takes the Eye soonest, and is the most disagreeable Sight in Society: an ugly offensive Distemper, that often hinders People from appearing abroad in Publick; which for that Reason, they most of all covet the Cure of, to be like other Persons in open View."[8] Characterized by often grotesque facial tumors, swellings, and infections, the illnesses lumped under the rubric of the king's evil invariably demonstrated a humiliating disfigurement that provided an ideal occasion for the staging of royal authority, charity, and divinity. All descriptions of the healing ceremonies where monarchs publicly demonstrated their power attest to the pathetic and even horrifying appearance of the sufferers, their very visible deformity emphasizing the grandeur, pity, and generosity of the royal physician. Commentators frequently evince wonder at the willingness of monarchs to mingle their majesty with the filth and infection of the sick, and during the seventeenth century both the French and English ceremonies included a ritual

"The Loyal Subjects hearty Wishes To King Charles the Second" (1660)

washing of the monarch's hands that highlighted the contrast between royal purity and the corruption of illness.

The monarchs of only two European countries, England and France, claimed the power to heal scrofula with a touch. Belief in this divine gift apparently originated in the latter, though patriotic English commentators have of course disputed this claim until the twentieth century. In this century, the two major historians of the royal touch, Marc Bloch and Raymond Crawfurd,[9] have argued that the initial formulation of the rite, as well as its further evolution and development, remain inseparable from the political and dynastic fortunes of the monarchs who used it to advance and consolidate their authority. This is certainly true of the first Tudor monarch, Henry VII (1485–1509), whose recuperation of a ceremony that stretches back at least to Edward I (1272–1307) betokens the relative insecurity of his claim to the throne.[10] Henry's elaboration of the ritual reflects a substantial transformation in its importance, the clearest indications of this the establishment of both a golden "Angel" as the healing token bestowed by the king on the sufferer, and a set "Office" that determined a fixed procedure for the state and religious function.

Under Henry the various elements that made up the rite—the giving of the coin, the touching of the sick, the signing of the cross—revolved around the reading of two gospels, Mark 16:14–18, and John 1:1–9. The sick were presented to the king as the first gospel was read; each time the king placed his hands on an individual's sores, the chaplain repeated, "They shall impose hands upon the sick, and they shall be whole." After all the supplicants had been touched, they were led back to the king as the second gospel was read. As the chaplain repeated the verse, "It was the true light which lighteth every man that cometh into this world," the king would cross the sore of the sufferer with the Angel, which was then placed around the neck of the diseased person, who was led away. The chaplain then read from John 1:10–14, and the ceremony concluded with a silent prayer.[11]

During the sixteenth century Henry's successors, more secure in a throne consolidated by their forebear, saw little need to amend the ceremony bequeathed them, though changes did result from the upheavals caused by the country's break from Rome. Yet his institutionalization of the rites governing the royal touch suggest technological as well as political considerations, the power of the press already inseparable from exhibitions of monarchical divinity. Magical rite and the printed word first converge in Henry's ceremony, where, as Crawfurd persuasively argues, "the growth of the printer's art naturally led to [the rite's] inchoate elements assuming a fixed and stereotyped form."[12] Though the various formal components of the service were already present, print contributed to their assumption of a standard, durable, and invariable shape. The ceremony, and the regal power it solemnized, achieved the "permanence" that Elizabeth Eisenstein has identified as one of the primary effects of the printing revolution.[13]

The conclusion of the sixteenth century saw the press intervene even more directly in the evolution of the royal touch, for the first three systematic treatises concerning the disease and its divine cure appeared within a space of twelve years: in 1597, Dr. William Tooker, chaplain to the queen, published in Latin his *Charisma: sive donum sanationis*; five years later, in 1602, William Clowes, a surgeon to the queen and St. Bartholomew's Hospital, published *A Right Frutefull and Approoved Treatise, for the Artificiall Cure of that Malady called in Latin Struma, and in English, the Evill, cured by Kings and Queenes of England*; finally, in 1609, André de Laurens, physician to the French king Henry IV, published *De mirabili strumas sanandi vi solis Galliae Regibus Christianis-simis divinitus concessa*, in which he disputes Tooker's claim that the English monarchy first enjoyed the gift of healing.

Why does the healing touch become a subject of public inquiry approximately three hundred years after its inception? What does it mean when a traditional practice first elicits such an academic consid-eration? Why should the turn of the century see this intrusion of print into the domain of symbolic theater and spiritual healing? The specific and formal shape achieved by the rite probably played an important part in this process, for its very stabilization made the form more amenable to examination and analysis. Moreover, this attention may suggest the enlargement of the object of scrutiny, the way in which a singular and determinate conformation made it worthy of sustained interrogation, of being a subject. The careful consideration of its history and meaning affirms the importance of the healing touch and renders explicit its significance as part of the royal identity.

At the same time, however, the involvement of the rite in self-conscious theorizing, its passage from practice to discourse, suggests its vulnerability, both in the reasons behind and consequences of the attention suddenly accorded the king's touch. At the commencement of the sixteenth century, print helped to fix the ceremony; the stability of the form, however, seems not to have been matched by perceptions of the regal power it glorified, for by the end of the century the press registers the changes in perception that must have occasioned these three works. What once was accepted as a miraculous instance of royal power now needs explanation, apologists who can expound on its history and meaning for—in England—a Protestant audience undoubtedly unhappy with certain aspects of a magical and idolatrous form of worship. Elizabeth, in fact, appears to have modified the healing office in response to Puritan pressures, removing a prayer that refers to the Virgin and the saints and performing the ceremony in English. Indeed, a related phenomenon, the royal blessing of "cramp rings" designed to heal the sick, disappears entirely during her reign.[14] In England, the appearance of two books on the king's evil during the last, difficult years of Elizabeth's reign may suggest the vulnerability of the royal powers it represents and exemplifies.

Legitimating a subject for public consumption, however, presents its own risks, even as it successfully counters a present danger. As we shall see in chapters 4 and 5, when dealing with Tudor and Stuart relationships to the print trade, the monarchy customarily regarded the press as a threat to the absolute power it coveted. When a subject enters the realm of print, the state's ability to control it is compromised, even when the state itself sponsors the initial assumption of a public stance, as in the case of the king's evil. All three books, written by men in the personal service of their rulers, demonstrate an unquestioning belief in the miraculous powers of monarchy; yet they initiate a public inquiry that within little more than a century was to call into question the very phenomenon they originally determined to celebrate.

Not, of course, that the eventual subversion of the royal touch can be glimpsed in these first works. Clowes's *A Right Frutefull and Approoved Treatise*, designed for a vernacular as opposed to a learned audience and written by a man who belonged to a circle committed to new medical ideas that might raise the status of the surgeon, probably generated the largest readership of the three.[15] Indeed, his book serves a practical purpose, aimed "unto the Junior or younger Chirurgions,"[16] and contains a number of cures that they might attempt with their patients. Clowes calls on his thirty years as a practicing surgeon to present a variety of treatments—including diet, powders, and plasters for which he provides a number of recipes, even incisions in radical cases in order "to cut them [the tumors] off, and then to pull them out" (26). Yet for all the treatise's attention to medical practice, it never presumes to rival or explain "the sacred hands of the Queens most Royall Majesty" that display "Divine inspiration and wonderfull worke and power of God, above mans skill, Arte and expectation" (A2v). A set of commendatory verses that open the treatise perfectly reflect Clowes's devaluation of his own art:

> Then Phisicke yeeld; give place Chirurgery;
> The Rational and Practicke for this paine
> Are both a like: her Peerelesse Majestie
> Healeth by God alone, Arte is but vaine.
> This she performes, to write I must surcesse,
> Her hidden skill no pen can well expresse.

Clowes represents a medical practice that knows its own place, never presuming to probe the mysteries of a divine and "hidden" power that rebukes the puny efforts of his experience and skill. The work begins by confessing its own inadequacy, the inability of the "pen" to even "expresse" the power of the royal miracle, and this insistence on its own deficiency marks the narrative strategy of the entire book. After outlining his own remedies, for instance, Clowes concludes his case studies with "a most miraculous Cure, healed onely by the Queenes most excellent Majesty, when neither Phisicke nor Chirurgery could take place or prevaile" (48). He attempted to help a patient for over a year until, unknown to him, this patient visited the queen. When Clowes finally sees the man again, he doesn't recognize the former sufferer who now appears perfectly healthy: "And that I should credit him the more, he shewed mee the Angell of golde which her Majesty did put about his neck, truly a cure . . . requireth divine honour and reverence: And here I doe confidently affirme . . . that (for the certaine cure of this most miserable Malady) when all Artes and Sciences doe faile, her Highnesse is the onely Day-starre, peerlesse and without comparison" (50).

Clowes can express himself "confidently" only when celebrating a power he can neither explain nor understand, his own "Artes and Sciences" humbled by the miraculous. The queen's "certaine cure" overwhelms Clowes's merely human powers, provides a healing alternative to the necessarily inadequate efforts of the medical community, and proves the unique and transcendent stature of England's beloved queen.

Unlike Elizabeth, James I, an austere Scottish Presbyterianism informing his religious beliefs, ascended the English throne distinctly uncomfortable with a ritual that he regarded as superstitious and idolatrous. This stalwart believer in the divine right of kings could hardly afford to dispense with a hallowed rite whose miraculous nature attested to the monarch's sacred identity, but even after assuming its duties, James remained uncomfortable with his office as royal physician. He made substantial changes in the ceremony, eliminating both the actual touching of the diseased spot and the signing of the cross with the Angel.[17]

Charles I, with a very different personal religion from his father, suffered none of the latter's qualms about the royal touch. In an innovation that indicates the centrality of the royal touch to the Stuart kingship, Charles includes the healing office in *The Book of Common Prayer* beginning in 1633. Accompanying the ceremonies for the consecration of church officials, the rite becomes a canonical part of the Church of England, an official miracle authorized by church doctrine and state ideology.[18] At the same time, Charles I's overthrow and execution provided the occasion for mystical rather than bureaucratic manifestations of belief in the king's touch. The royal martyr, first a prisoner and then a judicial victim, figures in numerous healings that, unencumbered by the traditional ceremonies and trappings of awful majesty, speak even more deeply to the popular desire to sanctify the person of the king. Numerous tales circulating both during his captivity and after his death testify to Charles's ability to heal without the golden Angel, when reduced to silver or even bronze during his time as a prisoner of Parliament. Cures occurred, in fact, when the sufferer could not even secure the king's touch, when vile guards prevented all but the king's "Bless you" from reaching the petitioners. Parliament found the public solicitations of their prisoner's healing powers so obnoxious, in fact, that, spurred by a letter of 20 April 1647 from Holdenby complaining of the "great Number of People . . . to be Touched for the Evil," they organized a committee to prepare a declaration "concerning the Superstition of being Touched for the Healing of the King's Evil," though this committee apparently never issued its report.[19]

The propaganda uses of Charles's power certainly did not escape his supporters, for shortly after the king's retirement from London in 1642 they published a petition *To the Kings Most Excellent Majesty. The Humble Petition of Divers Hundreds of the Kings Poore Subjects, Afflicted with . . . the Kings Evill.* Here they assert that "the cure . . . is one of the greatest of your royall Majesties prerogatives, which no force can deprive your Highnesse of, nor no humane mean hath power to annihilate; the rest of the Princely attribution hereditary to this Crowne of England, and its regall possessors, being subject to humane casualties, and dying with the possessors."[20] Though the logic here strikes me as tendentious—since the royal identity resided precisely in an immortal spiritual body that did not die with the individual monarch—the thrust of the passage remains clear: though parliamentary "force" has led the king to abandon his city and even now invades his "prerogatives," nonetheless his healing power remains as proof of his identity and right as the nation's lawful monarch. The "humane" confronts the "regall" and must finally, faced by the royal miracle of healing, admit its insufficiency. This lack, epitomized by the king's absence from his capital, reveals itself in the hopelessness of the sick, who cry out to their sovereign: "Oh the extremity of our griefes, the hideous and unexpresive nature of our sufferings, since your Majesties sad and lamented departure from these parts" (4). As long as Charles remains in Oxford, they cannot be healed, and the petition ends with a predictable conflation of the physical illness of the petitioners with the civic sickness of the state: "[return to] White-hall, where we all wish your Majestie, as well for the cure of our infirmitie, as for the recovery of the State, which hath languished of a tedious sicknesse since your Highnesse departure from thence, and can no more be cured of its infirmitie then wee, till your gracious returne thither" (8).

A little more than seventeen years after the publication of this petition, *The Parliamentary Intelligencer* printed the following notice, dated 27 June 1660 from Whitehall: "The Kingdom having for a long time, by reason of his Majesties absence, been troubled with the Evil, great numbers have lately flock'd for cure. His Sacred Majesty on Monday last touched Two hundred and fifty in the Banqueting-house. . . . His Majesty hath for the future appointed every Friday for the cure; at which Time Two hundred, and no more, are to be presented to him; who are first to repair to Mr. Knight his Majesties Chyrurgion . . . for their Tickets."[21] Though Charles I had returned to Whitehall, it was not to cure the nation but to suffer death; the petitioners' prayers were answered not by the father but the son, and after "a long time" probably unimagined by those desiring a cure from their "infirmitie." The state newsletter here announces that the royal physician has finally returned to his patients, the shepherd to his flock, his years in exile both noted and elided by the wonderfully politic term "absence."

As this brief note suggests, belief in the king's ability to cure the evil became one of the ways in which the restored Stuart monarchy sought to rewrite "exile" as "absence," to fashion the Restoration as an event that transcended the merely political. The return of the king as healer signals not a necessarily contingent and corrupt act of political compromise but the untainted working out of God's Providence. The royal physician has returned to heal both the individual who suffers from the king's evil and the state that has suffered under an unjust usurpation: in the words of John Browne, whose publication in 1684 of *Charisma Basilicon, Or, The Royal Gift of Healing* celebrates over two decades of the king's royal healing, Charles "cures not only His Subjects, but Preserves also His Three Kingdoms in Peace, Order, and Tranquility."[22]

Even more than his father, Charles exploited the political aspects of his healing office, organizing a massive deployment of state machinery to literalize, as it were, the metaphoric resonance of the monarch's identity as the nation's physician. The bureaucratization that the process of royal healing underwent during the course of his reign indicates how the royal touch played a significant role in his attempts to consolidate and extend his powers. The healing ceremony, for instance, became more strictly regulated, and even though the procedures laid down in *The Parliamentary Intelligencer* were apparently never followed, Char-

Engraving from John Browne's *Charisma Basilicon, Or, The Royal Gift of Healing* (1684)

les—who healed far greater numbers than any of his predecessors—did attempt to minister to a set number of patients chosen through a standardized procedure. First, sufferers were required to secure a certificate "signed and sealed under the Ministers and Churchwardens Hands that they were never before Toucht by his Sacred Majesty" (84). Then they were supposed to approach the king's physician in order to undergo an examination confirming that they indeed endured the king's evil; only after that could they acquire a ticket to a specific ceremony.

This care shown by Charles's government in determining who entered the healing ritual was matched by its concern for what flowed out: elaborate procedures governed the distribution of the king's gold. The clerk of the closet to his majesty took an account from the chief surgeon to his majesty of how many gold pieces were distributed during each ceremony; he then entered this number in a register book recording the numbers healed throughout the year, and gave a receipt to the exchequer for all the gold used in the rite. Though aspects of this system were used prior to the Restoration, its operation had never before been so carefully monitored. Browne uses this register to provide exact figures for the numbers touched by Charles through 1682. The total, 92,107, ostensibly provides statistical proof of Browne's boast earlier in his book that "more Souls have been Healed by His Majesties Sacred Hand in one Year, then have been cured by all the Physicians and Chirurgions of his three Kingdoms ever since His happy Restoration" (81-82).

Earlier monarchs, of course, had kept records of the dispersement of coins for the healing office, and historians have used almoner's rolls, as well as household and wardrobe accounts, to reconstruct patterns of giving and healing for kings as distant as Edward I.[23] Yet never before had a monarch quantified his healing office so precisely, providing a statistical measure of his miraculous powers. The accuracy of Browne's list, which he presents as a final and climactic confirmation of the royal miracle he has celebrated, is surely open to question,[24] but it nonetheless represents a remarkable instance of how the healing office became institutionalized as a routine, even commonplace feature of Charles's monarchical self-presentation.

Charles's decision to remove from circulation the golden Angel used during the healing rite represents another important indication of the transformation that the office underwent during his reign. Known then as "the healing piece," today as a "touchpiece," Charles first issued this special medal in 1665.[25] Though made of gold, this healing piece was not a coin but a medal, its monetary value lost to its status as a commemorative token. Not, of course, that the token was therefore valueless, for the gold maintained an approximate worth of ten shillings. Indeed, John Browne complained bitterly that far too many of those the king touched sold their medals: "were this not true, and very commonly put into practice, without all question His Majesties touching Medals would not be so frequently seen and found in Gold- Smith shops" (93).

Yet the transformation from coin to medal remains significant, reflecting a determination that the value of the token stem solely from its commemorative function and not its ability to circulate as coinage. As Louis Marin suggests in his examination of the medals issued by Louis XIV, "the medal, unlike the coin, is out of one kind of circulation but it enters into another: it is 'a durable monument, and made to transmit great events to posterity.' "[26] The healing piece's removal from circulation paradoxically increases its value, which now depends on its status as monument, as witness to and sign of the king's miraculous powers.

A great increase in the literature concerned with the king's evil accompanies these marks of the institutionalization of the healing rite. The public inquiry begun during the final years of Elizabeth continues and increases under Charles, as the healing power becomes a significant focus for a diversity of published works, including medical texts, millenarian prophecy, scientific speculation, and political propaganda. Such heterogeneous productions represent very different aims and perspectives, some concerned to explain the arcane numerological significance of the disease, others desirous of establishing its medical symptomatology and treatment, still others insistent on questioning the healing powers claimed by political rivals. Nothing in such disparate points of view explicitly questions Charles's royal touch; nonetheless, however respectful of royal prerogatives, this sustained attention to the king's evil contributes to a process that eventually calls into question the magical body of the king that lies at the heart of the royal power to heal.

Some of this material, in fact, endeavors to forestall precisely this possibility. The work of John Bird, published in 1661 to celebrate the providential return of God's anointed, reminds us that the millenarian rhetoric most familiar to us in the mouths of the monarchy's opponents played a significant role in articulations of the royalist project, for his long descriptive title exemplifies an apocalyptic vision: *Ostenta Carolina: Or The Late Calamities of England With the Authors of Them. The Great Happiness and Happy Government of K. Charles II Ensuing, Miraculously Foreshewn by the Finger of God in Two Wonderful Diseases, the Rekets and Kings-Evil: Wherein is Also Shewn and Proved, 1. That the Rekets After a While Shall Seize on No More Children, But Quite Vanish Through the Mercy of God, and By Meanes of K. Charles II. II. That K. Charles II is the Last of Kings Which Shall So Heal the Kings-Evil.*[27] Employing a typological method worthy of the three brothers in Swift's *Tale of a Tub*, Bird relays "a Message sent from Heaven for your Majesties acceptance" (A2). Depicting Charles as the "Antitype" of both Edward the Confessor and Christ, Bird can confidently assert "that our Royal Soveraign will be the last of the Kings of this Nation, to whom God will give the gift of healing the Kings-Evil" (75). Bird's direct access to heaven assures us of Charles's unique station in the divine order.

Yet for Bird, Charles's rank can be maintained only by a constant diligence that anxiously polices the medical field. Throughout western Europe there existed an ancient belief in the magical healing powers of the proverbial "seventh son." In both France and England these powers became attached specifically to the king's evil, this correspondence probably a reflection of the supernatural status of the disease already proven by its magical attachment to the crown.[28] In England, relations between the "rival" healers, royal and common, could be uneasy. The government of Charles I, for instance, quite rigorously prosecuted those who claimed to share in the powers and prerogatives of the monarch. In 1632 a Frenchman, James Philip Gaudre, or Boisgaudre, was imprisoned because he "took upon him to cure the king's evil." Boisgaudre apparently thought that because "he is the youngest of seven sons he performs that cure with better success than others, except the King," though Charles's officials wanted to attribute his cures to witchcraft. According to Sir Thomas Richardson, chief justice of the King's Bench, however, the state lacked evidence for such a charge, even though the necessity for punishment remained clear: "Not sufficient evidence to convict Boisgaudre of cozenage or of sorcery, but thinks he has committed a contempt worth punishment in taking upon him to cure the king's evil."[29]

Bird demonstrates a similar desire to protect Charles from rivals to his healing power, though he takes advantage of the numerological possibilities of the seventh son to further prove Charles's unique healing virtue, positing a wonderful system that fixes Charles as the seventh in line of descent from Henry VII, "so that our *Soveraign* last in order is the *seventh son of a seventh*, understand *Henry*" (77). For all of his delight in the mysteries of numerology, however, Bird evinces little desire to entertain the healing powers of others, recommending to the new king that he adopt stern measures to safeguard royal prerogatives: "I do humbly beseech the Kings Majesty, that a Law may be enacted by the King and his Parliament, for the deserved punishment of such diabolical impostures, as this in which is frequently committed in this land by seventh sons taking upon them the Royal Prerogative of our kings. . . . For the practice hereof tends much to the dishonour of God, and of our good King, and to the delusion of his Majesties Subjects" (78).[30]

In its tortured logic and desire to establish the king's exclusive rights to healing, Bird's *Ostenta Carolina* expresses a belief in the royal powers that Charles himself could not have shared, at least if the following anecdote in the Verney Papers provides an honest glimpse of the royal physician at work: "1677, Nov. 21. The King healed privately this day about six, whereof Lady Stewkely and Palmes were two. His healings are very uncertain, and everybody must take their fortune."[31] It had long been accepted that the king's touch was not infallible, even as confirmed a believer in Charles's powers as Browne aware that "although this method doth not always answer expectation, yet its Effects are wonderful, and its Cure most frequent" (111–12).[32]

What marks Bird as a zealot and measures his distance from medical and scientific interest in the king's evil is precisely the rigid separation he wishes to erect between the royal touch claimed by the king and the healing power claimed by others. The medical profession, as Clowes's 1602 treatise demonstrates, had long accustomed itself to accept the intimate relationship between their healing practices and those of the monarchy. Browne, for instance, however deep his belief in the miracle of the royal touch, implicitly accepts scrofula as a disease treatable by physicians and surgeons; indeed, his *Charisma Basilicon* is embedded in a medical text, merely a part of his larger *Adenochoiradelo-gia: Or, An Anatomick-Chirurgical Treatise Of Glandules & Strumaes, Or Kings-Evil-Swellings.*[33] And the same is true of the other important medical text dealing with scrofula published during Charles's reign, Richard Wiseman's *Severall Chiruricall Treatises* (1676). Wiseman, one of the most distinguished surgeons of his day, has no difficulty in accepting the efficacy of treatment of both surgeon and monarch. For Wiseman, in fact, each possesses a proper role, their powers complementary rather than competing: because the disease "frequently deludeth [the young Chirurgeon's] best care and industry, he will find reason of acknowledging the goodness of God; who hath dealt so bountifully with this Nation, in giving the Kings of it . . . an extraordinary power in the miraculous cure thereof."[34] Both Browne and Wiseman dedicate their books to the king, the latter suggesting the vital importance of the monarchy to the professional aspirations of the surgeons when he celebrates "our own Society in the City of London, established by Kings" ("Epistle to the Reader") as a mark of the increasing esteem enjoyed by himself and his colleagues.[35]

The king, in fact, reveals himself as far less jealous of his powers than Bird, even when challenged by claimants outside of the medical profession. In 1684, for instance, he pardoned Thomas Rosewell, a dissenting preacher convicted of treason for, among other reasons, ostensibly claiming that Charles did not possess the genuine healing touch.[36] An even more important encounter between Charles and a "rival" involves the case of Valentine Greatrakes, a popular Irish healer who visited London during spring 1666 and conducted a series of public healings. Greatrakes created an enormous stir in Restoration Ireland and England, not simply among the poor who flocked to him for treatment but among the well-to-do, the court, and members of the Royal Society. I wish to examine the career of Greatrakes in some detail, for the reception of Greatrakes in London and publicity generated by his notorious healings suggest the ways in which a fledgling scientific community, newly reconstituted around the institution of the Royal Society, attempted to understand and rationalize a magical power akin to that claimed by the king. In the controversy surrounding Greatrakes, the healing touch became the focal point of a sustained scientific and medical inquiry that eventually subverted the very royal prerogatives it initially meant to protect. Though this investigation never questioned Charles's miraculous powers—acknowledging them only to measure Greatrakes's inadequacy—it nonetheless accelerated a technological discourse that within fifty years would challenge the royal touch, claiming for the medical profession alone the power to police the body and heal disease.

Valentine Greatrakes—his last name variously spelled Greatracks, Gratrix, Greatres, and so forth—was born a gentleman in Affane, County Waterford, Ireland, 14 February 1629. During the years of civil upheaval he escaped with his family to stay with relatives in England before returning to Ireland, where he served as a lieutenant in Cromwell's army. He resettled in Affane in 1656 when much of the army was disbanded, becoming first clerk of the peace for the County of Cork and then, in 1663, high sheriff for County Wexford. His life appears unremarkable until about 1662, when, in the words of his own *A Brief Account of Mr. Valentine Greatraks* (1666), he began to have "an Impulse, or a strange perswasion in my own mind (of which I am not able to give any rational account to another) which did very frequently suggest to me that there was bestowed on me the gift of Curing the Kings Evil."[37] Though his wife very sensibly urged him to ignore these feelings, he eventually began to touch and cure people of this malady. His powers even continued to grow and finally, on "the Sunday after *Easter*-day, the 2^d of April, 65" (26), he feels another impulse, this one informing him that he now possesses the gift of healing.

As his powers grew, so too did his fame. At first merely a local phenomenon, by 1665 "the multitudes which came daily [to be healed] were so great" (36) that he was forced to leave his village. During this year Greatrakes came to the attention of the larger world, a series of dispatches from Dublin in Sir Roger L'Estrange's *The Intelligencer* during summer 1665 charting a public movement—even in the official government newspaper—from hostile disbelief to grudging skepticism:

> Dublin, July 5.—For this month last past there has been great talk of one Greatrates, and of strange cures he has done, only with touching or stroaking. . . . I was not willing to trouble you with the particulars of a story so idle and phanatick an appearance, but finding that many wiser than myself begin to be somewhat affected with the thing . . .

> Dublin, July 15.—the story of Greatrates is every day confirmed by more witnesses. . . . One letter I have seen from a lady whom I know to be a prudent and a very excellent person, who avers herself to have been an eye-witness in her own house of above three-score cured by him.

> Dublin, July 29.—The many and strange stories which for a long time have been told of Lieutenant Greatrates will be now brought to the test; he himself being arrived here upon Tuesday last.

> Dublin, Aug. 9.—During his continuance here, he passed divers examinations, both publick and private; and in the end there was not any thing criminal objected against him. I did myself see him stroak several, and about twenty of them declared themselves to be perfectly cured. . . . upon the whole matter the world is divided about him . . . for profit it is clear, that he aims not at it. . . . he has never yet been detected of any fraud or imposture.[38]

Greatrakes moved to the larger English stage in 1666 at the persistent urgings of Lord Conway of Ragley, Warwickshire, whose wife

Anne had suffered debilitating and apparently incurable headaches for years. In late July 1665 Lord Conway began to make inquiries about the Irish healer, spurred on by both "news book, and common report" that celebrated his cures. The response Conway first received from Michael Boyle, archbishop of Dublin, however, reveals an important religious official's hostility to the claims of such cures, couched in a language that emphasizes the dangers that Greatrakes might present to the state:

> I shal not deny but by the common report, especially of ordinary people, and of those who were on the same side with him in the last wars he is cryed up to have done divers cures, but this I know that severall of knowne integrity who have bin persuaded to make tryall of him, have return'd from him in the same condition they went unto him without the least improvement or alteration. . . . There are many others who have much severer thoughts of him in regard of his greate talking, and his little doeing, and of the society he most frequents who may have some ill designe to manadge under the countenance of his reputation, and possibly not without some grounds of reason; but as I will not chardge himselfe with any such seditious purposes, so I will not undertake to acquit those who follow him for though he himselfe may be led onely by the conduct of a wilde fantasy, yet his prosilytes may propound who themselves found other use of his esteeme among the vulgar.[39]

Though Boyle never explicitly contextualizes Greatrakes's cures in terms of the king's touch, his distrust of "ordinary people" and fears of sedition reveal all the hostility of John Bird or Thomas Allen confronting a rival to Charles's powers. Like Bird insisting that "a Law may be enacted . . . for the deserved punishment of such diabolical impostures," or Lord Chief Justice Richardson of Charles I's bench wishing for "evidence to convict Boisgaudre of cozenage or of sorcery," Boyle fears that an individual who imitates the king's power to heal can subvert the hierarchies of rank and dignity upon which the monarchy and kingdom depend. Though Boyle doesn't actually accuse Greatrakes himself of treason, he uses the healer's past service with Cromwell, as well as his present friends—former Cromwellian officers whom the government suspected of disaffection after the Dublin plot of 1663—to suggest the seditious nature of his undertaking and the way in which it encourages the ordinary, common, and vulgar. Boyle admits his fears of a popular movement that might define itself around the figure of the Irish healer.[40]

This was particularly a danger in the numerologically significant year 1666, when many in the nation apparently expected some type of divine sign. The anonymous pamphlet, *Wonders If Not Miracles Or, A Relation of the Wonderful Performances of Valentine Gertrux* (1665), an early testimony to the truth of Greatrakes's powers, twice notes that he might be considered one of the "Forerunners of those great things which [people] expect in that great year of Expectation 1666."[41] David Lloyd's attack on Greatrakes, on the other hand, *Wonders No Miracles; Or, Valentine Greatrates Gift of Healing Examined* (1666), uses this as a reason to particularly distrust what people say of the healer: "That the giddy multitude should follow any strange thing: that the *English* so notorious for their unsettledness, should gaze after a novelty at first, is no wonder, especially in such a year of expectation as this is."[42]

However negative Conway's first sources of information, he continued to show an interest in Greatrakes, and in January 1666 he convinced the healer to come to England. For Conway the event proved a personal disappointment, for Greatrakes found himself unable to heal Lady Anne. Yet during the weeks Greatrakes resided at Ragley, he performed numerous public cures before many skeptical observers. Indeed, Conway himself admits that "before his arrival, I did not believe the tenth part of those things which I have been an eye-witness of, and several others of as accurate judgment as any in this kingdom, who are come hither out of curiosity, do acknowledge the truth of his operations."[43]

Though Greatrakes did not satisfy everyone—he himself admits that of the "many hundreds [that] daily came to me from divers Counties . . . many were cured . . . and many were not"[44]—Ragley increased rather than diminished his fame and in late February he started for London, claiming "an Order from the Lord *Arlington*, by command of his Majesty, to come to *WhiteHall*."[45] Greatrakes remained in London until May, the center of a tremendous controversy over the efficacy of his powers. His lodgings in Lincoln's Inn Fields besieged by multitudes demanding cures, his reputation the object of malicious attack and spirited defense, an expected meeting with or public demonstration before the king apparently canceled, Greatrakes wrote his *Brief Account* to vindicate himself and then returned to Ireland, his family, and his duties, where he died on 28 November 1683.

The strange case of Valentine Greatrakes represents more than a mere freak of Restoration history, remarkable not simply because of the tremendous interest and controversy he generated, but because of the wide-ranging terms of the debate he raised in mid-seventeenth-century England. Michael Boyle's letter to Lord Conway demonstrates the complex interrelated issues of politics and social hierarchy that were necessarily implicated in evaluations of the "Irish stroker." The literature that survives concerning his comparatively brief years of notoriety testifies as well to the determined effort made by the medical and scientific communities to understand the powers that he displayed. Greatrakes's healing powers were not simply an object of belief or disbelief but the focus for a rigorous analysis of how healing took place and of the ways in which a medical and scientific community involved in a process of profound change defined its relationship to society: "Sir Heneage Finch says that I have made the greatest faction and disturbance between clergy and laymen that any one has these 1000 years. I have hardly a testimonial but there is the hands of 3 or 4 doctors of physic to it."[46] Though Greatrakes's pride in his accomplishments clearly speaks through Finch's alleged remark, it suggests as well not only the importance many attributed to the questions raised by Greatrakes but the degree to which both religious and medical communities became involved in and set at odds by the issues his powers raised; attempts to explain his ability to heal display the considerable pressures that would eventually divorce science from religion. Around this unusual figure range a host of questions involving relationships between political power, medical practice, social hierarchy, scientific knowledge, and religious belief.

Roy Porter suggests that for Greatrakes's contemporaries, considerations of the problems he raised began with two questions: "did he genuinely possess healing powers? (or was he a failure or a fraud?), and if he genuinely healed, were his healings by regular natural operations, or instead wonders and miracles?"[47] Those attempting to answer these questions often made a resolute effort to divorce science and medicine from politics. Though Greatrakes's healing touch would seem necessarily to invite comparison to the king's, many, particularly those associated with the Royal Society, practice a discreet silence on the correspondence between the two healers. George Rust, for instance, dean of Conner and one of those associated with the Cambridge Platonists, captures the heady atmosphere surrounding Greatrakes, and the way in which the stroker might be detached from political matters, when he writes from London to Joseph Glanvill: "The great discourse now at the *Coffee-houses*, and every where, is about Mr. G. the famous *Irish Stroker*. . . . He undergoes various censures here, some take him to be a *Conjurer*, and some, an *Impostor*, but others again *adore* him as an

Apostle." After meeting Greatrakes, Rust admits that "I confess, I think the man is free from all design, of a very agreeable Conversation, not addicted to any Vice, nor to any Sect or Party." Having determined to his satisfaction that Greatrakes "is free from all design," involved in no "Sect or Party," Rust can then treat him as a purely scientific problem: "I was three weeks together with him at my Lord *Conwayes,* and saw him, I think, lay his hands upon a thousand persons; and *really* there is something in it more than *ordinary.*"[48]

Henry Stubbe, a noted physician and vocal opponent of the Royal Society, and David Lloyd, a committed royalist and high-church divine, on the other hand, explicitly conduct their examinations of Greatrakes with his proximity to the royal physician in mind. The former, who does credit Greatrakes's powers, uses the stroker to vindicate his own contested doctrine of fermentation: "Considering that our life is but a Fermentation of the Blood, nervous Liquor, and innate constitution of the parts of our Body, I conceive I have represented those hints and proofs which may render it imaginable that Mr. Greataricks by his stroking may introduce an oppressed Fermentation into the Blood and Nerves, and resuscitate the oppressed Nature of the parts." Stubbe, who had himself served in the parliamentary army in Scotland from 1653 to 1655, attempts to finesse any embarrassment caused by his support of Greatrakes with the suggestion that the powers of the Irish healer function only to reaffirm the king's: "this gift of Healing was bestowed on him [Greatrakes], since the Restauration of his Sacred Majesty, and the restitution of the Doctrine and Discipline of the English Church."[49] Here Stubbe succeeds in making Charles's restoration responsible for Greatrakes's assumption of the healing touch, the popular healer empowered by the royal physician.

For Lloyd, however, working the opposite side of the argument, Greakrakes must be separated from the king, his pretended powers contrasted to Charles's genuine powers: "since the Wonder of his Majesties Restauration, evidencing the presence of God with his Person and Government; the men of Mr. Greatrates party have spent their time in venting and dispersing False Prodigies, to delude men into an Opinion of the displeasure of God against both" (12). In this formulation Greatrakes becomes a type of traitor because his attempt to claim the sovereign's prerogatives undermines belief in the providential nature of Charles's return; the Irish healer's "False Prodigies" represent a subversive affront to the real "presence of God" that distinguishes the king.

Lloyd's *Wonders No Miracles* derides Greatrakes's supposed cures by using the "imagination" and "unsettled . . . mind" to explain the behavior of both the healer and those he cures: "[Greatrakes] is troubled with Fancies and Imaginations, which he takes to be Impulses; and indeed it is not so much a wonder to me, that one should pretend these Impulses as that half the Nation doth not, since they have been so given over to Fantasies and inward suggestions, having lost almost the faculty, principles, and exercise of Reason" (9). Lloyd here participates in the favored solution for those who challenged Greatrakes's powers. Confronted by a host of apparently undeniable cures, those who refused to credit his healing touch assigned responsibility to the overheated imaginations of the sufferers themselves.[50] Lloyd draws a strict distinction between imagination and reason, between a giddy population given to vague fancies and impulses and those capable of employing a more rigorous vocabulary of the intellect. In such a formulation Greatrakes can be derided as a creature of the vulgar multitude, which is unable to distinguish between a scientific truth and a mere illusion.

For all their ignorance, however, the "common people" can present a terrible danger to the rational and principled elite. Lloyd expresses his fears of just how a man like Greatrakes might challenge the fragile edifice of the divine monarchy:

> And certainly (might a Melancholly, or a discontented man think) any man may work upon the imagination, as well as Princes; and finding it feasible by one or two experiments, [indecipherable] with other cunning peoples suggestions, might set up an Healing power as well as the king; levelling his Gift, as well as they would his Office . . . and when parity of reason led them to attempt in other Diseases, what with some success they had begun in the Kings Evil, they might not only out-do his Majesty, but be in a fair way to give Laws to the world. [13–14]

In dismissing "this nine daies Wonder of *Greatrakes*" (8), *Wonders No Miracles* assumes the difficult task of discrediting Greatrakes without at the same time calling into question the healing touch of the king. Lloyd fears the "levelling" of Charles's powers that can only work to degrade the royal person and office. However, as he recognizes here, in ascribing Greatrakes's cures to "the imagination," he runs the risk of doing precisely that. Many "Melancholly" and "discontented" individuals inhabit the kingdom, and they already regard the king's claims with some suspicion: "A cure I say, though so Generally owned, to the great honour of his Sacred Majesty of Great Brittain; yet cavilled at by the more morose sort of people" (13).

Greatrakes therefore presents an almost insoluble problem for Lloyd: to grant Greatrakes's claims to divine inspiration compromises the royal monopoly on healing, while to deny them by attributing his cures to the power of imagination inevitably raises questions about how the king himself heals. The strain on Lloyd's argument surfaces most obviously when he concludes by providing a list of "rules to discern true Miracles from false." A number of his formulations quite clearly undercut the monarchical miracles that he has tried so hard to protect: "2. Divine Miracles are done without means, forms, Rites, Ceremonies, Cuttings, Lancings, Plaisters, &c. . . . 3. Divine Miracles are done in an instant, nothing being able to oppose and consequently to delay the workings of a God. . . . 6. Neither were the Miraculous Cures only little Eases for the present, but perfect and compleat Cures, and that not of one or two of 500 that are touched, but of all" (37-38).[51]

Lloyd's interest in upholding authority and hierarchy extends not simply to the king himself, but to the medical community. Here, again, Lloyd will divide imagination and reason, identifying doctors with an intellectual vision that lies beyond the comprehension of most people. Only qualified professionals, Lloyd insists, can properly evaluate Greatrakes's claims and regulate his behavior: "this man began and set up among the Ignorant and Rude part of mankinde, the *Irish*, easily imposed on; (when he should by right have sate among the Doctors, as the greatest worker of Miracles did, and have answered them about the ground of this pretension, and have asked them *Questions*;) not appearing among the wise in publick, till his feats had prevailed with the more Ignorant in private" (18). This reference to Christ also marks, in a much more dramatic fashion, Henry Stubbe's conception of Greatrakes's relationship to the medical community, for he calls the Irish healer "this Antichrist of Physicians [who] may be of the greatest service to them in the World, if they preferre the recovery of their Patients before their Credit, or Rules of Art" (24). Both Lloyd and Stubbe reveal the substantial tension that not surprisingly existed between Greatrakes and the medical professionals whose powers he appropriated. Though Lloyd and Stubbe again take opposite parts—the former upset with Greatrakes's refusal to acknowledge professional regulation and authority, the latter concerned with what Greatrakes might teach his "colleagues"—both recognize the problem that he represents to those attempting to formulate and codify the "Rules of [their] Art."

At least part of this collision between the physicians and their Antichrist played itself out in print, in an exchange of satiric verses, though unfortunately only one side of the debate has apparently survived. "Rub for Rub: Or, An Answer To A Physicians Pamphlet, Styled, The Stroker stroked" (1666) presents itself as a response to a previous attack on Greatrakes launched by a physician who "play'd the Poet" in his desire to discredit the Irish healer.[52] In the response, this attempt to malign Greatrakes reveals the division of the professional community from "The Faith and Wisdom of the Multitude," an alienation, according to this anonymous supporter of Greatrakes, attributable to the doctor's envy of the healer's success:

> You envy't as his Happiness, and grutch
> Because you cannot grope where he doth touch:
> Doctor, your Practice is too scant I trow,
> Which makes you wound (anothers Credit) so.

The physician here suffers from a "Consumption in the Purse," his attempts to heal himself manifested in his "Jear" against a hated rival.

The poem's focus on the economics of healing suggests a popular rage against doctors that appears little different from such feelings in our own time. As Margaret Pelling notes, critics often attacked physicians—who represented the privileged, protected apex of the medical profession—for "discrepancies between the medical practitioners' professed claim to belong to a higher calling, and their economic behavior. Clergy, lawyers and physicians were all abused as having the profit motives of tradesmen."[53] Greatrakes's selflessness in healing for free provides a convenient contrast to the supposed rapacity of those who look upon healing as a profession:

> Alas, you fear your Craft should come to nought,
> Because such Wonders by his Hands are wrought,
> His Deeds pronounce his Worth: But let us know
> What honour we, to you Physicians owe.
> We're not beholding unto you I'm sure,
> Not you, but 'tis our Money gives us Cure.

This passage contrasts Greatrakes's "Wonders" to the physicians' "Craft," the latter stigmatized by its role as part of a financial transaction. True "Worth" is thus divided from the commercial and professional

worlds, which lose all "honour" by being characterized by their relationship to vulgar money. Using Greatrakes as a standard of selfless healing,
the poem presents doctors as rapacious, lecherous charlatans, their
professional identities belittled by the divinely inspired amateur whose
"hand is truly powerful." The attempt to expose Greatrakes thus becomes the self-interested strategy of a morally bankrupt profession
unwilling to share power or recognize the contributions of others to the
art of healing.

Greatrakes's period of fame during Charles's first years of rule brought
primarily medical and scientific questions to the fore. Even this brief
survey of responses to the stroker suggests the complexity of Restoration
attitudes toward a new science and the professional communities attempting to organize themselves around it. The distinction between a
rational, learned, scientific communication and the uneducated babble
of a superstitious multitude represents at least one way these communities endeavored to legitimate themselves. The charges of hypocrisy and
greed brought by "Rub for Rub" testify to the resistance that such elite
professionalization provoked. At the same time, the importance of
religious issues in judging and understanding Greatrakes—his creation
of "faction and disturbance between clergy and laymen"—reveals the
difficulties these new disciplines found in trying to reconcile themselves
to a dominant spiritual discourse.

    Though Michael Boyle and David Lloyd express great concern
for the political implications of Greatrakes's notoriety, such considerations seem peripheral to the popular response to and interest in the
stroker; they remain on the edge of the debate, always threatening to
overwhelm the medical and scientific transactions but never quite
imposing themselves. Indeed, despite all the concern about plots expressed by Boyle and Lloyd, a habitually paranoid government never
intervened. Greatrakes claimed that his journey to London was under-
taken at the command of the king, and the government apparently made
no effort to stop or arrest the stroker, though in March 1666 his petition
for the settlement of his lands in Ireland was rejected.[54] The expected
meeting between monarch and healer apparently never occurred, but
the reasons for this, too, remain obscure. Evidence exists, however, that
as highly placed an individual as Prince Rupert recommended a patient
to Greatrakes and even hosted the successful healing.[55] The king's
seeming indifference to the political implications of the healer's cures
suggests that intellectual curiosity and love of novelty rather than

political suspicion characterized the royal response to Greatrakes, in spite of the fact that Charles himself had suspended his public healings during much of 1665 and 1666 because of a particularly virulent outbreak of the plague.[56] Indeed, some of the anger directed against physicians in "Rub for Rub" may stem from the exodus of doctors from London during the worst of the plague.

During the last years of Charles's reign, however, other claims concerning the ability to cure the king's evil take on an explicitly political dimension. Challenges to the religious or medical community were no longer an issue when, as in the 1685 proceedings against Monmouth, the assumption of the touch carries with it royal pretensions:

> the said laite duke of Buckleugh did most treasonablie usurp the stile, honor, and kinglie name off the imperial crowns off Scotland, England, France, and Ireland, and caused himself to be proclaimed king, and did take upon him to be king, and was saluted by the people as king, and they kissed his hands and cryed "God blisse the king," and he was called Sir, and his majestie, and he was prayed for as king and commandit as king, and payed the armie, and touched children off the king's evill, and did exercise the other functions off royal dignitie.[57]

Shaped by the exigencies of the Popish Plot and Exclusion Crisis, Monmouth's claims regarding his ability to heal possessed a far different meaning from those of Greatrakes. What remained a scientific prodigy in the latter became an attempt by the former to share in and ultimately usurp Charles's royal identity.

Monmouth's claim to possess the royal touch antedated his invasion of 1685, belonging first of all to the turmoil of 1679-1681. During these years, with the fate of the Exclusion Bill still undetermined, Monmouth attempted to position himself as the preferred successor. Handsome, brave, popular, and Protestant, Monmouth seemed to possess all possible virtues except legitimacy, and during these years he did not despair of securing even that. On three separate occasions—in January and March 1679 and June 1680—Charles found it necessary to issue public declarations denying that he had ever married Monmouth's mother, Lucy Walter, so pervasive were rumors of a "black box" containing a secret marriage contract.[58]

Claiming the royal touch became another way of achieving this all important "legitimacy" and identifying himself as the true heir to the throne. Particularly after Monmouth's triumphant western progress during the latter half of 1680, reports of cures performed by the duke joined rumors about the black box.[59] In that year Benjamin Harris, one of the most active Whig publishers, provided London with an account of a healing performed by the duke while in Somerset (a county from which Monmouth recruited heavily during his later invasion).[60] Harris reprinted this chronicle early in 1681 in his newspaper *The Protestant (Domestick) Intelligence*, which narrates the events from "Crookhorn, January 1." The subject is a woman about age twenty, Elizabeth Parcet, who has suffered since her childhood from "the *Joint Evil*, being said to be the worst Evil."[61] Unable because of her poverty to travel to London and seek the king's touch, "God the Great Physitian Dictates unto her . . . to go and touch the Duke of Monmouth." She finds him at Sir John Sidenham's White Lodge and goes to great lengths to touch his naked skin with her own: "[she] broke her Glove, and brought away not only the Sores, but the Skin: The Dukes Glove, as providence would have it, the upper part hung down, so that his hand-wrest was bare: she prest on and caught him by the bare hand-wrest with her running hand: (saying, God bless your Greatness, and the Duke said, God bless you." Within ten days all her sores have healed.

Located precisely in place and time, emphasizing the girl's poverty and piety, this news story, which occupies two of the paper's four columns, insists on its truth and accuracy. It provides nine names, including a minister and two "Captains," who will verify it, assuring its London readers that their "Original" account can be found at the Amsterdam Coffee-house in Bartholomew Lane.[62] Lists of reputable witnesses, of course, were a standard feature of seventeenth-century accounts of prodigious occurrences, and Greatrakes had bolstered the *Brief Account* of his own miracles with fifty-four pages of testimonials, including statements from men like Robert Boyle, Ralph Cudworth, Andrew Marvell, and Benjamin Whichcott.

The unreliability of such measures of truth is surely one of the objects of attack in the Tory response to Monmouth's cure, an anonymous 1681 broadside entitled *A True and Wonderful Account of a Cure of the Kings-Evil, by Mrs. Fanshaw, Sister to His Grace the Duke of Monmouth*.[63] This begins by firmly placing his cure in the larger context of Monmouth's alleged legitimacy: "the extraordinary Cure of the Kings-Evil, lately perform'd by his Grace the Duke of *Monmouth*, in his Western Progress, has no doubt alarm'd many people, and open'd the eyes of the most unbelieving, to see Heaven by this Miracle proclaim his Legitimacy, and God Almighty himself declare for *The Black Box*." Here the western progress, black box, and royal touch all become part of a divine revelation; the testimony that will follow, "underwritten" by the six names put to the broadside, assures the truth of this new cure and should open all eyes to Monmouth's right to the throne.

Yet for all the certainty of this opening, and the documentary touches that it flourishes, the account rather quickly unmasks its satiric purpose. The cure, after all, concerns not Monmouth but his sister, born to Lucy Walter well after her liaison with Charles. The cure itself is presented in a straightforward manner, until the sex of her patient, one Jonathan Trott—"born of poor, but virtuous Parents," we are piously assured—becomes an issue: "he did not know why Mrs. *Fanshaw* might not receive from her Mother the curing of the ills of young men by a touch of her Naked flesh, as well as the Duke her Brother had from his father the curing of young women by a touch of his." The conclusion of the tale removes any doubts about its true purpose, for the allusion to the ancient myth that a lion would recognize the true king demonstrates the absurdity of the entire relation: "There is but one other natural Argument to prove the legitimacy of a Prince . . . and that is the Instinct by which Lions are taught to reverence and to do them homage, without ever hurting them. And this too I am told his Grace does design to shew the World in his own behalf: for it is credibly reported, that on Saturday next the Duke of *Monmouth* designs to be shut up with one of the greatest Lions in the Tower of *London*, there to be seen to the satisfaction of all that behold how secure he must needs be of his Legitimacy" (2).

This rather amusing attempt to make Monmouth ridiculous occasioned *An Answer to a Scoffing and Lying Lybell* (1681),[64] which reveals, in its desire to recuperate the duke's reputation, just how intricate and muddled the issue of the royal touch had become. The duke's defender has no doubt that "the Papistical Interest, and the promoting of the horrid Plot" lay behind *A True and Wonderful Account*, which by displaying Monmouth's ambitions hoped to awaken jealousies in the king's breast that would work to the advantage of the duke of York. Surprisingly enough, however, *An Answer* then blames Monmouth's supporters for having started the rumors concerning the cure in the first place: " 'twas a weak and most Ridiculous thing in the Duke of *Monmouth*'s Creatures to raise such a story of the Dukes Curing the Evil, to prove his Legitimacy lawful, and so heir to the Crown, for it is very well known, that the curing of the *Struma* . . . is no ways a mark of a Right and Legitimate successor . . . for it is not Intail'd to the Heir, but to the Crown it self." Yet *An Answer* then goes on to argue that the stories concerning Monmouth's cures may be true after all, for the royal touch, like the healing powers of seventh sons, depends simply on the imagination of the sufferer: "But what if this story of the Duke of Monmouth's Curing the Evil be true, is it so strange a thing, when we see it done by every Seventh Son, who at least pretend to it, and therefore if he did Cure it, or should again Cure it, that might better prove he was a seventh Son, then *Legitimate* or Heir to the Crown. But we know that Physitians who give Natural causes to things that seem Supernatural to the Vulgar, do attribute the Cause more to the parties Imagination, than to the Virtue of the Touch."

This desperately perplexed argument concludes by insisting that, because the curative powers of the touch can be explained without recourse to supernatural explanations, the duke may very well have succeeded in the cures attributed to him and that therefore it "might very well pass without this Libellers malicious and Defamitory story in Ridiculing the Action, and Scoffing at the person of this most Noble Peer." Caught up in the struggle between elite discourse and popular belief, *An Answer* betrays a hopelessly confused logic that attempts to satisfy the contradictory demands of both.

The debate joined by these three accounts of Monmouth's ability to touch suggests the important consequences of almost a century of printed, public deliberation concerning the nature and status of the royal touch. The disputation concerning Greatrakes in particular has inevitably affected understandings of the royal miracle, as another satire directed against Monmouth explicitly reveals. "A Canto on the New Miracle wrought by the D. of M." uses Greatrakes as a type of mountebank who can help us understand the duke himself:

> The Stroaker *Graitrix* was a Sot,
> And all his Feat-tricks are forgot;
> . . . .
> If seventh Sons do Things so rare,
> In You seven Fathers have a share;
> Shew us some more of these fine mocks,
> Show your *Black Art*, shew your *Black Box*.[65]

The way in which this virulent and caustic satire implicates the royal touch in Charles's sexual irresponsibility and Monmouth's bastardy demonstrates the corruption of the miracle's previous spiritual

resonance. Examinations of Greatrakes's career have helped to natural-
ize a once magical power, its supernatural significance debased though
not entirely erased by a scientific and medical community that has begun
to distinguish between a learned discourse of reason and a "Vulgar"
vocabulary of miracles and prodigies. This satire defames Monmouth by
leveling him with mere tricksters and seventh sons, celebrating him as
the "Great *Mountibank* of our sick State." By the 1680s, in fact, the touch
had become so ambiguous and contested a manifestation of royal power
that even the duke's supporters quarreled about the consequences of
claiming to share in it: Did it enhance his stature or make him ridiculous?
Did it help sustain his claim to legitimacy or merely enroll him in the
dubious ranks of seventh sons and folk healers? Belief in the miraculous
nature of the touch remains alive, but stigmatized by its relegation to
the common and vulgar it can no longer be deployed without generating
a contrary analysis that inevitably ironizes the first. Only this type of
process can explain the baroque logic of *An Answer*, which succeeds in
claiming the power of the royal touch for Monmouth only after having
irrevocably cheapened it. Such thoughtless inconsistency speaks to the
controversy that by the end of Charles's reign had come to characterize
the royal miracle.

In the forty years following Charles's reign, disputation becomes bathos;
by 1726 belief in the king's touch is little more than a form of Jacobite
nostalgia, kept alive primarily as part of the royal romance that the
Stuart pretenders tenaciously erected to keep their hopes of the throne
alive. The refusal of William and Mary to claim the power to heal surely
announced its political demise, even though "Great Anna" resumed the
practice during her brief reign. By the turn of the century the royal touch
had become irrevocably associated not with the throne of England but
with the Stuart dynasty, and their increasing political irrelevance marks
the demise of a living belief in the monarchical power to heal with a
touch.

Severed from legitimate expressions of a newly conceived royal
identity, and no longer protected by its royal practitioners, the king's
evil retains its importance only as an object of an increasingly powerful
medical fraternity. As we have seen, the seventeenth-century medical
profession—characterized by unstable and fluid boundaries between folk
and learned medicine—had little difficulty accommodating the royal
miracle to its scientific method; Clowes, Browne, and Wiseman all
integrated the touch with their medical understanding of and curative

practice involving struma. During the years 1697 through 1726, however, as licensed medical practitioners struggle to professionalize their industry, the medical community appropriates the disease for itself, relegating all cures by those outside the community to the status of fraud and quackery. While the medical profession had once conceived of the disease in ways that reflected the glory and authority of their royal patron, they now find in the king's evil only a confirmation of their own institutional power. Of the eight publications concerned with the king's evil that I've located during this twenty-nine year period, only three reveal a genuine belief in the royal touch: one of these is an example of Jacobite propaganda while the other two confirm their belief in ways that suggest the importance of a new and increasingly authoritative medical vocabulary. By attending to the triumph of this discourse, we can understand how the royal touch lost its privileged status, both as cure and object of belief.

The text published in 1697, Maurice Tobin's *A True Account of the Celebrated Secret of Mr. Timothy Beaghan, Lately Killed at the Five Bells Tavern in the Strand, Famous for Curing the King's Evil. In a Letter to Mr. William Cowper, Surgeon*, presents itself as little more than a particularly elaborate form of advertising. This pamphlet never actually reveals Mr. Beaghan's celebrated secret; though the author promises that he received it from Beaghan, he has passed it on to a qualified medical professional to whom the reader must apply: "all Persons Infected with the King's-Evil may repair to Doctor *Conner* . . . for his Advice."[66]

Defining itself quite frankly as part of a commercial transaction, Tobin's pamphlet nonetheless begins by admitting the difficulty the disease has presented to the medical community: "there is not one [Disease] in which Physicians and Chirurgeons have taken more Pains, and have had less Success then in Curing the King's Evil: For this Disease hath been hitherto reckon'd by Natural Means so Uncurable, that it was thought nothing but a Supernatural Vertue granted to Kings from Heaven could entirely Cure it" (3). About this supernatural power, however, Tobin has little to say: "It doth not belong to me to dispute whether even the Hands of Monarchs can Cure this stubborn Distemper, but I am convinced by several Experiences, as you your self and Hundreds of other People in this City know very well, that Mr. Timothy Beaghan . . . had almost an effectual Method to Cure this Disease" (4).

Tobin's mock humility fails to disguise the obvious disdain with which he regards the "Hands of Monarchs." For Thomas Allen, only thirty years before, those "Hands" had represented the link between monarchy and divinity, a miraculous cure for a terrible affliction; for Tobin they are merely an advertisement for a dubious rival. Though his admission that "it doth not belong to me to dispute" resembles the hesitancy of William Clowes when confronted by the royal miracle, Tobin clearly regards the royal touch as superstitious nonsense, particularly when measured against the surefire cure to which he can, for a slight fee, provide access. The tone of Tobin's pamphlet suggests nothing so much as one snake-oil salesman who has spotted a second.

Yet Tobin, at least, takes notice of the healing touch claimed by generations of monarchs; even in this slight self-promotional puff, published at a time when the reigning monarch no longer presumed to touch, Tobin must acknowledge the royal claims he discounts. How much more indicative of the disregard into which the royal physician had fallen is the 1712 publication of Dr. James Gibbs, *Observations of Various Eminent Cures of Scrophulous Distempers Commonly Call'd the King's Evil,*[67] a sixty-eight page treatise mingling medical explanations with case histories in which the king's touch receives not a single mention. Even though Gibbs's announced purpose is "to exhibit some considerations of the Causes and Observations of Various Eminent Cures of *Scrophulus Diseases*" (2), he never bothers to include the royal touch among those cures, in spite of his occasional reliance on Wiseman, the living example of Queen Anne, and the very name of the disease he considers.

The royal touch has simply become irrelevant to medical considerations of "Scrophulus Diseases." The problems that now animate its study are suggested by the following complaint near the conclusion of Gibbs's volume:

> And as for such Persons as Empirically pretend to Physic, without so much as the knowledge of their own Ignorance: I have often lamented the Public Damage, which has proceeded from no more than a pretence to a Secret, which, if they had, would be like a Sword in a blind Man's Hand, who by ill Management might Destroy the Person he would defend.
>
> Besides, how unreasonable it is to expect regular Cures of these Distempers, from such Persons as are not acquainted with the Rational Methods of the Medicinal Art. [67]

Gibbs's work clearly functions as part of a confrontation between licensed medical professionals, those "acquainted with the Rational Methods of the Medicinal Art," and those who possess merely an "Empirical" knowledge of their subject: during the seventeenth century "empirics," who treated disease on the basis of experience rather than theoretical study, could obtain royal licenses to practice healing and sell patent medicines without any formal medical training.[68] The "Secrets" claimed by these practitioners threaten the preeminence of Gibbs and his fellows, and this treatise attempts to defend the field, to create a market to which only the professional has access by erecting a rigid boundary between legitimate and quack medicine. In the context of this confrontation, the phenomenon of the royal touch excites interest primarily as an anomaly, no longer the defining characteristic of the disease but a matter of historical curiosity.

Indeed, the final victory of the eighteenth-century medical community over the royal miracle involves precisely how "history" will be written and understood. Official medicine claims the power not only to determine how a disease might be cured but how the chronicles of the nation's past might be read and interpreted. These issues form the focus of a debate occasioned by the anonymous 1721 publication of A Letter from a Gentleman at Rome, To His Friend in London; Giving An Account of some very surprizing Cures in the King's-Evil by the Touch, lately effected in the Neighborhood of that City. Wherein is contained, The compleatest History of this miraculous Power, formerly practised by the Kings of England, ever yet made publick; the Certainty of which is confirmed by the most eminent Writers of this Nation, both Catholicks and Protestants, as Malmsbury, Alured, Brompton, Polidore Virgil, Harpsfield, &c. and Tooker, Heylin, Collier, Echard, &c.[69]

This pamphlet presents an account of a series of healings from Rome; though it is discreetly silent as to the identity of the miracle worker, contemporaries would have recognized the Old Pretender, James Edward Stuart. The unnamed narrator, who travels in order to observe "the most remarkable Occurences that happen" (3), describes the excitement of those "miserable and deplorable Objects" who have "resorted from distant Parts to be touched, some deformed with large Swellings or Bunches under their Jaws, seemingly filled with corrupted Matter" (4). After observing the miracle of their healing, this "innocent" narrator draws the inevitable moral of his tale: "Into what a State of Degeneracy and Thoughtlessness is human Nature fallen, thought I? that have their Senses to testify the Power and Efficacy of this Divine Gift, and so little Reverence and Honour paid to the Hand that effects such surprizing Things" (4–5).

In fact, A Letter from a Gentleman at Rome attempts to persuade its audience not primarily through an appeal to our "Senses," to a description of the miraculous "Hand" at work, but by enlisting the authority of history. The *Letter* spends very little time recounting these Roman miracles, dwelling far more on the past than the present, fully three-quarters of its twenty-four pages recounting the long history of the royal miracle, with particular emphasis on its origins in Edward the Confessor and extraordinary manifestations during the life of the martyred Charles I. As the *Letter* surveys what its title styles "the most eminent Writers of this Nation," it clearly expects their "strongest Testimonies, even the Evidence of Eye-witnesses, to prove the Kings of *England* have enjoyed this supernatural Gift ever since the Reign of *Edward* the *Confessor*" (5).

In spite of its ostensible revelations concerning current healings, the *Letter* legitimates its claims by depending on antique accounts whose historical authority "proves" the power of the royal touch. The *Letter* does not pretend to interrogate the miracles it recounts, for it insists, rather like Clowes over a century before, that "What can we say to those Things? Can human Reason ever pretend to investigate such a supernatural Power? Ought we not rather suffer ourselves to be wrap'd up in Admiration, when we consider the transcending Effects of Miracles!" (17).

Not everyone was willing to wrap himself in such Jacobite "Admiration," and in 1722 William Beckett published an attack on the *Letter*. Identifying himself on the title page as "Surgeon, and F.R.S.," the long descriptive title of his work reveals the scientific perspective with which he intends to dismantle the "transcending Effects of Miracles" and the "compleatest History of this miraculous Power": *A Free and Impartial Enquiry Into the Antiquity and Efficacy of Touching for the Cure of the King's Evil. Written some time since, in Two Letters: The One to Dr. Steigertahl, Physician to his Majesty, Fellow of the College of Physicians, and of the Royal Society; the Other to Sir Hans Sloane, Bart. President of the College of Physicians, and Vice-President of the Royal Society. Now first published, in order to a compleat Confutation of that supposed supernatural Power, lately justified in a Pamphlet, intituled, A Letter from a Gentleman at Rome, to his Friend in London, &c. To which is added, A Collection of Records.*[70] For Beckett authority resides not in the questionable histories of writers like Polidore Virgil and William of Malmsbury, the sages who buttress the *Letter*, but in the scientific method exemplified by his correspondents, respected leaders in the College of Physicians and Royal Society. Allying himself with Steigertahl and Sloane, Beckett appropriates the banner of "*impartiality*," thankful that he lives in a "free and

inquisitive Age" (3) so that the royal miracle can be "candidly" examined.

Predictably, Beckett's "impartial" account concludes that the
royal touch cannot possibly be regarded as miraculous or supernatural;
if cures have been effected, they have depended on the imagination of
the sufferer and the awe occasioned by the royal presence. There can be
nothing miraculous about such cures, for even a man like Greatrakes
"cured a prodigious Number of Persons . . . by the stroaking with his
Hands" (30–31). Moreover, in surveying the literature on the royal
touch from Clowes and Tooker to Browne and Wiseman, Beckett
expresses a profound disdain for writers whose "Business was to exalt the
Power and Dignity of the Princes under whom they wrote, to influence
the Peoples Minds with a Belief, that they were capable of effecting
supernatural Things" (60). The gift of healing is "nothing more than
Impositions on the People; and the more it be enquired into, the more
its Mysteries will be exposed and set in a cleer Light" (53).

Beckett identifies this "cleer Light" with "a right Method of
Reasoning," which, along with "an unrestrained Freedom of Thought,"
have "become the happy Characters of this Age" (62). Beckett celebrates the new science, for it has liberated people from the superstitions
of the past, impositions that he specifically identifies with the clergy and
the monarchy. These two institutions are held responsible for a discourse
and practice that are denied the name of science. Representing the
modern institutions that now define medical knowledge and history,
Beckett strips past authorities of their legitimacy, dismissing the *Letter*
as a dated language, its rhetoric of "Divine Gift" and sacred "Hand" more
appropriate to 1660 than 1720. The language of divine healing doesn't
simply lose its privileged status, but becomes instead an explicitly
counterfeit vocabulary, designed to pretend to a knowledge and art that
lie well beyond it. The *Letter*'s subordination of reason to miracle is
stigmatized as a willful ignorance and naivety, proof for Beckett that it
participates not in a modern scientific method but in a backward-look-
ing politics of nostalgia.

It is nowadays commonplace to observe that history belongs to
the victors, and Beckett's attempt to rewrite the medical annals of the
nation participated in a long-term war waged in the popular press in the
late seventeenth and early eighteenth centuries between orthodox
medical professionals and a host of unlicensed and irregular practitioners. Along with their professional organizations, their literary propaganda eventually won for licensed medical personnel their special rank

as professionals, quackery the doom of those defeated.[71] The king's evil became part of that defeat, the royal touch, and the sacred monarchy it exemplified, reduced to a magical curiosity, the mark, according to Samuel Werenfels's *A Dissertation Upon Superstition in Natural Things* (1748), of "the Follies of a Fabulous Age."[72] During the seventeenth century medical science had helped to enlarge and celebrate the royal power; by the middle of the eighteenth century, however, a new medical community claimed jurisdiction over the powers of healing and in doing so transformed the monarch who would heal into just another quack.

3. The Monarch's Profane Body: "His scepter and his prick are of a length"

For more than three hundred years these opening lines of *Absalom and Achitophel* have remained the most famous characterization of Charles's sexual nature, an important though comic revelation of the masculine assumptions about power that buttressed Stuart ideals of monarchical authority:

> In pious times, e'r Priest-craft did begin,
> Before *Polygamy* was made a sin;
> When man, on many, multipli'd his kind,
> E'r one to one was, cursedly, confind:
> When Nature prompted, and no law deny'd
> Promiscuous use of Concubine and Bride;
> Then, *Israel*'s Monarch, after Heaven's own heart,
> His vigorous warmth did, variously, impart
> To Wives and Slaves: And, wide as his Command,
> Scatter'd his Maker's Image through the Land.[1]

In these lines the promiscuous play of male sexuality becomes a "pious" activity whose divine fire proves the legitimacy of an earthly king. The power of generation belongs to "man" alone, while "Wives and Slaves," "Concubine and Bride," passively serve and reflect this overwhelming male power, bearing the stamp of male vigor and warmth. The passage revels in a male Golden Age when "Nature," not arbitrary "law," defined man's state. The *ands* that level wives with slaves and concubine with bride insist on the illusory status of the social distinctions that might elevate women; one difference alone possesses meaning, that between man and woman. Man rules on earth as God in heaven, their power to create the mark of and connection between a celestial divinity and earthly authority.

Scholars have long admired these lines, particularly because they reveal Dryden's consummate skill in transforming Charles's sexual behavior, a frequent target of abuse and ridicule, into a potent symbol of his imperial power. A tactical maneuver in Dryden's program to defend the king, these lines reflect the ways in which Dryden's royalist sympathies could so brilliantly recuperate the king's identity in the service of Tory propaganda. We should recognize, however, that while the Whig opposition would have rejected Dryden's celebratory portrait of Charles, they would not necessarily have quarreled with his assumptions concerning the relationship of masculine power to political authority. These patriarchal assumptions had governed England long before a Stuart had occupied the throne, and they possessed, even after the execution of Charles I, an extraordinary vibrancy for the English people. Larry Carver notes that the designation of the country's leader as "father"—*pater patriae*—was a ubiquitous formulation during the seventeenth century, employed by Cromwell and William III as well as by the Stuarts, though he reminds us also that the title's meaning and significance could vary substantially.[2] Not everyone, to be sure, would have endorsed the divine sanction accorded the figure in Sir Robert Filmer's *Patriarcha*, where the authority of the father represents the very "law of nature": "I see not then how the children of Adam, or of any man else, can be free from subjection to their parents. And by this subordination of children is the fountain of all regal authority, by the ordination of God himself."[3]

"Regal authority," of course, had always depended on the laws of patrilineal descent, but the failure of the protectorate demonstrates their continued vitality even after the Civil War, execution of the king, and struggle to establish a new form of civic authority. Gerald MacLean's survey of seventeenth-century historical poetry reveals the absence of "a representation of political power that was not androcentric," the apparent impossibility of "imagining Cromwell as anything but a monarch, . . . of imagining any political state other than one ruled by a heroic leader."[4] Attempts to offer Cromwell the crown and the apparently inevitable decision to vest leadership in his son Richard after the lord protector's death demonstrate the lack of a mechanism for assuring the orderly transference of power that did not depend on patriarchal principles, the practical as well as imaginative difficulties the nation faced in forging a new political identity.

Yet there can be little doubt that Charles's return to England only temporarily relieved and soon exacerbated these problems. Charles's barren marriage to Catherine, compounded by the presence of his sundry illegitimate children, made succession an issue only a few years after his Restoration; as early as 1662, entries in Pepys's diary express foreboding about who will rule after Charles.[5] These concerns, which assumed extravagant proportions when James's conversion to Catholicism became public knowledge in the 1670s, eventually culminated in the hysteria of the Popish Plot and protracted Exclusion Crisis. English politics during both the 1670s and 1680s register the crucial importance of succession for the Stuart monarchy. Charles's failure to produce an heir and James's success precipitated major constitutional crises.

The problematics of succession had always been embedded in the figure of the father king, for in addition to its important political implications—through its origin in Caesarean Rome—it boasted a significant sexual component as well, the people's royal father also serving as the nation's passionate husband; for centuries the symbolic female body of the state had been wedded to the masculine body of the monarch, the very health of the kingdom assured by and imaged in the powerful erotic relationship between them.[6] Given Charles's notorious promiscuity, however, the awkward sexual implications of his identity as the nation's father were never far from the surface; in response to this title Charles himself allegedly remarked that "I believe that I am, of a good number of them."[7] Charles apparently never regarded discretion as a proper royal virtue, and his philandering had come to public notice very soon after the Restoration. Pepys, for instance, first mentions Charles's relationship with Barbara Palmer in July 1660—not two months after the king's triumphant return to London—and by December 1662 he complains that Charles's "dalliance with my Lady Castlemayne being public every day, [is] to his great reproach."[8] Such knowledge did not belong only to those who frequented court circles: in 1666 one Anthony Beele was indicted in Cumberland for publicly stating "Hang the King, he is a knave and a whore maisterly rogue."[9] And Tim Harris argues that the particularly violent bawdy house riots of 1668 in London reveal an important connection between the widely perceived licentiousness of the court and the issue of dissent.[10]

Even the fabulous vision of male power that opens Dryden's poem registers the difficulty of accommodating Charles's sexual behavior to the structures of seventeenth-century patriarchy. Dryden's discreet reinscription of Charles's sexual improprieties, for instance, depends on a suspicious privileging of nature over culture and law— "When Nature prompted, and no law deny'd"—that the poem's conclusion, with its emphasis on Charles as England's "*lawful* lord," will implicitly deny. In this opening stanza of the poem, the dichotomy between nature and culture is itself designed in the service of royalist and masculine power, useful here as a way to counter Whig outrage at Charles's sexual behavior, but abandoned when Charles asserts his proper legal authority. Dryden is not merely versifying Filmer; the political claims of the poem are surprisingly modest and concessional. For all their polemical insistence on the necessary relationship between male domination and social order, these lines reveal the tensions that undermine the simple equation of male sexuality with political dominance, for this opening stanza turns on the repeated "e'r" in lines one and four, the temporal marker indicating the loss of male sexuality's privileged status, which remains securely distanced in a biblical past.

These tensions and contradictions disclose the intricate relationship in Restoration England between the political, sexual, and literary. Considerations of law, authority, and political legitimacy were inextricably intertwined with considerations of sexual power and the social production of gender. The interrelationship between these problematics was certainly not peculiar to Restoration England; feminist scholarship of the last decade, in fact, would insist on the inevitable conflation of considerations of gender and politics. As Joan Wallach Scott explains, "politics itself is a gendered concept, for it establishes its crucial importance and public power, the reasons for and the fact of its highest authority, precisely in its exclusion of women from its work. Gender is one of the recurrent references by which political power has been conceived, legitimated, and criticized. It refers to but also establishes the meaning of the male/female opposition. To vindicate political power, the reference must seem sure and fixed, outside human construction, part of the natural or divine order."[11]

This, surely, represents the ideological charge of the opening to *Absalom and Achitophel*, where Dryden's comic celebration of masculine power wants to assure us of the unequivocal fixity of the binary opposition between male and female, the natural and divine orders that mandate the absolute subordination of women to men. Yet in *The Patriarch's Wife* Margaret Ezell reminds us that "at no time during the [seventeenth] century does one find authoritarian, rigidly patriarchal, or misogynistic opinions in theological or satirical writings left unchallenged,"[12] and this was particularly true after the dislocations of the Civil War, Interregnum, and Restoration: the last half of the seventeenth century witnesses a vigorous engagement between opposing attempts to both reaffirm women's traditional roles, and also question and transform those roles.[13]

Moreover, a good deal of this debate was carried on by women, who expressed themselves in print in increasing numbers: Elaine Hobby calculates that between 1649 and 1688 over two hundred women published their writing.[14] The important essays of Mary Astell during the final decade of the century may even suggest that we can locate the emergence of a "modern" feminist rhetoric in this debate, which was undoubtedly intensified and accelerated by the explosion of print after 1641.[15]

In the last chapter I examined one of the figures—the monarch as royal physician—used by the government to sustain the legal and theological relationship between the mortal body of the king and his divinity. In this chapter I will explore another of these representations, Charles as *pater patriae*, father of his country, and the way in which Restoration efforts to understand gender and delineate the opposition between male and female transformed a title fundamental to royalist ideology from an essential emblem of the patriarchal state into a specifically sexual critique of a mortal king. While scholars have long known that satirists used Charles's sexual behavior to subvert his political authority, little attention has been paid to the precise forms taken by this sexual subversion. We may ask, for instance, how a king noted for his prodigious heterosexual appetites could become a figure ridiculed, as we shall see, for his effeminacy, impotence, and homosexuality. What dynamic governed his metamorphosis from heterosexual libertinism to effeminacy and homosexuality? Why, situated at the apex of a patriarchal hierarchy, did Charles's notorious sexual prowess undermine rather than consolidate his political power? Indeed, we might even wish to ask why sexuality provided such an effective and flexible vocabulary for challenging Charles's authority. By looking at how Charles's subjects wrote his sexual identity, I wish to explain why it took the forms it did and what these figures can tell us about the relation between political and sexual power, the interaction between the law and desire.

I begin my inquiry with two descriptions of Charles's sexuality, the first from a 1663 entry in Pepys's diary, the second from the anonymous satire "The Fourth Advice To a Painter," published in 1667:

> the King doth mind nothing but pleasures and hates the very sight or thoughts of business. . . . my Lady Castlemayne rules him; who he [Sir Tho. Crew] says hath all the tricks of Aretin that are to be practised to give pleasure—in which he is too able, hav[ing] a large————; but that which is the unhappiness is that, as the Italian proverb says, *Cazzo dritto non vuoltconsiglio* [an erect prick doesn't want advice].[16]

As Nero once, with harp in hand survey'd
His flaming Rome and, as that burn'd, he play'd,
So our great Prince, when the Dutch fleet arriv'd,
Saw his ships burn'd and, as they burn'd, he swiv'd.
So kind he was in our extremest need,
He would those flames extinguish with his seed.
But against Fate all human aid is vain:
His pr—— then prov'd as useless as his chain.[17]

In juxtaposing these two depictions of Charles, I do not wish to
slight the important differences between them, particularly the disparity
between private and public with which I opened this book. Pepys's
remarks represent the intimate reflections of one who knew the king,
served in his government, and, however much he regretted Charles's
sexual irresponsibility, remained a staunch supporter of the monarchy.
The second quotation, on the other hand, belongs to a famous series of
poems that began with Edmund Waller's "Instructions to a Painter" in
1665 and culminated, two years later, in the publication of four responses to that poem, the "Second," "Third," "Fourth," and "Fifth
Advice To a Painter."[18] These answers to Waller's poem demonstrate
the considerable power of the press, which succeeded in transforming
Waller's celebration of James's naval victory over the Dutch at
Lowestoft into a comprehensive indictment of the government's conduct of the Second Dutch War. All four poems convert panegyric into
satire, and the "Fourth" and "Fifth," not hesitating to make public sport
of the king's sexuality, include explicit attacks on a king "grossly snar'd"
by women.

Yet in spite of their dissimilar contexts, both diary and poem
present Charles's sexuality in an almost identical fashion, charting a
corresponding movement from male sexual power to political or military
impotence. In the selection from Pepys's diary, the royal identity initially
manifests itself in Charles's formidable phallus, the sign of his sexual and
political authority. At the same time, however, Pepys insists that the
king cannot control his behavior because of his physical endowments;
Charles, in such a depiction, becomes the prisoner of his own penis. His
very manliness, asserted by his prodigious member, subverts his manliness, for it leads him to be "ruled" by a knowing woman who has learned
all the "tricks" of the most sophisticated sixteenth-century pornography
(Italian, of course). This short passage reveals the potentially subversive
force of sexuality, which here generates the collapse of conventional

hierarchies: a subject rules the king, a woman overpowers a man, decadent foreign wiles overcome proper English virtues.

The "Fourth Advice" responds specifically to this final inversion, historically realized in the humiliating English defeat in June 1677, when the Dutch captured the fort commanding passage into the Medway, sailed up the Thames—burning British shipping and taking the flagship of the Royal Navy as a prize—and established a naval blockade.[19] The poem's description of Dutch success reveals a constant undercurrent of sexual innuendo—the Dutch ships "big" and "swelling," the English defenses "weak," their ships "unmann'd," their "honor . . . lost"—which implicitly portrays the military action as the rape of an unprotected female. The satirist's anger at this violation lights on Charles, who has abandoned the nation he must protect. While the nation's ships, symbols of its military and economic might, "burn'd," the king "swiv'd," as fucking becomes a substitute for heroic action. The lines go on to suggest, however, that the king fails in *both* roles, for like his chain—which was supposed to guard the entrance to the Thames— his prick proves useless. This final image denies Charles's ability to fulfill his role as the male protector, as either father or husband, of his symbolically female kingdom.

Together these two passages provide a stark delineation of what, during the rest of Charles's reign, would become a conventional satiric passage from erotic promiscuity to sexual failure, a radical conversion of Charles's ascendant masculine power into various forms of submission, sterility, impotence, effeminacy, and homosexuality. While the king's phallic preeminence should enforce traditional patriarchal hierarchies—fixing unalterable boundaries between the masculine and the feminine—it functions instead to erode distinctions between male power and female passivity. The apparently paradoxical movement, from the royal phallus that signifies power to the captive penis that signifies weakness, defines the satirical correlation between political and sexual authority that governed attacks on Charles.

I begin with Pepys and "The Fourth Advice" to establish the paradigmatic structure within which Charles's protean sexual identities were enacted. But the conjunction of diary and poem discloses other important considerations that will dictate the logic of my argument. The first concerns my reliance on occasional satires—broadly encompassed under the title of "poems on affairs of state"—which participated in the creation of an oppositional vocabulary aimed at subverting and degrading Charles's royal identity. In depending on satiric appropriations of

Charles body, however, I do not mean to limit concern about the king's sexuality to his political opponents; the selection from Pepys demonstrates that the disquiet that generated this rhetoric cannot be restricted simply to the adverse party. Charles's sexual behavior provoked anxiety in a far more general fashion, his body the site of a radical gender instability for supporter and opponent alike.

Further, the very nature of the poems on affairs of state will necessarily lead me to depart somewhat from the major parameters of my study. If, as I have suggested, the responses to Waller's "Instructions" demonstrate the considerable power of the press, they reveal as well the impact of government censorship. Strenuous efforts to locate those responsible for the writing and distribution of the four "Advice" poems followed their publication, and George deForest Lord reminds us that in attaining printed form these poems had few imitators; hardly any of the satires collected in his edition of *Poems on Affairs of State* were published before the Glorious Revolution.[20] Yet lack of publication did not prevent these satires from entering the public arena: disseminated in manuscript through the many coffeehouses that composed one of the chief forums of opposition politics, they enjoyed a wide circulation, both politically and socially diverse. According to Lord, for instance, Pepys secured manuscript copies of each of the four "Advice" poems even before their actual publication.[21] I will look more closely at the relationship between coffeehouse and print trade in the next chapter, for now anticipating my argument that, in the distribution of oppositional literature, manuscript and print define not conflicting or mutually exclusive practices but collateral activities. Though manuscript and print could play distinct political roles, and placed readers into very different relations to the physical text as well as other readers, both functioned together to define a coherent strategy for constructing a subversive public literature. As Roger L'Estrange insisted in 1677 when recommending to Parliament that it amend the Licensing Act to include manuscripts as well as printed matter, "it is notorious that not one in forty libels ever comes to the press, though by the help of manuscripts they are well-nigh as public."[22]

Finally, I juxtapose Pepys and "The Fourth Advice" in order to insist that in dealing with Charles's sexuality we will be working not primarily with the "facts" of the king's sexual behavior but with the shapes given it by literary and political language. The fertile, powerful, and dominating male monarch of Dryden's *Absalom and Achitophel* was no less a fiction than the portrait in "The Fourth Advice" of a weak, impotent ruler overcome by female charms. Although generations of school children have grown up with the image of an irresponsible "merry monarch," recent historians have questioned the wisdom of naively accepting the truth of contemporary gossip and satire.[23] Charles certainly recognized as much when he remarked in a letter to his friend in exile Lord Taaffe that "they have done me to much honore in assigning me so many faire laydies as if I were able to satisfie the halfe."[24]

But Pepys's description of the royal phallus also participates in this process of fictive refashioning. Central to the passage, of course, is the fixation on the connection between a man's ability to give and receive pleasure and the size of his penis. This passage turns on the revelation that the royal body possesses a royal member, though Pepys, with his typical reserve, cannot bring himself to write the actual word. Instead, at the heart of the passage lies the knowing blank, the refusal to utter the truth that so effectively reveals that truth. Yet what is the status of this "truth," this unmentionable "fact"? How has Pepys discovered the contours of the royal anatomy, for he never explicitly claims to have actually seen Charles's prick. Is this knowledge then derived from Sir Tho. Crew? The passage confuses us here, for it is unclear just how far to take the "he says," which would seem to include only the information about Lady Castlemaine's expertise in the realms of pleasure. Is everything after the dash Pepys's own, or does Crew's gossip continue for the rest of the passage? Does Pepys, or Crew for that matter, merely repeat the common "knowledge" of the royal court? Even the specific information provided by Crew calls on aesthetic formulations, for his perceptions of Castlemaine's erotic sophistication depend on Pietro Aretino's pornographic sonnets. The passage's final movement to Italian rehearses a common procedure in the diary for dealing with sexual matters: whenever Pepys includes specific details of his erotic adventures he disguises them (from himself?) in a foreign language. The foreign tongue alone can articulate repressed content, speak the unspeakable. Does this perhaps suggest that Pepys presents here submerged autobiography, the uneasy and unconscious confession of a man who was himself, as the diary so often reveals, driven by an erect prick, the organ that refuses to be regulated by law, that is a law unto itself?

In this fashion Pepys's diary suggests the difficulty of distinguishing between the facts of Charles's sexuality and the myths that grew up around it, inventions that reveal as much about others as they do about the king. This recognition is crucial, for it suggests the centrality of representation and interpretation to figurations of Charles's sexual behavior, the extent to which Charles's sexual identity was the creation of his subjects, the product of the complex interaction between the needs, desires, and fears of a ruler and those he ruled.

We can approach this relationship between the monarch and his sub-jects, and the way in which it manifested itself in Charles's sexual metamorphoses, by examining the word *easy*, a term that frequently appears in descriptions of the king by those who knew him personally. The related but diverse meanings of the word generate a relatively straightforward subversion of Charles's power, sliding as the term does from compliment to criticism. Its debasement of the king, however, takes an explicitly sexual form, one that feminizes Charles by writing unexcep-tional male philandering in terms of whorish female promiscuity.

The most famous use of the term comes from Rochester's "Satyr on Charles II":

> I' th' isle of Britain, long since famous grown
> For breeding the best cunts in Christendom,
> There reigns, and oh! long may he reign and thrive,
> The easiest king and best-bred man alive.[25]

John Evelyn, in his diary, uses various forms of the word in his final judgment of Charles after the king's death: "A prince of many Virtues, & many great Imperfections, Debonaire, Easy of accesse, not bloudy or Cruel"; "Easily, & frequently he changed favorites to his greate preju-dice"; "his too Easy nature resign'd him to be menag'd by crafty men, & some abandoned and prophane wretches, who corrupted his otherwise sufficient parts."[26]

The many forms of *easy* appear as well in Halifax's *A Character of King Charles The Second*: "his spending was rather an Easiness in letting Money go, than any premeditated Thought for the Distribution of it"; "This Principle of making the love of Ease exercise an entire Sovereignty in his Thoughts, would have been less censured in a private Man, than might be in a Prince"; "In short, this Prince might more properly be said to have Gifts than Virtues, as Affability, Easiness of Living, Inclinations to give, and to forgive"; "If he had sometimes less firmness than might have been wished . . . I would assign the Cause of it to be his loving at any rate to be easy, and his deserving the more to be indulged in it, by his desiring that every body else should be so."[27]

A number of these uses of the word and its related forms refer to its primary meaning, given by the *Oxford English Dictionary* as "At ease; characterized by ease or freedom from pain or constraint." The phrase the dictionary employs to illustrate this meaning is *Free and easy*, and in this sense the term possesses a positive significance, a definite compliment, as in Evelyn's characterization of the king as "Easy of accesse," or in Philibert de Gramont's initial description of Charles in his *Memoirs*: "The king was inferior to none, either in shape or air; his wit was pleasant; his disposition easy and affable."[28] Even Rochester ostensibly uses the word in this fashion, particularly because he begins by contrasting the easy Charles to Louis XIV, "the French fool, that wanders up and down / Starving his people, hazarding his crown" (lines 6–7). Contemporary evidence suggests that Charles was indeed one of the most approachable and open of English monarchs, equipped with a pleasing condescension that made him extremely charming and socially adept.

Yet most often in Evelyn and Halifax the context of their remarks suggests the second important definition of the word: "Fond of ease, averse to taking pains or thought; not strenuous, indolent; careless, thoughtless, unconcerned." Many thought that throughout his reign Charles remained far too fond of his ease and pleasure. Pepys, especially, complains of a king who cared for little beyond his "lusts and ease": "everybody minding their perticular profit or pleasures, the king himselfe minding nothing but his ease—and so we let things go to wrack"; "[M. Wren] seems to hope that these people, the Duke of Buckingham and Arlington, will run themselfs off of their legs, they being forced to be always putting the king upon one ill thing or other, against the easiness of his nature."[29] Rochester clearly plays upon both meanings of the word when his initial distinction between Charles and Louis breaks down, discovering a king who "Restless . . . rolls about from whore to whore, / A merry monarch, scandalous and poor" (lines 20–21). This second meaning of the word thus points explicitly to the way in which Charles's sexual behavior influenced perceptions of his identity as a king. If Charles's "easiness" defines one of his chief virtues as a man, it also reflects one of his major liabilities as a king. Too fond of his lusts, Charles ignores the serious duties that should demand his attention. From this perspective Charles becomes a type of irresponsible king, the monarch who lets "things go to wrack" because his energies remain focused on his bedchamber rather than his council chamber. The term *easy* even begins to suggest Charles's inadequacy in his chosen field of combat: Halifax's sense that Charles possesses "less firmness than might have been wished" takes on an explicitly sexual meaning in Rochester's poem, where "poor, laborious Nelly" must employ "hands, fingers, mouth, and thighs, / Ere she can raise the member she enjoys" (lines 29-31).

This focus on the bedroom, however, evokes a further meaning of *easy* that transforms Charles's ostensibly male rakishness into female weakness: "Of persons and their dispositions: Moved without difficulty to action or belief; soon yielding, compliant, credulous. *Lady of easy virtue*: euphemistically for an unchaste woman." This definition in the *OED* reminds us that *easy* in a sexual context has long been a gender related term. In Shakespeare, for instance, when *easy* possesses a sexual meaning, it invariably refers to women, as in *Cymbeline*, when Jachimo taunts Posthumus about Imogen's "being so easy" (I.iv.47), or in *Alls Well That Ends Well*, when Lafew accuses Diana of being "an easy glove, my lord, she goes off and on at pleasure" (V.iii.277). Used to describe Charles, the term *easy* refers then not simply to the quantity of his amours but to the debasement of his proper male identity. Charles is led by his prick, his power as king diminished precisely because, in Rochester's wonderful lines, "His scepter and his prick are of a length; / And she may sway the one who plays with th'other." Charles surrenders his masculinity—and his potency as king—to the women he desires, putting himself, in Pepys's words, "at the command of any woman like a slave."[30] As king, Charles is "menaged," according to Evelyn above, not simply by "crafty men," but by "some abandoned and prophane wretches, who corrupted his otherwise sufficient parts." Here the contrast between "crafty men" and "prophane wretches," as well as the pun on the word "parts," suggests the female identity of those wretches. This connotation of *easy* thus explains a 1667 conversation between Pepys and Thomas Povey, treasurer for Tangier, where Povey complains "of the horid effeminacy of the king," for Charles "hath taken ten times more care and pains making friends between my Lady Castlemayne and Mrs. Steward when they have fallen out, then ever he did to save his kingdom."[31] Women, not politics or power, dominate Charles's life, and this inversion of proper authority, which demands that reason rule passion just as men rule women, exemplifies the weakness of his royal identity.

Both this complaint about the king, and the comfortable male fantasy that opens Dryden's *Absalom and Achitophel*, depend on the hierarchical imbalance between male and female. In Dryden's version of this sexual mythology, as we have seen, women are associated with a cultural law that has corrupted the active principle of masculine nature; Pepys and Povey assume the more conventional understanding of the relationship between law and nature when they identify women and passion with a nature that must always be subjected to men, reason, and culture. Though each writes this relationship in a different, indeed inverse, fashion, both use it to insist on the absolute distinction between men and women; in both versions power remains a male prerogative and hierarchy necessarily subjects women to male authority.

These discontinuities between men and women were supposedly written not simply in the political hierarchies of power but in the male and female bodies themselves. Marin de La Chambre, for instance, in his *L'art de connoistre les hommes* (1659)—translated into English in 1665 as *The Art of How to Know Men*—argues "that Man hath the vertues and qualities of the *Efficient* cause, and the Woman those of the *Passive* cause." The truth of this profound difference, for Le Chambre, is figured in the human anatomy: "to make this truth the more clear, we need onely consider the natural constitution of the Woman. For her weakness, as to the body; a smaller conformation of the parts; the fearfulness, which is natural to her; the delicacy and softness of the skin and flesh, and the many humours wherewith she abounds, are infallible demonstrations of the cold and moist temperament she is of."[32] Support for such a view could be sought in the authority of Aristotle, who, in James Howell's *The Parly of Beasts; or, Morphandra Queen of the Inchanted Iland* (1660), "doth affirm, that in the female ther is no active principle of generation, but that she is meerly passive, affording onely blood and the place of conception, the plastic formative vertu residing in the *Male's* seed."

In the latter half of the seventeenth century such views did not, as I have already noted, go unchallenged. The speaker in Howell's work who expounds on Aristotle's authority immediately derides it, for "this opinion is exploded by our modern Physitians and Naturalists, who assert that in the female also ther is an active and plastic principle of generation, with a procreative faculty."[33] The feminization of Charles II suggests that this battle is waged as well in the body of the king, for Charles's transformation calls into question the discontinuities between male and female upon which the conventional sexual mythology depends. Charles's sexuality provided such an efficacious idiom for interrogating monarchical authority precisely because his self-indulgent promiscuity undermines the patriarchal structures that his identity as father king ostensibly affirms. The royal phallus "observed" by Pepys becomes the contested ground for this questioning of the relationships between masculine authority and female weakness, political authority and sexual potency, law and nature. Celebrated in *Absalom and Achito-phel* as the "active principle of generation" who represents the nation's vigor and power, Charles also becomes the embodiment of a curious sexual mutability that explicitly contradicts Dryden's assertions of a strict and irrevocable division between the sexes. Charles's feminization reveals the instability of the triumphant male vision, as his *easy* nature discloses his passivity and subjection to women whose erotic powers master and tame him. These formulations of effeminacy and powerlessness question conventional assumptions about the nature of political and sexual power as the boundary between these ostensibly distinct activities and discourses is blurred and confounded.

In satires composed during the late 1660s, 1670s, and 1680s, the subtle modulations of gender visible in the various meanings of *easy* assumed much more extreme and subversive forms when attached to representations of Charles as the symbol of England's international ambitions. In "The Fourth Advice," as we have seen, this process of feminization manifests itself in an impotence at once both erotic and military. Indeed, if Anne Barbeau Gardiner correctly interprets the medal struck by the Dutch to commemorate the 1667 Peace of Breda, foreign nations, too, appreciated the connection between sexual and martial weakness: the United Provinces memorialized their victory over the English by displaying Charles's eviscerated and castrated body beneath their feet.[34]

    In the anonymous 1676 verse satire on Charles and his father, "A Dialogue between the Two Horses," Elizabeth participates in Charles's humiliation by accentuating his failings as a national leader when the poem calls for "A Tudor! a Tudor! We've had Stuarts enough, / None ever reign'd like old Bess in her ruff."[35] The stinging rebuke contained in the comparison between "old Bess in her ruff," the supposedly weak woman who exemplifies royal power, and the male Charles, who "will ne'er fight unless't be for queans," suggests at once the power of the mythology that had grown up around Elizabeth, and the way in which a nostalgia for her English Golden Age served to feminize Charles, whose ostensible male potency is mocked and debased through comparisons to Elizabeth's masculinized monarch. The contrast between a royal queen and a vulgar prostitute emphasizes Charles's failure to transform sexual superiority into political or martial power. The Whigs' Pope-burning processions, staged intermittently during the 1670s and 1680s on 17 November, the anniversary of Elizabeth's accession in 1558, implicitly contrasted her royal power and authority to Charles's weakness, measuring his inadequacies against Elizabeth's idealized and irreproachable historical standard.[36]

As a vision of past Protestant glory, Elizabeth functioned as a mythic figure, the personification of a national greatness and illustrious Protestant history now threatened by the possibility of a popish successor. Presented as part of a lost edenic past, Elizabeth, and the royal authority she exemplified, could be celebrated as a benign historical ideal. Louis XIV, on the other hand, a contemporary and rival monarch, reveals the ambivalence that many English must have felt for a monarch who wielded an unchecked political authority. Louis problematizes the question of royal sovereignty that the idealization of Elizabeth suppresses, and he does so by further complicating the presentation of Charles's sexuality.

To a large extent, satirists present the monarch of Catholic France as the antithesis of a proper English monarch. In "Britannia and Raleigh" (1674-1675), John Ayloffe embodies Louis as the tyrant king whose unjust authority Charles must resist and reject:

> A colony of French possess the court;
> . . . .
> I'th'sacred ear tyrannic arts they croak,
> Pervert his mind, his good intentions choke,
> Tell him of golden Indies, fairy lands,
> Leviathans, and absolute commands.
> Thus fairy-like the King they steal away,
> And in his place a Louis changeling lay.[37]

Here the demonic imagery emphasizes the baleful influence of the French, the way in which they attempt to transform a righteous English king into a French tyrant. In the opening of Ayloffe's poem Charles threatens to assume not a powerless female role but a frightening tyrannical identity.

Ayloffe measures the extent of England's danger by the type of comparison to Elizabeth that we have just examined. Ayloffe dramatizes Charles's perversion by contrasting the "Tudor's blest reign," her "virgin arms" and "golden days," to

> a dame bedeck'd with spotted pride,
> Fair flower-de-luces within an azure field;

Her left arm bears the ancient Gallic shield,
By her usurp'd, her right a bloody sword,
Inscrib'd *Leviathan the Sov'reign Lord.* [lines 60–64]

These two female figures struggle to shape Charles's royal identity, the result
of this battle indicative both of Charles's passivity, his male power subor-
dinated to female influences, and of England's troubled state:

But his fair soul, tranform'd by that French dame,
Had lost all sense of honor, justice, fame.
Like a tame spinster in's seragl' he sits,
Beseig'd by whores, buffoons, and bastard chits;
Lull'd in security, rolling in lust,
Resigns his crown to angel Carwell's trust. [lines 117–22]

Ayloffe appears to offer in his poem a straightforward condemnation of Charles in terms we have already examined. When Charles
becomes "a tame spinster in's seragl' " he completes a movement that
sees him first compared to Elizabeth's masculinized monarch, then
subjected to women, and finally transformed into a woman. His weakness for women makes him not only their tool but a womanish figure as
well, a female who no longer rules his own kingdom. This insistence on
Charles as a "tame spinster" has him betray both his kingdom and his
own manhood, his transformation into a woman marking one limit of
the king's sexual mutability. The Latin apostrophe to Charles—often
attributed to Rochester—found at the conclusion of the anonymous
"Fifth Advice To a Painter" (1667), rehearses an identical procedure:
"You shun battles and chase beauties, hate what is warlike and make
your wars in bed. Being fond of peace you love the weak. You seem like
bold Mars only in the works of Venus, but like Venus in the arms of
Mars" (lines 153–56). Figured as both "bold Mars" and weak "Venus,"
Charles is at once master and servant, the active symbol of potency and
the passive object of another's power. The contradictions that inform
these descriptions of Charles as a woman suggest the paradoxical nature
of Charles's sexuality, for he betrays the male mythology of power
precisely because he so assiduously pursues it. His sexual activity defines
at once his strength and his weakness, for his promiscuity expends his
sexual powers, disseminating his maleness rather than consolidating it.
    In Ayloffe's poem, however, the king's bisexuality becomes an
even more puzzling formulation, for this satire's presentation of Charles

contains a significant contradiction that it resolutely ignores. The poem begins, after all, by damning Louis for his insistence on "absolute commands," for his desire to rule as a tyrant, a "Leviathan." His influence over Charles, therefore, constitutes a danger because it would tempt the English king to "Taste the delicious sweets of sov'reign power; / 'Tis royal game whole kingdoms to deflower. / Three spotless virgins to your bed I bring" (lines 98–100). Louis would transform Charles into a male tyrant who would rape his three kingdoms, the very antithesis of the loving yet powerful "virgin" queen who defines proper English sovereignty. Yet the ultimate result of French influence is to make of Charles a weak, ineffective woman, a monarch unable to rule at all. Ayloffe accuses Charles of being at once a tyrant *and* a lascivious king who sacrifices duty to sex, a man who would rape his own kingdoms by assuming unlawful power *and* a "tame spinster," a besotted monarch who denies his very manhood by putting himself under the power of women.

What other satires involving the relationship between Charles and Louis reveal is that the contradictions that exist in Ayloffe's poem depend on ambivalent English perceptions of Louis and the type of monarch he represents. On the one hand, Louis frightens the English because he embodies a conception of tyrannical royal power that the English wish to reject; he symbolizes the ruler who would engross all power and destroy the vital but fragile British relationship between Parliament and sovereign. Yet Louis also attracts those who attack Charles because he exemplifies a royal authority that eludes the English king. Satires directed against Charles frequently evince a respect for, even an envy of, the French king whose monarchical power manifests itself in his military prowess. Marvell's "Further Advice to a Painter" illustrates a contempt for a king who spends all his energy "jigging it in masquerade" with "his play'r"—Nell Gwyn—by contrasting the "degenerate" Charles to Louis:

> Thus whilst the King of France with pow'rful arms
> Frightens all Christendom with fresh alarms,
> We in our glorious bacchanals dispose
> The humble fate of a plebian nose.[38]

Charles's bravery in revenging insults against his mistresses—revealed in the attack on Sir John Coventry[39]—is measured against Louis' potency as a warrior. Against Louis' "pow'rful arms" Charles can oppose only his active prick, as in the 1679 "A New Ballad":

> While the French take towns, with a hey, with a hey,
>   And the seamen get wounds, with a ho;
>   I have a French arse
>   For my unruly tarse,
>   With a hey tronny nonny nonny no.[40]

In these satires Louis XIV provides such a disturbing contrast to Charles precisely because as a successful military monarch he represents a masculine king to be at once admired and feared—admired because he embodies the greatness of his nation and feared not only because that greatness threatens England but because of the English ambivalence toward a monarchical figure of such absolute power. Louis and the nation he represents are thus instrumental in attempts to generate a coherent English political identity, which, in depending on a heroic male leader to embody its essential strength, dictates that Louis would necessarily function in Restoration satires as a figure generating both intense disquiet and respect. From this perspective the feminized Charles testifies to the divided sentiments of those who attack him, furious because his inadequacy undermines the kingdom but thankful because his sexual failures assure them that he cannot assume a tyrant's hegemony. In this way Charles's impotence functions almost as a form of wish fulfillment, which allows those suspicious of the monarchy to limit and deride its power.

Charles's feminization, and the contradictions that accompany its deployment in "Britannia and Raleigh," disclose a fundamental problem facing Restoration satirists, that of imagining a monarch both militarily vigorous and constitutionally responsible. The insistence on Charles's impotence in so many of the poems on affairs of state reveals the difficulty in Restoration England of integrating a traditional image of patriarchal monarchy with more recent conceptions of parliamentary authority, the pervasive doubts that the English held about themselves, about a nation recovering from decades of civil strife and governmental experimentation, about a monarchy recently reinstalled and legitimated. The ambivalence that regulates Charles's satiric transformation from sexual promiscuity to impotence thus demonstrates the essentially conservative character of these satires, which, in spite of their apparently radical appropriation of Charles's royal body, accept the normative character of conventional patriarchal authority.

Reestablishing the integrity of this patriarchal ideal therefore turns on attempts to stabilize Charles's polymorphous perversity by relocating the source of gender confusion, removing it from the monarchical body that should represent the wholeness of the kingdom and fixing it elsewhere. Evelyn's diary entry for 6 February 1685, part of which we have already considered, suggests just how such a task might be accomplished:

> An excellent prince doubtlesse had he ben lesse addicted to Women, which made him uneasy & allways in Want to supply their unmeasurable profusion. . . . certainly never had King more glorious opportunities to have made himselfe, his people & all Europ happy, & prevented innumerable mischiefs, had not his too Easy nature resign'd him to be menag'd by crafty men, & some abandoned & prophane wretches, who corrupted his otherwise sufficient parts. . . . those wiccked creatures tooke him [off] from all application becoming so greate a King.[41]

Evelyn's reflections reveal that the king's weakness cannot be separated from the insufficiency of the object of his passion. "Women" are the problem precisely because "their unmeasurable profusion" causes a "Want" in Charles. "His otherwise sufficient parts"—the sexual pun is particularly felicitous here—which might have made him "so greate a King," have been compromised by the female sex whose excess creates a lack in men. These reflections generate grief out of the disparity between what Charles might have been—"an excellent prince," "so greate a King," a monarch who could have made "his people & all Europ happy"—and what his passion for women, "wiccked creatures," made him. The object of these caustic reflections remains Charles, though their moral force depends on a prior construction of the dangerous and corrupt female. Political critique depends on misogynous rhetoric, royal inadequacy constituted primarily through female insufficiency. In such a disposition Charles emerges as an object of satire primarily because of the worthlessness of women.

Neither Evelyn's scapegoating of women nor his nostalgic evocation of a "lost" ideal are unusual; both participate in a conventional conservative rhetoric. We can observe this rhetoric at work in John Lacy's "Satire" (1677), which expresses a moral disgust for Charles's sexual behavior and partners, a weary familiarity with an "ill we've too long known."[42] Though the poem rather cleverly opens with a reference to one of the central images of Charles's royal iconography—"preserv'd by wonder in the oak, O Charles" (line 1)—it quickly undercuts this hint of panegyric by enunciating its central concern about Charles's sexuality: "Was ever prince's soul so meanly poor, / To be enslav'd to ev'ry little whore?" (lines 7-8). At issue in the poem is Charles's enslavement, his betrayal of royal stature, responsibility, and authority to the merely biological:

> The seaman's needle points always to the pole,
> But thine still points to ev'ry craving hole,
>
> . . . .
>
> C———t is the mansion house where thou dost swell.
> There thou art fix'd as tortoise is to shell,
> Whose head peeps out a little now and then
> To take the air and then creeps in again. [lines 9–10, 13–16]

The "craving" here characterizes Charles as well as his "holes," both the king and his mistresses driven by appetites that have become mechanical, like the pointing of a compass. These lines play with the distinction between expansion and contraction, spatial freedom and bondage. The female anatomy is at once spacious, a "mansion house" where the king can "swell," and restrictive, the ground where Charles is "fix'd." The initial sense of freedom provided by the female body gives way as that body becomes the sign of Charles's self-imprisonment, of constriction and an oppressive male vulnerability: Charles hides in his little shell, afraid to do more then "creep" in and out.

The diminution from swelling to creeping suggests a physical debility that the poem next figures in images of the king's sterility: "How poorly squander'st thou thy seed away, / Which should get kings for nations to obey!" (lines 19–20). Though the poem will later complain about Charles's bastards, these lines imply that the royal couple's barrenness can be blamed on Charles, who has been too prodigal in his spending to produce royal seed. Lacy here articulates a concern common to attacks on Charles, which frequently register the anxiety provoked by the uncertain succession. In references to Charles's "useless seed" in "The Fourth Advice" and the king's "dull, *graceless* ballocks" in Rochester's "Satyr on Charles II," we can glimpse, beyond the predictable moral outrage occasioned by Charles's sexual antics, the considerable fear raised by the king's failure to produce a legitimate heir. Charles has squandered the masculine and imperial power that should be his; he fails to propagate a genuinely royal line, for his betrayal of hierarchy makes him sterile, able only to engender a poor imitation of majesty: "Witness the royal line sprung from the belly / Of thine anointed Princess, Madam Nelly" (lines 23–24).

In the next twenty-seven lines, the royal mistresses Nell Gwyn and Barbara Palmer become the object of Lacy's attack, for they allow Lacy to castigate very different failings of the king. In Nell Gwyn he can express contempt "To see the bitch in so high equipage" (line 34), exploiting the ostensible difference in rank between a woman who "in the playhouse . . . took her degree" (line 29) and the king who should be engendering a "royal line." In Cleveland, on the other hand, Lacy portrays an aristocratic woman notorious for her greed, lust, and ambition. Through Cleveland he can then confront Charles's financial irresponsibility, the king's desire "T'enrich a harlot all made up of French" (line 43).

In spite of the fundamental distinction of rank that Lacy employs here to distinguish between Nell Gwyn and Barbara Palmer, the poem depends on establishing an identity between the two women, their portraits united by an undisguised contempt for female sexuality. As in the opening to *Absalom and Achitophel*, Lacy's poem insists upon the illusory nature of the social distinctions that might elevate women. Though the poem remains an assault directed at the king and his sexual failings, in this section of the poem Lacy's disgust detaches itself from Charles and becomes affixed to the two women. Charles, of course, remains responsible for the disorder of the kingdom, but now the women, not the king, have become the sign for that chaos. The public "curses" Charles for its plight, but Gwyn is "the monster" it sees; Charles has sent his "exchequer . . . into France," but Cleveland's "monstrous lechery" is the cause. The satiric logic of the poem moves to scapegoat the two women, condemning them for a sexual obsession initially located in the monarch. Both portraits insist on the erotic nature of women, which defines them much more surely than social hierarchy: Cleveland can be compared to the imperial Empress Messalina, while Nell can be characterized only through a common madam like Ross, but the point of both allusions remains the same: both women are fundamentally "whores."[43]

Charles, to be sure, suffers much criticism in this "Satire," but no lines seem quite as heated or nasty as those that deal with the sexuality of his two mistresses. Perhaps this impression arises from the simple lack of originality that marks these lines, which merely repeat the vulgar rhetoric of misogyny: both woman are "monsters," both "whores," both "bitches." Lacy characterizes both women as "beasts," Nell "with open throat" as she "cr[ies] fresh herrings e'en at ten a groat" (lines 25-26), Cleveland as the "bitch [who] wags her tail for more" (line 52). Lacy can see little beyond the sexual in these two women, and that sexuality arouses only disgust.

The poem's concluding stanza reveals the reason for this displacement of the poet's righteous anger from his ostensible subject, Charles, onto Charles's women. For all of Lacy's contempt for the king, he harbors yet the hope that Charles can reform himself:

> Heav'ns, to what end is thy lewd life preserv'd?
> Is there no God or laws to be observ'd?
> Nineveh repented after forty days:
> Be yet a king and wear the royal bays! [lines 65–68]

The opening rhetorical questions do not, after the venom of the rest of the poem, appear to elicit positive responses. They seem to look not toward Charles's salvation, but his damnation, the uselessness of his wasted life, which so completely denies the laws of God and man. By indulging his sexual appetites, Charles has called into question the cultural prohibitions that make civilized life possible. Yet for all of this, the second couplet asserts the possibility of reform. Charles can follow Nineveh's example; indeed, Charles *must* recreate his royal identity, according to Lacy's command.

The poet himself cannot really believe in Charles's reformation, and having commanded it he again denies its possibility:

> But Jonah's threats can never waken thee:
> Repentance is too mean for majesty.
> Go practice Heliogabalus's sin:
> Forget to be a man and learn to spin,
> Go dally with the women and their wheels
> Till Nero-like they drag thee out by the heels. [lines 69–74]

These lines represent the nadir of Charles's presentation in the poem; beyond this, for Lacy, there can be no worse, for Charles has not simply given up his power to women, but has himself become a woman. As Heliogabalus, the infamous Antonine emperor who played the role of Venus in palace theatricals and bathed in women's baths, Charles betrays not only his crown and royal authority, but his very manhood. Though Lacy has just insisted that Charles can "Be yet a king," here he concludes that Charles cannot even remember "to be a man." Though the tone of the poem would insist that Charles's transformation into a woman represents an unnatural perversion, the overthrow of essential biological categories—thus the horror of what the king has done to himself and the nation—Lacy's language suggests the primacy of cultural constructions: one can "forget to be a man," one can "learn to spin."

Charles has not learned his role properly, and the last lines of the poem present the radical therapy necessary for Charles to become himself. Again the poem holds out the possibility of reform, but this time only a cleansing act of violence can make that possible:

> Go read what Mahomet did, that was a thing
> Did well become the grandeur of a king,
> Who, whilst transported with his mistress' charms,
> And never pleas'd but in her lovely arms,
> Yet when his janizaries wish'd her dead,
> With his own hand cut off Irene's head. [lines 75–80]

For Lacy "the grandeur of a King" depends on the sacrifice of the desired, and for that reason frightening, female body. Men cannot remain unmoved by the erotic powers of women: Mahomet, like Charles, is "transported with his mistress' charms" and finds pleasure only "in her lovely arms." But the dictates of political power demand the subordination of the erotic; male power, in this poem, establishes itself through the erasure, indeed the annihilation, of women, whose beheading signals Charles's recovery of his royal identity:

> Make such a practice of thyself as this,
> Then shalt thou once more taste of happiness:
> Each one will love thee, and the Parliament
> Will their unkind and cruel votes repent,
> And at thy feet lay open all their purses. [lines 81–85]

The violent conclusion to Lacy's satire, directed not at the poem's ostensible object of attack, Charles, but at the women whom it ultimately holds responsible for his weakness, calls into question assumptions about the "natural" that structure the poem. The poem possesses an hysterical edge in its treatment of women that suggests the fragility of the male order that it wishes to define as proper and indeed inevitable. By the poem's conclusion, only violence can reestablish traditional hierarchies of rank and gender, the fundamental and supposedly unalterable distinctions between nature and culture.

Murder begets love in the conclusion to Lacy's poem, Charles's destruction of his women transforming the cruelty of those who before opposed him. By reasserting his masculine power, Charles can rediscover his royal power, making women of his opposition, who will "open" themselves and their purses at his feet. The open purses should remind us of the earlier criticism in the poem that Charles has "squander'st . . . [his] seed"; now that he will no longer spend his substance, he can consolidate his power. In righting the kingdom's sexual hierarchy, confirming the proper subordination of female to male, Charles can reestablish the rightful hierarchy between ruler and subject, and finally secure the authority that should animate his royal identity.

Lacy's imaginative reconstruction of a healthy kingdom locates Charles within an exclusively male world in which he flourishes anew as the object of a powerful male narcissism. The "janizaries" who demand Irene's sacrifice, the Parliament that finally celebrates Charles's sexual and political recovery, "Each one [who] will love thee" in line 83 are all implicitly male. Lacy rescues his king by dispossessing women, the achievement of national and monarchical unity symbolized in a self-regarding circle of masculine love and admiration.

Recent feminist criticism helps to explain the dynamics of such a gender system. In her analysis of *The Country Wife*, Eve Kosofsky Sedgwick argues that "men's heterosexual relationships in the play have as their raison d'etre an ultimate bonding between men; and that this bonding, if successfully achieved, is not detrimental to 'masculinity' but definitive of it."[44] According to Jane Gallop, "Men exchange women for heterosexual purposes, but the real intercourse is that exchange between men. The heterosexual object is irretrievably lost in the circuits, and the man is consoled by the homology."[45] Such formulations insist that heterosexuality, therefore, can only be understood as part of a larger disposition of homosocial relations;[46] heterosexual spending takes its meaning only from the homosocial economy that supports the sexual currency, relations between men the primary goal of heterosexual relationships. The conclusion of Lacy's poem, then, should come as no surprise, for it merely makes explicit the marginalization of women upon which such a sexual economy depends, and which it perpetuates. Charles triumphantly redeems his masculinity only when he sacrifices his women to secure his relationship with other men.

I will conclude this chapter by examining a work that might be said to begin where Lacy's poem ends, for the notorious *Sodom,* one of the most unusual literary products of Restoration England, dramatizes the sexual implications of Lacy's execution of the female body, erasing feminine desire entirely by enacting an unusual movement from the homosocial to the homosexual. Scholars normally regard this play as a bizarre freak and treat it almost entirely as a bibliographical curiosity.[47] Yet within the context of Restoration depictions of Charles's enigmatic sexual identity, *Sodom's* grotesque and singular logic can illuminate many of the questions with which this chapter began.

   Sodom neutralizes the threat women pose to masculine preeminence not through the patriarchal structures that normally limit women, but by their banishment altogether from the play's sexual economy. Within the western patriarchal system, women play a subservient though necessary role. They function, Gayle Rubin explains, as "the most precious of gifts," the currency upon which all gender relations depend: "If it is women who are being transacted, then it is the men who give and take them who are linked, the woman being a conduit of a relationship rather than a partner to it. . . . The relations of such a system are such that women are in no position to realize the benefits of their own circulation. As long as the relations specify that men exchange women, it is men who are the beneficiaries of the product of such exchanges—social organization."[48]

   Sodom fractures the sexual economy Rubin describes by attempting to remove women from the exchange between men. The rupturing of this current liberates a hatred and fear of women that, while an inherent part of the conventional system of exchange, must nevertheless be significantly repressed if that system is to function. In attempting to do away with women, the play can indulge a frank, even hysterical, renunciation of the female body, fashioning its infamous obscenity quite directly as a violent attack on women, an integral part of its attempt not simply to marginalize but to annihilate the female anatomy, a strategy and tone determined by perceptions of Charles's sexual weakness. Indeed, the play's sexual disgust with women cannot be separated from its political purposes, its attempt to revitalize the monarchy and the patriarchal structures that the king represents. In *Sodom* political and sexual anxiety join to create a powerful vision of the male desire for self-sufficiency and transcendence.

   Sodom begins by disingenuously ignoring its political involvement, imagining, in the first of its two extant prologues, an audience attending to matters not of state but of sex:

By Heaven a noble audience here to day
Well Sirs, you're come to see this bawdy Play
And faith it is Debauchery compleat,
The very name of 't made you mad to see't;
I hope 't will please you well, by Yove, I think
You all love bawdy things as whores love chink.
. . . .

It is the most debauch'd heroick piece
That e're was wrote, what dare compare with this,
Here's that will fit your fancy with delight
't Will tickle every vein, and please your sight,
Nay make your prick to have an appetite.[49]

The play's unusual frankness about its lascivious intent, its apparently single-minded desire to "make all pricks to stand and cunts to gape" (5), serves to obfuscate its far more dangerous political implications. Yet even as it affirms its goal of arousing desire, the play uses a literary vocabulary—insisting that it will be a "debauch'd *heroick* piece"—employing as the play opens with a speech by the king, Bolloxinion, an ironic discourse that places it securely among satires directed against Charles's sexuality:

Thus in the Zenith of my Lust I reign:
I eat to swive, and swive to eat again;
Let other Monarchs, who their scepters bear
To keep their subjects less in aw than fear,
Be slaves to crowns, my Nation shall be free—
My Pintle only shall my scepter be;
My Laws shall act more pleasure than command
And with my Prick, I'll govern all the land. [9]

Bolloxinion's rant, with its emphatic mock heroic accents, should immediately remind us of Buckingham's *Rehearsal* (1671), written probably within a few years of *Sodom* and directed at the same theatrical form, the heroic drama. *The Rehearsal*, however, directs itself chiefly against the literary sins of the form, its major targets Dryden, satirized in the absurd figure of Bays, and the dramatic conventions of the form itself. *Sodom*, on the other hand, focuses on the protagonist of the heroic drama, creating in Bolloxinion a monstrous sexual version of Dryden's Boabdelin, whose opening speech in *The Conquest of Granada* (1670) these lines parody. As this speech reveals, such a figure clearly satirizes Charles, the conventional identity between prick and scepter the most obvious indication of the play's political import. In his elevation of pleasure above power and easy desire to subordinate fear to freedom, Bolloxinion suggests Charles as well, though Bolloxinion represents Charles raised to the nth power, his desire to entirely replace scepter with prick—"My Pintle only shall my scepter be"—providing an outlandish comic exaggeration that moves the play into a realm of unrestricted sexual fantasy.

From the very beginning the play reveals the extraordinary violence against women that inhabits its fabulous sexual landscape; both versions of the prologue express a sensual obsession with women that cannot be separated from a pronounced disgust with the female body. The first begins by insisting that "cunts [are] Loves proper center," but follows this assertion with a long catalog of repulsive images:

> Their ulcer'd cunts by being so abus'd
> . . . .
> May well be styl'd, Love's nasty common sink;
> When e're your fancy is to fuck inclin'd,
> If they are sound or not, perhaps you'll find
> Some of their cunts so stufft with gravy thick
> That like an Irish Bogg, they'll drown your prick
> Some swive so much their hair's worn off the spot
> They're dead to sin and do beginn to rot; [3-4]

The second version of the prologue recapitulates this movement from defining cunt as "Loves proper center" to "Love's nasty common sink" by celebrating "Al . . . ty Cunts" even as it bewails "her tedious toyl" (5). By its end, the second prologue has concluded that "none but fops alone to cunts will bow," for "she that hath a cunt will be a whore" (6).

These bipolar perceptions of the female sex and body produce the central tension of the play, the obvious though unexamined contradiction that animates dramatic action when it becomes attached to the figure of Bolloxinion. As we have seen, Bolloxinion begins *Sodom* as a king who insists that political power can be understood and expressed only as a manifestation of his royal phallus, the male organ that generates and sustains the patriarchal structures of society. Pockenello, "Favorite of the King," endorses this vision of the political world, insisting that "Your Grace alone hath from the Powers above / A princely wisdom, and a princely Love" (10). In Pockenello's version of the royal state, which surely bears comparison with the opening of *Absalom and Achitophel*, the sexualized monarch possesses his warrant from heaven.

The uniqueness of *Sodom* lies in its conversion of this political sexuality from a heterosexual to a homosexual bias. What Evelyn regarded as an "addiction" to women is profoundly altered, the object of the king's desires transformed by the play's unstable depictions of the female sex. Though Bolloxinion's opening speech in no way restricts the objects of his lust, both the prologues and first-act set—"an Antichamber hung round with Aretine's Postures"—suggest a conventional heterosexual orientation. Immediately following Bolloxinion's speech, however, Borastus, the "Buggermaster-general," when asked to provide for the king's lust, admits that "I no longer Cunts admire; / The drudgery has worn out my desire— / Your Grace may soon to human arse retire" (11). This rejection of hetero for homosexual delights becomes the structural principle of the play, which portrays the nation's transformation into a homosexual state.

As political satire, this inversion of "normal" sexual practice is typical, Charles's ostensible male authority undermined and subverted by the feminization of his royal identity. The "Merry Monarch," notorious for his heterosexual promiscuity, becomes a worshipper of homoerotic delights, his masculinity transformed into an unmanliness that threatens the kingdom. Yet the play pursues its satiric "joke" so relentlessly, that it creates, and almost validates, a world in which men can abandon the female body. In this sexual fantasy produced by a terrible ambivalence toward female eroticism, the play generates a realm of homosexual machismo in which male virility grounds and proves itself on the male body, the female body a sign only of a sexual difference that haunts and frightens men. Though these two strategies appear contradictory—the first degrading Charles for his homosexuality, the second valorizing homosexuality—both depend on a reinscription of gender difference that privileges the male even as it questions male superiority. As in Evelyn, female insufficiency easily becomes male want.

Bolloxinion is at first hesitant to adopt the new homoerotic order, even though Act I reveals that the king and his court are no strangers to the pleasures of buggery. Though no homosexual novice, however, the king at first responds to Borastus's advice by insisting that "My pleasures for new Cunts I will uphold / And have reserves of Kindness for the old" (11). Yet he quickly admits that "As for the Queen her Cunt no more invites / Clad with the filth of all her nasty whites / Come, we miss-spend our time, we know not how / The choice of Buggery is

wanting now" (11–12). At the act's end he expresses his ambivalence
in a speech that, as Richard Elias has persuasively argued,[50] deliberately
burlesques Charles's 1672 proclamation concerning religious toleration:

> Henceforth Borastus, set the Nation free,
> Let conscience have its force of Liberty.
> I do proclaim, that Buggery may be us'd
> Thro all the Land, so Cunt be not abus'd
> That, the proviso, this shall be your Trust
>   (*to Borastus*)
> All things shall to your order be adjust.
> To Buggeranthos, let this charge be given
> And let him bugger all things under h . . ven. [13]

Bolloxinion's insistence that in sexual matters "conscience have
its force of Liberty" corresponds to Charles's desire to grant a liberty of
conscience to his Roman Catholic and nonconformist subjects. Here
the mingling of religious and sexual vocabularies reveals the sexual
apprehensions that regulate Bolloxinion's behavior. The speech begins,
after all, by insisting on the "force of Liberty" and that "Cunt be not
abus'd." Yet the rhetorical bombast of the final lines, with their insistence that Buggeranthos "bugger all things under h . . ven," expresses
not merely a taste for sodomic pleasures, but a forceful attempt on the
king's part to recreate the sexual universe. He determines not simply
that buggery shall be permitted, but that it shall form the chief pleasure
in all the land.

In imagining a world in which the king insists on the legitimacy
of buggery, the play suggests just how unsettling were perceptions of
Charles's sexual irresponsibility. The play subverts his power not because it necessarily takes seriously the charge that he enjoyed men, but
because the act of imagining such a "world turned upside down" reveals
the tremendous gulf between the dreams and ideals of Stuart absolutism
and the doubts and fears generated by the king himself. *Sodom* may be
understood as an inverted and perverse masque, in which the royal
presence assures not order, harmony, and proper perspective but chaos
and discord; the king becomes the symbol not of order's triumph, but of
its defeat, his erotic obsessions responsible for the nation's destruction
in a climactic sexual apocalypse.

From the ambivalences of the prologues and Bolloxinion's initial
adoption of buggery, these obsessions move forcefully to eradicate the

female body. Yet this procedure contains a grudging admission of female strength, a recognition that the female body possesses a power that cannot be denied. Indeed, the very extravagance of the play's antipathy toward women stems from this recognition of their necessary power; male power can assert itself fully only by eliminating the seductive and dangerous female body that can control and compel male desire.

Act III revolves around a scene that illustrates the play's forced and ambivalent recognition of this biological female strength. In it, the adolescent prince and princess, Pricket and Swivia, show their genitals to each other. Pricket, not yet fifteen, is still a virgin, though Swivia already possesses a sophisticated sexual knowledge. Pricket's reaction, as Swivia shows her "thing," emphasizes his astonishment that "the strangest Creature . . . I ever saw" could be "the Beards that keep men in such aw" (23). Swivia continues by insisting that

> This is the ware house of the world's chief Trade,
> On this soft anvil all mankind was made.
> Come 't is a harmless thing, draw near and try
> You will desire no other Death to dye. [24]

Swivia succeeds in seducing Pricket, providing the "plaisant pain" of his first sexual encounter. When he has recovered his senses they discuss the organ that has so overmastered him:

> Swivia.
> It was this Cunt, that made your Pintle weep
> And lull'd you so unto a gentle sleep.
> You gave those pleasures, which you waking thought
> On all my senses had amusement brought.

> Pricket.
> 't Is strange to think that such a homely seat
> With such delight, should all our senses treat,
> That such a gaping, slimy, hairy beast,
> Should from its maw give hungry Prick a feast,
> But its strange influence, I more admire
> My heart is glutted, yet I still desire
> And turn my freezing atoms into fire. [27]

Pricket's desire is again raised when Cunticula, one of the Maids of Honour, enters and frigs him until he spends. The act ends with the two women "*mournfully*" conveying the exhausted and now impotent prince to bed: "Tho he be living, he's as bad as dead" (32).

Act III of *Sodom* enacts, in a most unusual and even grotesque fashion, a primal scene wherein the young male comes to recognize the fundamental fact of sexual difference. In seeing the female "thing," and its absolute difference from his own organ, Pricket realizes the power of his penis. To some extent the scene dramatizes masculine superiority, as the attention lavished on the prince's prick by the two women provides what Irigaray has called the "woman's fetishization of the male organ [that] must indeed be an indispensable support of its price on the sexual market."

Yet the scene insists as well on the immense and frightening power of the female genitalia. Though Swivia assures the prince that hers is a "harmless thing," a "soft anvil," again and again Swivia talks of her power to make the prince die, to bring death and then "Resurrection," to "tickle you to live again." The sight of her cunt creates in Pricket "an agony," a "fire" that Swivia insists "I can allay." Pricket does assert that her "Cunt [is] a most obliging friend," but far more often he see it as "strange," "homely," "a gaping, slimy, hairy beast." Indeed, it is not the cunt that the scene figures, in Irigaray's language, as "nothing you can see . . . No Thing,"[51] but the shrunken penis after intercourse, that "poor little thing . . . as cold as steel," which only "cunt and Thigh" can raise again.

The rest of the play moves forcefully to counter this alien and frightening female power. By Act IV, Bolloxinion, who began the play uncertain about his taste for buggery, has determined that "Since I have bugger'd human arse, I find / Pintle to Cunt is not so much inclin'd" (36). He images the female genitalia as horrible and unnatural, characterized by a curiously absent presence:

> By oft fomenting, Cunt so big doth swell
> That Prick works there, like Clapper in a Bell.
> All Vacuum, no grasping flesh does hide
> Or hug, the brawny muscles of its side [36]

At once unpleasantly large, yet also hardly present—a contradiction revelatory of his fear of, and desire to efface, the female genitalia— women can no longer define "Loves proper center." This devaluation of cunt leads to a celebration of buggery, which comes to represent, for Borastus, a noble freedom peculiar to human kind: "Nature to them [animals] but one poor Rule does give / But man delights in various ways to swive" (36). Pockenello even applauds the act in terms that suggest the Promethean gift of fire: "May as the G . . ds his name immortal be / That first receiv'd the gift of Buggery" (37). By elevating buggery at the expense of conventional heterosexual sex, the play can remove women from the sexual economy of the kingdom. As Bolloxinion explicitly says, "Faces may change, but Cunt is but cunt still, / And he that fucks is slave to woman's will" (37). Act IV further introduces the movement of this court taste out into the nation itself. Buggeranthos, the General of the Army, enters to announce that his men have welcomed the king's proclamation: "They practise it in honour of your name; / If lust present they want no woman's aid / Each buggers with content his own comrade" (39). Men have become so enamored of this new taste for pleasure, in fact, that women have had to seek new forms of sexual release: "Dildoes and dogs, with women do prevail" (39). Banished from the kingdom's new sexual economy, women must seek their pleasure elsewhere, no longer part of the civilized order but devalued and forced into a bestial commerce. Buggeranthos tells the "moving" story of a woman he found "frigging with a bob'd Cur's tail"; since men have abandoned women, she has developed a passion for animals, particularly horses. Even here, however, women are scorned, for a horse whose "stateliest Tarse" she admires "Drew back his Engine": "At length I found his constancy was such, / That he would none but his dear M^rs touch" (40).

What this anonymous woman calls "this vile cunt starving land" suggests the relentlessness of the play's desire to punish women for their sexual power. Even when Bolloxinion takes pity on this woman, declaring that "She shall a Pintle have, both stiff and stout, / . . . She shall be mistress to an Elephant" (40), we recognize the male desire to humiliate the female body that Pricket first discovered in Act III. Ranged with dogs, horses, and elephants, women are effectively removed from a human world that now defines itself solely in masculine terms. Masculine delineations of the sexual world remain true even for the sex that has been banished, for nothing in the play suggests that women may themselves participate in a homosexual universe. In II.iii the frustrated Queen and her ladies attempt to satisfy themselves with dildoes, but these simulacra of the male organ provide no genuine satisfaction. Though one of the Queen's ladies, Fuckadilla, blames this lack on "Short Dildoes [that] leave the Pleasure half undone" (21), her mistress's desires fix themselves firmly on a man. The play, for all of its ostensible libertine freedoms, never imagines the possibility of women satisfying each other, for it wants to insist that only phallic power possesses genuine erotic potency.

The ruination that the king brings to his kingdom becomes intimately involved with contemporary politics when Bolloxinion receives an emissary from his brother monarch, Tarsehole of Gomorrah, who sends the king forty striplings as a present. There seems little doubt that "Brother Tarsehole" represents Louis XIV, particularly when the conversation immediately turns to war, the concern that Louis' relationship to Charles invariably raised in the minds of Englishmen humiliated by French might. Bolloxinion, of course, has no use for war, all his interest wrapped up in the soft peace that allows him to pursue his sexual desires. He forcefully proves this when choosing among the offerings sent by Tarsehole, elevating his pleasure above all else, his relations with a brother monarch reinforced not through the gift of women but of boys:

> Here my valued Gems, these are to me.
> _[pointing to the boys]_.
> More than the riches of my treasury—
> What does my crown and jewels do me good.
> Jewels and Gold are clay to flesh and blood. [43]

The introduction of Tarsehole speaks not only to contempt for Charles's passivity but to suspicion of his relationship with Louis. Throughout his reign, Charles's intimacy with and dependence on Louis generated a lack of trust between monarch and subject. This special relationship between Bolloxinion and Tarsehole perhaps gives a dangerous meaning to the former's boast during this scene that "I have fuckt and bugger'd all the land" (42)—suspected of being in league with Louis, Charles could be seen not as a protector, but despoiler of his own kingdom.

And this is precisely the role that Bolloxinion plays in the final scene of _Sodom_. Bolloxinion has paraded his heroic pride from the beginning of the play, his boast that "with my Prick, I'll govern all the land" revealing his extraordinary sexual narcissism. In this final scene we discover the full destructive fury of these outsized desires, which lead him to insist on his sexual domination of even the gods:

> I'll than invade and bugger all the G . ds
> And drain the spring of their immortal c . ds,

Then make them rub their arse till they cry:
You've frigg'd us out of immortality. [51]

Bolloxinion's rage stems from his failure to transform the sexual nature of his kingdom. He has attempted to deny male insufficiency by banishing the sexual other, forgetting, as David Lee Miller reminds us, that in modern constructions of gender, "the difference between male and female, then, is not that 'she' harbors a lamentable gap in being from which 'he' is exempt, but that 'he' projects onto 'her' a want of sufficiency that lurks within all subjects."[52] The desire in the play to erase the female body represents the passion for immortality, to bugger male gods in order to "drain the spring of their immortal c . ds." Such a desire cannot succeed because masculine identity requires a female other who testifies to male superiority. Evelyn pretends that female "profusion" generates male "Want," but the truth is that female want is the condition of male profusion. Without women Bolloxinion cannot recreate the land in his own sexual image, can only watch as a plague of biblical proportions ravages the land:

The heavy symptoms have infected all,
I now may call it epidemical.
Men's pricks are eaten of the secret parts
Of women, wither'd and despairing heart
The children harbor mournful discontents,
Complaining sorely of their fundaments.
The old do curse and envy those that swive;
Some fuck and bugger, tho they stink alive. [51–52]

The only redress for these evils, according to the king's physician, lies in restoring the kingdom's sexual balance: "Fuck women and let buggery be no more: / It doth the procreative End destroy" (53). Here the physician invokes the traditional rationale for condemnations of homosexuality, strictures articulated most systematically for medieval Europe in the *Summa theologica*, where Aquinas describes sodomy— "copulation with an undue sex, male with male, or female with female"—as one of four manifestations of "the unnatural vice." This vice contradicts "the natural order of the venereal act as becoming to the human race" precisely because it is not "in keeping with the end of human procreation."[53] Theologically as well as sexually and politically bankrupt, the king, like a Morat or Lyndaraxa, refuses to yield to conventional wisdom or natural law, determined to insist until the end on his own measure of heroic sexuality.

Bolloxinion's refusal to yield his sexual delights generates the nation's final destruction, as fiery demons announce the sexual apocalypse that will engulf the nation:

> Kiss, Rise up and Dally
> Prig, Swive and rally;
> Curse, blaspheme and swear
> Those that will witness bear.
> For the Bollox singes
> Sodome off the hinges,
> Bugger, bugger, bugger
> All in hugger-mugger,
> Fire doth descend:
> 't Is too late to amend. [53-54]

The childlike rhythms of this verse, which suggest a perverse nursery rhyme, point to both the approaching dissolution of the civilized order, as well as the infantile narcissistic desires that have led the nation to its destruction. Still refusing to sacrifice his mad heroic pride, however, Bolloxinion welcomes the approaching chaos, concerned only for his own safety and pleasures: "Let heaven descend, and set the world on fire— / We to some darker cavern will retire" (55). Here the play's ambivalence toward women prevents the masculine world from enjoying complete success. The attempt to obliterate female sexuality fails; the female body cannot, finally, be denied and Bolloxinion's homoerotic order remains unable to recreate itself or the royal power it comes to represent.

The play's conclusion, particularly its appeal to customary censures of sodomy, suggests that its ambivalences encompass not only the female body, but the male homosexuality that it attempts to present as an alternative to heterosexual sex. In spite of its grandiloquent delight in the male homoerotic, in fact, the play never presents two men satisfying themselves sexually on stage (as noted above, the play's phallic tyranny makes female homosexuality impossible). It shows us women masturbating with dildoes, women bringing men to orgasm with their hands, a dance that dissolves into oral and finally genital intercourse, a sister seducing her brother; though it constantly insists on the joys and virtues of buggery, that act must always take place off-stage, never presentable as a dramatic subject.

Though the play probably was not composed with an eye to its production, this curious absence in its sexual ragout suggests not simply the moral condemnation of the age—Restoration England no less homophobic than our own society[54]—but the impossibility of imagining a patriarchy that bases itself on homosexual rather than heterosexual sex. For all of its rhetorical celebration of buggery, the play cannot eroticize the sexual relationship of men, reveling instead in a conventional heterosexuality that possesses all the predictability of a pornographic movie. Without women to attest to their superiority, the men in Bolloxinion's court cannot establish or glory in their privileged masculinity. The feminized object of desire remains essential to the procurement not necessarily of male pleasure, but of male ascendancy; and however marginalized, the female body always poses a tremendous danger to the phallic order designed to obscure and erase it. Male anxiety can never be entirely overcome or resolved, the victories men win over women never complete enough to achieve the sexual omnipotence men desire.

The desire to banish the female body in order to realize a masculine fantasy of self-contained and omnipotent power is not in itself unusual in seventeenth-century England. Published approximately twenty years after the composition of *Sodom*, Richard Ames's *The Folly of Love* (1691) concludes by describing "some *Island* vast and wide, / Where *Nature's Drest* in all her *choicest Pride*; . . . / Producing all things which we useful call, / As *Edens-Garden* did before the *Fall*." This prelapsarian idyll preserves its serenity by removing women, defining a realm in which the narrator lives

> with a Score of *Choice Selected Friends*,
> Who know no private Interests nor Ends,
> We'd Live, and could we Procreate like Trees,
> And without *Womans Aid*—
> Promote and Propogate our *Species*.[55]

When Marvell imagines his edenic landscape in "The Garden," he, too, attempts to erase the female presence: "Such was that happy Garden-state, / While Man there walk'd without a Mate." In this "green Shade" Marvell contemplates an organic sensuality even more voluptuous than Ames's, in which "Ripe Apples drop about my head; / The Luscious Clusters of the Vine / Upon my Mouth do crush their Wine."[56]

In a more famous case, even Milton's Adam, while lamenting his plight after the fall, imagines a world blessed by the absence of women:

> O why did God,
> Creator wise, that peopl'd highest Heav'n
> With Spirits Masculine, create at last
> This novelty on Earth, this fair defect
> Of Nature, and not fill the World at once
> With Men as Angels without Feminine,
> Or find some other way to generate
> Mankind?

While James Turner correctly reminds us that in Milton's epic this "misogynistic yearning for 'some other way to propagate mankind' is revealed as a counsel of despair," he also admits that "there is clearly an undertone in the poem that points to the maleness of the good angels."[57] Indeed, Adam's reference to "Angels without Feminine" suggests that Milton has created the ideal homosexual world in *Paradise Lost*, where all good angels possess male names and enjoy a spiritual sexuality in which

> obstacle find [we] none
> Of membrane, joint, or limb, exclusive bars:
> Easier than Air with Air, if Spirits embrace,
> Total they mix, Union of Pure with Pure
> Desiring.[58]

These examples suggest that *Sodom* is not alone in its attempt to expel a sex that men apprehend as a "fair defect." The distinctiveness of the play, however, lies in its refusal to evade the problem of sexuality in the male single-sex economy. Ames, Marvell, and Milton's Adam remain discreetly obscure about the sexual potential of such a world, the first evoking an abstract organic state in which men "Procreate like Trees," the last simply asking for "some other way to generate / Mankind." All three create a "fantasy of non-sexual reproduction . . . [a] notion of holy asexuality," which, according to Turner, "recurred persistently in the visionary imagination."[59]

In *Sodom* the explicitly homosexual reconstruction of desire produces a significant alteration in this visionary strategy, the play's political anxieties transforming utopian vision into erotic apocalypse, a nightmare of fire, stink, and diseased, rotting genitalia; a sexual *Dunciad*, the play does not depend on a saturnian Dulness that helps to bring the "Smithfield Muses to the ear of Kings," but a sexual perversity and destruction that the king himself visits on the land. Though Charles's easy, self-indulgent sexuality may seem to have little in common with Bolloxinion's insistent taste for "men's beastly arses," the play's satirical transformation of the one into the other suggests the extent of the fears generated by Charles's antic behavior.

Sexually, for many of his contemporaries, Charles played his own fool, turning himself into a character in *The Country Wife*, where, as Sedgwick explains, "To misunderstand the kind of property women are or the kind of transaction in which alone their value is realizable means, for a man, to endanger his own position as a subject in the relationship of exchange: to be permanently feminized or objectified in relation to other men."[60] In this fashion Charles made his kingship a symbol not of an ordered and potent strength, but of a chaotic, frightening, and corrupting sexual weakness. Renaissance England created itself around the image of a Virgin Queen whose undiminished and uncorruptible sexuality bespoke the power of both the monarch and the nation.[61] Elizabeth presented herself as unique, uncirculated, "mint," aloof from the normal channels of sexual exchange. Charles, on the other hand, "spent" his erotic and political capital, his sexual extravagance degrading his masculine authority and making him, in the images analyzed in this chapter, less than a woman, impotent, sterile, effeminate, homosexual.

By redirecting Charles's desires through a homoerotic system of exchange, *Sodom* withdraws Charles from a circulation that threatens to invert the relationship between the male self and the female other. The play reveals, in its futile attempt to imagine an impossible ideal of masculine self-sufficiency, the tremendous resentment generated by this unwilling dependence on women, the intensity of male hatred of and contempt for the female body that normally lies submerged by the structures of our gender roles. The play practices a type of gender genocide, the intensity of its desire to annihilate the female commensurate with the futility of its attempt to imagine an alternative sexual economy.

Placed in the context of other satires directed against Charles's monarchical identity, his depiction as a royal homosexual in *Sodom* should not come as a surprise. In almost all of its representations, the king's sexual behavior arouses an intense anxiety, which reaches its climax in what Alan Bray has called the "shadow" world of seventeenth-century homosexuality: "it [homosexuality] was not conceived of as part of the created order at all; it was part of its dissolution. And as such it was not a sexuality in its own right, but existed as a potential for confusion and disorder in one undivided sexuality."[62]

In the movement from the comic certainties of Dryden's opening to *Absalom and Achitophel* to the apocalyptic vision of *Sodom* we can glimpse Restoration attempts to redefine the related categories of sexual and political authority after the frightening upheaval of the years 1642–1660. Dryden wishes to present a complacent male fantasy that assumes an identity between male sexual and political power. In subverting Charles's royal identity by means of his sexual behavior, however, Restoration satirists necessarily interrogate constructions of gender and the relationship between male sexuality and political authority. The implications of this dislocation of commonplace sexual and political assumptions play themselves out in the bizarre conclusion to *Sodom*. For all their differences, however, *Absalom and Achitophel* and *Sodom* attempt to create a patriarchal system of government that secures itself on the male domination or rejection of women. Both reveal a misogyny that would deny women a significant place in the social order. This is particularly true of *Sodom*, where Bolloxinion's celebrations of homoeroticism cannot be separated from the fears aroused by the female body. At the same time, however, the anxieties that generate the structure of *Sodom* stem from a monarch who is perceived to have threatened his kingdom by compromising his manhood.

Charles's betrayal of his masculinity is figured in a series of images whose contradictions demonstrate the ways in which a vocabulary of sexuality and gender—masculine, feminine, homosexual, heterosexual—has been coded in relation to authority, power, control, and autonomy. These contradictions suggest that what is at stake is not the king's actual behavior, but his symbolic meaning for Restoration England, his designation as "father" necessarily making him the focus of anxieties about, and attempts to rewrite, a national identity.

Figures for that identity in terms of Charles's feminization, impotence, and homosexuality thus reveal the doubts that lie behind the apparently self-possessed assertions of male power and political stability in a work like *Absalom and Achitophel*. In the opening to that poem, Dryden celebrates Charles's subordination of culture to nature, the king's unrepressed enactment of his sexual desires. Others, however, perceive Charles's promiscuous eroticism as a danger, for in refusing to renounce erotic for political power, Charles calls into question the suppression of our instinctual nature upon which civilization depends.

Charles's furiously erect penis generated a pervasive unease in Restoration England, for it in fact undermined the very phallic power that it should have represented. The political restoration of the king's power, which the escape narratives of chapter 1 figure in the ideal wholeness of Charles's fetishized body, cannot be understood or realized without a complementary "restoration" of the king's body; his political power and sexual power are inextricably intertwined in satires of the 1670s and 1680s, anxieties and doubts about the former mirrored and represented in projections about the latter. The transformations of Charles's hetero-sexuality examined in this chapter depend on the conflation of the sexual and the political, the nature and health of the body politic necessarily revealing itself in literary depictions of Charles's sexual identity.

That identity, as it emerges from attacks on Charles's kingship, turns on relations between the sexes. The sexual power of women threatens the patriarchal hierarchies upon which a coherent national and masculine identity "must" be founded, and all of the satires dealing with Charles's sexuality attempt in some way to control that feminine power. Figured as passive slaves and objects of male generation in *Absalom and Achitophel*, or as murdered sacrifices to male power in Lacy's "Satire," or as frightening, desirable, and therefore banished genitalia in *Sodom*, women must be controlled, marginalized, or destroyed for male power to assert itself. Charles's sexuality generates such powerful anxiety precisely because he is perceived as not understanding how women should be used in a male economy: he is soft when he should be hard, hard when he should be soft; he forms attachments to women when he should see them only as objects of use; he empowers their sexuality when it is his own identity and the nation's that must be concentrated, consolidated, and fetishized.

Part Two

The Language of Censorship

4. "The feminine part of every rebellion": The Public, Royal Power, and the Mysteries of Printing

Pope's *Dunciad* has proven so successful in enforcing its cultural vision, its portrayal of a climactic moment when transformations in the press released the horrors of social chaos, because to a large extent it obfuscates a genuinely historical understanding of the press's evolution in England: the poem defines a print "crisis" that had actually been under way for more than two centuries:

> Hence Bards, like Proteus long in vain ty'd down,
> Escape in Monsters, and amaze the town.
> Hence Miscellanies spring, the weekly boast
> Of Curl's chaste press, and Lintot's rubric post:
> Hence hymning Tyburn's elegiac lines,
> Hence Journals, Medleys, Merc'ries, Magazines:
> Sepulchral Lyes, our holy walls to grace,
> And New-year Odes, and all the Grub-street race.[1]

Indeed, in employing a vocabulary of the monstrous to depict the uncontrollable expansion of the print trade as a perverse and unnatural growth, Pope adapts a language used originally by the state in its attempts to regulate the press and secure for its own purposes the protean offspring of Gutenberg's invention.

This language suggests the revolutionary effects of the printing press on early modern Europe, in particular the unease generated by this first great manifestation of mechanical reproduction. There were, of course, other reactions to this new industrial process, and *The London Printer His Lamentation*, published in the year of Charles's return, testifies to the wonder it occasioned as well. For this anonymous author, the history of printing begins when people first traced letters with "Fingers, or litle Sticks in Ashes or Sand"; for centuries, however, "the Benefit accruing by that Invention tended no further than to the Composing of one single Manuscript at one Time, by the Labour and Inscription of one single Person." "Gottenburg" has changed all that, for now "In one Day's Time a Printer will print more, / Than one Man write could in a Year before."[2] A doggerel verse, to be sure, but nevertheless expressive of a printer's appreciation of and respect for the technology he commands. Here admiration displaces anxiety, the astonishing temporal compression of a year into a day registering the printing press's exciting potential to liberate and transform human labor.

The publication in 1979 of Elizabeth L. Eisenstein's magisterial *The Printing Press as an Agent of Change* marked a renewed determination by contemporary scholars to examine the specific cultural and economic innovations affected by Gutenberg's invention. For Eisenstein the printer became the nexus for a complex, interrelated series of changes in early modern Europe: "As pioneers in new manufactory and marketing techniques, early printers shared something in common with other urban entrepreneurs; but as pioneers in advertising and publicity, in agitation and propaganda, in lexicography and bibliography they must be placed in a class by themselves . . . focal points for every kind of cultural and intellectual interchange." Eisenstein's work has had a great impact on literary studies, particularly on the recent attention devoted to the figure of the author. Eisenstein recognized that "from the first, authorship was closely linked to the new technology,"[3] and in the last decade scholars have attempted to use her insights to examine what Michel Foucault has designated the "author function."

Attention to the author has primarily followed two principal directions. On the one hand, critics have emulated Foucault in his concentration on transgression and punishment: "Texts, books, and discourses really began to have authors . . . to the extent that authors became subject to punishment, that is, to the extent that discourses could be transgressive. In our culture . . . discourse was not originally a product, a thing, a kind of goods; it was essentially an act. . . . Historically, it was a gesture fraught with risks before becoming goods caught up in a circuit of ownership."[4] In such studies censorship governs the author's relationship to culture; literature itself, in the words of Annabel Patterson, is "conceived in part as the way around censorship."[5]

On the other hand, scholars have focused not on the repression of the author but on the progressive enlargement of authorial identity, the rights that in the seventeenth and eighteenth centuries began to accrue to professional writers.[6] In attending particularly to the evolution of copyright, these studies implicitly suggest that in regard to printed discourse at least, Foucault's distinction between the transgressive and commercial must be revised. Attempts by the English monarchy to regulate the press during the sixteenth and seventeenth centuries demonstrate that the "profits" of ownership cannot be separated from the dangers of transgression, that the relationship between royal authority and commercial printing is central to any consideration of literary form and authorial identity. As David Saunders and Ian Hunter argue,

> it was no simple matter to delineate the person of the expressive author in contrast to that of the artisanal book producer, to differentiate the economic interests of writers from those of publishers, or to determine the relation between a writer's legal personality . . . and his or her ethical or aesthetic personality. . . . Moreover, when these distinctions and relations began to be instituted, it was not as the sign of an emergence of the authorial subject or its illusion; it was as a set of makeshift solutions to problems arising from new circumstances and from the unforeseen interactions of legal, economic, technological, and ethical institutions.[7]

In this and the following chapter, I want to examine precisely the "makeshift solutions" devised by Charles's government to control the print trade during his twenty-five years as king. His struggle to master the press, to make it reproduce his conception of monarchical authority, depended for much of his reign on a complex series of laws and regulations, procedures and agencies developed for over a century by Tudor and Stuart monarchs. In the first of these two chapters, I will examine this system of press regulation and the ways in which Charles employed and refashioned these legal and commercial tools during the 1660s and 1670s as his government attempted to govern a restive press. I will focus particularly on the way in which the language of censorship determined the relationship between the printed word and a politically irresponsible populace, the metaphoric implications of a vocabulary designed to restrict access to a new and dangerous technology. During the sixteenth and seventeenth centuries, state power consistently defined itself in opposition to public discourse, which threatened to erode the system of rank and hierarchy that upheld social order. The Civil War proved a horrifying confirmation of such fears; after 1660 responsibility for the fall and execution of Charles I was attributed to the liberties of print and pulpit. Indeed, the very first act passed by Parliament after Charles

II's coronation, "An act for safety and preservation of his Majesty's person," established this position in law: "the growth and increase of the late troubles and disorders, did in a very great measure proceed from a multitude of seditious sermons, pamphlets and speeches, daily preached, printed and published, with a transcendent boldness, defaming the person and government of your Majesty and your royal father, wherein men were too much encouraged, and (above all) from a wilful mistake of the supream and lawful authority."[8] Print, and the public domain that it helps to create, "in a very great measure" destroy the fabric of royal power and civic order, overturning "lawful authority" and encouraging the "wilful" mistakes of "men." Here a singular authority stands in opposition to a chaotic power characterized by lawless multiplicity, unruly growth and increase. This distinction between the unitary authority of the state and the dispersed and decentered power of the press—especially as it evolved in the century prior to the Restoration—will form the subject of my first chapter.

In 1679, as the Popish Plot and Exclusion Crisis developed into a bitter contest against the Whig opposition, the lapsing of the Licensing Act of 1662 deprived Charles of the most formidable of his regulatory powers. The press had voiced and exploited fears generated by the plot even before the act lapsed on 10 June, and during the years 1678–1682 the kingdom witnessed an explosion of print unrivaled since the early 1640s, much of it explicitly concerned with the relationship between national politics and public discourse. In the second chapter I will argue that during the years 1681–1683, in three trials for high treason, Charles's government formulated authorial identity in a fashion that allowed the king not simply to successfully assert his control over the press, but to question the right of "the people" to participate in political affairs. Charles sought to stabilize the dynamic and fluid field of print by defining the author as a fundamental object of punishment and agent of transgression, restricting public access to matters of state by fixing responsibility for the dispersed power of the printed word in the author. In making the author the prime mover of book production, shifting responsibility for the economy of printed matter from the publisher and printer to the author, Charles brutally manifested his own royal power and created a "privileged" author as a locus of legal correction and discipline.

Hardly fifty years after the establishment of the first press in England, Henry VIII issued the first royal proclamation containing a list of prohibited books, "Enforcing Statutes against Heresy; Prohibiting Un-licensed Preaching, Heretical Books" (1529): "his highness is credibly informed that some of the said errors be already sown and spread within this his realm, partly by the corruption of indiscreet preachers, partly by erroneous books copied, printed, and written as well in the English tongue as in Latin and other languages, replete with most venomous heresies, blasphemies, and slanders intolerable to the clean ears of any good Christian man."[9] At this early stage of the print revolution, when printed books still shared the market with those "copied . . . and writ-ten," when the vocabulary of prohibition remains associated with the "ears" rather than the eyes, the chief danger to state authority did not necesarily lie in the printed book. The violent compaigns against the Lollards, for instance, in the fourteenth and fifteenth centuries, had employed a similar rhetoric against scribal editions produced in great numbers and aggressively circulated. And the pulpit remained an even more effective tool for resistance and subversion than either manuscript or book; as G.R. Elton notes, "to an administration engaged in putting through disturbing innovations, nothing could be more troublesome than public expressions of resistance and especially denunciations from the pulpit, easily the most effective platform for influencing the popular mind."[10]

Even so, this proclamation establishes the primary image of the book as a sower and spreader of poisons. In a proclamation issued a year later, the government not only proscribes specific books, but fashions the first licensing system; in spite of the formal legal rhetoric, the proliferating images reveal the anxiety provoked by an invention that apparently cannot be brought under the strict control of the state:

> divers heresies and erroneous opinions have been late sown and spread among his subjects of this his said realm, by blasphemous and pestiferous English books, printed in other regions and sent into this realm, to the intent as well to pervert and withdraw the people from the Catholic and true faith of Christ, as also to stir and incense them to sedition and disobedience against their princes, sovereigns, and heads, as also to cause them to contemn and neglect all good laws, customs, and virtuous manners, to the final subversion and desolation of this noble realm.[11]

From poison to plague, from slanders "intolerable to the clean ears" to blasphemies that have actually begun to penetrate and work on "the people," corrupting them, stirring them up, incensing them against all good laws, the movement from the one proclamation to the next testifies to the hyperbolic inflation of a language designed to stop a spreading contagion that seems to possess a life of its own, one apart from the severe limits of legal discipline.

In 1529 Henry legislates against a short list of specific books. In 1530 a list proves insufficient; effective prohibition requires the licensing of "any book or books in English tongue concerning Holy Scripture."[12] In 1538 "sinister opinions have, by wrong teaching and naughty printed books, [so] increased and grown within this his realm" that Henry makes the first attempts in England to license all printing: "no person or persons in this realm shall from henceforth print any book in the English tongue, unless upon examination made by some of his grace's Privy Council, or other such as his highness shall appoint, they shall have license so to do."[13] By 1546 printing has created a world where the "corrupt and pestilent teaching as hath of late secretly crept in by such printed books" requires a bitter course of healing: "So as now the purging of that which is noisome and hurtful cannot, without taking away some part of that being tolerable, be put in execution, being the books increased to an infinite number, and unknown diversities of titles and names, whereby specially to revoke, annul or condemn the same, the King's majesty is enforced to use his general prohibition, commandment, and proclamation." This general prohibition includes not only two paragraphs of interdicted authors—in which we discover names like Tyndale and Coverdale, Wycliffe and Frith—but further refinements on the licensing system: "from henceforth no printer do print any manner of English book, ballad, or play, but he put in his name to the same, with the name of the author and day of the print, and shall present the first copy to the mayor of the town where he dwelleth, and not to suffer any of the copies to go out of his hands within two days next following."[14]

In many ways these first seventeen years of press censorship encapsulate the sensibility and procedures that govern official attempts to control the print industry over the next century and a half. They demonstrate, first, the centrality of printing to the structures that support social hierarchy and rank. All of these proclamations depend on a characterization of "the people" that assumes their inferiority, their unreadiness to participate in the world of print. Indeed, at a time when probably less than a fifth of the male and a tenth of the female population could read, we might wonder at a language that seems so prone to rhetorical excess. To some extent this reflects the ways in which printed material could make its way in a primarily oral culture; ballads, broadsides, and chapbooks were available to "hearers" as well as "readers," and the 1540s saw a rapid increase in the production and distribution of cheap printed literature.[15]

But we may also attribute the hyperbole in these proclamations to the fundamental changes of the Reformation. England was a deeply divided nation in the 1530s and 1540s; though Henry and Cromwell accomplished the break from Rome and reconstruction of the church in England with remarkable ease, discontent and opposition—which did break out in the northern risings of 1536–1537—were a genuine concern.[16] Though, as David Loades notes, there seems little recognition by the state before 1520 that printing had created a new set of problems in regard to censorship, during the troubled decades of the Reformation governmental misgivings about the effects of print on the kingdom dramatically intensified.[17] Though there had been earlier administrative crusades directed against Lollard writings circulating in manuscript, the proclamations from the 1530s and 1540s increasingly blame social unrest specifically on the press, which becomes demonized as the power that corrupts the kingdom by perverting "the people," infecting them in ways that inevitably threaten the body politic. At a time when the political nation was restricted to gentlemen and the enfranchised burgesses and yeomen, when the vast majority of the population, in the words of William Harrison, had "neither voice nor authoritie in the common wealth, but are to be ruled, and not to rule other," "the people," stirred up, incensed, made neglectful through the press, could themselves readily symbolize the infection that desolates the realm.[18] The 1530 proclamation that institutes the first licensing system is entitled "Prohibiting Erroneous Books and Bible Translations," its yoking of licensing and translation, prohibition and language, indicative of the state's recognition that social authority and subordination depend upon control of the Word: "his highness hath therefore semblably thereupon consulted with the said Primates and virtuous, discreet, and well-learned personages in divinity foresaid: and by them all it is thought that it is not necessary the said Scripture to be in the English tongue and in the hands of the common people, but that the distribution of the said Scripture, and the permitting or denying thereof, dependeth only upon the discretion of the superiors, as they shall think it convenient."[19] Language must be kept from their tongues, books from their hands, for the hierarchy that sustains the gulf between the "common people" and their "superiors" depends on state control of the productions and distribution of the new print technology. Power most profoundly reveals itself in its ability to impose itself on the words subjects speak and read.

The medical terminology associated with print in so many of these proclamations indicates just how frightening the state found a print technology that stubbornly evaded its repeated efforts at control. Imagistically the printed word becomes the Black Death that repeatedly ravaged the kingdom during the fifteenth and sixteenth centuries, a power unhealthy, infectious, subtly and mysteriously contagious. Books become a corruption, a pestilence that violates the kingdom, penetrating a once-sound body and making it unclean. This medical language, fused with images of growth, of sowing and reaping, suggests a contamination of the organic processes of reproduction, a terrible inversion of the natural order. A plague has invaded the body of the kingdom, fragmenting a unity and wholeness that prohibitions and licensing procedures always attempt to recapture. Behind the multitudinous rules and regulations that will eventually define the legal status of the press, lies an edenic past free from the promiscuous fruits of mechanical reproduction, which inevitably corrupt the kingdom.

If such a language reveals the anxiety produced by print technology, it also suggests a magical apprehension of books and printing; however formal the language of these state proclamations, at times they betray a potent sense of the mystery and wonder with which people regarded this astonishing invention. To some extent we can see this in the anthropomorphizing of the book, the way in which merely reproducible objects take on lives of their own. For the most part the proclamations move forcefully from the books to the "divers lewd and evil-disposed persons" who created them, recognizing the human presence behind the object. Occasionally, however, the book becomes sundered from the human agency that produced it, the book, not the author or printer, "worthy to be damned and put in perpetual oblivian," the book itself "naughty."[20]

In the occasionally fantastic rhetoric that disrupts their bland official surfaces, these proclamations disclose a terrible sense that print has destabilized and disjointed the "natural" hierarchies that shape society and protect privilege. The proclamation of 1530 needs hardly a paragraph before it has conjured up "the final subversion and desolation of this noble realm," while in 1546 the state confronts a world in which "books increased to an *infinite* number, and *unknown diversities* of titles and names." Such a language depicts a kingdom that has become divided, manichaean, in which the world of law is threatened by a dark and secret realm of books that mysteriously propagate themselves. This type of hyperbole recalls *The Dunciad*, with its polemical insistence on the vast numbers of Dulness's minions:

> Millions and millions on these banks he views,
> Thick as the stars of night, or morning dews,
> As thick as bees o'er vernal blossoms fly,
> As thick as eggs at Ward in Pillory.[21]

In state instruments such language suggests not Pope's excitement and malice, but the profound bewilderment and frustration generated by a mechanical process that cannot comfortably be integrated within the social structures that have produced it. Books manifest a power that the state cannot entirely understand or control, participating, as Jean Baudrillard writes, in an "industrial revolution [that] gave rise to a whole new generation of signs and objects. These were signs with no caste tradition, which had never known the restrictions of status, and which would not have to be *counterfeited* because they were being *produced* on such a gigantic scale."[22] The frightening implications of this change in scale become apparent in the hysterical references to "infinite number" and "unknown diversities," in the suspicion that "status," the essential and "natural" gulf between the common people and their superiors, would be eroded and finally destroyed.

The necessity for prohibition occasioned by such anarchic increase meant that the growth of the print industry would be matched by the expansion of the mechanisms for regulation, as the crown assumed a greater and greater control over the products of the press. Inevitably this control expressed itself in the bureaucratization of the process of censorship, the ceaseless growth of rules, proscriptions, limitations. In 1530 only books dealing with scripture need approval, their fitness for publication signified by the name of the printer and the examiners. By 1546, when all books have become part of the licensing process, the name of the author and date are required as well, and advanced copies and delays in distribution are now mandated.

Confronted by an apparently infinite production of objects, the state reacted in a predictable fashion, creating an increasingly complex array of structures designed to restrict numbers by insisting on number. At various times in the sixteenth and seventeenth centuries there will be regulations regarding the number of cities that might maintain presses—only London and occasionally York and Finsbury, except for the university presses of Oxford and Cambridge—the number of master printers in the kingdom, the number of apprentices they might employ, the number of individual presses they might own; there will be instructions about which names must appear on a book, the proper number of copies to be given to the proper number of officials, and the proper number of days distribution must be delayed. Such formulations pretend that, like Lilliput, the state can imprison the Gulliver of printing if only enough frail threads can be spun about its monstrous and frightening bulk. Yet the language of these proclamations suggests the futility of such attempts to bound and limit the "infinite" and "unknown." While the specific provisions of censorship amass the press into a figurative leviathan, their very language discloses the fear that the power they seek to restrain is by its very nature dispersed, magical, and evasive. In following the complex web of royal proclamations and decrees concerned with censorship during the sixteenth and seventeenth centuries, one witnesses the inexorable accretion of regulation, the almost geological growth of legal discourse as each new law incorporates what it finds and adds another layer of prohibition. Laws directed toward press regulation become more lengthy and byzantine as they attempt to impose strict and concrete limits on an invention whose powers of reproduction always seem to fly one step ahead of the law.

The history of censorship in England through the middle of the seventeenth century reveals only one important conceptual reformulation, introduced in 1557, when Mary and Philip granted a Charter of Incorporation to the "free men of the mistery or art of Stationery of our City of London."[23] Peggy Kamuf, in her study of the institution of authorship, reminds us that "censorship must aim to suppress not ideas 'as such' but their reproduction and dissemination,"[24] and the truth of this insight is borne out by the decision to assign the chief responsibility for enforcing the labyrinthine complex of regulations created by the state to the individuals responsible for the production and marketing of books. Prior to this time, though there had existed a Craft of Stationers since the early sixteenth century, printers and publishers belonged to other city companies, primarily the Drapers and Grocers, through whom many books were sold.[25] With the creation of their own craft organization, however, the stationers gained a monopoly on the printing of books. Mary and Philip did not grant this valuable privilege simply to elevate and enrich the Stationers' Company, as the opening of the charter makes explicit: "certain seditious and heretical books rhymes

and treatises are daily published and printed by divers scandalous malicious schismatical and heretical persons, not only moving our subjects
and lieges to sedition and disobedience against us, our crown and
dignity, but also to renew and move very great and detestable heresies
against the faith and sound catholic doctrine of Holy Mother Church"
(xxviii).

According to one print historian, "the skillful use of the corporate
organization of printers and publishers in the suppression and control of
undesirable printing has long been considered a masterstroke of Elizabethan politics."[26] The Stationers' Company became the state's chief
defense against printing, a policy that remained basically unquestioned
until the reign of Charles I. The charter provides the power for the
company to perform this work by granting it the right of search and
seizure:

> it shall be lawful for the Master and Keepers or Wardens aforesaid and their
> successors for the time being to make search whenever it shall please them
> in any place, shop, house, chamber, or building of any printer, binder,
> or bookseller whatever within our kingdom of England . . . for any books
> or things printed, or to be printed, and to seize, take, hold, burn or turn
> to the proper use of the foresaid community, all and several those books
> and things which are or shall be printed contrary to the form of any
> statute, act, or proclamation, made or to be made. [xxxi]

In his history of the Stationers' Company, Cyprian Blagden notes that
only the goldsmiths and pewterers possessed a similar privilege.[27] The
crown did not lightly grant the power to institute national searches, and
in this case it clearly reveals the importance that the state attached to
the job the stationers were commanded to do.

As agents of the state they now possessed the right to police their
own industry, to control the creation and flow of books in the kingdom.
This power, in fact, would increase substantially during the next seventy-five years, a Privy Council Order in 1566 and Star Chamber Decree
in 1586 expanding their right of search and seizure.[28] In 1637 another
Star Chamber Decree grants the "Master and Wardens of the Company
of Stationers . . . or any two licensed Master-Printers . . . power and
authority, to take vnto themselves such assistance as they shall think
needfull, and to search what houses and shops (and at what times they
shall think fit)." In addition, all books had not only to receive a license
from the state, but before publication "shall be also first entred into the

Registers Booke of the Company of Stationers; vpon paine that euery Printer offending therein, shall be for euer hereafter disabled to use or exercise the Art or Mysterie of Printing."[29]

This reference to the Stationers' Register represents official recognition of a copyright system that had begun even before the original incorporation of the company in 1557. During the fifteenth and early sixteenth centuries, rights to a particular book or type of book could be established either through a royal grant or by putting on record publications not protected by royal privilege. Though the charter granted by Mary and Philip said nothing specifically about such matters, it gave the Master and Wardens of the Company power to "establish, for the good and sound rule and government of . . . the foresaid community, ordinances, provisions and statutes whenever it shall seem to them to be opportune and fit" (xxx). For the original ninety-seven members of the company, such "good and sound rule" required the protection of their rights and privileges through legitimation of a system that could combat the piracy of their printed works. The Stationers' Register allowed them not only to collect fees for the permission to print but to create a copyright that protected their interest in a work. This copyright, moreover, had little to do with the author. Rights to a publication under this system were vested solely in members of the company, those entrepreneurs who bore the financial risk associated with the enterprise. Books were the property not of the author but of the men responsible for making and marketing the physical object.

The right of search and seizure, central to the charter, thus appealed to both crown and company for very different reasons: for the first it represented a way to control seditious and heretical books; for the second, a way to halt infringement of their copyrights. As Alfred Pollard amusingly notes, "this Stationers' copyright was, in fact, the outcome of one of the most conspicuous instances of Tudor statecraft. The Tudors understood, as the Stuarts never did, that if they wanted to get something for themselves they must help other people to get something."[30] This relationship between the crown and the Stationers' Company was in no way unusual, for such reciprocal collaboration characterized the monarchy's governance of the London livery companies.[31] Nonetheless, more than any other royal act, the crown's creation of the Stationers' Company and legitimation of its copyright suggests the important link between state censorship and commercial profit, the intertwining of political and economic considerations in the production of literature and the attempt to restrict its circulation.

In concentrating on these first years of press regulation, I have been less interested in the specifics than in the language of censorship and what it reveals about the conflicting powers of state and press and about the government's concern with the relationship between print and the public. To a remarkable degree, Elizabethan and Stuart press sanctions all share the same imagistic complexity, the same assumption of an untrustworthy and vulnerable "people," visible in these Henrician proclamations issued during the first half of the sixteenth century. Such sentiments, moreover, cannot condescendingly be attributed to a monarchical system of government soon overcome by the swift march of time and progress, for after 1641 the same language informs parliamentary attempts to regulate the press. In 1647 Parliament worries about how the growth of printing has worked "to the great abuse and prejudice of the People," while two years later it laments the "subversion" of good government carried out by "lies and false suggestions, cunningly insinuated and spread amongst the people, and by malicious misrepresentation of things acted and done, to take off and divide their affections from that just Authority which is set over them for their good and safety."[32] In 1649 Parliament complains of "Presses erected in by-places and corners, out of the Eye of Government," and in 1653 it makes explicit what has always been implicit in the metaphors of dispersion, propagation, and secrecy: "many of the Evils and Exorbitances . . . appear to have been much occasioned through the multiplying of Printing-houses, without any Warrant or Authority, and by reason of the Artifice and Subtilty of restless Spirits, unwilling to be confined within the limits of orderly Government."[33]

For these early modern governments, confinement and limit define the nature and effect of state power; authority, whether royal or parliamentary, expresses itself in these proclamations as the ability to impose its shape and hierarchies on the kingdom, to recreate that kingdom in its own image. Print technology, by its very nature, must threaten that power; geared toward the efficient production and multiplication of images, the printing press and books that issue from it become emblems of those anarchic forces that frustrate the omnipotence of those who rule. The state sees itself as absolute, unquestioned, all-seeing: "the Eye of Government" would go everywhere, its gaze coextensive with the kingdom. By its sheer powers of replication the press reveals this flattering self-image as illusion, and the inevitability of the tension between state authority and the press.

The mid-seventeenth-century document that most profoundly

captures the power of and anxiety raised by printing, as well as the intimate connection between constructions of the press and the people, is Milton's *Areopagitica*, not itself a legal text but an argument against just such a text. In his critical response to the June 1643 "Ordinance for the Regulating of Printing," Milton employs the same language of growth, breeding, confinement, and fragmentation that we have followed in the previous century of governmental censorship. Yet writing from outside that legal tradition—Milton was not to become a licenser himself until his appointment in 1649 as Latin Secretary—he can recognize not just the genuine potency and truth of these metaphors and images, the way in which they contradict the very arguments employed by the state, but the necessity to transform such a language in order to bring into being an honest and conscientious citizenry. This undertaking, however, which according to Abbe Blum involves Milton in a "drama which only partly conceals the interdependence of author and authority," at the same time reveals the high price such a public citizenry must pay for its empowerment.[34]

When Milton explains that books "are as lively and as vigorously productive as those fabulous dragon's teeth; and being sown up and down, may chance to spring up armed men," he echoes the imagery of sowing and reaping used by Henry VIII in the 1530s and 1540s. The language of Henry's proclamations reveals the hope that proscription and licensing can halt this terrible growth; Milton's use and transformation of the image, on the other hand, suggests the impossibility of the task as books become "armed men," no longer passive objects but aggressive presences. Henry's proclamations reflected the magical apprehension of printing in references to "naughty" books of "infinite" number, but Milton's essay moves this recognition into an entirely different and more serious key: "books are not absolutely dead things, but do contain a potency of life in them to be as active as that soul was whose progeny they are; nay, they do preserve as in a vial the purest efficacy and extraction of that living intellect that bred them."[35]

Milton's notable reanimation of the legal discourse of censorship stems from a recognition that licensing is not simply an immoral but an impossible task; the metaphoric language used to limit the press reveals the futility of the very effort, for books are not simply physical objects. They are too alive, too quick, too spirited to suffer confinement: "truth and understanding are not such wares as to be monopolized and traded in by tickets and statutes and standards" (736–37). Milton can move from the licensing of books—and the stationers' monopoly that supports such an abhorrent system—to the licensing of truth and understanding because he comprehends that the object of interrogation is not the book itself but the intellectual being that it represents and reproduces.

In a similar fashion, Milton's famous use of "the mangled body of Osiris" for "the virgin Truth, hewed . . . into a thousand pieces, and scattered . . . to the four winds" (742) participates in all the images of fragmentation that characterize the legal discourse of censorship from Henry through the protector. Yet, again, Milton uses the image to suggest the impossibility of regaining a past golden age. In this world such perfection can never be achieved: "We have not yet found them all, Lords and Commons, nor ever shall do, till her Master's second coming. He shall bring together every joint and member, and shall mold them into an immortal feature of loveliness and perfection. Suffer not these licensing prohibitions to stand at every place of opportunity, forbidding and disturbing them that continue seeking, that continue to do our obsequies to the torn body of our martyred saint" (742). Writing, as he so often does, with an emphatic sense of the distinction between divine and human time, Milton can insist that perfection lies only in the former, the "immortal" realm; and that licensing, a product of the latter, can never achieve its stated end, can never remove all impurity and infection in what must be a futile attempt to return us to a perfection that lies only before us.

Milton, in fact, subverts the promise of regulation by imagining a kingdom of infinite proscription: "If we think to regulate printing, thereby to rectify manners, we must regulate all recreations and pastimes, all that is delightful to man" (732). He follows this with a series of increasingly ludicrous confinements, in which everything from bagpipe to garment becomes an occasion for rule and law. Only after reducing licensing to absurdity does Milton suggest an appreciation of its opposite: "This justifies the high providence of God, who, though he command us temperance, justice, continence, yet pours out before us, even to a profuseness, all desirable things, and gives us minds that can wander beyond all limit and satiety" (733).

Milton here rejects the legal language of confinement, undermining the logic of a century of press censorship through images of profusion and increase that suggest the uncontrollable reproductive powers of print technology: "They are not skilful considerers of human things who imagine to remove sin by removing the matter of sin. For, besides that it is a huge heap increasing under the very act of diminishing, though some part of it may for a time be withdrawn from some persons, it cannot from all, in such a universal thing as books are" (733). Milton's insistence that "truth . . . opens herself faster than the pace of method and discourse can overtake her" (731) can be seen as a reflection of a print industry that has changed the nature of truth and learning. Stanley Fish, without explicitly making the connection to the mystery of printing, nonetheless grasps the dynamic nature of truth in Milton's essay: "The image here is one that will loom larger and larger: it is of a truth that is always running ahead of any attempt to apprehend it, a truth that repeatedly slips away from one's grasp, spills out of one's formulations, and escapes the nets that for a moment promise to catch it."[36] The power that has made truth so slippery and vigorous, so lively and active, is the power of printing, which becomes a figure of excess that defies the state's ineffectual attempts to assert itself by limiting and confining the truth.

This celebration of truth's potency through the printed book, however, goes hand in hand with an appreciation of the responsibility books must therefore bear: "I deny not but that it is of greatest concernment in the church and commonwealth to have a vigilant eye how books demean themselves as well as men; and thereafter to confine, imprison, and do sharpest justice on them as malefactors" (720). This sentence introduces Milton's insistence that books are "not absolutely dead things," and it suggests the debt that books must satisfy in Milton's treatise for their metaphoric manhood. The magical language in Milton that equates books with people reflects both the power of printing and the vigilance that it therefore demands. In unfolding the metaphorical implications of his language, Milton magnifies the power of the book while at the same time exaggerating its responsibility within the state; confinement and imprisonment return as emblems of "sharpest justice."

Indeed, books can be subjected to this justice precisely because Milton demands it for the people. Where the legislation of censorship has always assumed the worst of the citizenry it protected—justifying itself through their legal incompetence—Milton argues passionately for their maturity, their accountability as responsible individuals: "Nor is it to the common people less than a reproach; for if we be so jealous over them as that we dare not trust them with an English pamphlet, what do we but censure them for a giddy, vicious, and ungrounded people, in such a sick and weak estate of faith and discretion, as to be able to take nothing down but through the pipe of a licenser" (737). Milton specifically rejects here the characterization of "the common people" familiar from a century of press regulation, though, as Francis Barker emphasizes, this metamorphosis occurs only through a complementary change in modes of subjection: "The decisive moment of control is now to be not so clearly the sanction of punishment, as the inner discipline, the unwritten law, of the new subjection. . . . The state succeeds in penetrating to the very heart of the subject, or more accurately, in pre-constituting that subject as one which is already internally disciplined, censored, and thus an effective support of the emergent pattern of domination."[37]

Milton's portentous argument against licensing is therefore carefully framed by its introductory insistence that "I deny not" the need for "a vigilant eye" and "sharpest justice" and its concluding vision of how such vigilance and justice will function: "no book be printed, unless the printer's and the author's name, or at least the printer's, be registered. Those which otherwise come forth, if they be found mischievous and libellous, the fire and the executioner will be the timeliest and the most effectual remedy that man's prevention can use" (749). Identifying the book primarily with the mechanical means of production in the figure of the printer,[38] Milton insists that ultimate control of the press lies with the executioner. If books are indeed like people, then the infection they bear—"remedy" and "prevention" suggesting the medical terminology of early censorship legislation—can be controlled only through the destruction of the diseased members.

Three documents from the first years of Charles's reign suggest the new king's difficult and ambivalent relationship to both the press and the long and complex history of state censorship that he inherited; and none of these documents, to be sure, acknowledge Milton's attempt to redefine the connection between print and a politically responsible populace. In 1660 there appeared in London a broadside entitled *The Original and Growth of Printing* in which the anonymous author rewrote the then accepted history of printing in England. He argues that even before William Caxton founded his press at Westminster in 1476, Henry VI had established a press in 1468 at Oxford. For proof, the author claims both that "a Book came to my Hands Printed at *Oxon. Anno Dom.* 1468," and that he has been entrusted with a manuscript from Lambeth House that tells of "a Hollander," Frederick Corsells or Corsellis, adept in the mysteries of printing, who was brought surreptitiously to England by Mr. Robert Turnour, "of the Roabs to" Henry VI. Henry, along with Thomas Bourchier, archbishop of Canterbury, had funded the project in the amount of 1500 Marks, because of which, even after two presses were set up in London, no printer could "exercise that ART, but only

such as were the Kings sworn Servants; the King himself having the
Price and Emolument for Printing Books."[39]

In 1664 this broadside was reissued as a pamphlet, its argument
swollen to twenty-four pages, its author proudly acknowledged as Richard Atkyns, even its title bearing signs of its metamorphosis: *The Original
and Growth of Printing: Collected Out of History, and the Records of this
Kingdome. Wherein is also Demonstrated, That Printing appertaineth to the
Prerogative Royal; and it is a Flower of the Crown of England.* This new
edition contains two introductory epistles, one to the king and the other
to Parliament; Loggan's print of Charles II, Archbishop Sheldon, the
earl of Clarendon, and the duke of Albemarle facing the title page; and
a license granting the permission to print of Mr. Secretary Morice. Thus
armed, Atkyns insists, in a much more spectacular fashion than in 1660,
on the proper lessons drawn from his research:

> That Printing belongs to Your Majesty, in Your publique and private
> Capacity, as Supream Magistrate, and as Proprietor, I do with all
> boldness affirm; and that it is a considerable Branch of the Regal Power,
> will no Loyal Person deny: for it ties, and unties the very Hearts of the
> People. . . . If the Tongue, that is but a little Member, can set the Course
> of Nature on Fire; how much more the Quill, which is of a flying Nature
> in it self, and so Spiritual, that it is in all Places at the same time; and so
> Powerful, when it is cunningly handled, that it is the Peoples Diety. . . .
> this Power . . . is intire and inherent in Your Majesties Person, and
> inseparable from Your Crown.[40]

As a historian of print, Atkyns must be judged an abysmal failure.
The book upon which he bases his argument was shown in the eighteenth century to have been misdated—an omitted numeral X causing
the difficulty—while the manuscript containing the story of Henry VI
and Corsellis has never been found.[41] Atkyns, however, may not have
grieved too much about his scholarly reputation, for though he insists
that he contradicts the common opinion partially because "I am a Friend
to Truth," his major interest, he candidly admits, is "not to lose one of
my best Arguments of Intituling the King to this ART in his Private
Capacity" (3). Atkyns designed his history to substantiate his royal
patent rights for the printing of all common-law books, a claim vigorously opposed by the Stationers' Company. By demonstrating the king's
proprietary control of print technology, its inseparability from the
crown, Atkyns reinforces his own commercial rights.

Frontispiece to Richard Atkyns's *The Original and Growth of Printing*
(1664)

In spite of his evident self-interest and factual inaccuracy, however, Atkyns writes eloquently of the primitive fascination of printing, his language of spatial and temporal displacement—"in all Places at the same time"—evoking the sheer wonder of an invention that had transformed books from rare and precious commodities to the stuff of daily life. Atkyns possesses as well a sure sense of the influence this has given the press, of the way in which its "Paper-pellets became as dangerous as Bullets" (7). He understands that in a century and a half printing has become a fundamental attribute of political authority, an essential part of state power and identity. Yet for all of his polemical insistence in this passage on how printing resides "intire and inherent in Your Majesties Person," he recognizes the fragility of the crown's relationship to the press: "I dare positively say, the Liberty of the Press, was the principal furthering Cause of the Confinement of Your most Royal Fathers Person; for, after this Act [which overturned the Court of Star Chamber and its regulation of the press], every Male-content vented his Passion in Print" (B2). Losing that which should have been inherent in his person, Charles I lost his crown, the immortal royal body that made him a king sundered from the physical body that suffered confinement and finally death. Here Atkyns dramatically figures the contradiction between a singular and unitary royal authority and the dispersed and fragmentary power of the press, between the divine status of a monarch and a mechanical invention capable of becoming "the Peoples Diety."

Atkyns's *The Original and Growth of Printing* presents a royalist fantasy, a vision of monarchical wish fulfillment in its insistence that only by returning printing to the prerogative of the king can England reestablish its past stability:

> Printing is like a good Dish of Meat, which moderately eaten of, turns to the Nourishment and health of the Body; but immoderately, to Surfeits and Sicknesses: As the Use is very necessary, the Abuse is very dangerous. . . . How were the Abuses taken away in Queen Elizabeth, King James, and the beginning of King Charles his time, when few or no Scandals or Libels were stirring? Was it not by Fining, Imprisoning, seizing the Books, and breaking the Presses of the Transgressors, by Order of the Council-Board? Was it not otherwise when the Jurisdiction of that Court was taken away by Act of Parliament, 17 Car. If Princes cannot redress Abuses, can less Men redress them? [sig. B^v-B2]

Writing as if *Areopagitica* had never been written, Atkyns employs the familiar tropes of a past golden age and present corruption and sickness in order to insist on the king's right, proven by a century of historical example, to regulate the print trade. By attributing to Elizabeth, James, and Charles I a firm control of the press, Atkyns can locate the present fall from grace in Parliament's "Act for the regulating of the privy council, and for taking away the court commonly called the star-chamber" (1640, 16 [not 17] Caroli. c. 10).

Though Atkyns certainly exaggerates the success of Tudor and early Stuart attempts to regulate the press—surely none of those monarchs would have recognized as their own a time "when few or no Scandals or Libels were stirring"—he correctly understands the importance of Parliament's assumption of the power to regulate the press, a process in which they had played a relatively insignificant part prior to the Interregnum. The monarchy had early assumed this function, and until 1641 the royal proclamation and order of the Star Chamber—which began as the king's privy council sitting in a judicial capacity—constituted the primary weapons in the campaign against unlicensed and unlawful printing. Thus by abolishing the Court of Star Chamber and overturning its decrees, Parliament succeeded in bringing press censorship under its own jurisdiction. Atkyns's insistence that this power be returned to the king must have impressed Charles: perhaps the difference between Atkyns's insignificant 1660 broadside and its handsome 1664 republication testifies to royal encouragement and support.

During his reign Charles continued to claim the prerogative powers that had made control of the press for over a century a predominately royal exercise of power. A suit in the Court of King's Bench, for instance, in 1677, affirmed the king's authority to issue patents assigning any book or type of book to an individual publisher, while in May 1680—during the heat of the Exclusion Crisis—the king's judges unanimously agreed that in the interests of civil order the king might by proclamation prohibit all unlicensed news books and pamphlets.[42] Both before the Licensing Act was passed in 1662 and after it lapsed in 1679, Charles intervened in the print trade by right of his royal prerogative. Yet the clearest indication of Charles's failure to regain past rights and privileges and of his realistic assessment of his monarchical powers lies in the 1662 "Act for preventing abuses in printing seditious, treasonable, and unlicensed books and pamphlets, and for regulating of printing and printing-presses." As Alfred Pollard remarks, "when Charles II faced the problems of the book-trade he showed his unwillingness to go on his travels again by embodying much of the Star Chamber decree of 1637 in the form of an Act of Parliament instead of relying on the old doctrine that everything which concerned printing came specially under the royal prerogative."[43] When Charles attempted to subordinate the "Peoples diety" to his own he inevitably turned to Parliament.

The Licensing Act of 1662—given this title because the act insists that the license actually be printed at the beginning of each book—represents the legal text that articulates the relation between state power and the press for much of Charles's reign; as such it reiterates the restrictive structures of monarchy's relationship to its subjects, as well as Parliament's new relationship to the king, for the act mandated its periodic renewal by Parliament. Little in the act can be called new: it opens by alluding to "the general licentiousness of the late times," which encouraged "many evil disposed persons" to print books "dishonoring . . . Almighty God . . . indangering the peace of these kingdoms, and raising a disaffection to his most excellent Majesty"; twice the act laments the "secret printing in corners" that disfigures the kingdom.[44] And if the language of the act imitates past legislation, the same is true of the specific regulations detailed in its twenty-five headings. As Pollard notes above, for the most part it repeats the decree of 1637, concerned primarily with details of the licensing procedure and precise limits on the number of master printers, letter founders, apprentices, individual presses, and so forth.

The major change in press censorship that arose from the act involved the state's relationship to the Stationers' Company. The company certainly remained essential to the regulation of the press: entries made in their register-book still conveyed a copyright, while the master and wardens of the company continued to take part in the search and seizure both of imported goods and domestic printing establishments. Yet the act relegates the company to the role of only another player in the censorship drama, no longer the primary buttress and extension of state power. The scrutiny of imported goods, for instance, is placed under the jurisdiction of the archbishop of Canterbury and bishop of London, while the company shares the right of search and seizure with the king's principal secretaries of state, the same individuals responsible for licensing, or appointing someone to license, "all books of history, concerning the state of this realm, or other books concerning any affairs of state."[45] Even before the act had passed, the Clarendon government had appointed Sir John Berkenhead as licenser of the press in October of 1660. In February of 1662 Roger L'Estrange succeeded to the post of surveyor of the press, and in August of 1663 he was appointed "Surveyor of Printing and Printing Presses,"[46] a position from which he would police the company for over two decades.

L'Estrange was a perfect choice for the job, a brilliant propagandist, a rigorous monitor of the company, and a tireless investigator who relentlessly pursued illegal presses and unlicensed publications. His *Considerations and Proposals In Order to the Regulation of the Press*, published just months before his appointment to his new post, reveals the siege mentality that he brought to his position, his conviction that the press was being manipulated by a faction working "upon the *Passions* and *Humours* of the *Common People*; and when they shall have put *Mischief* into their *Hearts*, their next *Business* is to put *Swords* in their *Hands*, and to Engage them in a direct *Rebellion*."[47] L'Estrange runs from print to sword, persuasion to rebellion, without the slightest hesitation, reiterating even more urgently Atkyns's movement from "Paper-pellets" to "Bullets."

L'Estrange opens his essay with a proposition with which, during the seventeenth century, only the Levellers might have disagreed: "I think no man denys the *Necessity* of Suppressing *Licentious* and *Unlawful Pamphlets*, and of *Regulating the Press*, but in what *manner*, and by what means This may be Effected, That's the question" (1). This proposition certainly seemed self-evident to Thomas Hobbes, who explains in *Leviathan* that "it is annexed to the Soveraignty, to be Judge of . . . what, men are to be trusted withall, in speaking to Multitudes of people; and who shall examine the Doctrines of all bookes before they be published. For the Actions of men proceed from their Opinions; and in the wel governing of Opinions, consisteth the well governing of men's Actions, in order to their Peace, and Concord."[48] If L'Estrange, Hobbes, and Milton represent three different strands of mid-century political thought, all nonetheless agree on and suggest the almost universal belief in the necessity for press censorship. Indeed, when L'Estrange later provides a list of books that should be suppressed, many of which are older works dealing with the execution of Charles I, his language reminds us of Milton's insistence on the immense responsibility books bear for properly demeaning themselves: "If it be objected that This looks too farr Back; It may be Answer'd that *Persons* are Pardon'd, but not *Books*. . . . 'tis not the Date, that does the Mischief, but the Matter and the Number" (8 and 9). All three men take books seriously enough to demand of them a strict accounting.

L'Estrange's questions, then, concern not the task but the method, and his doubts about the present system, and the Stationers' Company in particular, surface even in his dedication to the king, where he implicitly condemns the company for its divided interest: "Diverse of the very *Instruments*, who are *Entrusted* with the *Care* of the Press, being both *Privy*, and *Tacitly Consenting* to the *Corruptions* of it; by virtue of which *Connivence*, many *Hundred-Thousands of Seditious Papers*, since your Majestyes Return, have passed *Unpunished*" (A4ᵛ). For L'Estrange the company cannot properly function as a state censor because it represents not the state, but the private interests of its various members: "the *Question* is *Here*, how to *Prevent a Publique Mischief*, not how to *Promote a Private Trade*. . . . both *Printers* and *Stationers*, under Colour of Offering a service to the *Publique*, do Effectually but Design *One upon another*" (27).[49] Predictably, L'Estrange's final recommendation looks toward the office he would shortly assume: "the *smaller Interest* should *give place*, and be *Subordinate* to the *Greater*: That is, The *Master*, and *Wardens*, to Manage the Business of their Respective *Trade*, but withall, to be Subjected to some *Superior Officer*, that should over-look them *Both* on behalf of the *Publique*" (28).

L'Estrange insists on the need for a "*Superior Officer*" to oversee the company because he possesses a keen awareness of the ways in which economic self-interest interfered with its commitment to censorship. A year later, Atkyns provides a more explicit explanation of what hinders the company, when his 1664 edition of *The Original and Growth of Printing* considers some of the specific practices that fatally compromise booksellers in their contradictory roles as private businessmen and public censors: "There are at least 600 Booksellers that keep Shops in and about London, and Two or three Thousand free of the Company of Stationers; the Licensed Books of the Kingdom cannot imploy one third part of them. . . . But this is not all, 'tis not onely for their Interest not to Suppress them, but to Maintain them: An unlicensed Book bears Treble the price of another; and generally the more Scandalous a Book is, by so much the more dear" (16). In these complaints against the Stationers' Company, both L'Estrange and Atkyns certainly argue to advance their own interests. Yet John Hetet, who has recently examined the accounts of the company during the reign of Charles, affirms the accuracy of their charges. While the warden and masters of the company posed as zealous supporters of state censorship, they aided colleagues in the surreptitious printing of unlicensed material; they secured their own monopolies by seizing the presses of competitors, and confiscated unlicensed books so that they could resell them at higher rates.[50]

Yet tensions between L'Estrange and the company involved factors other than economic. To some extent they reflect the protracted contest between customary rule and the increasing centralization of the government, which no longer cared to grant so much power to the London companies. Ideology also played an important role in the company's failure to satisfy L'Estrange and the government he represented. Individuals like Benjamin Harris, Richard Janeway, and Francis Smith—to mention only the most famous opposition booksellers, printers, and publishers—were willing to suffer constant harassment and repeated imprisonment for using their positions in the trade to circulate political and religious views that challenged Charles and his government. These individuals responded to both economic and ideological pressures, forces that together determined the evolution of the print industry in the latter half of the seventeenth century.

For L'Estrange, therefore, the question of how to control the print trade turns on the state's relationship with the company, his *Considerations and Proposals* chiefly concerned with regulating the stationers in ways that would serve the government's interests. Yet L'Estrange does turn his attention to another of the *"Grand Delinquents"* liable for corrupting the press, and he does so in a way that suggests a desire to combat the protean and diffused power of the press by assigning to the author an originary responsibility and power:

> Touching the *Adviser, Author, Compiler, Writer,* and *Correcter,* their Practices are hard to be Retriv'd, unless the One Discover the Other.
> This Discovery may be procur'd partly by a *Penalty* upon *refusing to Discover,* and partly by a *Reward,* to the *Discoverer;* but let both the *Penalty,* and the *Reward* be *Considerable* and *Certain:* and let the *Obligation* of *Discovery* run quite Through, from the *first Mover* of the Mischief, to the *Last Disperser* of it. That is to say; *If any unlawful Book shall be found in the Possession of any of the* Agents, *or* Instruments *aforesaid, let the* Person *in whose possession it is* found, *be Reputed, and Punish'd as the* Author *of the said Book, unless he* Produce *the Person or Persons, from whom he Receiv'd it.* [2]

L'Estrange argues here that each figure in the long chain of book production be understood as a progressive manifestation of the *"first Mover,"* who becomes the putative object of correction in every stage from composition to distribution. Such a formulation doesn't deny the importance of printers or booksellers, but it does reconfigure them within an economy of punishment directed at an ostensible "source" located in the author, the unique individual who precedes the dangerous dispersive powers of the trade. Near the conclusion of his pamphlet, L'Estrange returns to the author, convinced that "for the *Authors*, nothing can be too *Severe*, that stands with *Humanity*, and *Conscience*. First, 'tis the way to cut off the *Fountain* of our Troubles. 2dly There are not many of them in an Age, and so the *less work* to do" (32). Within seventy-five years, of course, Pope would find incredible the suggestion that "there are not many of them in an Age"; but detached from the industrial process of reproduction, the author here seems an easy mark, the originary point—"the *Fountain*"—from which to disrupt the dangerous multiplicity of the press and its products.

Early in 1664, in fact, the government practiced with grim results the strategy recommended by L'Estrange in his *Considerations and Proposals*, executing John Twyn for printing *The Execution of Justice*, popularly known as *Mene Tekel or The Downfall of Tyranny*. Probably written by Captain Roger Jones, an officer in Cromwell's army, the book advocated not simply deposing Charles, but killing him as well.[51] For the government the publication of *The Execution of Justice* was particularly offensive because it coincided with an abortive plot and uprising in Yorkshire. This affirmed the already potent connection between the printed word and the deed, the conviction that "Paper-pellets" lead directly to "Bullets," that "Dispersing seditious books is very near a-kin to raising of tumults; they are as like as brother and sister: raising of tumults is the more masculine; and printing and dispersing seditious books, is the feminine part of every rebellion."[52] But Twyn also suffered because he refused to identify the book's author; unwilling to lead the government back through the chain of production, Twyn accepted a penalty that was indeed "*Considerable* and *Certain*." Though in Twyn's case the search for the "*Fountain* of our Troubles" was frustrated, the connection between authorship, treason, and printing remained for Charles, as we shall see in the next chapter, a significant way in which not only to safeguard but to generate and enhance his monarchical identity.

The writings of L'Estrange and Atkyns, along with the Licensing Act of 1662, suggest the compromises forced upon Charles in his attempts to control the press. He recognized, for instance, that Parliament could no longer be ignored in matters relating to the print trade; at the same time, he sought to increase his prerogative powers whenever possible, using both the courts and the surveyorship to advance his own interests. Charles also seems to have recognized the weaknesses of the regulatory system he inherited, particularly regarding the role of the Stationers' Company. Yet the company remained indispensable to the policing of the press, and Charles settled for pressuring its members to subordinate personal to state interests.

Until the lapsing of the Licensing Act in 1679, such a jerrybuilt system seems to have enjoyed reasonable success. For all the conviction and fury of royal proclamations and Star Chamber decrees before 1641, the licensing system had never worked as efficiently as its creators would have liked. Both the Catholics and the Puritans had for decades suc-ceeded in printing unlicensed books and pamphlets: the latter had maintained a minority press in England since the 1550s, while the former managed, through a combination of secret presses and materials smuggled from abroad, to circulate more than six hundred unlawful religious books and pamphlets during the years 1603–1640. As H.S. Bennett notes, "there was a considerable gap between theory and practice in the regulation of the book trade at this period. A series of edicts, an impressive licensing system, a duty imposed on the Stationers' Company to enforce the governmental regulations—all seem to have been rather ineffective."[53]

Success in regulating the press, then, cannot be measured by an absolute standard. By many specific criteria Charles's attempts might seem to have failed. Certain provisions of the Licensing Act were apparently ignored from the start—including rules regarding the num-ber of master printers—while under L'Estrange's tenure, according to Frederick Siebert, no more than half of the pamphlet literature publish-ed was properly licensed. Yet Siebert also suggests that enforcement of printing regulations was at its most stringent during the reigns of Elizabeth and Charles.[54] Christopher Hill goes even further, claiming that after the relative freedom of the Interregnum, Charles's reign represents a substantial reintroduction of censorship. In spite of parlia-mentary acts that increasingly resembled Star Chamber decrees and royal proclamations, Hill argues that the Interregnum saw the publica-tion of a large amount of literature that could not have been published after the Restoration: "The consequences of this sudden reversal of press freedom were drastic and have never been properly analysed. A great deal of self-censorship must have been exercised." Ronald Hutton would agree, arguing that while the Licensing Act of 1662 "did not entirely prevent the production and dissemination of the literature it was designed to curb . . . it destroyed the atmosphere of free debate . . . which had made most of the two previous decades so exciting and disturbing."[55]

Such judgments may be unduly pessimistic. In two books devoted to the radical underground in England during the years 1660–1677, Richard L. Greaves convincingly argues that "the revolution of the 1640s and 1650s lived on because the government failed in its efforts to choke off the propagation of radical ideas, either in press or in pulpit."[56] The alacrity with which the opposition took advantage of the lapsing of the Licensing Act in 1679 suggests that both an audience for political literature and the structures for producing and distributing such material had survived and even prospered during the first two decades of Charles's reign. Indeed, concentrating too intently on printed matter alone may blind us to the ways in which "free debate" could flourish in apparently adverse circumstances.

We can appreciate the problems that Charles's government faced in attempting to limit public debate by looking briefly at the coffeehouse and the part it played in the dissemination of news, unlicensed and even unpublished literature. During the last half of the seventeenth century, the coffeehouse functioned as a necessary adjunct of the print trade because it fulfilled two roles denied the press. In the first place, in a society without a consistent and legitimate source of news, the coffeehouse provided a sanctioned space where the population might meet to discuss current events, a precinct where a "public" citizenry could in fact be constructed. From 1666 until 1679 the kingdom possessed only one newspaper, the official *London Gazette*, which printed primarily royal proclamations and sanitized versions of foreign news.[57] For thirteen years the kingdom suffered without a reliable printed source of domestic news, and to a great extent coffeehouses fulfilled this function later usurped by the print medium.

At the same time, the coffeehouse also provided a public conduit for the circulation of unlicensed literature, which included not only printed matter but unpublished manuscripts as well. During the seventeenth century, when the character of the author had yet to assume the substantiality or importance that it does today, publication was not an essential part of an author's identity. Circulation in manuscript was not only a legitimate method of acquiring a readership, but for many a more respectable alternative to vulgar publication. And unpublished manuscripts possessed particular attractions for writers engaged in the potentially dangerous world of politics, for the Licensing Act, as we have seen, covered only printed material.

At least one career, that of the notorious Captain Robert Julian, the "Secretary to the Muses," depended on the reliable transmission of unpublished manuscripts. Active during the latter years of the seventeenth century, Julian distributed libels and satires through the coffeehouses and taverns of Restoration London, at one point standing in the pillory for circulating copies of a satire on Charles II, "Old Rowley the King." During the early eighteenth century, Tom Brown has Julian describe himself as a man "whose Business was so publick and so useful," though an anonymous poem written during Charles's reign treats him less kindly:

> Thou common shore of this poetic town,
> Where all our excrements of wit are thrown—
> For sonnet, satire, bawdry, blasphemy
> Are empti'd and disburden'd all on thee.[58]

As this little rhyme suggests, promiscuity rather than specialization defined Julian's trade, and, according to the anonymous "News from the Coffee-House" (1667), this virtue characterized as well the coffeehouses that Julian haunted:

> There's nothing done in all the world, from *Monarch* to the *Mouse*,
> But every day or night 'tis hurl'd into the Coffee-House.
> What *Lillee* or what *Beoker* can by Art not bring about,
> At Coffee-House you'l find a man can quickly find it out.[59]

Though the movement from "*Monarch* to the *Mouse*" suggests no specific focus to coffeehouse activities and functions, their notoriety during the 1660s, 1670s, and 1680s stemmed from their position as centers of unofficial political activity, the "matrix," according to Peter Fraser, "of independent journalism," where expensive newsletters might circulate among those ordinarily unable to afford them.[60] David Allen has shown that political clubs met all over Restoration London, in taverns and private houses as well as coffeehouses, but for the government the relative cheapness of coffeehouses, which encouraged the participation of the "middling" elements of society, made them particularly dangerous.[61] L'Estrange complained that "every *Coffee-House* [is] *furnished* with *News-Papers* and *Pamphlets* (both *written* and

Printed) of *Personal Scandal, Schism,* and *Treason,*" while the anonymous
"New Satirical Ballad of the Licentiousness of the Times" (1679) mocks
the pretensions of those who gathered there to discuss state affairs:

> I' the coffee-house here one with a grave face,
> When after salute, he hath taken his place,
> His pipe being lighted begins for to prate,
> And wisely discourses the affairs of the State.[62]

While such prattle may seem harmless enough, for the government "affairs of state" were precisely that, matters that concerned the
state and not private individuals. Charles's government inevitably interpreted all unofficial political activity as oppositional; coffeehouses
seen in this light became centers of sedition and potentially illegal
activity. According to Sir Roger North, members of the important
Green Ribbon Club "were carriers up and down, or Dispersers of seditious Talk, at proper Times, as Blood from the Heart, to nourish Sedition
all over the Town, to the *Exchange, Westminster,* Coffee-Houses, and
Sub-Coffee-Houses, in wonderful Harmony of Discovery."[63] For the
government, of course, this seditious harmony can only occasion discord, and L'Estrange captures the government's fears of the leveling
tendencies inherent in a forum that might discuss everything from
"*Monarch* to the *Mouse*" when in an issue of *The Observator* he includes
a mock petition from Charles "To his Majesty, *Millenarius Coffee-man,
King* (among the Saints) for 1000 Years."[64] As previous governments,
both royal and parliamentary, understood, the unlicensed spread of
domestic news and intelligence threatened the hierarchies upon which
state power depended.

Charles addressed this problem in a proclamation of 12 June
1672, where he singled out coffeehouses as centers of "bold and Licentious Discourses": "men have assumed to themselves a liberty, not onely
in Coffee-houses, but in other Places and Meetings, both publick and
private, to censure and defame the Proceedings of State." Another
proclamation, in 1674, repeated this prohibition against "any Writing
or Speaking to utter or publish any false News or Reports," for such
rumors "endeavour to create and nourish in the minds of his Majesties
good subjects an evil opinion of things they understand not."[65] Such
language assumes that "good subjects" will remain obedient unless led
astray by pernicious influences, here located not simply in the press
itself, but in all forums that permit unlicensed communication between
the king's subjects.

In 1675 Charles's government took what must have seemed a logical step, attempting to close all coffeehouses, which it now identified as the very center of seditious dissent: "Whereas it is most apparent, that the Multitude of Coffee-Houses of late years set up and kept within this Kingdom . . . and disaffected persons to them, have produced very evil and dangerous effects. . . . for that in such Houses, and by occasion of the meetings of such persons therein, divers False, Malicious and Scandalous Reports are devised and spread abroad, to the Defamation of his Majesties Government, and to the Disturbance of the Peace and Quiet of the Realm."[66] The suppression of coffeehouses, however, proved not only unpopular but legally questionable as well; not two weeks after the first order, Charles issued "An Additional Proclamation Concerning Coffee-Houses," in which he allows them to remain open—ostensibly because of their large stocks of teas and coffees—as long as they post a five hundred pound bond to meet the following condition: "the above-bound A.B. shall at all times hereafter . . . use his utmost and endeavour to prevent and hinder all Scandalous Papers, Books, or Libels concerning the Government, or the Publick Ministers thereof, from being brought into his House, or to be there Read, Perus'd or Divulg'd; And to prevent and hinder all and every person and persons from declaring, uttering and divulging in his said House, all manners of False or Scandalous Reports of the Government, or any Ministers thereof."[67]

At the root of the abuses represented by the coffeehouse lies "all Scandalous Papers, Books, or Libels" that have escaped state censorship. Attempts to close the coffeehouses, then, became another way not simply to control the press, to thwart the distributive networks formed by an increasingly sophisticated "communications industry," but to inhibit a reading public that increasingly threatened the government's power to define the nature of and restrict access to political discourse. During the Interregnum, to frustrate the dispersal of unlicensed publications it had seemed sufficient to legislate against "the Hawker, Pedler or Ballad-singer," threatening them with forfeiture of their stocks and "also to be whipt as a Common Rogue."[68] By the middle of Charles's reign, a far more complex system of print and manuscript distribution was in place, one that granted people, in the words of "A New Satyricall Ballad," the liberty "to talk and write what they please." For this anonymous poet, as for generations of monarchs, such activities denote not a right or proper freedom, but "an Epidemical Disease," whose infection of the population manifested itself in the momentous events of 1678-1682.

Just as the issue of exclusion predates the introduction of the first Exclusion Bill before Commons on 15 May 1679, the press's intervention in the Popish Plot and Exclusion Crisis anticipated the lapsing of the Licensing Act on 10 June 1679. Nonetheless, the importance of this latter date should not be underestimated, for the lapsing of the act severely impeded the government's ability to prevent the press—and through the press, the public—from playing a substantial role in the extended political crisis that gripped the nation during the years 1678-1682. Within a month Benjamin Harris had published the first edition of his newspaper, *The Domestick Intelligence*, and by the autumn of 1682, when the government finally regained control of the press, almost forty different newspapers had presented the politics of plot and exclusion to the kingdom.[69] The combined Popish Plot and Exclusion Crisis became one of the three or four most written about occasions during the seventeenth century.[70]

The excitement generated not simply by the crisis itself but by the press's role in defining the historical moment may be gauged by the anonymous attempt to survey contemporary published accounts responding to the extraordinary press of events: *A Compleat Catalogue of All the Stitch'd Books and Single Sheets Printed since the First Discovery of the Popish Plot, (September 1678.) to January 1679/80.* Under "Folio's" on the subject of "Plot" this thirty-two page pamphlet lists eighty-eight titles; under "Quarto's" on "Papist" it includes sixty-three. In addition, many of the titles placed under the categories of "Miscel" and "Poetry" clearly relate to the politics of popery and exclusion. This *Catalogue* promises on the title page that "The continuation is intended by the Publisher," and two supplements, in fact, were issued: the first carrying the list to 25 June 1680, the second to Michaelmas Term 1680.[71] Like his or her more famous predecessor, this anonymous Thomason possessed a sure sense of the press's importance in the unfolding of a historical crisis.

In our own era, when print, television, and radio combine to saturate us in "the news," it is difficult to recognize how novel and unexpected, exciting and disconcerting, the sudden proliferation of printed news must have seemed to contemporaries. Charles's government certainly appears to have been caught unawares, for it proposed no bill to extend the Licensing Act and didn't seriously consider the problem until late May.[72] Peter Fraser reminds us that even the government could not have "consciously suppressed the kind of journal that appeared in 1678": "The modern concept of a free press, in the journalistic sense, had not found any recognition in England before that date. It was generally thought that news could be easily and generally recognized as true or false, important or unimportant. The modern notion that comment and editorial viewpoint are inseparable elements in all news was unknown."[73] At least some of the bitterness generated by the press wars of 1678–1682 can be attributed to the unprecedented interpretive demands of a "modern" political debate in which the complexities of the relationship between news and propaganda had yet to be recognized or articulated. In *A Letter of Advice to the Petitioning Apprentices* (1681), a government supporter insists that though these are mutually exclusive catagories—the lies and seditions of false "oracles" clearly distinguishable from the truth of government and monarch—the nation does not possess an informed citizenry with the necessary skills to discriminate between them: "For now a days no plague so Infectious as the Plague of Faction and Fanaticism, that seems even to threaten the downfal of the Nations Tranquility, and none so likely to be Infected as Raw Youths in the height of their Blood, who are apt to embrace the words of a Seditious Teacher for the voice of an *Oracle*."[74]

By 1678 the press freedom of the early 1640s could only have been a memory for most people, and a frightening one at that, for throughout the crisis the Tories linked past horrors to present abuses as they successfully played on the connection between the excesses of the press and the breakdown of social order. Current troubles constantly remind government supporters of the late rebellion, the force of the parallel, even if exaggerated for the purposes of propaganda, indicative of just how seriously Charles's government felt itself under threat. In February 1680, Narcissus Luttrell, for instance, notes that "About this time many libells are thrown about to disaffect the king and his people, and turn all to 41."[75] Predictably, Roger L'Estrange makes great capital of this charge, insisting that in both 1641 and 1681 an uncontrolled press functions not simply as a symptom of the nation's distress, but as its very cause: "Libels were not only the *Fore-runners*, but in a high Degree, the *Causes* of our late *Troubles*: . . . If we look well about us, we may find this kingdom, at this Instant laboring under the same Distempers; the Press as *busie* and as *bold*; Sermons as *Factious*; Pamphlets as *seditious*; the Government *defam'd*."[76] In *The Observator*, in fact, he insists that a perfect continuity of publication links the factions of 1641 and 1681: "How many thousand Libells has your Faction Publish'd from *One and Forty* to *this very day*, against all sorts of Persons that have been converted to the Exercise and acknowledgment of their Duties both to Church and State?"[77]

After 10 June, the debate about the Popish Plot and Exclusion Crisis that took place in newsletters, pamphlets, books, ballads, and broadsides, in prose, verse, and song demonstrates a self-conscious awareness of the changes that had taken place in the public consumption of news. To a large extent people saw the political crisis that enveloped the nation as a print crisis, the latter both a cause of and emblem for the former. Laments about the excesses of the press, of course, could function simply as another excuse for partisan propaganda, as in the anonymous attack on weekly Tory newsletters, *The Character of Those Two Protestants in Masquerade, Heraclitus, and The Observator* (1681): "They are Teeming Animals, that swell with Noise and Nonsence, but onely bring forth a Penny Pamphlet. No sooner is the Travel over, but the Weekly Infants are snatch'd from the Bosom of their Parents, and being hurried into Publick, they create a Disturbance with their clamorous Shricks. No sooner do the troublesom Brats yelp themselves into silence, and expire, but another Issue is successively continued."[78] Here the productions of a Tory press become the satanic issue described in Milton's allegory of Sin and Death.

The Tories, in a similar fashion, damned the Whig pamphleteers, describing them in "Scandal Proof" (1681) as rebels who would foment chaos in an otherwise healthy body politic: "Come on ye Scribling *Rebels* of the Age, / Come on I say, advance upon the Stage; / Arm'd with *Phanatick* Malice Zeal and Rage." In this poem Richard Janeway, the notorious Whig printer, becomes the champion of the *"Phanatick* Scriblers who Bully-all,"* an exemplar of the seditious Whig upstarts who meddle in serious matters that do not concern them:

> So like a *Janus*, does *Dick Janeway* look,
> We see his Double Face in every Book;
> In which wee'r Weekly Plagu'd with's Impudence,
> Offensive to all Loyal men of Sense,
> Who hate both *Dick*, and's Damd'd Impertinence.[79]

Yet the print explosion that accompanied and, in contemporary minds, exacerbated the Popish Plot and Exclusion Crisis occasioned far more than the simple venting of partisan prejudices. The press's active role in politics was deeply disturbing to many—no matter their political sympathies—a phenomenon that most people neither entirely understood nor countenanced. As J.A. Downie notes, "contemporaries were bewildered by the development of a 'fourth estate.' They were astonished by the sheer volume of political propaganda that the party presses managed to turn out."[80] Luttrell, for instance, sounds contemptuous of and discouraged by the fractious and irresponsible tone of both sides: "About this time [April 1681] the presse abounds with all sorts of pamphlets and libells; one side running down the papists and upholding the dissenters; the other side cryeing down both, asperseing the last two houses of commons and ridiculing their proceedings, and sounding nothing but 41; publick intelligencers or pamphlets of news abounding, every day spawning two, sometimes three, filling the town and country with notorious falsehoods." Not five months later he again expresses concern for a "violent paper scuffle" that has generated "a great divition and animosity between those that call themselves church of England men and those that are dissenters."[81]

Often such responses to the crisis took a comic tone, as in "Whig and Tory, Or the Scribling Duellists" (1681), where the anonymous author identifies the two sides as snarling but fearful dogs:

> You've seen how two domestick Curs will grin,
>   Yet fearing with each other to ingage,
> Will threw loud *Challenges* about in din
>   And stifle the revengeful heat of rage.

For this author the two embattled contestants appear equally absurd and untrustworthy, though they flaunt their irresponsibility in very different guises:

> Arm'd thus, he [Whig] boldly marcheth out, and sees
>   His Bravery applauded by the Crowd,
> Whilst *Herald*-like *Courants*, and *Mercuries*,
>   Proclaim revengeful Challanges aloud.
> . . . .
> Splendid as is the Morn he [Tory] dith advance,
>   Each Play commits a flourish to his care,
> Whilst scraps of *History* tagg'd with *Romance*,
>   Like Pantaloons doth dangle here and there.[82]

Here differences in genre signal distinctions of rank, the Whig playing to the "Crowd" in common newsletters while the Tory, characterized by an epic simile, employs the higher forms of drama, history, and romance. The issue of rank was central to the controversy that greeted the press warfare of 1678-1682. For many, a print crisis existed precisely because the loss of effective controls over the press placed it in the hands of the "Crowd," those who by right should play no part in the political deliberations of the kingdom. The Popish Plot and Exclusion Crisis reveal the press in the act of becoming a popular medium, its considerable power apparently available to all: "Now every Scribler does the Press invade, / And what was a Diversion's grown a Trade." This couplet from "A Satyr Against the Pen-Men and Speech-men of the Times" (1679) captures Tory outrage at both the promiscuous invasion of what should be a privileged activity, as well as the economic consequences of this subversion. The print industry was in the process of assuming a modern form, and the term "trade" already suggests the extraordinary contempt that Pope would later level at "the Grub-Street Race" who took advantage of the new economic and political opportunities it offered. Even the anonymous author of this satire, in spite of evident Tory sympathies, despises the opportunism of both sides; if the Whigs are "bold knave[s]" who dare to express themselves about "to whom the Crown belongs," the Tory propagandists are nonetheless equally presumptuous:

> But now lest ill opinion spread too fast,
> Another with his Rhymes to Press makes hast,
> And thinks by them to give a helping hand
> To the great Right, which of it self can stand.[83]

The press simply has no business intruding in such affairs, its influence pernicious no matter what the aim of its trespass; the medium, for this poet, is the message, the press inviting by its very presence in such matters of national policy a new, and dangerous, relationship between the state and its subjects.

These satires turn on the recognition that an aggressive press allowed the public to participate in political activity to an unprecedented extent. In affirming this version of the years 1678-1682 we need not accept the melodramatic Tory portrayal of a struggle between a ruling elite and "the people," a vast and undisciplined underclass attempting to grasp the reigns of power by asserting their own control over the technology of print. Though Charles's government would certainly use this sensational image to enhance its own power, employing an antipopulist rhetoric that exploited fears of social leveling, the contest between the government and the opposition involved a conflict—concerned especially with matters of religion and the nature of government—between competing factions of the traditional ruling elites. But as this struggle intensified, both sides found it necessary to court "public opinion," to create a public and claim it for themselves. Government and opposition became Tory and Whig precisely because they could each assert that they represented a public constituency, that they gave voice to a definable segment of the population. The creation of parties, one of the most significant transformations of the political landscape to emerge from Restoration politics, could not have occurred without an active press, both opposition and government, which helped both to create a public identity for a political party and to stimulate a wide popular appeal for its positions.[84]

The Whigs certainly took the lead in this process, not simply by exploiting the lapsing of the Licensing Act to bring their case to the public but through the House of Commons' decision in 1680 to allow official publication of its votes, and in 1681 of its proceedings.[85] The 1640s had seen short-lived experiments involving accounts of parliamentary news, while in the late 1670s unauthorized reports on Parliament's activities could be found in the newsletters making the rounds of the coffeehouses. But in 1660 both houses had prohibited published reports of votes and debates, and only in 1680 did the Commons, and shortly after the Lords, sanction the public scrutiny of their business. This certainly represented a calculated political decision by the opposition, an attempt to preserve public support for exclusion, since the privilege of printing the reports went to members of the Stationers' Company politically sympathetic to the Whigs.[86] Nonetheless, the recognition that Parliament might expose itself to public review by acknowledging the power of press and print suggests an important change in apprehensions of the way in which political business could be conducted. Recent decisions by the American Congress and British House of Commons to allow television cameras into their sacred chambers reveal a related realization about the nature of politics and communications: in both cases a medium at once feared and despised becomes an indispensable part of the political process, its previous exclusion now impossible.

When Charles denied the Whigs the public forum provided by Parliament—dissolving the First and then proroguing the Second Exclusion Parliament, elected in August and September of 1679 and not permitted to sit until October 1680—the Whigs again attempted to mobilize public support by orchestrating a series of petitions asking for the immediate assembly of the new Parliament. Part of the Whigs' brilliant propaganda campaign designed to force Charles into accepting the Exclusion Bill, these petitions brought into the political arena a part of the population normally excluded from the political process; and this, of course, is precisely what angered the court party and the king. In a meeting between the privy council and the mayor and aldermen of London on 10 December 1679, Luttrell notes the lord chancellor's insistence that "his majestie was resolved by no means to suffer" the "tumultuous and seditious petitions goeing forward in the citty and country."[87] Two days later, on 12 December, Charles issued a proclamation "Against Tumultuous Petitions," warning that proceedings soliciting "the Hands or Subscriptions of multitudes of his Majesties Subjects . . . are contrary to the Common and known Laws of the Land, for that it tends to promote Discontents amongst the People, and to Raise Sedition and Rebellion."[88] Like printing, petitions must be denied a population too easily swayed and excited, the biases of rank inherent in such legal formulations made explicit in A Letter of Advice to the Petitioning Apprentices (1681), an anonymous response to a petition collected among the London apprentices: "But why [Charles] should be loaded by a Petition from the meanest of his Subjects, to councel him in the greatest of his Affairs, I am not sensible."[89] Petitions, like books, subvert the hierarchies upon which the royal identity depends, for they give "Hands," a public identity and voice, to the "multitudes."

In spite of the judiciary's support of the king's right to prohibit the collection of petitions—a decision related in the public's mind to the judges' support of press censorship—the government's prohibition enjoyed little success.[90] Eventually, in fact, the Tories were forced to answer the Whigs in kind, encouraging addresses to the king that denounced the illegal petitions. For L'Estrange, the conflict between Whig petitions and Tory addresses illuminated the distinction in rank between an irresponsible multitude and a loyal, obedient citizenry: "What Privilege have the Petitioners more then the Addressers? Or is it Lawfull for them to Print odious Reflections upon the Kings Authority, and Administration; and Unlawfull for the Addressers to give the People a Fairer understanding of the State of the Nation? Is it Lawfull for them to Brag of their Thousands, and to write themselves all the COMMONERS of England, and is it not Lawfull for the Addressers to shew the People their Mistake, and to Count Noses with 'em?"[91]

J.S. Morrill and J.D. Walker have written of a seventeenth-century "process of growing social differentiation" that questioned "the validity of the unitary description of those below the level of the gentry as 'the people' ";[92] and the confused and awkward distinction that L'Estrange tries to draw here between "Addressers" and "Petitioners" speaks directly to this process. On the one hand, L'Estrange takes great pains to separate the "Addressers" from "the People": the former act as teachers, giving "the People" a *"Fairer* understanding of *the State,"* a just appreciation of "their *Mistake."* In associating the "Petitioners" with "their *Thousands"* and "all the COMMONERS *of England,"* the passage wants to refuse this distinction to the "Petitioners," who are symbolically sunk in the undifferentiated mass of "the People," that ignorant multitude whose attempt to "write themselves," to formulate their own public identity disturbs L'Estrange, for in doing so they inevitably question the *"Kings Authority,* and *Administration,"* the royal attempt to identify itself as the state. On the other hand, L'Estrange's final challenge to "count Noses" reveals his desire to claim that the "Addressers" are every bit as popular and numerous as the "Petitioners." The confusions and evasions of this passage point to the cynicism of an appeal to the public that depended on an antipopulist rhetoric.

Such cynicism, of course, characterized Whigs as well as Tories. The 1681 elections to the Oxford Parliament, for instance, were accompanied by an unexampled series of addresses to the newly elected representatives that recommended particular policies and the passage of specific legislation once Parliament met. Published as pamphlets and reprinted in *Smith's Protestant Intelligence,* these addresses, presented as spontaneous expressions of popular electoral support for Whig positions, were actually orchestrated by the opposition leaders. As J.R. Jones notes, "their purpose was not so much to subordinate Members of Parliament to the people, a doctrine which nearly all Whigs would have abhorred as leveling, but to preserve Whig unity."[93] During the years 1678-1682 "the People" enter the theatre of national politics not primarily because of a principled decision to comprehend in the political process the excluded and disenfranchised, but because for both Whig and Tory it became expedient and finally necessary to do so.

The press and printed word, of course, were not alone responsible for the political transformations that accompanied the mounting crisis; we should instead see the press as part of a intricate and interrelated network of social, economic, and cultural institutions that would include the pulpit, the Whig pope-burning and Tory presbyter-burning processions, the Restoration theaters and popular fairs, the coffeehouses and penny post, even the courts and elections, all of which played significant roles in the political drama of the years 1678–1682.[94] Nathaniel Thompson, the most famous Tory printer, provides a fantastic illustration of the press's vital interaction with other cultural forms in his introduction to *A Choice Collection of 120 Loyal Songs*:

> Amongst the several means that have been of late years to reduce the deluded Multitude to their just Allegiance, this of Ballads and Loyal Songs has not been of the last influence. While the . . . Heads of the Factions were blowing up Sedition in every corner of the Countrey, these joying Choristers were asserting the Rights of Monarchy, and proclaiming Loyalty in every street. The mis-in-form'd Rabble began to listen; they began to heer to Truth in a Song, in time found their Errors, and were charm'd into Obedience.

Publishing his collection in 1684, when the dimensions of the Whig defeat were clear, Thompson could well afford to brag about his role in "reduc[ing] the deluded Multitude" and educating the "mis-in-form'd Rabble." But his astonishing representation of the orphic power of song, of "joying Choristers" gadding about the streets, suggests the way in which humble ballads, printed and sung, shared between readers and listeners, could play a role in the larger political processes and changes initiated by the conflict between Whig and Tory.

Nonetheless, both sides recognized the centrality of the press to the political crisis of 1678-1682, not only as a precipitating cause but as part of a potential solution; a resolution of the crisis, many recognized, depended on who could establish control over the press. Thompson certainly believed this, for his self-applause continues: "without ostentation, I may say, I printed my News-Papers (that always vindicated the King and Government) to undeceive the People, who were daily impos'd upon by Curtis, Smith, Harris, Care, Vile, Baldwin, Janeway, &. when no body else would or durst."[95] The Stationers' own Horatius at the bridge, Thompson portrays himself defending the monarchy against a barbarous horde of Whig printers, booksellers, writers, and publishers, who themselves would have shared the conviction that royal power could not maintain itself against a public voice articulated through the press.

This was certainly the understanding of Francis Smith. Committed to Newgate for promoting petitioning as early in the crisis as

December 1679, Smith was returned by the government to Newgate on 14 April 1681, this time, according to Luttrell, "for high treason, for some words he had spoken, as if he would never leave writing news till he had reduc'd this kingdome to a common wealth."[96] Violence and rebellion in such a formulation depend on words not cannon, the press and not the military the way to reduce and ultimately destroy the monarchy.

5. "The very Oracles of the *Vulgar*": Stephen College and the Author on Trial

Lord Chief Justice Scroggs's concern for the hungry children of the nation, enunciated at the trial of Henry Care on 2 July 1680 for a libel contained in *The Weekly Pacquet of Advice from Rome*, reveals the government's frustration at its continued inability to curb the press even a year after the lapsing of the Licensing Act:

> [A] public notice to all people, and especially printers and booksellers, that they ought to print no book or pamphlet of news whatsoever, without authority. . . . But if so be they will undertake to print news foolishly, they ought to be punished, and shall be punished if they do it without authority, though there is nothing reflecting on the government as an awful thing. The reason is plain: so fond are men in these days, that when they will deny their children a penny for bread, they will lay it out for a pamphlet. And it did so swarm, and the temptations were so great, that no man could keep two-pence in his pocket because of the news.[1]

From his seat of judgment Scroggs confronts a kingdom swarming with newsbooks and pamphlets, a people tempted and maddened by the innumerable issue of an unregulated and ungovernable press. In his vision of a foolish population frenzied by print, sacrificing money and even children to an unnatural obsession with the news, Scroggs realizes the nightmare behind a century and a half of government censorship.

During the Second Exclusion Parliament later that year, the government attempted to revive the Licensing Act or obtain new legislation, but its efforts met with no success.[2] Yet in spite of Parliament's refusal to help the government, the king nonetheless remained in possession of considerable legal powers. He had maintained throughout his reign that regulation of the print industry remained a matter of monarchical prerogative, and after the lapsing of the act a flurry of royal proclamations sought to impose control over the press. In August 1679 the Chancellor, Lord Finch, issued an ordinance revising the by-laws of the Stationers' Company; it specifically noted that all changes in the governance of guilds and fraternities must be approved by the crown to avoid the "disinheritance or diminution of the Prerogative of the King." To assure its legal standing, the ordinance was approved not just by Finch, but by the lord chief justices of both the Kings-Bench and Common-Pleas, Sir William Scroggs and Sir Francis North.[3]

On 31 October 1679 Charles issued a proclamation "For the Suppressing of Seditious and Treasonable Books and Pamphlets," while 12 December 1679 saw publication, as we have seen, of an order "Against Tumultuous Petitions." On 12 May 1680 the king used the legal opinion of his judges, sought earlier in the month, as support for his proclamation "For Suppressing the Printing and Publishing Unlicensed News-Books, and Pamphlets of News," which led to the July trial of Care.[4] Sir George Jeffreys opened that trial by insisting that "all the judges of England having been met together . . . they gave it in as their resolution, that no person whatsoever could expose to the public knowledge any thing that concerned the affairs of the public, without license from the king."[5] Here Jeffreys provides an explicit statement of the doctrine that public affairs are not a matter of public knowledge unless the king so determines.

By far the most frequent charge brought by the government against those in the print trade was that of seditious libel, which Frederick Siebert has described as the most effective method of restricting the press during the latter part of the seventeenth century.[6] From September 1679 to September 1681, Luttrell's account of the political turmoil in the kingdom contains over thirty entries concerning the appearance of seditious or blasphemous publications and the government's efforts to suppress the material or punish the malefactors. In February 1680, for instance, Luttrell includes a number of accounts concerning the important trial of the Whig publisher Benjamin Harris. On the fifth, at Guildhall, Harris "came to his tryall for publishing a scandalous and seditious pamphlet called the Appeal from the Country to the Citty, and was found guilty of the same." On the twelfth he "came up to receive his judgment, and was sentenced to stand in the pillory, to pay 500¹. fine to his majestie, and to give good security for his good behaviour for three years." Yet for Luttrell the justice and severity of the punishment was compromised by the behavior of the crowd on the

seventeenth, when Harris "stood for an hour in the pillory over against
the old Exchange . . . [but] he and his party hollowed and whooped, and
would permit nothing to be thrown at him."[7]

The government also sought to silence Harris's "party" by mounting its own press campaign, led by L'Estrange and Nathaniel Thompson,
whose self-congratulatory vaunting possesses at least some justification.
Both historians and literary critics agree that Tory propaganda played a
significant role in transforming the political landscape of the early
1680s, turning the considerable fear of Papists into an even greater
anxiety about civil order.[8] But using the press to combat the press only
compounded the government's problems, for such a strategy contributed
to the already unwelcome public debate, implicitly legitimating the
press's transgression into affairs of state. However effective government
propaganda and however skillful the Tory journalists, Charles, as Jeremy
Black notes, "wished not to conduct a propaganda war but to terminate
one."[9]

In this chapter I will argue that in order to do so Charles's
government exerted increasing pressure on the writer, displaying a
renewed determination to define the author—in the terms developed
by L'Estrange fifteen years earlier in his *Considerations and Proposals*—as
the primary agent of public discourse, the unitary source from which the
power of the press ultimately flowed, and the cynosure of judicial
discipline. Printers, publishers, and booksellers certainly remained important targets of legal action and government harassment, but, as Lord
Chief Justice North explained to Benjamin Harris before sentencing, "if
you expect any thing in this world, of this kind of favour, you must find
out the author; for he must be a rebellious, and villainous traitor."[10] The
October 1679 proclamation "For the Suppressing of Seditious and
Treasonable Books and Pamphlets" offers a forty pound reward to
anyone discovering the author or printer of a seditious book or pamphlet,
and, more significantly, makes a serious effort to penetrate the chain of
production that tended to protect an author's identity. The proclamation extends pardon to hawkers and disposers of seditious books who will
discover the bookseller or printer, "and likewise to any Bookseller or
Printer of any such Books or Pamphlets, who shall Discover and make
known the Authors thereof."[11]

The government possessed a clear sense of how difficult it could
be to unravel the complex trade practices that led back to the author:
as Scroggs noted during Care's trial, "It is hard to find the author, it is
not hard to find the printer." But Scroggs also insisted that "one author

found is better than twenty printers found,"[12] and during the years 1679-1683 the nation's courts and judges increasingly stressed the author's preeminence in the legal economy of censorship. In the two and a half years following the Oxford Parliament, the government brought three men to trial for high treason, Edward Fitzharris, Stephen College, and Algernon Sidney, whose cases illuminate the related issues of authorial accountability and textual dissemination. All three were indicted for conspiring against the king, but in each instance the government's prosecution depended on establishing the defendant's responsibility for composing a libel. To a surprising extent, given the government's emphasis in these trials on violent plots against the king, Fitzharris, College, and Sidney were punished primarily as authors, and their executions helped to reaffirm the king's supremacy over the press.

Central to all three trials was the issue of authorial identity, the government's desire, according to Peggy Kamuf, to make "the signature on a book or commodity . . . function as the proper name of the subject who can be held accountable for whatever effects the law deems dangerous to its own order."[13] Indeed, part of the government's intent in these cases was to place "signatures" on anonymous texts, to insist that unacknowledged publications, in the cases of Fitzharris and College, and even unpublished manuscripts, in that of Sidney, had authors who could be held legally culpable. Yet these trials concern not the author alone, but that figure's relationship to the public for which he wrote. Particularly in the case of Stephen College, which I will examine in this chapter, questions of authorship become intertwined with the construction of "the public," authorial identity and the public's role in political affairs inseparable features of the government's attempt to limit and control print technology.

For the government's conception of authorship and its assumptions concerning the role and character of the writer, we should turn to another speech by Scroggs, this delivered on the first day of Michaelmas-term, 1679. Earlier in the year Scroggs presided over the acquittal of George Wakeman, the first of the Popish Plot trials not to secure a conviction. Public outrage at this first legal questioning of the plot included charges that Scroggs had accepted money from the Papists, and he suffered vilification in the Whig press for months before taking this unusual method of defending himself. In his speech, which he subsequently published, Scroggs doesn't simply justify his conduct at the

trial of Wakeman, but promises revenge against "those hireling scribblers . . . who write to eat, and lie for bread":

> I intend to meet with them another way, for they are only safe whilst
> they can be secret; but so are vermin, so long as they can hide them-
> selves. And let their brokers, those printers and booksellers by whom
> they vend their false and braded ware, look to it; some will be found,
> and they shall know that the law wants not power to punish a libellous
> and licentious press, nor I a resolution to execute it.
>
> And this is all the answer is fit to be given (besides a whip) to those
> hackney-writers, and dull observators, that go as they are hired or
> spurred, and perform as they are fed, who never were taught.[14]

Scroggs's outrage and contempt light on the shame and dishonor,
which we have seen before, of writing for hire. Like Pope a half century
later, Scroggs must despise men who write for bread, though, like Pope
again, his attempts to degrade and dismiss them tend to contradict the
importance he attributes to them. Thus Pope, at the end of the third
book of The Dunciad, includes a note from Scriblerus comparing the
Grub-street race to the water rats who have destroyed the dikes of
Holland: "Do not gentle reader, rest too secure in thy contempt of the
Instruments for such a revolution in learning, or despise such weak
agents as have been described in our poem, but remember what the
Dutch stories somewhere relate, that a great part of their Provinces was
once overflow'd, by a small opening made in one of their dykes by a
single Water-Rat."[15] In Scroggs's speech this same contradiction appears
when we contrast his initial insistence that printers and booksellers are
simply "brokers" for the author to his later characterization of authors
as merely "hired" labor who "perform as they are fed." The first locution
defines authors as the power behind the print trade, the figures who
control the elaborate economic industry that serves to propagate their
views and protect their persons; the latter describes them as nothing
more than hirelings who serve the whip and the economic interests of
their masters. Here a more traditional disdain for the writer jars against
a newer sense of the author as a significant figure.

Scroggs's speech expresses not simply his personal rage but the
state's considered arguments for refusing to allow the public access to
the press: "The extravagant boldness of mens pens and tongues is not to
be endured," for "if once causes come to be tried with complacency to
popular opinions, and shall be insolently censured if they go otherwise,

all public causes shall receive the doom as the multitude happen to be possessed; and at length every cause shall become public, if they will but espouse it." The introduction of the insolent "multitude" into the affairs of state, the creation of a "public" realm within which the decisions and actions of the government can be examined and judged, represents for Scroggs the destruction of the hierarchies that properly order society. Writers become dangerous precisely because "the extravagant boldness of mens pens" helps to define and construct such a "public." Predictably, Scroggs eventually plays the government's trump, damning the opposition as irresponsible radicals who would level all social distinctions by introducing the multitude into matters of state that should not concern them: "No act of oblivion ought to make us forget by what ways our late troubles began, when the apprentices and porters mutined for justice, in their own sense."[16] Here the dreadful specter of 1641 reaffirms the government's insistence that abuses of the press lead inevitably to chaos in the state, that when apprentices and porters can possess "their own sense" of justice, rebellion cannot be far behind. For L'Estrange, in *A Word Concerning Libels and Libellers*, it was precisely the "intolerable License" of the press that helped turn the political world upside down, for "that stripp'd the *Magistracy* of their *Privileges* and *Ornaments*, and set-up *Thimble-makers*, *Dray-men* and *Coblers* for their *Lords* and *Masters*."[17]

This strategy, linking press, public, and rebellion, increasingly came to depend on the elevation of the writer, that figure, encouraged by the Whig's exploitation of the press, who bears responsibility for making "every cause ... public." In the following year L'Estrange provides an even more explicit example of this process in *A Short Answer to a Whole Litter of Libels*, where he rails against libels "popp'd into the world by stealth, (as an Authority to the Rabble) by some Little Mercenary Scribler that sponges for his very Bread, and commonly cousons the Printer too, into the Bargain." In this description of authorial power, mercenary writers deceive even the printer as they pursue their venal and secret ambition to serve as "Authority to the Rabble": "And yet not withstanding the Contempt that I have for these sneaking and Insidiary Hirelings, the Practice is never the lesse of so Bloudy and Dangerous a Consequence, that it is Impossible to preserve the Peace either of Communities, or Private families, where this License is permitted. . . . For all people are not fortify'd alike against the force of Evill Impressions."[18]

In attempting to oppose the public's dangerous intrusion into affairs of state, both Scroggs and L'Estrange necessarily grant formidable power to a previously insignificant and despised figure, the hack, the hired scribbler created by the expansion of the print industry during the late sixteenth and early seventeenth centuries.[19] Out of the trade's growth at the turn of the century there arose, as Richard Helgerson demonstrates, "a system of authorial roles," but these empowered chiefly the "poets," the "self-crowned laureates" who could distinguish themselves from the mere hirelings exploited by the booksellers and publishers who increasingly dominated the expanding literary marketplace.[20] Ben Jonson achieved his hard-won dignity only by detaching himself from the company of those lowly professional writers who found it necessary to "sponge" for their "very Bread."[21] For Scroggs and L'Estrange such wretched creatures begin to assume an importance out of all proportion to their rank, thus necessitating the constant assertions that such "sneaking and Insidiary Hirelings" can indeed threaten the peace of both state and family in spite of their base inconsequence.

In the trial of College, which took place on 17 August 1681— within five months of the dissolution of the Oxford Parliament—these issues played a prominent role not only because of the libels attributed to the defendant, but because of his social and economic rank. For the Tories, the "Protestant Joiner," as he was popularly known, became a convenient symbol of the Whig's desperate and irresponsible appeal to a segment of the population that should have had no voice in matters of national politics. Sir Roger North makes quite clear the issues of station and hierarchy that induced the government to bring College to trial: "*Stephen College* . . . was a Joiner by Trade, but, being a pragmatical Man, and a Fanatic, was set up as a prime Operator in the desperate Doings of the Party. . . . this Handycraft's Man was made famous by the Title of the *Protestant Joiner*; and his Province lay in managing of Sedition and Treason among a lower Order of Men."[22]

North's assessment plays on all the popular fears and prejudices that the government exploited in its campaign against the Whigs. In his *Notes Upon Stephen College*, for example, L'Estrange emphasizes the absurdity of a mere "Handycraft's Man" intruding himself in matters of state when he reports the following remark to College from "a Gentleman": "you know I have my self at Cornbury heard you many times talk undutifully of the Government. Now methinks, you that are but a Mechanick should not presume to meddle with things so much above ye."[23] The emphasis on College as a "Joiner by Trade," a "Handycraft's Man," and "Mechanic" displays the government's fears of social leveling, their outrage that men of College's degree should take part in political matters. College's own account of how he received his nickname provides a perfect example of the type of behavior that the government would have found so objectionable:

> the last Session of Parliament at *Westminster* they sent for me to the *Sun* Tavern behind the Exchange, and when I came, the Duke of *Monmouth* and several Lords were together, and I believe above 100 Parliament men of the Commons: The duke of *Monmouth* called me to him and told me he had heard a good report of me, and that I was an honest man and one that may be trusted; and they did not know but their Enemies the Papists might have some design to serve them as they did in King *James's* time by Gun-powder, or any other way: And the Duke with several Lords and Commons did desire me to use my utmost skill in searching all places suspected by them, which I did perform: and from thence I had as I think the Popular name of the Protestant Joyner, because they had instructed me before any man in *England* to do that Office.[24]

Though College's introduction to the duke and assembled lords and members of commons takes place at a tavern rather than a coffeehouse, the scene—proudly related by College, with its promiscuous mixing of individuals from several stations, conspiratorial atmosphere of plot and counterplot, and recruitment of a craftsman into affairs of state—represents all that the government most feared during the turmoil of the Popish Plot and Exclusion Crisis.

Yet College is portrayed as a dangerous figure not simply because he presumes above his station, but because he was deliberately "set up" by the Whig leadership, according to North, to spread rebellion among the "lower Order of Men." The government regarded College as a conduit between the leaders of the party and "the multitude," as explained in *A Letter from a Gentleman in London to his Friend in the Countrey, on the Occasion of the Late Tryal of Stephen College*: "The *Fears* and *Jealousies* they [the Phanatical Party] so much pretend, are first created chiefly by the great *Donns* of the *Party*, and then most impiously infus'd into the minds of the *Vulgar* and *Ignorant*, who believe what the Leaders of the *Faction* deliver to them with as steadfast a faith as the *Heathens* of old did to their *Oracles*."[25] Precisely because he belonged among and appealed to the "Vulgar and Ignorant," College's involvement in politics, particularly his composition and transmission of political literature, became a significant factor in his trial.

Because of the emphasis on rank and station in his prosecution and trial, I want to examine more precisely College's social and economic position in Restoration society, particularly as the government's determined efforts to situate him among the "lower Order of Men" obscures any appreciation of the divisions that might exist within this undifferentiated "multitude." At the opening of his trial, College identified himself as "a freeman of London, and I am not impleadable by the charter of London any where out of the liberties of the city."[26] Though the court rejected College's assertion that his status protected him from trial in Oxford, his position as a "freeman of London" indicates that he enjoyed a relatively privileged status in Restoration London. As a citizen, College exercised full economic and political rights within the city; freeman householders voted in elections for the aldermen and Common Council, could alone buy or sell goods within the precincts of the city, and participated in governance of the wardmotes, which Valerie Pearl has identified as "the primary units of City government for police, taxation and electoral purposes" in seventeenth-century London. Indeed, Pearl argues that the wards experienced "a new vigor" during "the growth of political consciousness" in that century, providing an important platform for expressions of public opinion in the city.[27] Tim Harris estimates that during the late 1670s and early 1680s fifteen thousand freemen voted in municipal elections, which would place freemen, in a population of approximately 120,000, among the most privileged 10 percent of the inhabitants of the city.[28] Pearl cautions us, however, not to see the freemen as an elite but as constituting "the great majority of male householders in the city."[29]

As a freeman, then, College cannot simply be dismissed as a part of the lower orders of society who had no political role whatsoever in the nation. Like the freeholder on the land, the freeman in town possessed a genuine political identity in matters of local government and administration. Though Edward Chamberlayne, in *Angliae Notitia, or The Present State of England* (1669), draws a sharp distinction between freeholder and freeman, assuring his readers that "the Law of *England* hath conceived a better opinion of the Yeomanry that occupy Lands, then of Tradesmen," the latter would have shared in the rights and privileg s that Chamberlayne assigns to the former: they are "lookt upon as not ap to commit or omit any thing that may endanger their Estates or Credi s . . . wherefore they are judged fit to bear some offices, as of Constabl , Churchwarden, to serve upon Juries, to be Train-Souldiers, to vote in the Election of Knights of the Shire for Parliament."[30] In this context the government's prosecution of College, and insistent efforts to diminish and disregard his status, suggest its determination not to allow this segment of the population to expand its influence within the state, to translate its considerable local authority into a more prominent national political power. Indeed, John Crowne ridicules their political pretensions in his comedy *City Politiques* when the "Catholic Brick-layer," his parody of College, first introduces himself by insisting " 'Tis well known what I am, I am a freeman of Naples, a bricklayer by trade."[31] College's assertion of his legal and political rights evokes the satirist's scorn and contempt for a character described in the Dramatis Personae as merely "a bold, saucy, factious fellow."

In degrading College's station, Charles's government was un-doubtedly aided by the relative unimportance of the gild through which he almost certainly enjoyed his status as a freeman. In sixteenth-century London, according to Steve Rappaport, "seven of every eight men became freemen" through apprenticeship, and figures provided by D.V. Glass suggest that proportion had changed little by the end of the seventeenth century.[32] If College had been born in London he would have gained citizenship through his father (if his father was a citizen when College was born); otherwise he undoubtedly achieved it by successfully completing his apprenticeship and becoming a journeyman in the Company of Joiners. The joiners, however, had never been a particularly prosperous or prestigious company; during the time of Henry VIII, it ranked forty-second out of forty-eight companies, and in a 1603 assessment to raise ten thousand quarters of corn and four hundred pounds, it was ranked forty-first, responsible for forty-one quarters and less than two pounds. (Rich companies like the Merchant Tailors and Drapers were assessed over seven hundred quarters and thirty pounds.[33])

The growing division during the seventeenth century between retailers and craftsmen—which created a considerable tension between booksellers and printers within the Stationers' Company—would not have improved either the economic or the social position of the joiners. According to Glass, figures provided by the 1692 poll tax place joiners among those groups in which "less than half" could pay the tax; the majority of stationers, for the sake of comparison, proved capable of paying the required amount.[34] And in calculating the number of hearths per dwelling in twenty London parishes in 1666, M.J. Power places joiners near the bottom of the scale, well below almost all trades involved in selling, and comparing unfavorably even with most other craftsmen: "It is very clear that the selling groups live in the largest dwellings, craftsmen in much smaller homes, and semi-skilled workers in the smallest of all. . . . people in trade or with some professional skill were the wealthiest groups in pre-industrial society; . . . skilled craftsmen were considerably less prosperous."[35] Social prestige may not be a direct reflection of economic status, but the government's contemptuous references to College as a "Mechanic" and "Handycraft's Man" suggest that as a craftsman his trade did not inspire a great deal of respect. When Edward Chamberlayne distinguishes among "Tradesmen," merchants and retailers enjoy a distinct preeminence over the "Mechanics or Handy-craftsmen" who occupy the bottom of his ranking.[36]

Yet such figures can be misleading: Glass reminds us, for instance, that even those groups that had difficulty in paying their poll tax "constituted the 'wealthier sort' in the city within the Walls," and Jeremy Boulton warns that "occupational groups were not socially homogeneous. Behind the bland labels of many trades and crafts lay a wide range of wealth and status."[37] All that we know about Stephen College suggests that he had, in fact, achieved both social prominence and a degree of wealth through his trade as a joiner. Henry Laverock Phillips argues that the "Philip Colledge" who became a liveryman within the company in 1675 can be identified as Stephen College. If true, this indicates that College had joined the company's elite, for taking up livery would have eventually made him eligible to become an assistant, warden, or master, those individuals who managed the company and its trade. Indeed, from these positions within the companies came the men who sat on the Common Council and possessed responsibility for governing London.

I do not regard Phillips's identification of College as conclusive, however;[38] yet even if College did not achieve livery, there can be little doubt that he had gained considerable prominence as a joiner. During his trial we learn that he owned a horse, gun, sword, even a suit of silk armor, signs not just of economic independence and even wealth but of genuine social distinction.[39] Though his politics must certainly have played an important part in bringing him to the attention of the Whig leaders, there is evidence that his eminence within the trade also helped him to make his way in Restoration London. According to the eighteenth-century historian James Granger, College "was a man of more enlarged understanding than is commonly found in mechanics. His ingenuity in his trade procured him employment among persons of rank; some of whom he was afterwards permitted to visit upon the foot of a friend."[40] Granger's condescension reveals the social taint that even a century later marked the "mechanic," but his remarks indicate as well that it did not disable College from moving in circles that we might have thought closed to him.

Attempting to locate Stephen College more precisely within the complex cultural and economic hierarchies that governed life in Restoration England is, as A.J. Fletcher and J. Stevenson remind us, an endeavor that would not have proven easy even in 1681: "The criteria of social rank included birth, wealth, occupation, and the life style that accompanied their gradations. Historians do not agree, any more than did contemporary commentators, on the precise weight to be given to these various criteria."[41] The publicity surrounding College's trial, however, provides a way for us to evaluate the government's strenuous efforts to sink him within "the multitude," to recognize that this strategy was designed not simply to exploit fears about the imminent collapse of social order, but to deny a more influential place in the political nation to the "middling sort," who were increasingly assertive in seeking a greater voice in the kingdom. Especially in London, where urban life put a particular strain on the traditional hierarchies and signs of deference and obligation, the government found itself confronted by individuals no longer content with their anonymous place among the undifferentiated mass of "the people."

The government brought Stephen College to trial for treasonable offenses that ostensibly culminated in a plot to seize the king during the meeting of the Oxford Parliament. The king's decision to convene Parliament in Oxford rather than London had generated some controversy. The Whigs, of course, contested the unusual change in location because it removed them from their center of power in London; their opposition, the dissolution of the Second Exclusion Parliament in January, and ferociously contested elections that followed, along with the great anticipation that preceded the sitting of Parliament, had given the meeting in Oxford an air of uncertainty and even crisis. Luttrell, for instance, notes on 11 March that "Severall papers have been scattered and reports spread about, that there would be a massacre at Oxford; but these are thought to be devices to terrifye and amuse people."[42] Transparent as these rumors seemed to Luttrell, during the trial the government used the anxiety surrounding the March meeting to lend credence to its charges against the "Protestant Joiner."

Getting College to trial proved a difficult process, indicative of the highly polarized state of the nation in the months following the

Oxford Parliament. The *Calendar of State Papers* first mentions College on 28 June, when it notes the warrant to Thomas Atterbury for "apprehending Stephen Colledge, commonly called the Protestant joiner."[43] The government brought College before a London grand jury in early July, but that jury dismissed the charges by returning a vote of "*ignoramus*," a verdict that both frustrated and disturbed the government; a letter of 11 July to the bishop of London complains that "our Non-conformists are building several new meeting-houses and since last Friday that the grand jury acquitted College they grow impudent."[44]

Government attempts to prosecute stationers had elicited identical verdicts from packed juries since the summer of 1680, when Slingsby Bethel and Henry Cornish had been elected sheriffs of London.[45] In this case, however, another letter of 11 July, from Secretary of State Jenkins to Lord Norreys, reveals the government's ability to counter the Whig strategy: "His Majesty has directed an indictment to be preferred at the Oxford Assizes against Stephen College. . . . His Majesty desires you to have all the care you possibly can that there be a good, honest, substantial grand jury for the county and the like for the city and particularly that both consist of men rightly principled for the Church and the king. He forsees that some will appear at the assizes there, as it was at the Old Bailey, in order to put a discountenance on the proceedings against College."[46] Because College had traveled to Oxford to attend the meeting of Parliament in March, he could be indicted and tried there, isolated from the Whig's power and influence in London.

These communications provide a glimpse of both the behind-the-scenes maneuvering that would decide College's fate and the great public importance of and interest in the legal proceedings against College. For the government, the very visible demonstrations of support for the "Protestant Joiner" threatened to subvert the judicial rituals designed to affirm royal power. According to John Brewer and John Styles, the courts represented the state's "chief means of exercising authority and enforcing regulations. It was in the courtroom or, at least, in the presence of the justice of the peace and his clerk, that men were most aware of the powers that were wielded over them." Yet they also warn against regarding the seventeenth-century legal system "as simply an instrument of an elite. . . . The discretion and voluntaristic nature of the legal system that aided patrician power also enabled others to exploit the law."[47] The rival grand juries—that in London reflecting the Whig power of selection, the one in Oxford demonstrating the government's power—illustrate one of the ways in which the judicial system could be manipulated by opposing interests. In this battle to control the judiciary, however, the king possessed far greater power than the Whigs; according to legal historian A.F. Havighurst, the judiciary under Charles, particularly after 1680, functioned not as an independent arm of government but as a "monarchical administration whose effective elements still sprang largely from royal authority": "By free use of the power of appointment and removal, and by the power of persuasion which comes from royal prestige, Charles gradually moulded the judiciary into an instrument of personal power. It came to be of assistance in stifling the Popish Plot, in controlling the opposition press."[48]

For many in seventeenth-century England, "the rule of law" played an important part in constituting the unique nature of English society and its superiority over other European countries. In the press the government cleverly used this pride in traditional English values by presenting the rival grand juries as an emblem of the Whig's lack of respect for the law. *A Modest Vindication of the Proceedings of the late Grand-Jury at the Old Baily* begins by ostensibly celebrating the London grand jury "for giving more Credit to the solemn Protestation of *One* of their own *Religion* and *Party*, than to *Half a dozen* Oaths of *Church-Papists* or *Masquerading-Protestants*."[49] It seems to argue that the prosecution of College represents an attempt to obfuscate the Popish Plot, to "dexterously transubstantiate the *Popish Design* into a *Presbyterion Conspiracy*." During his trial, in fact, College frequently insisted that charges against him signal the government's desire to transform the Popish Plot into a Protestant one. Yet *A Modest Vindication* mounts, and then parodies, such arguments only to reduce them to absurdity. All the witnesses against College, it concludes, must have been "hired by the *Pope*, or suppose the *Devil*, or at least by some of their Emissaries, the *Jesuits*." And College himself is tellingly associated with "Wat Tyler's Insurection [when] the Rabble were in a uproar at St. Albans," and compared to Greyndcob, one of the "Ringleaders, . . . (a bold impudent Fellow, not much inferior to *Colledge*)."

When speaking in its own voice, the government's propaganda machine piously insisted that in reaching a different verdict the Oxford grand jury had merely attended to the facts of the case without considering religion at all. For weeks L'Estrange's *The Observator* railed at Whig jurors who admit that they accept a witness "against a *Papist*; but the very *same Evidence* against a *True Protestant*, we look upon no otherwise then as a *Sham*, or *Subornation*."[50] In *A Letter From the Grand-Jury of*

Oxford To the London-Grand-Jury, a clever Tory writer has the Oxford jury tell its London counterpart that "surely the *Evidence* that will hang a *Popish Traytor*, may serve well enough for a *Protestant One*." In this broadside the Oxford jury confesses that it can only "admire how you [the London jury] could salve the Reason and Dictates of your Consciences, in acquitting a notorious Traytor in a publick Court of Judicature; that had so abominably affronted our Excellent King, by such Words and Actions, in so many Seditious *Coffeehouses*. . . . Yea, the very mentioning of his Traytorous Speeches stinks in the Nostrils of all Loyal and honest Christians."[51] College's association with "Seditious Coffeehouses" occurs throughout his trial and, along with the emphasis here on abominable words and "Traytorous Speeches," it suggests the importance that language would assume in College's case.

Indeed, College's grim end illuminates the complexities of the late-seventeenth-century print industry not only because his trial concerns issues of authorship and textual dissemination, but because the case itself became an object of intense press scrutiny; a relatively large body of literature charts College's relatively short period of notoriety. Not two weeks after the order of 28 June to apprehend College, he first appears in *The Observator*, where L'Estrange reports in the issue of 7 July (no. 31), that "the *Protestant-Joyner* is gone over to the *Popish Lords* in the Tower."[52] After that College figures in almost every number through 52 (10 September), either unmistakable allusions or direct references charting his course from apprehension and trial to execution and posthumous publication. College's case received great play in the opposition newsletters as well: *The Impartial Protestant Mercury* contains items on College's progress from July through September, the issue after his trial devoting almost the entire first sheet—an exceptionally long story for this publication—to a description of the trial, both as a legal event and public spectacle: "The Lords *Lovelace* and *Norris* were in Court, with several others of the Nobility and Gentry."[53]

In addition to weekly items in newsletters, College's case occasioned the publication of numerous pamphlets and broadsides that dealt with just about every stage of his inexorable march from prison to execution. There are publications dealing with the rival grand juries, "letters" claiming to be both to and from College during his imprisonment before and then after the trial, various accounts of the trial itself, numerous "last speeches and confessions" and accounts of the execution, as well as elegies, lamentations, condemnations, and even two verses claiming communication with College's ghost.[54] Stephen College achieved his fifteen minutes of fame well before Andy Warhol recognized the incredible promiscuity of the modern media and communications industry.

Perhaps even more indicative of the press's centrality to College's case and the issues it raises is the way in which figures from the print industry become part of the literature surrounding his trial. Tory propaganda, for instance, consistently associates College with notorious Whigs in the industry in order to demonstrate his political sympathies, suggest his deep involvement in the cause, and "prove" his identity as a writer and publisher of seditious literature. *A Letter Written from the Tower by Mr. Stephen Colledge (the Protestant-Joiner) To Dick Janeways Wife* tries to blacken College's name by involving him in an adultery with the wife of Richard Janeway, publisher of the important opposition newspaper, *The Impartial Protestant Mercury*. Pretending to be from College, this broadside opens with the joiner lamenting his imprisonment because it has interfered with his carnal delights: "My Commitment was the more surprising to me, in that it broke those measures we had taken for a *Rendezvous* that Evening, where we were to repeat those satisfactions Thee and I have often mutually tasted from the solaces of *Venus* abroad, while *Dick Janeway* toil'd contentedly upon his *Mercury* at home." Even as College betrays his friend, he encourages Janeway's wife to support the cuckolded publisher in his political activism: "Encourage thy *Dick* to go on, though I can no long assist, in the *True Protestant Cause*, yet he is hard enough for all their *Observators*, *Heraclitus*, and other *Tantivy-Scriblers*; and (as I often told Thee) our best Friends are still behind the Curtain, *Men* whose Talent is declaiming, and that can out-bark all their *Towzers*, and out-do that She-Tory *Joa—Br—*. with all her *Guns* and *Crackfarts*."[55] This wonderful tissue of double entendre, scurrilous lies, and insinuations works on the Swiftian principal of "scribler, out of thy own mouth I damn thee." By masquerading as College, this anonymous propagandist can ridicule two important Whigs, demonstrating the sexual hypocrisy of the one and the sexual humiliation of the other. Such a strategy implies a relatively sophisticated knowledge of the print industry on the part of its audience. A broadside like this makes little sense if a reader does not recognize the identity of Dick Janeway or Joanne Brome (a Tory publisher responsible for *The Observator* and many of L'Estrange's literary efforts). It reveals that in London, at least, the reading public knew a good deal about the personalities involved in the print industry and that the most notorious figures were not writers but printers, publishers, and booksellers.[56]

A *Letter Written from the Tower* further demeans the scribbling and publishing of College and Janeway by portraying them as willing tools of the important figures who remain "behind the Curtain." This suggests not only the involvement of prominent Whigs like Shaftesbury in this sordid world of publication but the existence of the type of dangerous "conspiracy" that the Tories constantly attributed to the Whigs. Indeed, Shaftesbury—who was also arrested and imprisoned in July—was clearly a target in the government's action against College, and just days after College's indictment there appeared *Some Modest Reflections upon the Commitment of the Earl of Shaftesbury, Arising from the Late Indictment against Mr. Stephen Colledge*, in which a Whig supporter adopts the Tory pose of denigrating College's birth in order to distance him from the noble peer:

> But what will it amount unto, towards the Proof of a Protestant-Plot, wherein my Lord of Shaftesbury, and many other great and worthy Persons, are said to be conceiv'd; if some rash and unadvised Words, should be proved against Colledge and Whitaker? Shall other Men, and the best and wisest in the Nation, under his Majesty, be immediately judged Traitors, because one or two warm and inconsiderate Persons have talked foolishly and extravagantly? We are fallen into a strange World, if a Body of Men must be made accountable for the Giddiness of some, and those such as they had little Converse with.[57]

This anonymous writer takes great care to separate the "inconsiderate" College, a rash, giddy, and foolish fellow, from Shaftesbury, one of the "best and wisest" men in the nation.

The attention received by College in the press both reflected and intensified the interest in his trial on 17 August, which became a political event of some weight, not simply a dispassionate exercise in blind justice but a judicial ritual affirming royal authority. John Kenyon has described all of the Popish Plot trials as species of "baroque entertainment,"[58] and, like executions or progresses through the city, such trials served as public spectacles designed to manifest the grandeur and inevitability of the king's power. The government certainly took the trial seriously, a letter to Secretary Jenkins from the officer responsible for transporting College from the Tower to Oxford for his trial speaking of "10 or 12 of the warders on horseback with carbines," and rather melodramatically promising that "if College's party attempt to take him out of my hands, they shall never have him alive."[59] At the same time, the Whigs rallied to College's support, particularly, if we can trust the disgusted Sir Roger North, the "lower Orders" that the joiner ostensibly represented: "This made the whole Party engage, as *pro Aris & Focis*, with all the Skill and Interest they had, to boom off this Fire-Ship, and save their Friend. . . . And the Attendance was accordingly, for there was scarce a pragmatical Town Party-Man absent; and Abundance of the Vulgar Sort of them. . . . With this Armament and Attendance, not unlike that which was at the Meeting of Parliament, this Protestant Joiner came down to be tried at *Oxford.*" This crowd, according to North, "had posted themselves in the view of the Prisoner, and made Signals at all Times with Winks and Lipbitings."[60] The trial lasted from noon until two in the morning, when the jury, "after half an hours Consideration, [brought] him in Guilty, with a great Shout upon the Verdict." The court then adjoined until ten in the morning "when he received the sentence of death, as in cases of high treason."[61]

The indictment against College with which his trial begins includes not a word about libels, his plot to forceably seize the king during the Oxford Parliament emphatically at the center of the charges against the joiner:

> Stephen Colledge . . . in the county of Oxford aforesaid; falsely, maliciously, subtilly, advisedly, devilishly and traiterously didst prepare arms, and warlike offensive habiliments to wage war against our said sovereign lord the king. . . . didst say and declare, that it was purposedly designed to seize the person of our said sovereign lord the king at Oxford aforesaid. . . . And that thou the said Stephen Colledge, in prosecution of thy traitorous purpose aforesaid, would be one of them who should seize our said sovereign lord the king at Oxford. [568–69]

Yet the indictment does conclude by alluding to College's "most wicked treasons and traiterous imaginations, composings and purposes aforesaid the sooner to fulfil and perfect, and discords between our said sovereign lord the king, and his people to move, cause, and procure" (569). The legal language of "composing and imagining" refers to the most important medieval statute concerning treason, 25 Edward III, c.2, "A declaration which offenses shall be adjudged treason," and specifically to the clause stating that "*treason shall be said* . . . When a man doth compass or imagine the death of our lord the King."[62] According to John Bellamy, between 1352 and 1485 "the most important development in the interpretation of the law of treason" involved this clause, for in considering intention as well as action "the category could be extended to embrace a wide variety of offences." Extended interpretations of "imagining and compassing the king's death" came under the title of "constructive treason," which the early modern state found particularly useful in cases involving "words and writings which commented on the king and his behavior in what was regarded as a malicious manner."[63]

After the Restoration the act of publication was regularly associated with the language of "compassing and imagining": the first statute passed by the Cavalier Parliament, "An act for safety and preservation of his Majesty's person and government against treasonable and seditious practices and attempts" (1661), specifically stated that "such compassings, imaginations, inventions, devices or intentions . . . shall express, utter, or declare, by any printing, writing, preaching, or malicious and advised speaking," while at the trial of John Twyn, Justice Kelyng advised the jury that "printing and publishing such wicked positions, was an overt act declaring the treason of compassing and imagining the King's death."[64]

College's prosecution, as Lord Chief Justice North asserted during the trial, rested on the application of both of these statutes: "a seizing of the king, and endeavour to do that, is a constructive intention to the death of the king; for kings are never prisoners, but in order to their death. And therefore it hath been held in all times, that by the statute of Edw. the 3d that was treason; but then the statute of this king [Charles II], in the 13th year of his reign, is more strong; for there it says, If any man shall by any words, or malicious speaking shew the imagination of his heart, that he hath any such intention, that is treason too" (619).

Because the publications attributed to College furnished the best proof of "the imagination of his heart," they became as important to the trial as the plot, and the attorney general touched on both when first addressing the jury after the reading of the indictment. He begins by promising to reveal both College's accomplices and that "he had prepared arms in an extraordinary manner, arms of a great value, for one of his condition, who is by trade a joiner" (589); he even jeers that College had "boasted of himself, that he should be in a little time a colonel . . . a great preferment for a joiner" (590), revealing from the very start the considerations of rank that would work against College throughout the trial. The libels appear at the end of the attorney general's speech in order to show that College's malice against the king "was not a sudden unpremeditated thing": "we shall produce to you the evidence that he drew the king's picture, and exposed him in all the reproachful characters imaginable, and that the picture might be the better understood, he adds a ballad to it: and that he may not have the confidence to say this is not true, we shall produce to you a whole bundle of these papers . . . and we shall prove him to be the author of them" (591).

Following his opening statement, the attorney general questioned the government's first witness, Stephen Dugdale, immediately leading him from disparaging remarks made by College about the king—"the king was a papist himself, that he was as deep in the plot as any papist of them" (592)—to College's specific plans for Oxford: "we must look to arm ourselves, and that he would arm himself, and be here at Oxford; and he told me here in the town accordingly when I came out of the country, and he said that he had several stout men that would stand by him in it" (593). Having quickly established the "particulars" of the alleged plot, the attorney general then questions Dugdale at length about College's relationship to various "pictures and papers." Indeed, the libels attributed to College dominate the trial for the rest of Dugdale's testimony and cross examination, obviously causing a great deal more excitement than revelations about the plot.

Dugdale begins by producing a piece that he calls "the Letter pretended to be intercepted to Roger L'Estrange."[65] Dugdale swears that College admitted "he was the author of it himself; and he shewed me it in manuscript before it was printed." The attorney general examines the paper and damningly notes its connection to the earlier trial of Edward Fitzharris: "It is a letter, and a great part of Fitzharris's libel is taken out; it seems Colledge was the author, and this is the original of the libel." Fitzharris's guilt, proven before the same court only two months before, when he was sentenced to death for writing a libel, is skillfully used to ensnare College. After establishing that College had provided copies not only to Dugdale but to two other gentlemen, the attorney general has the libel read aloud to the court. After this reading the attorney general asks Dugdale about further libels, when George Jeffreys, who had aggressively questioned and disparaged Fitzharris during that trial, interrupts to ask specifically of "A Raree Shew," the ballad that the government clearly most wanted to lay to College's charge.[66] Accompanied by a woodcut, this combined "picture and print" provided a sensational occasion for the government to produce textual evidence for College's antipathy to the king. Next to the often vague charges concerning

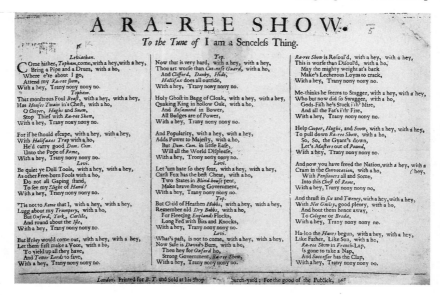

Stephen College's "A Ra-ree Show" (1681)

College's plot, the specificity of the ballad and its accompanying print proved an irresistible opportunity for the government to savage its judicial victim.

Dugdale begins by claiming that he heard College sing the ballad on a number of occasions, that College admitted he had written the ballad and made the picture, and that College explained "he would get it printed": "He told me he was the author of this cut, and he gave me one, and we sang it together presently after it was printed." An examination of the print, in which five members of the court participate, elicits from Dugdale a detailed description of how College himself interpreted the cut. At one point, in fact, Jeffreys gets carried away and provides his own gloss on the picture, the lord chief justice having to intervene in order to ask Dugdale "Did he [College] make this explication to you?" When the clerk reads the ballad in court, the attorney general's response suggests the impact that the libel has had on the courtroom: "This shews you what a sort of man he is" (596).

Dugdale's revelations about College's career as an author did not end with his remarks on "A Raree Show." Dugdale concludes his testimony with "a word or two more about a libel in manuscript . . . [that College] told me the printer durst not print it, it was so dangerous. . . . it was the worst I ever heard in my life against the king and government" (598), while during College's crossexamination Dugdale even produces, and has read in court, "one picture that I have not shewed yet, which you have explained what the meaning was" (602). Yet Dugdale, and the other witnesses, always return to "A Raree Show," the text that most fully represents both College's treason and his authorial identity. Indeed, during College's crossexamination, Dugdale insists on College's authorship of the ballad by noting a variation between printed and manuscript texts (line 73 in Lord's version):

> *Dugdale.* And in one place . . . the king was termed a rogue; but they put him in by another name. *Jefferies.* Where is it? *Dugdale.* It is in Rary Shew; in the manuscript it was, "Now now the rogue is down." *Jefferies.* Let me see it; I took notice of it,"Now, now the giant is down." (602)

Bibliographical scholarship becomes one of the tactics used by the court to convict College, Dugdale providing the most detailed examination of textual detail and specificity of interpretation.[67]

To leave no doubt of College's relationship to "A Raree Show," the government next called Robert Stevens and Thomas Atterbury, the two in charge of the search of College's house that discovered his papers. Both swear that during the search they found "the first draught" in College's bed-chamber, "an original drawn with a pencil upon Dutch paper" (603), but to the considerable dismay of the court the original could not be found among the mass of papers in evidence against College. The testimony of Atterbury and Stevens ends in a good deal of confusion, College insisting that "I am sure you could never find the original of any such thing in my house," Stevens assuring the court that "Sure I am, it was taken when we searched the house" (604).

After the embarrassment with Atterbury and Stevens, the government called only those witnesses who specifically linked College to the Oxford plot. Along with Dugdale, Edward Turberville testified to College's behavior while in Oxford, corroborating that College went armed—"he himself had a case of pistols, a sword, and I believe he might have his armour on"—and boasted that should the king not satisfy his party "we will secure him till he comes to those terms we would have from him" (615). Two other witnesses, John Smith and Bryan Haynes, provided testimony concerning College's activities in London before and after the Oxford session, both reporting particularly damaging conversations allegedly held with the defendant. Smith, for instance, gave a detailed description of College's personal weapons and armor, including "his head-piece, which, if I am not mistaken, was covered over with camblet, it was a very fine thing." According to Smith, College concluded a display of his armaments with the statement that "these are the things which will destroy the pitiful guards of Rowley, that are kept up contrary to law and justice, to set up arbitrary power and popery" (605). Haynes's testimony was even more sensational, including charges that College bragged of having access to "1,500 barrels of powder, and . . . 100,000 men ready at an hour's warning." Haynes included in his testimony as well a number of disrespectful remarks made by College about "that beastly fellow Rowley," including a genealogy of the Stuart line that emphasized what the packed courtroom would have regarded as sexual perversity: "and speaking of the king, [College] said, he came of the race of buggerers, for his grandfather king James buggered the old duke of Buckingham; and he called him [Charles] captain, and sometimes the king, and sometimes Rowley" (609).

The government returned to College's literary activity only with its final witness, Sir William Jennings, who testified to a number of encounters with College in coffeehouses, including one that describes precisely the type of public behavior that so incensed the government: "But there was a picture looking on by 7, or 8, or 10 people, I believe more or less, and I coming crowding in my head among the rest, looked upon this picture. After the crowd was over, Mr. Colledge takes a picture out of his pocket, and said he, I will give you one of them if you will. So he gives me a picture; which picture if I could see, I could tell what it was; it was written 'Mac a Top,' and there were several figures in it. (Then the picture was shewed him.)" (617). All of the witnesses against College consistently associated him with the coffeehouses, Haynes at one point implying that it was a common sight to "have seen you [College] in the coffee-houses bawling against the goverment" (610). *City Politiques* presents College as such a "tempestuous disputer in coffeehouses that as ever you appeared in one both sides would run away" (II.i.113-15).

While reading the record of College's trial we should remember North's complaints about the size and activity of the crowd attending the trial: justices, witnesses, and defendant played their parts before a throng of spectators. Like a play, the trial was a dramatic event, an encounter between audience and actor in which the bare "text" carries only part of the performance's meaning. Just about everyone involved in College's trial shows an acute awareness of not only the jury who will decide College's fate, but the crowds that pack the courtroom. Bryan Haynes's charges about "1,500 barrels of powder and 100,000 men" went unsubstantiated during the course of the trial—the government never attempted to produce even one barrel—but their impact nonetheless may have been considerable; his references to College's remarks concerning a "race of buggerers" had no bearing on the alleged plot but nonetheless such sensational stuff served the government's purposes.

Clearly the government's emphasis on College's literary involvement proceeded not entirely from legal considerations but from its canny appreciation of the dramatic effect of textual demonstration, of concrete evidence produced through readings and the examination of prints. College himself shows an awareness of this when he complains that "here are a great many things made use of that serve only to amuse the jury, I can conjecture nothing else they are brought for; I desire to know whether the pictures produced are part of the treason" (616). A few minutes later the lord chief justice answers College's question, implicitly recognizing both the legal and the dramatic aspects of College's alleged ballads and pictures: "For a conspiracy in you, if the witnesses speak truth, there is a plain proof, and of the degrees of it: first of all, by your publishing libels, and pictures to make the king odious and contemptible in the eyes of the people, and that you should be the author of some of those pictures, and they were found in your custody" (619). North goes on to enumerate the further "degrees" of proof, listing College's preparation of arms and his journey to Oxford, for these decisively transform "bare words" into "the overt-act." In spite of their judicial weight, however, such acts, in the context of the courtroom, could not have seemed as "real" as College's identity as an author, proven by the literary artifacts that demonstrably "make the king odious and contemptible in the eyes of the people." Examined by a miscellaneous crowd of "7, or 8, or 10 people" in a public coffeehouse, such poems and pictures challenge the king's identity and authority; as part of a judicial ritual, however, they demonstrate royal power, their dramatic impact turned back upon their ostensible author.

College attempted to thwart this strategy by consistently maintaining that he had nothing to do with any of the libels or pictures attributed to him. During his defense he called two witnesses to testify that the papers found in his house were planted there by people unknown to him. His maid, Elizabeth Hunt, claimed that a porter—"I never saw the man since nor before"—brought "three bundles" of papers to College's house insisting that they must be left. College explains that somehow "they were put in a box and left in my compting-house: I never touched them, but there they staid, for ought I know, till they were taken" (669). College's sister, Sarah Goodwin, tells an even more mysterious tale, claiming that other papers were planted in her house by a "waterman, I suppose, that belonged to his majesty, for he had a coat marked with R.C." (672).

College tried to bolster his insistent claims that "I neither know the printer nor the author, I declare it upon my life" (674), by presenting himself as a simple, plain, honest man, suggesting through this guise that literary endeavors were quite beyond him. He opens his summation to the jury, for example, by complaining that "I have no flourishes to set off my defense. I cannot take the jury nor the court with an oratory; I am unhappy in those things" (675). College denies any facility with words or speech, "unhappy" in those talents that would allow him to sway a jury or, by implication, a coffeehouse crowd. In defining himself here in relationship to language, College at the same time makes a statement about rank, implying that this trial pits his simple, sturdy, yeoman virtues against the sophisticated learning and eloquent speech of the court. The issue of rank, of who in the kingdom have a right to concern themselves in public affairs, was absolutely central to College's trial, revealing itself most tellingly in regard to both arms and print.

Numerous witnesses testified that College went about armed. Those produced by the government claimed a design against the king; those called by College noted only his fear of the Papists. College himself admitted that "all that know me, know I was never without a case of pistols and an horse, though I was but a joiner" (650), the last clause suggesting precisely the prejudices that the government exploited in emphasizing his carrying of weapons. Throughout the trial the government implied that nothing could justify College's pretensions in going about armed, and during his summation the solicitor general explicitly castigated College for attempting to move beyond his proper social sphere: "he came down in an equipage not suitable to his profession; for you see he was by trade a carpenter or a joiner, but armed on horseback with a case of pistols, things that do not become such men to travel with" (696).

College was particularly vulnerable to such charges because he possessed not only arms but a suit of armor whose richness a number of witnesses recalled. Smith, as we have already seen, had described the camblet-covered headpiece as "a very fine thing" (605), while Turberville believed that College wore the armor during his visit to Oxford. Even witnesses called by College alluded to the armor: when Thomas Smith described it as "a suit of armour made of silk to wear under a coat," College nervously insisted that "it was silk-armour only for the thrust of a sword. And I assure you, my lord, I had but one suit, one case of pistols, and but one horse" (649). In the courtroom the attention paid to College's armor ostensibly involves questions about his aggressive intentions, though a description of such armor in Sir Roger North's *Examen* reveals the subtext concerning College's station:

> There was much Recommendation of silk Armour, and the Prudence of being provided with it, against the Time that Protestants were to be massacred. And accordingly there were abundance of those silken Back, Breast, and Potts made and sold, that were pretended to be Pistol Proof; in which any Man dressed up was safe as in an House, for it was impossible any one could go to strike him for laughing: so ridiculous was the figure, as they say, of Hogs in Armour; an Image of Derision insensible, but to the View as I have had it. This was Armour of Defense.[68]

North does not question the defensive nature of this type of armor, but he also has little doubt about the unsuitability of such armor for men of College's rank. Government references to College's armor during the trial represent a subtle attempt to emphasize both the danger of allowing the "Vulgar" to rise above their station, and the absurdity of such pretensions, which can only produce "Hogs in Armour."

The government indulged a similar strategy in its emphasis on College as an author. The libels attributed to him are dangerous not only because they attempt to make the king odious in the eyes of the people but because they reveal a restive "multitude" asserting control over a powerful technology. Early in the trial Jeffreys asserts that College's activity as a Whig propagandist "is your common trade it seems" (602), and throughout the trial College's "trade" and "profession" come under intense scrutiny, particularly from Jeffreys, whose constant snipping at College inevitably reveals a contempt for the joiner's rank. When the matter of College's pistols first arises, Jeffreys jeers that "I think a chissel might have been more proper for a joiner" (601); and when College tries to argue about the politics of the Long Parliament with the lord chief justice, Jeffreys dismisses the defendant as "a mighty learned gentleman, to talk of those points indeed" (691).

During his summation to the jury, Jeffreys makes explicit the connection between rank, arms, and printing that explains the government's decision to portray College not just as a man plotting against the king, but as an author:

> this gentleman, whose proper business it had been to manage his employment at London for a joiner, is best seen in his proper place, using his proper tools of his trade. I think it had been much more proper for him, and I believe you will think so too, than to come with pistols and those accoutrements about him, to be regulating of the government; what have such people to do to interfere with the business of the government? God be thanked, we have a wise prince, and God be thanked he hath wise counsellors about him, and he and they know well enough how to do their own business, and not to need the advice of a joiner, though he calls himself the Protestant Joiner. What had he to do to engage himself, before his advice was required? How comes he to concern himself, so much that after he had writ this libel, wherein he is pleased to take notice of tyrants, afterwards should go to make a print, I mean the Rary Shew? [705]

In condemning College as a rebel and as an author, the two words that Jeffreys cannot help repeating are *proper* and *business*. Both suggest his desire to reaffirm hierarchy, to insist on social categories that he defines not as arbitrary constructions, but as natural, inevitable, and immutable manifestations of the understanding "God" who has placed a wise king and counsellors over us. To know one's "proper" place is to know a divine order sanctioned by the lord and overseen on earth by a sacred king; to know one's "business" is to know one's place in the increasingly complex economic system that organizes Restoration society. Between the joiner's "trade" and "the business of the government," Jeffreys wishes to erect a gulf vast and unbridgeable, and his movement from arms to print suggests the two forces that most threaten the strict hierarchy he would create.

In College's trial the government aggrandizes the author precisely so that it could more easily control the productions of the press. By emphasizing College's publishing activities, the government reveals its determination to create in the figure of the author a primary site of regulation and punishment. Though the alleged plot against the king provided an easy way for the government to secure a conviction against College, the government's concern to prove him an author suggests the importance attributed to publication. During the trial, in fact, College as overreaching author seemed far more dangerous to the king than College the conspirator, for while the alleged plot never became more than a series of rash threats, the pile of papers attributed to College was tangibly present and possessed a dramatic power that could be demonstrated, could be tapped, and in effect reversed, through public reading and interpretation. Indeed when, after the trial, Secretary Jenkins communicates to the sheriff of Oxfordshire the king's instructions regarding the execution, he reveals Charles's recognition that College's power lay in his relationship to language and the press:

> He [the king] further recommends it to your care that at his [College's] execution some persons be present, that can write shorthand, to take his last words, to prevent a misinformation and scandalous reports. You are likewise desired to restrain any extravagant or undutiful excursions of his tongue and particularly the distributing of any papers, which you are desired to seize, if any such thing be offered.
>
> Since there are lodged in your hands already a great many prints and cuts, most of them scandalous and seditious, his Majesty thinks fit that all papers and prints you have should be burnt by the hangman at the time and place of execution.[69]

The careful orchestration of College's execution reveals the king's concern for control of the word. Shorthand must be employed to provide an accurate account of College's final "words" so that false reports can be given the lie. All care must be taken to "restrain his tongue" to prevent both "undutiful" speech and "papers" from disturbing the significance of his death, which the simultaneous execution of College and his papers perfectly represents: College becomes an emblem of the king's struggle to wrest the press from the hands of the vulgar and refashion it as an instrument of royal power.

After College's condemnation, the government and the opposition struggle over his meaning in the press, each side seeking to appropriate him as a symbol for its cause. A Tory writer, for instance, impersonates College in *A Letter Written from Oxford By Mr. Stephen College To his Friends, in London, &c.*, claiming that the piece is "Written by himself, Immediately after his Condemnation."[70] This broadside takes great delight in presenting College as an overweening traitor, punning frequently on his name and the university town where he plotted his mischief: "they were well-wishers to the *Colledges*, and were carrying that tall Gentleman there to the *University*. What to do, says the man? for in my mind he looks as if he were too old to learn." The writer presents College as a man puffed up with pride, his head so turned with self-importance that he thinks to "leave off *Joyning* and turn *Statesman*." The broadside concludes with a witty reference to the press war in which College's public significance will be determined: "Gentlemen, receive my Last Salutes with as upright and good Hearts, as I send them, and tell Mr. J——y, that if it were in my Power to appoint, no body should have leave to Print my Story but Himself, as well for His sake, as my own; For if any such fellow as N.T. should Transmit my Memory to Posterity, I shall scarce be Nam'd twice in a Page, without the Appellation of Traytor." Here the old association between College and Janeway serves not simply to reinforce College's ties to the opposition press, to emphasize his identity as a literary figure, but to suggest how the public can establish his true voice amidst the conflicting claims about him. This final attention to the print industry will particularly amuse the careful reader who notes that "N.T."—Nat Thompson—allegedly published this broadside, providing a Swiftian irony that suddenly calls into question its own veracity.

Authenticity becomes an important issue especially in regard to College's behavior on the day of his execution. The popular genre of "the last speech and confession" had become particularly important during the Popish Plot, every execution being followed by written accounts ostensibly providing exact relations of the victim's final words. In the case of College, the government very much wanted a confession that would not only vindicate their charges against the Protestant Joiner, but implicate more substantial figures, particularly Shaftesbury, in his plots. On 22 August, for instance, Secretary Jenkins notes in a letter to the bishop of Oxford that "His Majesty is perfectly of opinion that, if College be truly relenting, he is conscious of a great many things that may be of consequence to be known and that he can't be truly penitent without revealing them for the safety of the King and kingdom." College clearly refused to cooperate, for a letter to Jenkins on the twenty-seventh reports that "College . . . still refuses to say anything more than that he spake rash words." The government continued to hope, however, and as late as the twenty-ninth, Jenkins is comforted by "news here that College is come to a second penitence and makes very candid confessions."[71]

The first published account of College's execution answered almost all of the government's hopes, for *The Last Speech and Confession of Mr. Stephen Colledge* presents College as a genuine penitent. He declares that at his trial "I had more favour shown me than I could have imagined would be allowed to any person in my circumstances" and admits that his vanity and pride led him beyond his station: "I am sensible I have had the eye of the World upon me for some little time past, which I here declare was occasioned by my own inconsideration in hearkening to the allurements of this vain world."[72] He displays the proper understanding of his position by explaining just how a subject should revere his king: "I have sinned against the best of kings, in not having before my eyes that Aw, that Fear and Reverence that became me as a Subject, to the greatest Tyrant in the world. For, as His Majesty is the undoubted Father of our Countrey, we ought to pay him Paternal Reverence, and sincere Love." Finally, and perhaps most important, "College" here confesses his responsibility as an author: "I have sinned against my Countrey in spending most part of my time for some years past in inventing of Seditions, tending not only to the disturbance of its Peace, but to the utter subversion of those wholsom laws that have been made by our Ancestors."

Though this confession fails to implicate more important members of the opposition in College's plotting and printing, in every other way it fulfills the government's fondest expectations. As Alan Sinfield and Jonathan Dollimore have explained, "to be sincerely validated by former opponents—especially when their confessional self-abasement is in excess of what might be expected from the terms of their defeat" is "one of the most authoritative ideological legitimations available to the powerful."[73] This "College" admits his guilt, praises the justice of his trial, confesses his failure to respect hierarchical distinctions, and describes kingship in terms worthy of Sir Robert Filmer. Such a figure fully vindicates the government's case. Unfortunately for the government, however, the opposition immediately denounced *The Last Speech and Confession* as a forgery. Dick Janeway's *Impartial Protestant Mercury* of August 30–September 2 unhesitatingly informs its readers that "this is certain. That the half sheet which came out pretending to be [College's] last Speech, said to be printed by A. *Banks*, is wholly a Cheat and a Forgery; and was in truth Printed by that Notorious *Thompson*. But his true Speech delivered under his own Hand, will shortly be made Publick."[74] "That Notorious Thompson," his role in blackening College's name foretold by the anonymous author of *A Letter Written from Oxford*, apparently used Banks as a cover to provide the Tories with a College ideally suited for their propaganda purposes.[75]

College's relation, Edith College, published the Whig account of

College's execution, *A True Copy of the Dying Words of Mr. Stephen College*. This document contains little to cheer the government, for though College is respectful, he provides no penitent confessions of guilt or wrongdoing. On the contrary, he most emphatically denies his responsibility for the libels attributed to him: "As to the Printed Papers which *Dugdale* produced in the court, I do declare I never saw them called *The Raree Show*, and *Intercepted Letter*, in his hand before that time, and therefore could not and did not decypher any of the Pictures to him, it's utterly false. I was not the Author of those Verses called the *Raree Show*, neither do I know who was, or the Printer; or ever owned myself the Author of either of them Papers to him in my Life."

In *A True Copy* College also claims that the government had persisted in attempts to link him to the Whig leadership: "the Messenger who brought me a Message of my Death, told me I might have my Life would I confess who was the cause of my coming to Oxon, and upon what account. I answered him, I was glad the confessing the truth of that would do it, and said, I came voluntarily of my self, I rode my own Horse, spent my own Money, and neither was invited or had dependency upon any Person."[76] The government steadfastly insisted that the accoutrements of a gentleman enjoyed by College must betoken his support by the party. L'Estrange questions College's assertion here by reporting that "the people of the *Red Lyon* in *Henly*" swear that all of College's expenses were "plac'd to the Account of another Person."[77]

College's unfortunate notoriety did not quite pass with his death, for after his execution he continued to serve the propaganda purposes of both parties. The Whigs, not surprisingly, portray him as the victim of a corrupt legal system, "And Thou, Undaunted Soul, that now must fall / A *Legal Victim* to their Gall," using his death to establish his credentials as a Protestant martyr: "This carry to the Grave: *Though* Live *you cann't*, / *You yet may Die a* Protestant."[78] Tory writers, on the other hand, emphasize the issues of rank and hierarchy that dominated College's trial. "The Whiggs Lamentation for the Death of their Dear Brother Colledge, The Protestant Joyner," though presenting itself as a sincere tribute, praises College in terms that reveal its government bias:

> Our dear Brother States-man, tho' bred in a Saw-pit,
> Had internal *Genious*, enough to or'throw Wit:
> He fram'd a new Moddel, to limit the K——,
> In hopes Crown and Sceptre might truckle to him.

Here again the government fastens on College's overreaching, the destructive potential of an individual of inferior station who aspires to be "both Champion and Carver of Laws." College would simply invert the natural hierarchies that properly order society, his "Saw-pit . . . Genious" concerned primarily with its own vain advancement. This poem wishes as well to assume the victory of Tory beliefs, claiming that "the Popish Plot, has now quite lost it's Name, / And none thy bright Blunderbush dare to maintain."[79] College becomes the ragtag standard-bearer of a lost cause.

Though College's final speech had failed to serve the government's purposes, neither implicating others nor confessing his publishing activities, this didn't stop the government's propaganda machine from insisting on the truth of their "College." In "Stephen Colledge's Ghost to the Fanatical Cabal" he is made to admit his role as

> an active Puppet and was proud,
> To squeak out *Treason* to the listning Croud,
> Whilst S—— behind the *Curtain* sate,
> And taught my busie babling tongue to prate.[80]

For the government College always remained too inconsiderable a fellow to have been alone responsible for his own actions. In the heated and paranoid atmosphere of the late seventies and early eighties, both sides consistently saw political action in terms of secret plots and conspiracies.

After implicating Shaftesbury in his plots, "College" turns to the press, implicitly confessing his literary identity and explicitly damning the press's excesses:

> Now for the scribling Tribe, my last advice
> Is seasonable Caution to be nice,
> Too boldly in their function they transgress,
> Too fatally Licentious is the Press.
> The giddy and believing Rout they please
> With Mercuryes and Impartiallities,
> Whilst into the unpleasant Dose is thrown,
> *Protestency* to make the Cup go down.

From the medical imagery to the contempt for a "giddy and believing Rout," these lines recapitulate the government's traditional belief in the dangers of the press and the necessity for keeping it out of the public's hands. At once fearful of the press's "function," the government nonetheless has little but contempt for "the scribling Tribe" that live by manipulating a credulous public. In this text of sin and transgression, where College admits his punishment "where death and everlasting horror dwells," the press becomes a demonic instrument, "fatally Licentious" in its the debasement of true religion for partisan purposes.

As a topic for political commentary, College lingered on as late as 1683, when *City Politiques*—first performed in January—and *Strange News from Newgate; Or, A Relation how the Ghost of Colledge the Protestant-Joyner, appeared to Hone the Joyner since his Condemnation* brought his career to an inglorious close.[81] Another Tory production that impersonates College in order to have him degrade himself, the broadside opens with his confession of *"Treasonable Intentions, and Raree-Show Tricks."* Rather than stressing his literary activity, however, *Strange News* dwells on College's identity as a mechanic, presenting him as a proud "Joyner in Ordinary to the Commonwealth of Fiends, where the Earl of Shaftesbury is received into favour, and created one of the Governing-members of the Luciferian Associates." Hell recapitulates the hierarchical structures of Restoration England, the piece expressing a pervasive mistrust of the lower orders in the figure of Hone, who continues the conspiracy and design among tradesmen and handycraftsmen begun by College.

The play, on the other hand, makes a good deal of College's literary profession, dramatizing precisely the type of perverse world of print portrayed by Scroggs at the trial of Care: "As paper in Holland passes for money, pamphlets with us pass for religion and policy. A bit of paper in Holland, from a man of credit, takes up goods here, pays debts there; so a pamphlet will take up fools here, make fools there. A pamphleteer is the best fool-maker in the nation" (IV.i.4-10).

In such a society College flourishes, the rapacious scribbler motivated not by principle but simply by money. Early in the play he offers to switch sides if only the government will provide a pension, the Governor's indignant response indicative of the play's attitude to those who seek to involve themselves in a politics that is simply above them: "A pension! A whip, you rascal. . . . Follow your trade and mind all of you your own matters; leave state affairs to your governors, we have more to lose than any of you" (I.ii.114-17).

These half-dozen ballads and poems occasioned by College's death present the dead joiner primarily as a caricature, either as the heroic martyr or demonic rebel of Whig and Tory propaganda. By far the most important consideration of College after his death came from the pen of Roger L'Estrange, whose fifty-page pamphlet, *Notes Upon Stephen College*, represents a serious attempt to deal with some of the issues raised by his unusual career and fate. L'Estrange clearly writes as a voice of the government, concerned to vindicate its behavior and damn College's. Yet L'Estrange goes about this task in a fashion that explains a great deal about the government's understanding of and relation to literary texts. Indeed, L'Estrange's short pamphlet participates in the creation of the modern literary text, for the questions he insists on raising and answering suggest those enumerated by Michel Foucault in his description of the "author-function": "literary discourses came to be accepted only when endowed with the author-function. We now ask of each poetic or fictional text: from where does it come, who wrote it, when, under what circumstances, or beginning with what design?"[82]

Though the pamphlet deals with a number of questions about College, particularly his religious beliefs,[83] literary matters occupy L'Estrange for almost the entire pamphlet. L'Estrange begins by considering the question of authorship, concerned to prove, in spite of College's consistent denials, "that he went off the Stage with a Sad account to answer for upon this very Point" (11). L'Estrange produces an array of evidence designed to make College's identity as the author of "A Raree Show" "as clear as the light it self" (11). Some of this evidence merely reiterates points already made by the government during the trial: L'Estrange notes that many report hearing College sing the ballad, while others confess that they received copies of the ballad from College himself. Yet L'Estrange also provides information not presented during the trial, particularly a link between College and the printer of "A Raree Show": "The *Printer* confesses and declares upon the sight of one of the Papers found at *Colleges*, that it was wrought at *his Press*; that he did it for *Franck Smith*" (12). L'Estrange uses this admission to speculate about College's connection to the notorious Francis Smith, who was prosecuted as late as 1684 for printing "A Raree Show": "undoubtedly *Franck Smith* receiv'd the *Manuscript* [from College]; and *College*, it seems, told *Smith* no more upon this occasion" (13).[84]

Aware, perhaps, that such speculation cannot actually prove

College's guilt, L'Estrange presents a far more specific piece of evidence, using textual scholarship to connect College to the poem:

> There was a Paper of *College's Intercepted*, which upon Examination he utterly *deny'd* at *first*; but finding himself *Discover'd*, he *confess'd* it. This was some few days before his Execution. The Paper here intended, was the *speech*, word for word, that was Printed for *Edith College*; which being shew'd to the *Joyner*, he acknowledg'd it to be of his own *Hand-writing*; and so is the *Manuscript* also of the *Raree-show*, from whence that Ballad was Printed; and I have the *Original* at this Instant by me, to satisfie any man that shall make a doubt whether or no it was of *Colleges Writing*. [13–14]

Here L'Estrange describes two "original" manuscripts, the similarity of handwriting linking them to one author. By using the "proper" edition of College's final speech—the one published by Edith College and not the one by A. Banks—L'Estrange makes a bold attempt to subvert the assertions made in the very manuscript he presents as evidence, using the text to both contradict and discover the author, to make it the "property" of College in spite of its explicit denials.

L'Estrange particularly enjoys working with texts, secure in the knowledge that he possesses an ocular proof that can "satisfie any man that shall make a doubt." Though L'Estrange admits that "the Capital Branch" of the charges against College involved "the Design of *Seizing the king*" (24), at first he ignores the plot, aware, perhaps, that on this question the government could produce few particulars that went beyond rash words. By working with texts, however, both printed and in manuscript, L'Estrange, like any literary scholar, can point to an "objective" array of facts and evidence. This I suspect explains L'Estrange's dependence on imagery of light and sight throughout the pamphlet, his insistence that the truth is available to those who would see: "I cannot but deplore the Infatuated blindness of this Unhappy Creature, that should now at his last Extremity, instead of discharging his soul by a publique and Sincere Repentance, be troubling of his head with Shifts and Reservations, as if he were contriving how to cast a mist before the Eyes of God and Men; and in a case so open too, that half an eye sees thorow it" (14). In this case, L'Estrange insists, the truth discovers itself, for texts possess a life of their own that the author cannot control. College's denials are frivolous, for what he has written and published reveals the truth, transparent in spite of his attempted obfuscations: "the

Treason of his *Heart* is laid as open in those Cuts, as that of his *Tonge* was at his *Trial*" (28).

As L'Estrange continues, he develops the extent of College's treason through a close, critical reading of "A Raree Show" and its accompanying print. L'Estrange plays the literary critic here, the interpreter careful to do justice to his text: "I shall not force these words of his beyond a fair Congruity with the tenour of what he says in other places" (41). He looks, for instance, at the lines "For fleecing England's flocks / Long fed with bits and knocks" (lines 53–54), arguing that they "denote the *king* to be a *Tyrant* and an *Oppressor*" (34). In explaining the significance of such lines, the way in which they undermine the authority of the king, L'Estrange makes the traditional government argument against public involvement in the print industry. In poems like "A Raree Show," L'Estrange assures his readers, we see "all the *Fore-runners* of, and *Dispositions* to a *Rebellion*, as clear as the Noon-day, and *College* deeply engag'd in every Point" (34–35). An unrestricted press presents a danger to the stability of the country because the general population cannot be trusted to judge the truth of what they read: "How many Impudent and Ridiculous *Shams*, by Counterfeit Tickets, and Letters were Expos'd in the daily Papers of Intelligence, which at that time were swallowed whole, as the very Oracles of the *Vulgar*" (35–36).

As L'Estrange's reading of the poem continues, however, he uses the ballad not simply as a manifestation of dangerous antimonarchical sentiments that may upset the people, but as proof of the existence of the plot itself: "That there was a Plot to be Executed at *Oxon*, will be granted, I presume, by any man that has but eyes in's head, and looks that way" (35). Again, L'Estrange insists that there can be no question about his assumptions concerning authorial intention: one need only have "eyes in's head" to see the truth of L'Estrange's assertions. He cites, for instance, "So, so the giant's down, / Let's masters out of pound" (lines 73-74) to reveal "both the Design of Dethroning the king, and in the word MASTERS the Doctrine of the Supremacy of the Two Houses" (33-34). Such a reading uses the text to insist on the reality of College's plot, literary evidence transformed from a revelation of College's malice toward the king to a representation of College's rebellious political activity: "In that *Doggrel copy* there is Chalk'd out the very Train of the whole *Conspiracy*; and so plainly too, that it will not bear any other Construction" (43).

L'Estrange again uses the tools of textual scholarship to reveal even more "plainly" the implications of the poem, examining textual differences in the line "Haloo! the hunt's begun, with a hey, with a hey" (line 86): "I have in my hand the *Manuscript of Colleges own writing*, from whence this Ballad was Printed; where it is to be noted, that instead of *Halloe*, it was in the Original, *Stand to't*; but *that struck out*, and *Halloe interlin'd* in the *place* of it; the other being too broad a discovery of the Violence they intended. Let me further observe, that this Song was Calculated to *Oxford*; that is to say, both for the *Time*, and the *Place*, *When*, and *Where* this Exploit was to have been executed" (44-45).

Though L'Estrange began his *Notes Upon Stephen College* by ignoring the plot, by the pamphlet's conclusion the poem has itself become that plot, particulars in the poem taken for specifics of the conspiracy. L'Estrange gives no play to the literary imagination, for "A Raree Show," possessing no life of its own, exists solely as a representation of political action. The text has itself become the deed, for L'Estrange ultimately reads the poem as a "Song of *Triumph*, as for a thing *already* done, [rather] then a bare *Project* and *Exhortation* towards the doing of it: Insomuch that they have in this Ballad delineated the very *Scheme* of their Intentions" (45). In his insistence that the poem leaves us no doubt about College's intentions, L'Estrange reveals what Peggy Kamuf regards as the central issue involved in the act of censorship: "An author may disavow the opinions he or she nevertheless represents, or intend them ironically or satirically, or be unable himself or herself to affirm one intention to the exclusion of another, which is clearly the most troubling possibility for a law that has to suppose an immanence of intentionality to itself as represented by a signature. The issue of censorship is always finally about the disjunction of intentions and utterances."[85] In treating the poem as he does, L'Estrange dissolves any disjunction between intention and utterance, any distinction between literal meaning and figurative language. College is guilty of a plot precisely because the poem can be read as that plot. In an attempt to confirm its own power, the government affirms the power of the author and his creations, transforming "bare words" into "overt acts" and "hireling scribblers" into the priests who tend "the very Oracles of the *Vulgar*."

Conclusion

Unlike Stephen College, Algernon Sidney was entitled by birth to participate in the most important political affairs of the kingdom. The second son of Robert Sidney, second earl of Leicester, Algernon, even though an unfortunate younger son, possessed a most illustrious pedigree: Sir Philip Sidney, his great-uncle; Penshurst, his family seat; his mother, Dorothy Percy, daughter of the ninth earl of Northumberland. Almost twenty when the Civil War broke out, Sidney fought briefly against the king before being wounded at Marston Moor, serving afterward as military governor of Chicester before being elected to Commons in 1646. Thereafter he became governor of Dover Castle and was even appointed one of the commissioners for the trial of Charles I, though he took no part in the trial nor signed the king's death warrant. He sat on the Council of State both before and after Cromwell's protectorate, from which he remained aloof. On an embassy to Denmark during the events leading to the Restoration, Sidney chose a European exile after Charles's assumption of the crown. He returned to England in 1677 to attend to personal and financial affairs but became involved in the campaign against Danby and the politics of the Popish Plot and exclusion, standing four times, unsuccessfully, for a seat in Parliament during the years 1678–1681. He was arrested on 26 June 1683 after the discovery of the Rye House plot, tried and sentenced in November, and executed on 7 December. The original sentence of hanging and quartering—carried out in the case of College—was graciously commuted by the king to beheading.[1]

Because of Sidney's noble birth, the matters of rank and hierarchy that figured so prominently in the prosecution of Stephen College played no part in Sidney's trial. The issue of authorship, however, proved crucial, particularly because the manuscript attributed to Sidney had been neither completed, published, nor circulated. Found in Sidney's study when his rooms were searched, the fragmentary manuscript—part of his *Discourses concerning Government*—therefore raised the question not simply of whether Sidney had actually written this particular libel but the larger questions of what act or acts define an author, a text, the moment of composition. When can a text properly be said to exist? Where does the act of composition take place? At what point must an author assume responsibility for a text? During Sidney's trial, of course, no one asked these questions directly nor were they articulated within a specifically literary context. Indeed, this trial concerned issues of literary categorization as well, for the government demonstrated a great reluctance to distinguish between letters and philosophy, occasional essays and theoretical speculation. For the government all generic difference was obliterated by the political, which rendered superfluous all other judgments. Sidney's trial suggests that during the seventeenth century there existed no strictly literary realm, at least in the way we often think of the "literary" today. The very category of the literary is determined by the complex interaction between judicial traditions and political necessity, forged from the untidy confrontation between competing forces vying for power in elections, through the courts, and on the page.

The indictment read at the opening of his trial accused Sidney of conspiring "with divers others traitors . . . [to] deprive and cast down the said lord the king . . . not only from the regal state, title, power and rule of his kingdom of England; but also to kill, and bring and put to death the same lord the king."[2] According to this indictment, the conspiracy had two concrete effects: first, "Algernon Sidney as a false traitor . . . maliciously, advisedly and traiterously did send one Aaron Smith into Scotland to invite, procure, and incite divers evil-disposed subjects of our lord the king"; second, "the aforesaid Algernon Sidney to fulfil and perfect those most wicked, horrid and devilish treasons, and traitorous compassings, imaginations and purposes aforesaid . . . did make, compose and write . . . a certain false, seditious and traitorous libel" (819). Because there was some question as to whether the government had provided the two witnesses legally necessary to prove Sidney guilty of treason,[3] the libel played a particularly important role during the trial, and the indictment ends with two quotations from it, the second contending that "we may therefore change or take away kings, without breaking any yoke, or that is made a yoke which ought not to be one, the injury is therefore in making or imposing, and there can be none in breaking it" (819).

Sidney's trial, then, turned not simply on the question of authorship—Sidney consistently eschewed the honor—but on the nature and consequences of the act of writing itself. As Sidney noted during his able and aggressive defense, "I say first, it [the libel] is not proved upon me; and secondly, it is not a crime if it be proved" (867). Sidney's first assertion may be rather disingenuous, since the papers were found in his house and his handwriting identified by a number of witnesses. Yet in pursuing his second line of argument, Sidney forced the court to confront the implications of its charge that private papers could constitute an overt act of treason.

In the first place, he argued that the work in question seemed—Sidney carefully spoke as if he had never before seen the libel produced in court—only "a polemical discourse, it seems to be an answer to Filmer, which is not calculated for any particular government in the world" (866). In Sidney's view the offending work consisted only of a theoretical argument designed to counter the writings of Sir Robert Filmer, whose *Patriarcha* had first been published in 1680, though it had circulated in manuscript for at least twenty-five years before that: "if a commoner of England write his present thoughts, and another man looking on his book writes his present thoughts of it, what great hurt is there in it?" (866). Sidney's argument highlights the tremendous differences between the excerpts read in court from the libel attributed to him and those read from the work charged to College, which, as we have seen, contained specific and inflammatory references to Charles. By reading College's libels in court, the government demonstrated the challenge presented by literary texts to the person and authority of the king.

The portions of the work attributed to Sidney and read in court, however, contain no direct charges against the king or his brother; Sidney provides a speculative context for words that the government regarded as resurrectionary in intent: "He [Filmer] says, that the power of kings is for the preservation of liberty and property. We may therefore change or take away kings without breaking any yoke which ought not to be one; the injury is therefore in making or imposing, and there can be none in breaking it" (856). For Sidney, therefore, such passages, as abstract reflections on the theory of government, fall within the rights and privileges of a free-born Englishman, "a commoner of England" in Sidney's telling phrase. For the government, however, the absence of personal attacks on the king cannot mitigate the treasonous object of the work's argument: "the whole design of this treatise is to persuade the people of England, that it is lawful, nay, that they have a right to set aside their prince in case it appear to them, that he hath broken the trust laid upon him by the people" (839). Such sentiments, the government prosecution of Sidney insists, cannot be permitted no matter how chaste the language.

Nor how private. Sidney's second line of defense depended on the government's failure to prove that the work had been published or even that it was intended for publication.[4] In his address to the jury, Sidney argues that "found papers" cannot be accounted treason: "If any man can say I ever printed a sheet in my life I will submit to any punishment" (878). The implications of the act of publication dominated Sidney's defense, and the following confrontation between the defendant and Lord Chief Justice Jeffreys reveals the extraordinary powers the state claimed over the use of language and the act of writing:

> Sidney. . . . and will you, my lord, indict a man for treason for scraps of paper found in his house, relating to an ancient paper, intending as innocently as any thing in the world, and piece and patch this to my lord Howard's discourse, to make this a contrivance to kill the king? Then, my lord, I think it is a right of mankind; and it is exercised by all studious men, that they write in their own closets what they please for their own memory, and no man can be answerable for it, unless they publish it. L.C.J. Pray do not go away with that right of mankind, that it is lawful for me to write what I will in my own closet, unless I publish it; I have been told, Curse not the king, not in thy thoughts, not in thy bedchamber, the birds of the air will carry it. I took it to be the duty of mankind, to observe that. [868]

In *Censorship and Interpretation*, Annabel Patterson has explored the way in which our very concept of "literature" depends on the rules of censorship, upon the complex relationship that developed in early modern Europe between rulers and writers. For Patterson literature "was essentially a joint project, a cultural bargain between writers and political leaders."[5] Sidney's trial reveals the fragility of that cultural bargain, as the writer's attempt to defend a "right of mankind" collides with the government's opposing desire to describe the "duty of mankind." Sidney insists on the private nature of the act of writing, the fundamental "innocence" of composition, which takes place in that personal and private space defined by the memory and the closet. For the protection of the writer, writing and publishing must be two very different acts, the private act unregarded by the state until it passes, by the act of publication, into the public realm. For the state, however, such a distinction can only compromise its ability to defend and extend its own power, which inevitably seeks to deny all distinctions between public and private. In Orwell's nightmare vision of the totalitarian state, *1984*, the protagonist's rebellion begins with the ostensibly simple act of putting words on a page. In its refusal to withdraw from either the closet or the bedchamber, Charles's government begins to suggest such a world, where, according to Jeffreys, even "thy thoughts" are legitimate objects of state scrutiny.

Later in the trial Sidney attempts to provide legal evidence for the "right of mankind" he asserts: he reads from a book of "old Hale's" and insists that both Hale and Coke agree that "compassing by bare words is not an overt-act" (888). In response, Jeffreys explains that "though some judges have been of opinion that words of them selves were not an overt-act: but my lord Hale's, nor my lord Coke, nor any other of the sages of the law, ever questioned but that a letter would be an overt-act, sufficient to prove a man guilty of high treason; for *scribere est agere*." Jeffreys' reply betrays not simply a deplorable logic in its failure to address the difference between a letter and a political treatise, but the frightening conviction that because words are themselves deeds, the act of writing is necessarily a public act. Because of this Jeffreys can assume that though "the imagination of a man's heart is not to be discerned; but if I declare such my imagination by an overt-act . . . it will be sufficient evidence of treason within that act" (889). Though subsequent developments in the history of English copyright and censorship would deny Jeffreys' conception of the relationship between authorship and treason, the trial of Algernon Sidney demonstrates an inexorable logic of censorship, which can move with a terrible inevitability from words to deeds, from the multiplicity of print to the individual's study and imagination.

Notes

Introduction

1. Samuel Pepys, *The Diary of Samuel Pepys*, ed. Robert Latham and William Matthews (Berkeley: Univ. of California Press, 1970–1983), entry for 25 May 1660, 1:158.

2. *Englands Joy or A Relation of The Most Remarkable passages, from his Majesties Arrivall at Dover, to His entrance at White-hall* (London, 1660), pp. 5–6.

3. John Evelyn, *The Diary of John Evelyn*, ed. E.S. De Beer (Oxford: Clarendon Press, 1955), entry for 29 May 1660, 3:246.

4. *The Quenes Maiesties Passage through the Citie of London to Westminster the Day before her Coronacion*, ed. James M. Osborn (1558; rpt. New Haven: Yale Univ. Press, 1960), pp. 48–49. For a detailed discussion of this pageant and the tradition of civic pageants, see David M. Bergeron, *English Civic Pageantry, 1558–1642* (Columbia: Univ. of South Carolina Press, 1971), pp. 11–23.

5. For a study of the part played by this traditional festive culture in the Civil War, see David Underdown, *Revel, Riot, and Rebellion: Popular Politics and Culture in England, 1603–1660* (Oxford: Clarendon Press, 1985).

6. Paula R. Backscheider, *Spectacular Politics: Theatrical Power and Mass Culture in Early Modern England* (Baltimore: Johns Hopkins Univ. Press, 1993), pp. 1–66.

7. Buchanan Sharp, "Popular Political Opinion in England, 1660–1685," *History of European Ideas* 10 (1989): 13. See also Carolyn A. Edie, "The Popular Idea of Monarchy on the Eve of the Stuart Restoration," *Huntington Library Quarterly* 39 (1976): 343–73. She suggests the difficulty of determining just "what people think" when print always aims "to sway the minds of those who read" (345).

8. For estimates about the mass of publication occasioned by these events, see O.W. Furley, "The Whig Exclusionists: Pamphlet Literature in the Exclusion Campaign, 1679–81," *Cambridge Historical Journal* 13 (1957): 19; and Lois Potter, *Secret Rites and Secret Writing: Royalist Literature, 1641–1660* (Cambridge: Cambridge Univ. Press, 1989), p. 4.

9. On the effectiveness of Tudor and Stuart censorship, see H.S. Bennett, *English Books and Readers, 1603 to 1640: Being a Study in the History of the Book Trade in the Reigns of James I and Charles I* (London: Cambridge Univ. Press, 1970); Christopher Hill, "Censorship and English Literature," in *Writing and Revolution in 17th Century England*, vol. 1 of *The Collected Essays of Christopher Hill* (Brighton, Sussex: Harvester Press, 1985), pp. 32–71; Leona Rostenberg, *The Minority Press and the English Crown: A Study in Repression, 1558–1625* (Nieuwkoop, Netherlands: B. De Graaf, 1971); and Frederick Seaton Siebert, *Freedom of the Press in England, 1476–1776: The Rise and Decline of Government Control* (Urbana: Univ. of Illinois Press, 1952). In his *Index of Dedications and Commendatory Verses in English Books before 1641* (London: Bibliographical Society, 1962), Franklin B. Williams, Jr., notes that "a survey of the licit output of the London trade in 1640, when control was rigorous, shows that . . . fully 65 per cent. of the books are without imprimatur" (237). In his essay "The Laudian Imprimatur," *Library*, 5th series, 15 (1960): 96–104, he surveys the period 1634–1640 and concludes that "it appears that after seven years of turning the screw Laud managed to get his imprimatur into a maximum of 35 per cent. of the books" (97–98).

10. Proclamation No. 110, "A Proclamation touching D. Cowels booke called the Interpreter," in *Royal Proclamations of King James I, 1603–1625*, vol. 1 of *Stuart Royal Proclamations*, ed. James F. Larkin and Paul L. Hughes (Oxford: Clarendon Press, 1973), p.243; Proclamation No. 129, "Prohibiting Erroneous Books and Bible Translations," in *Tudor Royal Proclamations*, ed. Paul L. Hughes and James F. Larkin (New Haven: Yale Univ. Press, 1964–1969), 1:194.

11. David Cressy, *Literacy and the Social Order: Reading and Writing in Tudor and Stuart England* (Cambridge: Cambridge Univ. Press, 1980), p. 47.

12. For an account of Thomason's collection, see G.K. Fortescue's preface to the *Catalogue of the Pamphlets, Books, Newspapers, and Manuscripts Relating to the Civil War, the Commonwealth, and Restoration, Collected by George Thomason, 1640–1661* (London: British Museum, 1908). His calculations concerning the number of pieces in the collection are found in 1:xxi. For figures on the growth of the newspaper industry, see Joseph Frank, *The Beginnings of the English Newspaper, 1620–1660* (Cambridge: Harvard Univ. Press, 1961).

13. Bennett, *English Books and Readers*, p. 1.

14. For a study of the newspaper in England, see Frank, *Beginnings of the English Newspaper*; on the relationship between contemporary history and panegyric, see M.L. Donnelly, "Caroline Royalist Panegyric and the Disintegration of a Symbolic Mode," in *"The Muses Common-Weale": Poetry and Politics in the Seventeenth Century*, ed. Claude J. Summers and Ted-Larry Pebworth (Columbia: Univ. of Missouri Press, 1988), pp. 163–76; on heroic poetry, see Gerald M. MacLean, *Time's Witness: Historical Representation in English Poetry, 1603–1660* (Madison: Univ. of Wisconsin Press, 1990); on verse satire, see George deForest Lord, *Classical Presences in Seventeenth-Century English Poetry*

(New Haven: Yale Univ. Press, 1987), chap. 5; on the writing of history, see Achsah Guibbory, *The Map of Time: Seventeenth-Century English Literature and Ideas of Pattern in History* (Urbana: Univ. of Illinois Press, 1986). See J. Paul Hunter, *Before Novels: The Cultural Contexts of Eighteenth-Century English Fiction* (New York: Norton, 1990), particularly chap. 7, for a more general account of the significance of the way in which "the quick flash of the present moment was to be the new focus of experience and the center that would control modes of thought, systems of value, and the content and form of literature" (109).

15. In *Time's Witness*, MacLean, while considering the new power of the print industry, and its necessary role in the Restoration settlement, notes that "the Restoration was . . . the first royal occasion that could, and indeed had to, make use of an already established commercial printing industry that employed people who had become fully aware of their political power" (263–64).

16. Roger L'Estrange, *The Intelligencer*, No. 1, Monday, 31 Aug. 1663, pp. 1–2.

17. See Guibbory, *Map of Time*, for a survey of historiographical modes current during the seventeenth century; MacLean deals with this subject as well.

18. Richard Ollard, *The Image of the King: Charles I and Charles II* (New York: Atheneum, 1979), p. 54.

19. Gordon S. Wood, "Conspiracy and the Paranoid Style: Causality and Deceit in the Eighteenth Century," *William and Mary Quarterly* 39 (1982): 410. See Hunter's *Before Novels*, pp. 180–82, for a similar account of the way in which conspiratorial explanations of history displaced providential explanations.

20. Lawrence Stone, "Literacy and Education in England 1640–1900," *Past and Present* 42 (1969): 121. For a more theoretical consideration of the relation between signing and literacy, see R.S. Schofield, "The Measurement of Literacy in Pre-Industrial England," in *Literacy in Traditional Societies*, ed. Jack Goody (Cambridge: Cambridge Univ. Press, 1968), pp. 311–25.

21. Cressy, *Literacy and the Social Order*, pp. 145–47. There seems at least some agreement between social historians that figures for the ability to sign probably underestimate the number of people who could read. According to Margaret Spufford, *Small Books and Pleasant Histories: Popular Fiction and Its Readership in Seventeenth-Century England* (London: Methuen, 1981), "an account of 'literacy' based on the only measurable skill, the ability to sign, takes no account of the implications of the fact that reading was a much more socially diffused skill than writing" (27). Keith Thomas, "The Meaning of Literacy in Early Modern England," in *The Written Word: Literacy in Transition*, ed. Gerd Baumann (Oxford: Clarendon Press, 1986), pp. 97–131, also questions the relationship between signing and reading: "the calculations based on [signing] greatly underrate the number of people who could read print with relative ease" (102). Hunter, in *Before Novels*, argues that literacy figures based on the ability

to sign one's name may particularly underestimate the number of female readers: "we just don't know how accurate the 'signing' test was for women . . . but if a distinction is to be made . . . between signing and the ability to read, the distinction is more likely to be important for women" (75).

22. Hunter, *Before Novels*, p. 66.

23. Cressy, *Literacy and the Social Order*, p. 145. On the question of literacy and social hierarchy, see also Hunter, *Before Novels*, pp. 61–88, and Stone, "Literacy and Education in England," pp. 107–11.

24. Peter Burke, "Popular Culture in Seventeenth-Century London," in *Popular Culture in Seventeenth-Century England*, ed. Barry Reay (London: Croom Helm, 1985), p. 49; Valerie Pearl, "Change and Stability in Seventeenth-Century London," *London Journal* 5 (1979): 6. For an extended consideration of the unique character of London during the late-seventeenth century, see Tim Harris, *London Crowds in the Reign of Charles II: Propaganda and Politics from the Restoration until the Exclusion Crisis* (Cambridge: Cambridge Univ. Press, 1987).

25. Cressy, *Literacy and the Social Order*, p. 14. For analyses of the dynamic relation between oral and written cultures, see Pearl, "Change and Stability in Seventeenth-Century London," pp. 4–7; Bernard Capp, "Popular Literature," pp. 198–243; and Barry Reay, "Popular Culture in Early Modern England," pp. 1–30, both in Reay, *Popular Culture in Seventeenth-Century England*. Thomas, in "Meaning of Literacy," insists that "the interaction between contrasting forms of culture" characterizes the entire period 1500–1750 and "gives this period its particular fascination" (98).

26. The refusal of writers to enter the published literary marketplace during the latter half of the seventeenth century is discussed by David M. Vieth, *Attribution in Restoration Poetry: A Study of Rochester's Poems of 1680* (New Haven: Yale Univ. Press, 1963), pp. 15–28, and Margaret J.M. Ezell, *The Patriarch's Wife: Literary Evidence and the History of the Family* (Chapel Hill: Univ. of North Carolina Press, 1987), particularly chap. 3. George deForest Lord discusses the effect of censorship on the decision to publish, and the circulation of politically subversive manuscripts, in his introduction to *Poems on Affairs of State: Augustan Satirical Verse, 1660–1714*, ed. Lord, et al. (New Haven: Yale Univ. Press, 1963–1975), 1:xxxi–xlii.

27. On the dual nature of ballads, see Harris, *London Crowds in the Reign of Charles II*, pp. 27, 102, and Spufford, *Small Books and Pleasant Histories*, pp. 9–12. On a politics that blends oral and written activity see Pearl, "Change and Stability in Seventeenth-Century London," pp. 5–7, and Harris, *London Crowds in the Reign of Charles II*, pp. 15–28.

28. MacLean, *Time's Witness*, p. xii.

29. Social historians concerned with seventeenth-century England are increasingly attentive to the ways in which politics were open to a larger percent of the population than we have traditionally imagined. Harris, *London Crowds in the Reign of Charles II*, for instance, would have us revise "a polarized model

of social and political relations, and instead adopt a participatory model" (17). For complementary arguments, see Burke, "Popular Culture in Seventeenth-Century London," and Pearl, "Change and Stability in Seventeenth-Century London." In "Meaning of Literacy," Thomas even argues that illiteracy could prove compatible with political activism.

30. Jurgen Habermas, *The Structural Transformation of the Public Sphere: An Inquiry into a Category of Bourgeois Society*, trans. Thomas Burger and Frederick Lawrence (Cambridge: MIT Press, 1989), p. 57; Sharp, "Popular Political Opinion in England," pp. 13–14; Franco Moretti, " 'A Huge Eclipse': Tragic Form and the Deconsecration of Sovereignty," in *The Power of Forms in the English Renaissance*, ed. Stephen Greenblatt (Norman, Okla.: Pilgrim Books, 1982), p. 7. In *Spectacular Politics*, Backscheider describes the Interregnum and Civil War era as the "pivotal moment" when "both an individual sense of selfhood and the concept of public opinion began to form" (33).

31. See Susan Staves, *Player's Scepters: Fictions of Authority in the Restoration* (Lincoln: Univ. of Nebraska Press, 1979), for a discussion of many of these issues. Note her remark that "there were no pamphlet wars in 1485. Especially during the interregnum, printing and protestantism had combined to help the citizen see himself as an individual creature apart from the state" (202).

32. Hunter, *Before Novels*, pp. 81, 85.

33. J.R. Jones, *Charles II: Royal Politician* (London: Allen and Unwin, 1987), describes how "one can talk of 'politics' and 'public opinion' after 1667 in an almost modern sense" (5).

34. Pearl, "Change and Stability in Seventeenth-Century London, p. 16.

35. Harris, *London Crowds in the Reign of Charles II*, p. 15.

36. Both contemporary reactions to the execution of Charles I are quoted in Nancy Klein Maguire, "The Theatrical Mask/Masque of Politics: The Case of Charles I," *Journal of British Studies* 28 (1989): 3,4.

37. Pepys, *The Diary*, entry for 25 May 1660, 1:158.

38. Christopher Hill, *Some Intellectual Consequences of the English Revolution* (Madison: Univ. of Wisconsin Press, 1980), p. 27. Steven N. Zwicker, "Lines of Authority: Politics and Literary Culture in the Restoration," in *Politics of Discourse: The Literature and History of Seventeenth-Century England*, ed. Kevin Sharpe and Steven N. Zwicker (Berkeley: Univ. of California Press, 1987), pp. 230–70, makes a similar point when he reminds us that "there was a widespread desire to forego division, to believe once again in that powerful fiction of unitary politics" (234–35). See as well Edie, "The Popular Idea of Monarchy," p. 356, and Douglas Brooks-Davies, *The Mercurian Monarch: Magical Politics from Spenser to Pope* (Manchester: Manchester Univ. Press, 1983).

39. Two important early works dealing with Elizabeth's monarchical self-fashioning are Frances A. Yates, *Astraea: The Imperial Theme in the Sixteenth Century* (London: Routledge & Kegan Paul, 1975), and Roy Strong, *The Cult*

of Elizabeth: Elizabethan Portraiture and Pageantry (London: Thames and Hudson, 1977). More recent scholarship in this area would include Louis Adrian Montrose, " 'Shaping Fantasies': Figurations of Gender and Power in Elizabethan Culture," *Representations* 1 (1983): 61–94; Leah S. Marcus, "Shakespeare's Comic Heroines, Elizabeth I, and the Political Uses of Androgyny," in *Women in the Middle Ages and the Renaissance: Literary and Historical Perspectives*, ed. Mary Beth Rose (Syracuse: Syracuse Univ. Press, 1985), pp. 135–54; Leonard Tennenhouse, *Power on Display: The Politics of Shakespeare's Genres* (London: Methuen, 1986); Philippa Berry, *Of Chastity and Power: Elizabethan Literature and the Unmarried Queen* (London: Routledge, 1989).

40. Hill, *Some Intellectual Consequences*, pp. 28–31. Gerard Reedy, "Mystical Politics: The Imagery of Charles II's Coronation," in *Studies in Change and Revolution: Aspects of English Intellectual History, 1640–1800*, ed. Paul J. Korshin (Menston, Yorkshire: Scolar Press, 1972), pp. 19–42, provides an account of Charles's coronation procession through London that confirms Hill's suggestion that after the Civil War the monarchy could be exploited in ways not possible before. For a survey of the various royal iconographies employed by Charles after his return, see Nicholas Jose, *Ideas of the Restoration in English Literature, 1660–71* (Cambridge: Harvard Univ. Press, 1984).

41. Potter, *Secret Rites and Secret Writing*, argues that royalist culture survived during the protectorate through its ability to exploit the subversive potential of the press. N.H. Keeble, *The Literary Culture of Nonconformity in Later Seventeenth-Century England* (Leicester: Leicester Univ. Press, 1987), similarly insists that "writing was essential to the survival of nonconformity" after the Restoration (283). For the importance of the press to radical and nonconformist culture, see as well Richard L. Greaves, *Deliver Us from Evil: The Radical Underground in Britain, 1660–1663* (Oxford: Oxford Univ. Press, 1986) and *Enemies under His Feet: Radicals and Nonconformists in Britain, 1664–1677* (Stanford: Stanford Univ. Press, 1990).

42. Richard W.F. Kroll, *The Material Word: Literate Culture in the Restoration and Early Eighteenth Century* (Baltimore: Johns Hopkins Univ. Press, 1991), p. 21. In line with this assertion, Kroll observes that the Restoration saw "the establishment of the publication industry as a distinct subculture" (44).

43. Richard Helgerson, "Milton Reads the King's Book: Print, Performance, and the Making of a Bourgeois Idol," *Criticism* 29 (1987): 14.

44. See Jonathan Goldberg, *James I and the Politics of Literature: Jonson, Shakespeare, Donne, and Their Contemporaries* (Baltimore: Johns Hopkins Univ. Press, 1983), for an exciting discussion of this theatrical metaphor and royal power. See as well Christopher Pye, "The Sovereign, the Theater, and the Kingdome of Darknesse: Hobbes and the Spectacle of Power," *Representations* 2 (1984): 85–106.

45. The works of Michel Foucault, of course, are essential to modern formulations concerning discourse and power. For an essay devoted particularly

to an analysis of the subject and subjectivity in Foucault, see Patricia O'Brien, "Michel Foucault's History of Culture," in *The New Cultural History*, ed. Lynn Hunt (Berkeley: Univ. of California Press, 1989), pp. 25–46. For two particularly interesting reconstructions of this transformation of the modern state, see Francis Barker, *The Tremulous Private Body: Essays on Subjection* (London: Methuen, 1984), and Nancy Armstrong, *Desire and Domestic Fiction: A Political History of the Novel* (Oxford: Oxford Univ. Press, 1987).

46. Theodore B. Leinwand, "Negotiation and New Historicism," *PMLA* 105 (1990): 479; Carolyn Porter, "Are We Being Historical Yet?" *South Atlantic Quarterly* 87 (1988): 743–86. Both Porter and Leinwand try to formulate alternatives to the subversion/containment debate that has occupied new historicism and cultural materialism in the last few years; both provide extensive bibliographies surveying these modes of scholarship and their discontents. For an anthropologist's analysis of cultural change and power relationships that complements the positions of Leinwand and Porter, see Aletta Biersack, "Local Knowledge, Local History: Geertz and Beyond," in *The New Cultural History*, ed. Hunt, pp. 72–96.

47. Backscheider, *Spectacular Politics*, p. 64.

48. Leinwand, "Negotiation and New Historicism," p. 479.

49. Barker, *Tremulous Private Body*, describes the relationship between monarch and nation as "a condition of dependent membership . . . incorporation in the body politic which is the king's body in its social form. With a clarity now hard to recapture, the social plenum *is* the body of the king, and membership of this anatomy is the deep structural form of all being in the secular realm" (31–32).

50. "An Act for the abolishing the kingly office in England and Ireland, and the dominions thereunto belonging, 17 March 1649," in *The Stuart Constitution: Documents and Commentary*, ed. J.P. Kenyon (Cambridge: Cambridge Univ. Press, 1986), pp. 306–7.

51. The classic work on the legal and theological implications of the king's sacred body is Ernst H. Kantorowicz's *The King's Two Bodies: A Study in Mediaeval Political Theology* (Princeton: Princeton Univ. Press, 1957).

52. Peter Burke, *Popular Culture in Early Modern Europe* (New York: New York Univ. Press, 1978), pp. 150–53.

53. For accounts of the legend of "Alfred and the Cakes," see P.J. Helm, *Alfred the Great* (London: Robert Hale, 1963), pp. 98, 178–85; and "Appendix I: Alfred and the Cakes," in *Alfred the Great: Asser's Life of King Alfred and Other Contemporary Sources*, trans. Simon Keyes and Michael Lapidge (London: Penguin, 1983), pp. 197–202.

54. Larry Carver, "The Restoration Poets and Their Father King," *Huntington Library Quarterly* 40 (1977): 344–45.

55. "The Answer of Mr. Waller's Painter to his Many New Advisers," in *Poems on Affairs of State*, ed. Lord, 1:153–56, lines 39–43.

56. Andrew Marvell, *The Rehearsal Transpos'd*, in *The Rehearsal Transpos'd and The Rehearsal Transpos'd, The Second Part*, ed. D.I.B. Smith (Oxford: Clarendon Press, 1971), pp. 4–5.

57. Proclamation No. 577, "Ordering Arrest for Circulating Seditious Books and Bulls," in *Tudor Royal Proclamations*, ed. Hughes and Larkin, 2:341.

58. For a discussion of College's place within the tradition of graphic satire, see M. Dorothy George, *English Political Caricature to 1792: A Study of Opinion and Propaganda* (Oxford: Clarendon Press, 1959), pp. 53–60.

59. Stephen College, "A Raree Show," in *Poems on Affairs of State*, ed. Lord, 2:426–31.

60. George Monck, duke of Albemarle, *Observations Upon Military and Political Affairs* (London, 1796), p. 215.

61. Helgerson, "Milton Reads the King's Book," p. 7.

62. Abraham Cowley, *Ode, Upon The Blessed Restoration and Returne of His Sacred Majestie, Charls the Second* (London, 1660), p. 16.

63. Alexander Pope, *The Dunciad*, "Martinus Scriblerus, of the Poem," in *The Complete Poetry of Alexander Pope*, Twickenham edition, ed. John Butt, *et al.* (London: Methuen, 1939–1969), 5:49. All references to the poetry of Pope are to this edition. For intriguing discussions of Pope's relation to changes in the literary marketplace see Laura Brown, *Alexander Pope* (Oxford: Blackwell, 1985); and Brean S. Hammond, *Pope* (Brighton, Sussex: Harvester Press, 1986), particularly chaps. 3 and 4.

1. Restoration and Escape

1. [John Wade], "The Royall Oak: Or, The wonderful travells, miraculous escapes, strange accidents of his sacred Majesty King *Charles the Second*" (London, n.d.). In *A Bibliography of the Literature Relating to the Escape and Preservation of King Charles II after the Battle of Worcester, 3rd September, 1651* (Aberdeen: The Univ. Press, 1924), William Arthur Horrox suggests the uncertainty of the ascription to Wade, and provides a tentative date of 1660 for publication.

2. John Ogilby, *The Entertainment of His Most Excellent Majestie Charles II . . .* (London, 1662), p. 37.

3. Pepys, *The Diary*, entry for 23 May 1660, I: 155–56.

4. *An Exact Narrative and Relation Of His Most Sacred Majesties Escape from Worcester . . .* (London, 1660).

5. *A Summary of Occurrences, Relating to the Miraculous Preservation Of our late Sovereign Lord King Charles II. After the Defeat of his Army at Worcester in the Year 1651. Faithfully taken from the express Personal Testimony of those two worthy Roman Catholics, Thomas Whitgrave of Moseley, in the County of Stafford Esq; & Mr. John Hudleston Priest, of the holy Order of St. Bennet; the eminent Instruments under God of the same Preservation* (London, 1688). This version,

published subsequent to Charles's death, demonstrates the tremendous versitility of the escape narratives, which could be exploited for a variety of causes. A *Summary of Occurrences* participated in James II's campaign for Catholic toleration, as its long subtitle, and publication by "Henry Hills, Printer to the King's most Excellent Majesty, for his Household and Chappel," suggests. Unlike earlier accounts published during Charles's lifetime, which treat with discretion the awkward fact that most of the people who helped Charles were Catholic, *A Summary of Occurrences* calls attention to their religion in order to give substance to Charles's alleged promise that "If it please God I come to my Crown, both you, and all of your Perswasion, shall have as much liberty as any of my Subjects" (p. 32). Over a quarter of a century after its first appearance as a way to celebrate and legitimate Charles's Restoration, the escape still possessed significant propaganda value, capable of taking on new meanings in a radically different political context. For a discussion of the accuracy of this account of the escape, see Ronald Hutton, *Charles the Second King of England, Scotland, and Ireland* (Oxford: Clarendon Press, 1989), p. 69.

6. Pepys's collection of Worcester narratives, as well as an excellent discussion of the whole affair from escape through publication, can be found in *Charles II's Escape from Worcester: A Collection of Narratives Assembled by Samuel Pepys*, ed. William Matthews (Berkeley: Univ. of California Press, 1966). Another, more miscellaneous collection of escape narratives can be found in *The Royal Miracle: A Collection of Rare Tracts, Broadsides, Letters, Prints, and Ballads concerning the Wanderings of Charles II after the Battle of Worcester (September 3 October 15, 1651)*, ed. A.M. Broadley (London: Stanley Paul, 1912). For a bibliography of publications concerning the escape from the seventeenth to early twentieth century, see Horrox, *A Bibliography*. For a reconstruction of the escape, see Richard Ollard, *The Escape of Charles II after the Battle of Worcester* (London: Hodder and Stoughton, 1966); and the accounts in Hutton, *Charles the Second*, pp. 66–70, and Antonia Fraser, *King Charles II* (London: Macdonald Futura, 1980), pp. 112–28.

7. Michael McKeon, *The Origins of the English Novel, 1600–1740* (Baltimore: Johns Hopkins Univ. Press, 1987), pp. 212–14.

8. Burke, *Popular Culture in Early Modern Europe*, pp. 152–53.

9. See Hayden White, *Metahistory: The Historical Imagination in Nineteenth-Century Europe* (Baltimore: Johns Hopkins Univ. Press, 1973), for a consideration of the Romantic conception of history. Capp, "Popular Literature," briefly discusses the complementary question of the relationship of disguise narratives to carnivalesque inversions of social order, pp. 209–11.

10. Goldberg, *James I and the Politics of Literature*, p. 177.

11. *Englands Triumph. A More Exact History of His Majesties Escape After the Battle of Worcester* . . . (London, 1660), p. 107.

12. Simon Ford, ΠΑΡΑΛΛΗΛΑ; *Or The Loyall Subjects Exultation For the Royall Exiles Restauration*. . . . (London, 1660), p. 36.

13. Francis Gregory, *David's Returne From His Banishment.* . . . (Oxford, 1660), p. 26.

14. Ibid., p. 24.

15. Sir Richard Baker, *A Chronicle of the Kings of England From the time of the Romans Government unto the Death of King James.* . . . (London, 1670), p. 771.

16. Sir Richard Bulstrode, *Memoirs And Reflections Upon the Reign and Government of King Charles the Ist. and K. Charles the IId.* . . . (London, 1721), p. 217.

17. Sir Percy Herbert, *The Princess Cloria: Or, The Royal Romance.* . . . (London, 1661), sig. A^v. The first part of this work was published in 1653 under the title *Cloria and Narcissus.* A second part was added in 1654; only after the Restoration were the final three parts added and the whole published under the title used in the bibliography.

18. For an excellent discussion of the nature and scope of providential belief in Restoration England, see Derek Hughes, "Providential Justice and English Comedy, 1660–1700: A Review of the External Evidence," *Modern Language Review* 81 (1986): 273–92.

19. For an explanation of the relationship between these two views in Restoration and eighteenth-century politics, see Wood, "Conspiracy and the Paranoid Style," particularly pp. 411–20.

20. Michael McKeon, *Politics and Poetry in Restoration England: The Case of Annus Mirabilis* (Cambridge: Harvard Univ. Press, 1975), p. 162. See also Reedy, "Mystical Politics," who discusses the dynamics of contradictory typological readings of history.

21. John Dauncey, *The History of His Sacred Majesty Charles the II.* . . . (London, 1660), pp. 131–32.

22. Francis Eglesfield, *Monarchy Revived, in The Most Illustrious Charles The Second.* . . . *(London, 1661), pp.* 185–86.

23. Gregory, *David's Returne From His Banishment,* p. 24. For an analysis of contemporary readings of Charles's providential history, see Anne Barbeau Gardiner, "John Dryden's Reading of the Ultimate Meaning of History," *Ultimate Reality and Meaning* 12 (1989): 16–29.

24. "Colonel Gounter's Report," in *Charles II's Escape,* ed. Matthews, p. 148.

25. "Father Huddleston's Original Account," in *Charles II's Escape,* ed. Matthews, p. 113.

26. " The King's Account of His Escape," Pepys's transcription, in *Charles II's Escape,* ed. Matthews, p. 42.

27. Ibid., p. 76.

28. *An Exact Narrative,* p. 17.

29. Baker, *A Chronicle of the Kings of England,* p. 628.

30. *An Exact Narrative,* p. 3.

31. Eglesfield, *Monarchy Revived*, p. 177.

32. *Englands Triumph*, pp. 14–15.

33. Hutton, *Charles the Second*, suggests that "the man who could play his expected part to perfection at a coronation, in a royal court, or in a manor house in Jersey now brought this talent to the role of warlord" (66). And Fraser emphasizes that "extreme courage is the verdict of all those present—with the exception of Buckingham . . . [who] was still gravely displeased at being denied command" (*King Charles II*, 110).

34. Eglesfield, *Monarchy Revived*, p. 181. Even the "two horses" are prone to a suspicious growth. See a ballad by Henry Jones, "The Royal Patient Traveller, or, The wonderful Escapes of His Sacred Majesty King Charles the Second from Worcester-Fight . . ." (n.p., n.d.), in Broadley, *The Royal Miracle*, pp. 93–97: "King Charles mounting himself so brave, / three times his Horse was shot" (p. 94). Broadley notes that a publication date of 1660 was "added in Antony Wood's hand."

35. Dauncey, *The History of His Sacred Majesty Charles the II*, pp. 113–14.

36. Ibid., p. 113; Dauncey, *An Exact History of the several Changes of Government In England* . . . (London, 1660), p. 85.

37. Baker, *A Chronicle of the Kings of England*, p. 626. A personal confrontation between Charles and Cromwell could serve parliamentary interests as well, at least in 1651. *A full & perfect Relation of the great & bloody fight At Worcester on Wednesday Night Last Being the 3, of Septemb. 1651 between the Parliaments Forces & the King of Scots* (London, 1651)—which Horrox, *A Bibliography*, identifies as "probably the earliest printed account" of the battle and Broadley, *The Royal Miracle*, as "the earliest parliamentary account"— promises just such a clash in the rest of its newsworthy title: *With the true particulars thereof, and the manner of the Fight shewing How Charles Stuart (their Captain Gen) & Major Gen Massey charged in the Van, and his Excellency the Lord General Cromwell in person against them. Together with the taking or killing of the said Charles Stuart* . . . (in Broadley, *The Royal Miracle*, pp. 299–301). Unfortunately, the actual account of the battle belies these thrilling promises, for nothing in it places Charles near Cromwell.

38. *Englands Triumph*, pp. 93–94. Scenes like this were replayed in many cities and towns throughout the kingdom; see Underdown, *Revel, Riot, and Rebellion*, pp. 271–75, for descriptions of some of the popular festivities celebrating Charles's return.

39. Herbert, *The Princess Cloria*, sig. A.

40. Ibid., pp. 421, 422.

41. Thomas Blount, *Boscobel: Or, The History of His Sacred Majesties Most miraculous Preservation After the Battle of Worcester, 3. Sept. 1651* (London, 1660), "To the Reader."

42. Bulstrode, *Memoirs And Reflections*, p. 221.

43. *Englands Triumph*, p. 108.

44. Ibid., p. 84.

45. Louis Marin, *Portrait of the King*, trans. Martha M. Houle (Minneapolis: Univ. of Minnesota Press, 1988), p. 32.

46. *An Exact Narrative*, p. 6.

47. John Evelyn, *The Diary*, entry for 6 September 1651, 3:40.

48. Blount, *Boscobel*, pp. 17.

49. Ibid., p. 29.

50. *A Summary of Occurrences*, pp. 19–20.

51. "Father Huddleston's Original Account," in *Charles II's Escape*, ed. Matthews, p. 112.

52. Gregory, *David's Returne From His Banishment*, pp. 26–27.

53. "Colonel Gounter's Report," in *Charles II's Escape*, ed. Matthews, p. 160.

54. *Englands Triumph*, pp. 26, 27.

55. Baker, *A Chronicle of the Kings of England*, pp. 627–28.

56. Thomas Whitgreave, "An Account of Charles the Second's Preservation," in *Charles II's Escape*, ed. Matthews, p. 120.

57. "Father Huddleston's Original Account," in *Charles II's Escape*, ed. Matthews, p. 106.

58. "The King's Account of His Escape," Pepys's transcription, in *Charles II's Escape*, ed. Matthews, pp. 70, 52, 64, 60.

59. Stephen Greenblatt, *Shakespearean Negotiations: The Circulation of Social Energy in Renaissance England* (Berkeley: Univ. of California Press, 1988), p. 76. See also Capp, "Popular Literature," who reminds us that "there is no direct challenge to the political or social order in these tales" (p. 210).

60. Henry Vaughan, "Thalia Rediviva: The King Disguis'd," in *The Works of Henry Vaughan*, ed. L.C. Martin, 2nd ed. (Oxford: Clarendon Press, 1957), pp. 625–26, line 40; John Cleveland, "The Kings Disguise," in *The Poems of John Cleveland*, ed. Brian Morris and Eleanor Withington (Oxford: Clarendon Press, 1967), pp. 6–9, lines 5–8. The relationship of these poems to royal panegyric is discussed at length by Donnelly, "Caroline Royalist Panegyric," pp. 168–73.

61. Pope, "Imitation of Epistle II.i," in *The Complete Poetry*, 4: 229, lines 390–95. See Jose, *Ideas of the Restoration*, particularly chap. 9, for an excellent critical explanation of why royal panegyrics celebrating the Restoration settlement consistently fail to "achieve any very penetrating understanding of politics and history in action" (164).

62. Pope, *The Dunciad in Four Books*, in *The Complete Poetry*, 5, Book IV, p. 394, lines 521–24.

2. The Monarch's Sacred Body

1. Thomas Allen, ΧΕΙΡΕΞΟΚΗ *The Excellency or Handy-Work of the Royal Hand* (London, 1665), pp. 25, 8.

2. For a description of a public healing held in Holland before the king's departure for England, see Sir William Lower, *A Relation in Form of a Journal, of the Voyage and Residence which the most Excellent and most Mighty Prince Charles the II King of Great Britain, &c. Hath Made in Holland, From the 25 of May, to the 2 of June, 1660* (The Hague, 1660), pp. 74–78.

3. "The Loyal Subjects Hearty Wishes to King Charles the Second" (London, n.d.). For date of publication the Wing catalog suggests "1660?"

4. Lucinda McCray Beier, *Sufferers and Healers: The Experience of Illness in Seventeenth-Century England* (London: Routledge and Kegan Paul, 1987), p. 31.

5. Margaret Pelling and Charles Webster, "Medical Practitioners," in *Health, Medicine and Mortality in the Sixteenth Century,* ed. Charles Webster (Cambridge: Cambridge Univ. Press, 1979), pp. 165–66.

6. For recent considerations of the relationship between Newton's science, religion, and magic, see *Standing on the Shoulders of Giants: A Longer View of Newton and Halley,* ed. Norman J.W. Thrower (Berkeley: Univ. of California Press, 1990). In "Newton's 'Sleeping Argument' and the Newtonian Synthesis of Science and Religion," pp. 109–27, James E. Force argues that Newton regarded the discovery of design in nature and scripture as "corollary" enterprises. In "Newton as Alchemist and Theologian," pp. 128–40, B.J.T. Dobbs insists that "Newton himself saw his diverse studies as constituting a unified plan for obtaining Truth and that his methodology was essentially the same in all areas of study" (p. 129).

7. William Vickers, *An Easie and Safe Method for Curing the King's Evil. . . .* 5th ed. (London, 1711), p. 35. Vickers, whose cure for the king's evil went through no less than twelve editions between 1707 and 1719, was embroiled in a ferocious dispute with the physician Thomas Fern over precisely the question of licensed versus unlicensed medical practitioners. For the grounds of this debate see Fern's *A Perfect Cure for the King's Evil* . . . (London, n.d). Fern's attack on Vickers was probably published in 1709, the date he appends to his preface.

8. Fern, *A Perfect Cure for the King's Evil,* sig. B.

9. The two pioneering twentieth-century studies of the king's evil date from the first quarter of the century: Raymond Crawfurd, *The King's Evil* (Oxford: Clarendon Press, 1911); Marc Bloch, *Les rois thaumaturges: etude sur le caractere surnaturel attribue a la puissance royale, particulierement en France et en Angleterre* (Publications de la Faculte des lettres de l'Universitie de Strasbourg, fasc. 19, Paris/Strasbourg, 1924). All citations from the latter refer to the following translation: Marc Bloch, *The Royal Touch: Sacred Monarchy and Scrofula in England and France,* trans. J.E. Anderson (London: Routledge and Kegan Paul, 1973). For the history of the king's evil I have depended as well on Frank Barlow, "The King's Evil," *English Historical Review* 95 (1980): 3–27, and Keith Thomas, *Religion and the Decline of Magic: Studies in Popular Beliefs in Sixteenth- and Seventeenth-Century England* (New York: Scribners, 1971). On

the specific question of the origins of the healing power of kings, Barlow is far more skeptical than either Bloch or Crawfurd, both of whom hypothesize a continuous healing rite from the eleventh century in France and twelfth in England; see Bloch, pp. 12–27, and Crawfurd, pp. 11–33. Barlow, on the other hand, concludes that "it would be credulous to believe that in France there was an established, continuous, and flourishing custom from Philip I to Louis IX. And for England it is incredible that the custom should have begun with Henry I" (p. 26).

10. Bloch, *Royal Touch*, pp. 65–67; Crawfurd, *King's Evil*, pp. 48–50.

11. The Latin Office of Henry VII is reprinted in Crawfurd, *King's Evil*, pp. 52–56. The English translation used here was first published during the reign of James II in 1686, and is reprinted in Crawfurd, pp. 132–36.

12. Crawfurd, *King's Evil*, p. 52.

13. Elizabeth L. Eisenstein, *The Printing Press as an Agent of Change: Communications and Cultural Transformations in Early-Modern Europe*, 2 vols. (Cambridge: Cambridge Univ. Press, 1979). She writes specifically about "the preservative powers of print" and the significance of "typographical fixity" in 1:113–26.

14. On the healing ceremony under Elizabeth, see Bloch, *Royal Touch*, pp. 189–92, and Crawfurd, *King's Evil*, pp. 68–78. On the subject of cramp rings see Bloch, 92–107.

15. For brief discussions of Clowes and his place in the medical community see Margaret Pelling, "Medical Practice in Early Modern England: Trade or Profession?" in *The Professions in Early Modern England*, ed. Wilfrid Prest (London: Croom Helm, 1987), pp. 115–16; Pelling and Webster, "Medical Practitioners," p. 177.

16. William Clowes, *A Right Frutefull and Approoved Treatise* . . . (London, 1602), p. 8. All references are to this edition.

17. For details of James's relation to the royal touch, see Bloch, *Royal Touch*, pp. 191–92, and Crawfurd, *King's Evil*, pp. 82–90.

18. For details of Charles I's relation to the royal touch, see Bloch, *Royal Touch*, pp. 207–11, and Crawfurd, *King's Evil*, pp. 90–102.

19. *Journals of the House of Commons* 5 (1646–1648): 151. Keith Thomas notes that he has failed to find a "trace of any resulting declaration" (*Religion and the Decline of Magic*, p. 197 n. 4).

20. *To the Kings Most Excellent Majesty. The Humble Petition of Divers Hundreds of the Kings Poore Subjects, Afflicted with the Kings Evill* . . . (London, 1643), p. 4. All references are to this edition.

21. *The Parliamentary Intelligencer*, No. 28, from Monday July 2 to Monday July 9, 1660, pp. 436–37.

22. John Browne, *Charisma Basilicon, Or, The Royal Gift of Healing Strumaes, Or Kings-Evil* . . . (London, 1684), sig. Cc8^v. All references are to this edition.

23. For a discussion of the archival evidence available to the historian concerning the rite in England, see Bloch, *Royal Touch*, pp. 246–50.

24. It is difficult to know precisely what to make of Browne's figures. Their accuracy, certainly, can be called into question, for we know that however rigorous the examination of patients appeared on paper, in fact it was less than ideal. In his description of the screening process, Browne complains at length of the cheating that inevitably occurred, and sets forth very definite measures for amending loopholes and tightening controls. Indeed, in confirmation of Browne's fears, William Vickers's *Easie and Safe Method* contains the admission that "I was stroaked twice by King Charles II. and thrice by King James II" (4).

25. Helen Farquhar, "Royal Charities," *British Numismatic Journal* 12 (1916): 39–135; 13 (1917): 95–163; 14 (1918): 89–120; 15 (1919–1920): 141–84.

26. Louis Marin, "The Inscription of the King's Memory: On the Metallic History of Louis XIV," *Yale French Studies* 59 (1980): 27.

27. John Bird, *Ostenta Carolina: Or The Late Calamities of England With the Authors of Them. . . .* (London, 1661). All references are to this edition.

28. For a discussion of belief in the magical power of the seventh son, see Bloch, *Royal Touch*, pp. 168–76. For the currency of such beliefs in late seventeenth-century England, see John Aubrey, *Miscellanies* (London, 1696), p. 97: "several Persons have been Cured of the Kings-Evil by the touching, or handling of a Seventh Son. (It must be a seventh Son, and no Daughter between, and in pure Wedlock)."

29. For information on the case of Boisgaudre, see the *Calendar of State Papers. Domestic. 1631–1633*, pp. 347–48. In 1637 the King's Privy Council concerned itself with another case, that of William Gilbert (alias Yeaton) of Priestleigh, Somerset, whose seventh son, Richard, began "curing the king's evil, wens, and other swellings" at the age of five. Because it was determined that neither father nor son had received gifts other than trifles, "nor had they used any imposture or deceit, but had been merely carried away by a simple credulity, which made them a little vainglorious," they were not punished, only warned to stop their cures. For information on this case, see the *Calendar of State Papers. Domestic. 1637*, pp. 419, 450, 467, 548–49. Crawfurd, *King's Evil*, discusses another case involving Charles I's prosecution of a rival healer, that of James Leverett in 1637 (pp. 95–97).

30. Thomas Allen joins Bird in maintaining that " 'tis not lawful for ordinary persons to assume so great a power, their skill in healing is not the Gift of God, as appeareth by the quality of the persons; who are generally ignorant, and prophane" (*XEIPEΞOKH*, 5). God, for Allen, operates only through kings, the "ignorant, and prophane" not a fit vehicle for the miraculous.

31. Verney Papers, in *Historical Manuscripts Commision Reports: 7th Rept.*, p. 494.

32. Both Bird and Allen admit that the king's healing touch can fail. When they do, however, they must draw from it a providential lesson that places the blame squarely on the patient and not the physician: "Nor is it done to perfection in all, some being remediless, which are touch'd, that we may know that corruption in justice, unsoundness in faith and doctrine, shall not and cannt be so universally taken away by our Good King, but that some (do what he can) tares, and wicked men will continue among the wheat, and good men" (Bird, *Ostenta Carolina*, 90–91); "if there be weakness and folly in them that approach to receive it, if you vacate the Gift, and frustrate the intent of the Donor, 'tis not the kings fault, nor aught to be laid to his charge, charge your selves with it" (Allen, *XEIPEΞOKH*, 30). Such are the shifts required by their insistence on a mystical apprehension of the healing touch.

33. The *Charisma Basilicon* was nonetheless a most important part of *Adenochoiradelogia*; the full title of Browne's work suggests just how central to his medical text was his examination of the royal touch: *Adenochoiradelogia: Or, An Anatomick–Chirurgical Treatise of Glandules & Strumaes, Or Kings-Evil-Swellings. Together with the Royal Gift of Healing, Or Cure thereof by Contact or Imposition of Hands, Performed for Above 640 Years by Our Kings of England, Continued with Their Admirable Effects, and Miraculous Events; and Concluded with Many Wonderful Examples of Cures by Their Sacred Touch* (London, 1684). The larger work presents itself proudly under the king's patronage. Browne describes himself on the title-page as "One of His Majesties Chirurgeons in Ordinary, and Chirurgeon of His Majesties Hospital," while the text itself opens with a statement expressing Charles's "great Liking and Satisfaction" in Browne's "Performance," as well as the royal grant of a copyright for the work, an important favor when copyright normally resided in printers or booksellers (A2^v–A3). Browne dedicates the book to both Charles and his brother James, using the royal touch as a metaphor to describe the relationship of his medical treatise to royal power: "These Anatomical Exercitations of the Glandules, and the Treatise of Strumaes, or Kings-Evil-Swellings, lie prostrate at Your Majesties Feet, humbly imploring Your Majesties Sacred Touch" (A4–A4^v).

34. Richard Wiseman, *Severall Chiruricall Treatises* (London, 1676), p. 245. All references are to this edition.

35. For a discussion of the increasing prestige of surgeons within the medical community during the years after 1660, see Geoffrey Holmes, *Augustan England: Professions, State and Society, 1680–1730* (London: G. Allen & Unwin, 1982), pp. 193–205.

36. The trial, appeals, and pardon of Thomas Rosewell can be found in *A Complete Collection of State Trials and Proceedings for High Treason and Other Crimes and Misdemeaners From the Earliest Period to the Year 1783*, ed. T.B. Howell and T.J. Howell (London: 1816–1828), vol.10, cols. 147–308.

37. Valentine Greatraks, *A Brief Account of Mr. Valentine Greatraks* . . . (London, 1666), p. 22. All quotations are from this edition.

38. Sir Roger L'Estrange, *The Intelligencer*, 13 July, 27 July, 7 Aug., 21 Aug., 1665, quoted in Reverend Samuel Hayman, "Notes on the Family of Greatrakes. Part I," *The Reliquary* 4 (1863): 88. For "Part II" see *The Reliquary* 4 (1864): 220–36.

39. Michael Boyle, archbishop of Dublin, to Lord Conway, Dublin, 29 July 1665, in *Conway Letters: The Correspondence of Anne, Viscountess Conway, Henry More, and Their Friends, 1642–1684*, ed. Marjorie Hope Nicolson (New Haven: Yale Univ. Press, 1930), pp. 262–63.

40. For a more politically radical interpretation of Greatrakes see J.R. Jacob, *Robert Boyle and the English Revolution: A Study in Social and Intellectual Change* (New York: Burt Franklin, 1977), pp. 164–76. I do not deny the political dimensions of the Greatrakes controversy that Jacob delineates; both Michael Boyle and David Lloyd articulate precisely the fears of sedition that concern Jacobs. Nonetheless, neither Charles nor his government seem to have taken Greatrakes seriously enough as a political danger to warrant state intervention in his short but brilliant career.

41. *Wonders If Not Miracles Or, A Relation of the Wonderful Performances of Valentine Gertrux* . . . (London, 1665), pp. 3, and 4–5.

42. David Lloyd, *Wonders No Miracles; Or, Mr. Valentine Greatrates Gift of Healing Examined* . . . (London, 1666), p. 21. All quotations are from this edition.

43. Lord Conway to Sir George Rawdon, Ragley, 9 Feb. 1665–66, in *Conway Letters*, ed. Nicolson, p. 268.

44. Greatraks, *Brief Account*, p. 30.

45. Greatraks, *Brief Account*, p. 39; in the *Calendar of State Papers. Domestic. 1665–1666*, Henry Muddiman notes on 1 March from Whitehall the arrival of Greatrakes in London: "Greatres, the healer, is come to London, and is followed by many for cure" (p. 281).

46. Greatrakes to Lord Conway, received 3 May 1666, in *Conway Letters*, ed. Nicolson, p. 272.

47. Roy Porter, "The Early Royal Society and the Spread of Medical Information," in *The Medical Revolution of the Seventeenth Century*, ed. Roger French and Andrew Wear (Cambridge: Cambridge Univ. Press, 1989), p. 288.

48. George Rust to Joseph Glanvil, quoted in Glanvil's *Saducismus Triumphatus: Or, Full and Plain Evidence Concerning Witches and Apparitions*. . . . (London, 1681), pp. 90–92. A complete version of this letter can be found in the *Conway Letters*, ed. Nicolson, p. 274. For accounts of scientific attempts in the seventeenth century to explain Greatrakes's healing powers—a fascinating story unfortunately outside the scope of my argument—see the following: Eamon Duffy, "Valentine Greatrakes, the Irish Stroker: Miracle, Science, and Orthodoxy in Restoration England," in *Religion and Humanism: Papers Read at*

the Eighteenth Summer Meeting and the Nineteenth Winter Meeting of the Ecclesi-
astical History Society, ed. Keith Robbins, Studies in Church History 17 (Oxford:
Basil Blackwell, 1981), pp. 251–73; Barbara Beigun Kaplan, "Greatrakes the
Stroker: The Interpretations of His Contemporaries," *Isis* 73 (1982): 178–85;
Porter, "Early Royal Society," pp. 288–90; Nicholas H. Steneck, "Greatrakes
the Stroker: The Interpretations of Historians," *Isis* 73 (1982): 161–77.

    49. Henry Stubbe, *The Miraculous Conformist: Or An Account of Severall
Marvailous Cures performed by the stroaking of the Hands of Mr. Valentine
Greatarick* ... (Oxford, 1666), p. 14, sig. A2^v. All quotations are from this
edition.

    50. Saint-Évremond, for instance, living in London during the brief
period of Greatrakes's celebrity, satirizes the healer in *A Novel*, a brief account
of an "Irish-man . . . [who] passed for a great Philosopher, and a mighty performer
of Wonders, according to the opinion of the Credulous, and his own perswasion." The climax of the tale occurs at a large public healing at St. James's,
where the urbane and skeptical narrator offers the following explanation for the
mob behavior that so offends, and eventually effects, his sensibilities:

> Already did the Blind suppose they saw that light they did not see; already did
> the Deaf imagine they heard, and heard not; the Lame already thought they
> were grown well, and the impotent resumed in imagination the first use of their
> members. A Strong Idea of Health had made the Sick forget their Distempers—
> and imagination which was no less active in the curious, then in the Sick, gave
> the first, a false prospect out of a desire of seeing, as it did a false Cure to the
> second, out of a desire of being Cured.
>
>   Such was the power of the Irish-man upon our minds. Such was the force
> of our Minds upon our Senses.

See Marguetel de Saint-Denis, Charles, seigneur de Saint-Évremond, *A Novel*,
in *Miscellany Essays: By Monsieur de St. Evremont, Upon Philosophy, History, Poetry,
Morality, Humanity, Gallantry, &c* (London, 1692–94), 2:92, 110–11.

    51. Lloyd's task is so difficult, and his argument so confused, that I think
he has misled Jacob, who argues that Lloyd regarded the king's power to heal as
a mere "trick" dependent on the imagination of the "lowly patient" (*Robert Boyle
and the English Revolution*, 165–66). For Lloyd only "a Melancholly, or a
discontented man" believes this. Lloyd himself insists that "our Kings can heal
by a bare stroake" (*Wonders No Miracles*, 13), and this apparently explains why
Lloyd did not regard this checklist of the miraculous as a subversion of the royal
touch.

    52. "Rub for Rub: Or, An Answer To A Physicians Pamphlet, Styled,
The Stroker stroked" (London, 1666). Marjorie Hope Nicolson, in *Conway
Letters*, pp. 250–51, identifies this verse broadside as an attack on Greatrakes,
as does A. Bryan Laver in "Miracles No Wonder! The Mesmeric Phenomena
and Organic Cures of Valentine Greatrakes," *Journal of the History of Medicine*

33 (1978): 35–46. As my analysis of the poem suggests, however, the terms of its satire can best be understood as an attack against a privileged medical monopoly that in the popular mind had, in Stubbe's words, preferred "their Credit" to "the recovery of their Patients" (24). A notation in the British Library catalogue identifies the piece as "A reply to an attack upon the cures said to be wrought by V.G."; this position seems to me to lead to a more coherent reading of the poem.

53. Pelling, "Medical Practice in Early Modern England," p. 115.

54. *Calendar of State Papers. Domestic. 1665–1666.* The entry for 15 March, Whitehall, includes a communication from Muddiman to Edw. Dyer of Dover: "People flock after Greatres still, but several who have been stroked by him decry him. His petition for settlement of his lands in Ireland is rejected by Council" (p. 300).

55. Letter from Henry Oldenburg to Robert Boyle, London, 13 March 1665/66, in *The Works of the Honourable Robert Boyle*, ed. Andrew Millar (London, 1744), 5:352–53: "Monsieur *de Son* hath been stroked by him [Greatrakes], and he tells me, that whereas he hath been for several years troubled with great back-aches . . . he now finds himself, upon being stroked, very well, insomuch that he purposes, in case of continuance, to go to sea with prince *Rupert*, in whose lodgings this cure was performed; his highness, as the patient told me, having urged him to suffer that friction."

56. Crawfurd, *King's Evil*, p. 112. Browne provides no figures for these two years in his list of Charles's cures.

57. *A Complete Collection of State Trials*, ed. Howell and Howell, vol. 11, cols. 1059–60.

58. The history of Charles's attempts to end such rumours can be found in his *Declaration To All Loving Subjects*, Whitehall, 2 June 1680, in *The Letters, Speeches, and Declarations of King Charles II*, ed. Arthur Bryant (London: Cassell, 1935), pp. 311–13.

59. For a complete account of Monmouth's political career from 1679 to his rebellion, see Robin Clifton, *The Last Popular Rebellion: The Western Rising of 1685* (London: Maurice Temple Smith, 1984).

60. *His Grace the Duke of Monmouth Honoured in His Progress In the West of England . . .* (London, 1680). This is, except in minor details, essentially the same account that appears both in *The Protestant (Domestick) Intelligence* and *A Choice Collection of Wonderful Miracles, Ghosts and Visions* (see below, note 65).

61. *The Protestant (Domestick) Intelligence. Or, News both from City and Country*, No. 86, Friday, 7 Jan. 1680 [1681].

62. The Amsterdam Coffee House appears to have been intimately connected with the Whigs. In 1677 one "Kidd," identified as its "keeper," was included in a warrant issued by the secretary of state; the charge may have concerned "publish[ing] and dispers[ing] false news." And in 1684 Titus Oates was arrested here after calling the duke of York a traitor. See Bryant Lillywhite,

London Coffee Houses: A Reference Book of Coffee Houses of the Seventeenth, Eighteenth, and Nineteenth Centuries (London: Allen and Unwin, 1963), pp. 80–81.

63. *A True and Wonderful Account of a Cure of the Kings-Evil, by Mrs. Fanshaw, Sister to His Grace the Duke of Monmouth* (London, 1681).

64. *An Answer to a Scoffing and Lying Lybell Put Forth and Privately Dispersed Under the Title of A Wonderful Account of the Curing the Kings-Evil, by Madam Fanshaw the Duke of Monmouth's Sister* (London, 1681).

65. "A Canto on the New Miracle wrought by the D. of M. curing a young Wench of the Kings Evil, as it is related at large by B. Harris in his Prot. Intelligence, publish'd Friday Jan. 7th. 1681. to prevent false Reports." This poem represents the right-hand column of a broadside issued with no date or place of publication. On the left side is another verse attack on Monmouth, "The Oxford Alderman's Speech to the D. of M. when his Grace made his Entrance into that City about Sept. 1680." "A Canto" was apparently reprinted with minor changes of punctuation and capitalization as "A Canto upon the Miraculous Cure of the Kings-Evil, performed by His Grace the D. of M.," in *A Choice Collection of Wonderful Miracles, Ghosts, and Visions* (London, 1681), p. 4. The otherworldly title of this odd collection belies its political significance. This four-page pamphlet contains eight parts, each a supernatural account of the current political situation designed to place Monmouth in a ridiculous light just prior to the meeting of Parliament in Oxford. Three of these concern the royal touch and are reprints, little changed, of the news story in *The Protestant (Domestick) Intelligence, A True and Wonderful Account*, and "A Canto." The collection thus contains a "true" account of a royal healing designed to suggest Monmouth's legitimacy, a "false" account of a healing designed to remind us of his illegitimacy, and a straigtforward satire that ridicules his healing pretensions. This volume purports to be "printed for Benjamin Harris," but I suspect it is a Tory impersonation of the celebrated Whig publisher, who had published the original account of Monmouth's Somerset healing.

66. Maurice Tobin, *A True Account of the Celebrated Secret of Mr Timothy Beaghan . . .* (London, 1697), p. 7. All quotations are from this edition.

67. Dr. James Gibbs, *Observations of Various Eminent Cures of Scrophulous Distempers Commonly Call'd the King's Evil* (London, 1712). All quotations are from this edition.

68. For a description of the status and licensing of "empirics," see Roy Porter, *Disease, Medicine and Society in England, 1550–1860* (London: Macmillan, 1987), p. 20; see also Beier, *Sufferers and Healers*, pp. 19–32.

69. *A Letter from a Gentleman at Rome, To His Friend in London; Giving An Account of some very surprizing Cures in the King's-Evil . . .* Translated out of the Italian (London, 1721). All quotations are from this edition.

70. William Beckett, *A Free and Impartial Enquiry Into the Antiquity and*

Efficacy of Touching for the Cure of the King's Evil . . . (London, 1722), p. 58. All quotations are from this edition.

71. For considerations of this press war, see Beier, *Sufferers and Healers*, pp. 32–50; Holmes, *Augustan England*, p. 167; Roy Porter, "The Language of Quackery in England, 1660–1800," in *The Social History of Language*, ed. Peter Burke and Roy Porter, Cambridge Studies in Oral and Literate Culture 12 (Cambridge: Cambridge Univ. Press, 1987), pp. 73–103; Andrew Wear, "Medical Practice in Late Seventeenth- and Early Eighteenth-Century England: Continuity and Union," in *The Medical Revolution of the Seventeenth Century*, ed. French and Wear, pp. 294–320. Charles Webster, in *The Great Instauration: Science, Medicine and Reform 1626–1660* (New York: Holmes and Meier, 1976), locates the 1650s and 1660s as the decades that first saw a popular demand for a vernacular medical literature (p. 265).

72. Samuel Werenfels, *A Dissertation Upon Superstition in Natural Things. To which are added, Occasional Thoughts On the Power of Curing the King's-Evil Ascribed to the Kings of England* (London, 1748), p. 73.

3. The Monarch's Profane Body

1. John Dryden, *Absalom and Achitophel*, in *The Works of John Dryden*, ed. H.T. Swedenberg, Jr., *et al.* (Berkeley: Univ. of California Press, 1956–), 2:5–36, lines 1–10.

2. Carver, "Restoration Poets and Their Father King," pp. 340–47.

3. Sir Robert Filmer, *Patriarcha*, in *Patriarcha and Other Political Works of Sir Robert Filmer*, ed. Peter Laslett (Oxford: Basil Blackwell, 1949), pp. 63, 57. For a rather amusing literary attempt to realize or parody—it is difficult to decide which—Filmer's patriarchal state, see Henry Neville, *The Isle of Pines, or, A late Discovery of a fourth Island in Terra Australis, Incognita* (London, 1668). And for a critical analysis of the way in which patriarchal assumptions were figured and transformed in late sevententh-century literature, see Richard Braverman, "Capital Relations and *The Way of the World*," ELH 52 (1985): 133–58. As Braverman notes, "Sovereignty and the ability to reproduce it—renewal and repetition—are exclusively within the male domain, for in reproduction woman is represented as totally passive, subject to the all-potent male will" (144–45).

4. MacLean, *Time's Witness*, pp. 152–53.

5. Pepys, *The Diary*, entry for 31 Dec. 1662, 3:303. Pepys's foresight deserves quotation: "The Duke of Monmouth is in so great splendour at Court and so dandled by the king, that some doubt, if the king should have no child by the Queene (which there is yet no appearance of), whether he would not be acknowledged for a lawful son. And that there will a difference follow upon it between the Duke of York—and him—which God prevent."

6. For literary elaborations of this sexual relationship between state and

monarch during the sixteenth century, see Berry, *Of Chastity and Power*; David Lee Miller, "Spenser's Poetics: The Poem's Two Bodies," *PMLA* 101 (1986): 170–85; and Phyllis Rackin, "Genealogical Anxiety and Female Authority: The Return of the Repressed in Shakespeare's Histories," in *Contending Kingdoms: Historical, Psychological, and Feminist Approaches to the Literature of Sixteenth-Century England and France*, ed. Marie-Rose Logan and Peter L. Rudnytsky (Detroit: Wayne State Univ. Press, 1991), pp. 323–45. For the particular articulations it took under Charles, see Jose, *Ideas of the Restoration*, pp. 41–42; and Edie, "Popular Idea of Monarchy," p. 356.

7. Quoted in Carver, "Restoration Poets and Their Father King," p. 333.

8. Pepys, *The Diary*, entries for 13 July 1660 and 31 Dec. 1662, 1:199, 3:302.

9. Sharp, "Popular Political Opinion in England," p. 18.

10. Harris, *London Crowds in the Reign of Charles II*, pp. 82–91.

11. Joan Wallach Scott, *Gender and the Politics of History* (New York: Columbia Univ. Press, 1988), pp. 48–49.

12. Ezell, *Patriarch's Wife*, p. 61.

13. This debate concerning the nature and status of women can be charted in the following, selected list of sources: Richard Ames, *Sylvia's Revenge, Or; A Satyr Against Man; in Answer to the Satyr Against Woman* (London, 1688); Judith Drake, *An Essay in Defence of the Female Sex* (London, 1696); *Female Excellence: or, Woman Displayed, in Several Satyrick Poems* (London, 1679); Sarah Fyge Egerton, *The Female Advocate: Or, An Answer To a Late Satyr Against the Pride, Lust and Inconstancy of Woman* (London, 1686); Charles Gerbier, *Elogium Heroinum: Or, The Praise of Worthy Women* (London, 1651); Margaret Askew Fell Fox, *Womens Speaking Justified, Proved and Allowed of by the Scriptures* (London, 1667); Robert Gould, *Love Given O're: Or, A Satyr Against the Pride, Lust, and Inconstancy, Etc. of Woman* (London, 1682); Bathsua Makin, *An Essay to Revive the Antient Education of Gentlewomen* (London, 1673); *Mysogynus: Or, A Satyr Upon Women* (London, 1682); François Poullain de La Barre, *The Woman as Good as the Man: Or, The Equality of Both Sexes* (London, 1677) [first English translation of his *De l'egalite des deux sexes*]; William Walsh, *A Dialogue Concerning Women, Being a Defence of the Sex. Written to Eugenia* (London, 1691). For recent critical considerations of seventeenth-century feminism, see Moira Ferguson, *First Feminists* (Bloomington: Indiana Univ. Press, 1985); Sara Heller Mendelson, *The Mental World of Stuart Women: Three Studies* (Brighton, Sussex: Harvester Press, 1987); Hilda L. Smith, *Reason's Disciples: Seventeenth-Century English Feminists* (Urbana: Univ. of Illinois Press, 1982); Dale Spender, ed. *Feminist Theorists* (New York: Random House, 1983); Linda Woodbridge, *Women and the English Renaissance: Literature and the Nature of Womankind, 1540–1620* (Chicago: Univ. of Chicago Press, 1984).

14. Elaine Hobby, *Virtue of Necessity: English Women's Writings, 1649–88* (London: Virago, 1988), p. 1. Hobby also suggests that hers is a conservative

figure, for much undiscovered women's writing may be embedded in male texts and collected or catalogued under male names: "if my speculation is correct . . . many more women wrote and published in this fragmentary way than ever set their names to an entire book or pamphlet" (207). For another examination of the publications of women, see Patricia Crawford, "Women's Published Writings, 1660–1700," in *Women in English Society, 1500–1800*, ed. Mary Prior (London: Methurn, 1985), pp. 211–82. She indicates that for the entire seventeenth century "231 named women wrote most of the 658 first editions" (214).

15. For a consideration of Astell's life and writings, see Ruth Perry, *The Celebrated Mary Astell: An Early English Feminist* (Chicago: Univ. of Chicago Press, 1986); she provides a "Bibliographical Checklist" on pp. 459–66. In the forward, Catherine R. Stimpson writes that Astell was "arguably the first systematic feminist theoretician in the West" (xi). For a more conservative reading of Astell, see Joan Kinnaird, "Mary Astell and the Conservative Contribution to English Feminism," *Journal of British Studies* 19 (1979): 53–75. Crawford notes that even if we accept Kinnaird's position, Astell nonetheless constructed the "most sustained arguments of the century for a reassessment of women's place in society" ("Women's Published Writings," 230).

16. Pepys, *The Diary*, entry for 15 May 1663, 4:136–37.

17. "The Fourth Advice To a Painter," in *Poems on Affairs of State*, ed. Lord, 1:141–46, lines 129–36.

18. All four "Advice" poems, as well as Waller's "Instructions," can be found in vol. 1 of Lord's edition of *Poems on Affairs of State*. All quotations from these poems are from this volume. Lord discusses their publication in his introduction to each poem, as well as in his general introduction to the volume, specifically on pp. xxxiv–xlii. In speaking of these poems as a "series," I do not mean to imply that they were the only responses to Waller's poem. As Lord notes, dozens of poems circulated that adopted the same "advice" form.

19. For a study devoted to this campaign, see P.G. Rogers, *The Dutch in the Medway* (Oxford: Oxford Univ. Press, 1970).

20. *Poems on Affairs of State*, ed. Lord, 1:xxxi–xlii.

21. *Poems on Affairs of State*, ed. Lord, 1:xxxvii.

22. Sir Roger L'Estrange, "Minutes of a Project for Preventing Libels," quoted in Lord, *Classical Presences*, p. 115; J. Walker discusses L'Estrange's proposal in "The Censorship of the Press during the Reign of Charles II," *History* 35 (1950): 229.

23. J.R. Jones insists that along with Sir Arthur Bryant he wishes to break "with the traditional picture of Charles as an immoral and frivolous king, who possessed neither principles nor objectives and refused to commit himself to the tedious business of governing" (*Charles II: Royal Politician*, 2). And in his recent biography, Ronald Hutton acknowledges that "at the time it was widely

assumed that [Charles's mistresses] had great influence upon policy-making," but he concludes "that, on the whole, such a notion was false" (*Charles the Second King of England*, 451).

24. Letter dated 5 March 1659, in *Charles II to Lord Taaffe: Letters in Exile*, ed. Timothy Crist (Cambridge: Rampant Lions Press, 1974), p. 35.

25. John Wilmot, earl of Rochester, "A Satyr on Charles II," in *The Complete Poems of John Wilmot, Earl of Rochester*, ed. David M. Vieth (New Haven: Yale Univ. Press, 1968), pp. 60–61, lines 1–4.

26. Evelyn, *The Diary*, entry for 6 Feb. 1685, 4:409–11.

27. George Savile, marquis of Halifax, *A Character of King Charles The Second: And Political, Moral and Miscellaneous Thoughts and Reflections* (London, 1750), pp. 44, 46, 50–51, 55.

28. Anthony Hamilton, *The Memoirs of Count De Gramont*, ed. Allan Fea (London: Bickers and Son, 1906), p. 99.

29. Pepys, *The Diary*, entries for 27 July 1667, 3 Sept. 1665, and 25 Nov. 1668, 8:354–55; 6:210; 9:375.

30. Pepys, *The Diary*, entry for 27 July 1667, 8:356.

31. Pepys, *The Diary*, entry for 24 June 1667, 8:288. The term *effeminate* participated in the transformations that overtook the homosexual identity after the seventeenth century. During the seventeenth century the word possessed multiple uses, describing cross-dressed boys, as well as men, like Charles in this example, excessively fond of women. As a descriptive term, *effeminacy* became almost exclusively attached to male homosexuals only after the seventeenth century. For discussions of this change in meaning see the two essays by Trumbach listed in note fifty-four to this chapter.

32. Marin Cureau de La Chambre, *The Art of How to Know Men*, tr. John Davies (London, 1665), p. 11.

33. James Howell, *The Parly of Beasts; or, Morphandra Queen of the Inchanted Iland* (London, 1660), p. 55. For an intriguing survey of Renaissance medical lore dealing with the relationship between male and female bodies, see Stephen Greenblatt's *Shakespearean Negotiations*, chap. 3.

34. Anne Barbeau Gardiner, "The Medal That Provoked a War: Charles II's Lasting Indignation over Adolfzoon's Breda Medal," *The Medal* 17 (1990): 11–15.

35. "A Dialogue between the Two Horses," in *Poems on Affairs of State*, ed. Lord, 1:274–83, lines 149–50.

36. For a consideration of how idealizations of Elizabeth had developed during the seventeenth century, see R. Malcolm Smuts, *Court Culture and the Origins of a Royalist Tradition in Early Stuart England* (Philadelphia: Univ. of Pennsylvania Press, 1987).

37. John Ayloffe, "Britannia and Raleigh," in *Poems on Affairs of State*, ed. Lord, 1:228–36, lines 25, 29–34. All references are to this edition of the poem.

38. Andrew Marvell, "Further Advice to a Painter," in *Poems on Affairs of State*, ed. Lord, 1:164–67, lines 35–38.

39. For further information about the notorious Coventry incident—in which Sir John Coventry had his nose slit in December of 1670 for remarks in Parliament concerning the king's extra-dramatic interest in the theater—see the *Dictionary of National Biography* and *Poems on Affairs of State*, ed. Lord, 1:168. For Coventry's remarks, and the parliamentary debate that followed his disfigurement, see *Cobbett's Parliamentary History of England From the Earliest Period to the Year 1803* (London, 1806–1820), 4:460–61. Lord also includes in his first volume three satires that deal with the Coventry affair: "The King's Vows," pp. 159–62; "Further Advice to a Painter," pp. 164–67; "A Ballad Called the Haymarket Hectors," pp. 169–71. I consider these three poems and the Coventry affair in my essay "Charles II, George Pines, and Mr. Dorimant: The Politics of Sexual Power in Restoration England," *Criticism* 32 (1990): 193–221.

40. "A New Ballad," in *Poems on Affairs of State*, ed. Lord, 2:176–79, lines 61–65.

41. Evelyn, *The Diary*, entry for 6 Feb. 1685, 4:410–11.

42. John Lacy, "Satire," in *Poems on Affairs of State*, ed. Lord, 1:425–28, lines 2–3. All quotations are from this edition of the poem.

43. Unlike Castlemaine and Portsmouth, who invariably appear in poems on affairs of state as objects of loathing, Nell Gwyn could on occasion fare rather well at the hands of satirists. In "Nell Gwynne" (*Poems on Affairs of State*, ed. Lord, 1:420), for instance, she is congratulated for not interfering in politics: "She hath got a trick to handle his p———, / But never lays hands on his sceptre" (lines 3–4). And in "A Dialogue, Between The Dutchess of Portsmouth, and Madam Gwin, at parting" (London, 1682), she succeeds in upholding the honor of her country against a French, Catholic intruder.

44. Eve Kosofsky Sedgwick, *Between Men: English Literature and Male Homosocial Desire* (New York: Columbia Univ. Press, 1985), p. 50.

45. Jane Gallop, *Thinking through the Body* (New York: Columbia Univ. Press, 1988), p. 37.

46. I am using the term *homosocial* as defined by Sedgwick to refer to "social bonds between persons of the same sex" (*Between Men*, 1). As Sedgwick explains in her introduction, our society is marked by a radical disjunction between male homosocial and homosexual structures and desires.

47. I do not mean here to slight the bibliographical questions concerning *Sodom*, which are indeed complex and fascinating. For an important if brief review of the problems of authorship see Judith Milhous and Robert D. Hume, "Attribution Problems in English Drama, 1660–1700," *Harvard Library Bulletin* 31 (1983): 5–39. For a more recent and more detailed discussion of authorship, which takes issue with the conclusions reached by Milhous and Hume, see J.W. Johnson, "Did Lord Rochester Write *Sodom?*" *The Papers of the Bibliographical Society of America* 81 (1987): 119–53. Johnson presents a strong, but conjectural

case for Rochester's authorship; in my judgment, without further evidence no definitive attribution of authorship seems possible. Rochester is certainly an attractive candidate, but I here treat the play as anonymously composed. An exception to the general refusal to consider the play as a literary text, Richard Elias provides the best analysis of the play's political import in "Political Satire in *Sodom*," *Studies in English Literature* 18 (1978): 423–38.

48. Gayle Rubin, "The Traffic in Women: Notes on the 'Political Economy' of Sex," in *Toward an Anthropology of Women*, ed. Rayna R. Reiter (New York: Monthly Review Press, 1975), pp. 173, 174.

49. *Rochester's Sodom. Herausgegeben nach dem Hamburger Manuscript*, ed. L.S.A.M. von Römer (Paris: H. Welter, 1904). All references are to this edition. In spite of its inconsistent punctuation—in fact, because of the whole-sale changes it would demand—I have decided against correcting the text. For a discussion of the most important surviving texts of the play, see Larry D. Carver, "The Texts and the Text of *Sodom*," *The Papers of the Bibliographical Society of America* 73 (1979): 19–40. Carver concludes that given the relation-ship between surviving manuscripts of the play, there can be "no authoratative text of *Sodom*" (27). He argues that "the number, nature, and variety of the extant texts suggest that *Sodom* was often copied and circulated widely" (30), and that the Hamburg manuscript used here "almost certainly derive[s] from the 1684 anonymously printed version" (29). No examples of this printed text have survived.

50. Elias, "Political Satire in *Sodom*," pp. 432–34.

51. Luce Irigaray, *Speculum of the Other Woman*, trans. Gillian C. Gill (Ithaca: Cornell Univ. Press, 1985), pp. 53, 48.

52. David Lee Miller, "The Death of the Modern: Gender and Desire in Marlowe's 'Hero and Leander,' " *South Atlantic Quarterly* 88 (1989): 779.

53. St. Thomas Aquinas, *Summa theologica*, trans. Fathers of the English Dominican Province (New York: Benziger Brothers, 1947), 2:1825, 1811.

54. The last decade has seen a tremendous increase in scholarship devoted to recovering the history of homosexuality; two good introductions to this research are David F. Greenberg, *The Construction of Homosexuality* (Chicago: Univ. of Chicago Press, 1988); and *Hidden from History: Reclaiming the Gay and Lesbian Past*, ed. Martin Bauml Duberman, Martha Vicinus, and George Chauncey, Jr. (New York: New American Library, 1989). For particular attention to questions concerning transformations of the homosexual identity that occurred during the seventeenth and eighteenth centuries, see G.S. Rous-seau, "The Pursuit of Homosexuality in the Eighteenth Century: 'Utterly Confused Category' and/or Rich Repository?" *Eighteenth-Century Life* 9 (1985): 132–68; Randolph Trumbach, "Sodomitical Subcultures, Sodomitical Roles, and the Gender Revolution of the Eighteenth Century: The Recent Historiog-raphy," *Eighteenth-Century Life* 9 (1985): 109–21; and Randolph Trumbach, "Sodomitical Assaults, Gender Role, and Sexual Development in Eighteenth-

Century London," *Journal of Homosexuality* 16 (1988): 407–29. For an important study of homosexuality that also considers *Sodom*, see Alan Bray, *Homosexuality in Renaissance England* (London: Gay Men's Press, 1982).

55. Richard Ames, *The Folly of Love; Or, An Essay Upon Satyr Against
Woman*, in *Satires on Women*, ed. Felicity A. Nussbaum, Augustan Reprint
Society 180 (Los Angeles: William Andrews Clark Memorial Library, 1976),
pp. 26, 27.

56. Andrew Marvell, "The Garden," in *The Poems and Letters of Andrew
Marvell*, ed. H.M. Margoliouth, 2nd ed. (Oxford: Clarendon Press, 1952),
1:48–50, lines 34–36.

57. James Grantham Turner, *One Flesh: Paradisal Marriage and Sexual
Relations in the Age of Milton* (Oxford: Clarendon Press, 1987), pp. 172, 291.

58. John Milton, *Paradise Lost*, in *John Milton: Complete Poems and Major
Prose*, ed. Merritt Y. Hughes (New York: Odyssey Press, 1957), X.888–95,
VIII.624–28.

59. Turner, *One Flesh*, pp. 161–62.

60. Sedgwick, *Between Men*, pp. 50–51.

61. Both Berry, *Of Chastity and Power*, and Montrose, " 'Shaping Fantasies,' " suggest that in spite of Elizabeth's impressive manipulation of her sexual identity, her presence on a male throne nonetheless generated significant anxiety in Renaissance England. I do not mean here to ignore or obscure
this.

62. Bray, *Homosexuality in Renaissance England*, p. 25.

4. "The feminine part of every rebellion"

1. Alexander Pope, *The Dunciad in Four Books*, in *The Complete Poems*,
5, Book I, pp. 272–74, lines 37–44.

2. *The London Printer his Lamentation; or, The Press oppressed, or overpressed, September, 1660*, in *The Harleian Miscellany: Or, A Collection of Scarce,
Curious, and Entertaining Pamphlets and Tracts . . .* (London, 1744–1746),
3:277–78.

3. Eisenstein, *The Printing Press as an Agent of Change*, 1:23, 153.

4. Michel Foucault, "What Is an Author?" in *Textual Strategies: Perspectives in Post-Structuralist Criticism*, ed. Josue V. Harari (Ithaca: Cornell Univ.
Press, 1979), p. 148.

5. Annabel Patterson, *Censorship and Interpretation: The Conditions of
Writing and Reading in Early Modern England* (Madison: Univ. of Wisconsin
Press, 1984), p. 63. For other works dealing with the relationship between
censorship, literature, and authorial identity, see Goldberg, *James I and the
Politics of Literature*, pp. 1–17; and Arthur F. Marotti, *John Donne: Coterie Poet*
(Madison: Univ. of Wisconsin Press, 1986). On the development of censorship

itself, see Siebert, *Freedom of the Press in England;* Rostenberg, *Minority Press;* and Donald Thomas, *A Long Time Burning: The History of Literary Censorship in England* (London: Routledge & Kegan Paul, 1969).

6. For studies by literary critics of the relationship between copyright and author, see Joseph Loewenstein, "For a History of Literary Property: John Wolfe's Reformation," *English Literary Renaissance* 18 (1988): 389–412, and "The Script in the Marketplace," *Representations* 12 (1985): 101–14; Mark Rose, "The Author as Proprietor: *Donaldson v. Becket* and the Genealogy of Modern Authorship," *Representations* 23 (1988): 51–85; Martha Woodmansee, "The Genius and the Copyright: Economic and Legal Conditions of the Emergence of the 'Author,' " *Eighteenth-Century Studies* 17 (1984): 425–48. For considerations of copyright from other disciplines, see Lyman Ray Patterson, *Copyright in Historical Perspective* (Nashville: Vanderbilt Univ. Press, 1968); E.P. Skone James, Sir John Mummery, J.E. Rayner James, and K.M. Garnett, *Copinger and Skone James on Copyright,* 13th ed. (London: Sweet & Maxwell, 1991); R.F. Whale and Jeremy J. Phillips, *Whale on Copyright* (Oxford: ESC, 1983).

7. David Saunders and Ian Hunter, "Lessons from the 'Literatory': How to Historicize Authorship," *Critical Inquiry* 17 (1991): 485.

8. "An act for safety and preservation of his Majesty's person and government against treasonable and seditious practices and attempts," 13 Caroli II.c.1 (1661), in *The Statutes at Large, From Magna Charta to the Eleventh Parliament of Gt. Brit., Anno 1761,* ed. Danby Pickering (Cambridge, 1762–1869), 8:2.

9. Proclamation No. 122, "Enforcing Statutes against Heresy; Prohibiting Unlicensed Preaching, Heretical Books," in *Tudor Royal Proclamations,* ed. Hughes and Larkin, 1:182.

10. G.R. Elton, *Policy and Police: The Enforcement of the Reformation in the Age of Thomas Cromwell* (Cambridge: Cambridge Univ. Press, 1972), p. 13. On the connection between ears and censorship, see Patterson, *Censorship and Interpretation,* chap. 2, "Prynne's Ears; or, The Hermeneutics of Censorship," pp. 44–119. For an examination of the Lollards and their literature, see Anne Hudson, *Lollards and Their Books* (London: Hambledon Press, 1985), and *The Premature Reformation: Wycliffite Texts and Lollard History* (Oxford: Clarendon Press, 1988).

11. Proclamation No. 129, "Prohibiting Erroneous Books and Bible Translations," in *Tudor Royal Proclamations,* ed. Hughes and Larkin, 1:194.

12. Ibid., p. 195.

13. Proclamation No. 186, "Prohibiting Unlicensed Printing of Scripture, Exiling Anabaptists, Depriving Married Clergy, Removing St. Thomas a Becket from Calendar," in *Tudor Royal Proclamations,* ed. Hughes and Larkin, 1:270, 271.

14. Proclamation No. 272, "Prohibiting Heretical Books; Requiring

Printer to Identify Himself, Author of Book, and Date of Publication," in *Tudor Royal Proclamations*, ed. Hughes and Larkin, 1:374, 375.

15. For estimates on literacy in early-sixteenth-century England, see Cressy: "Aggregate figures for the sixteenth century are not readily available, but a reasonable guess might place male illiteracy around 80% and female illiteracy close to 95% at the time of the accession of Elizabeth. A projection back to the reign of Henry VII would find perhaps 90% of Englishmen illiterate at the turn of the century, with illiteracy claiming as many as 99% of the women" (*Literacy and the Social Order*, 176). It should be emphasized that these are aggregate figures—considerations of geography and profession would obviously change these percentages enormously—and, based solely on the ability to sign, they may significantly underestimate the percentage of the population that could read. On the audience for cheap printed matter during the sixteenth century—particularly its inclusive nature—see Tessa Watt, *Cheap Print and Popular Piety, 1550–1640* (Cambridge: Cambridge Univ. Press, 1991). On the increase in cheap printed matter after 1540, see David Loades, *Politics, Censorship and the English Reformation* (London: Pinter, 1991), pp. 113–14.

16. On the extent of national discontent during the 1530s and 1540s, see Elton, *Policy and Police*, and D.M. Palliser, "Popular Reactions to the Reformation during the Years of Uncertainty 1530–70," in *Church and Society in England: Henry VIII to James I*, ed. Felicity Heal and Rosemary O'Day (London: Macmillan, 1977): 35–56. On the northern risings in particular, see C.S.L. Davies, "The Pilgrimage of Grace Reconsidered," in *Rebellion, Popular Protest and the Social Order in Early Modern England*, ed. Paul Slack (Cambridge: Cambridge Univ. Press, 1984), pp. 16–38, and "Popular Religion and the Pilgrimage of Grace," in *Order and Disorder in Early Modern England*, ed. Anthony Fletcher and John Stevenson (Cambridge: Cambridge Univ. Press, 1985): 58–88.

17. Loades, *Politics, Censorship and the English Reformation*, p. 110. Loades presents a lucid and informative discussion of censorship in and before the sixteenth century; see part II of his book, pp. 91–147.

18. *Harrison's Description of England In Shakespeare's Youth. Being the Second and Third Books of His Description of Britain and England. Part I. The Second Book*, ed. Frederick J. Furnivall (London: N. Trubner & Co., 1877), p. 134. For a consideration of how English society looked to sixteenth- and seventeenth-century eyes, see David Cressy, "Describing the Social Order of Elizabethan and Stuart England," *Literature and History* 3 (1976): 29–44; Cressy provides as well an outline for a twentieth-century description of the various levels of social and economic hierarchy in early modern England. For detailed attempts to reconstruct hierarchy in sixteenth-century England see Cressy, *Literacy and the Social Order*, particularly pp. 118–41; and Steve Rappaport, *Worlds within Worlds: Structures of Life in Sixteenth-Century London* (Cambridge: Cambridge Univ. Press, 1989).

19. Proclamation No. 129, in *Tudor Royal Proclamations*, ed. Hughes and Larkin, 1:196.

20. Proclamations Nos. 272, 129, 186, in *Tudor Royal Proclamations*, ed. Hughes and Larkin, 1:373, 194, 270.

21. Pope, *The Dunciad in Four Books*, in *The Complete Poems*, 5, Book III, p. 322, lines 31–34.

22. Jean Baudrillard, "The Structural Law of Value and the Order of Simulacra," in *The Structural Allegory: Reconstructive Encounters with the New French Thought*, ed. John Fekete, Theory and History of Literature 11 (Minneapolis: Univ. of Minnesota Press, 1984), p. 62.

23. "Charter of Incorporation of the Stationers Company," in *A Transcript of the Registers of the Company of Stationers of London; 1554–1640 A.D.*, ed. Edward Arber (1875–1894; rpt. Gloucester, Mass.: Peter Smith, 1967), 1:xxviii. All quotations are from this edition.

24. Peggy Kamuf, *Signature Pieces: On the Institution of Authorship* (Ithaca: Cornell Univ. Press, 1988), p. 60.

25. For detailed accounts of the history and development of the Stationers' Company, see Siebert, *Freedom of the Press in England*, pp. 64–87; Cyprian Blagden, *The Stationers' Company: A History, 1403–1959* (London: G. Allen & Unwin, 1960); Marjorie Plant, *The English Book Trade: An Economic History of the Making and Sale of Books*, 3rd ed. (London: G. Allen & Unwin, 1974).

26. Siebert, *Freedom of the Press in England*, p. 64.

27. Blagden, *The Stationers' Company*, p. 21.

28. "Privy Council Order against seditious books, 1566," in *The Tudor Constitution: Documents and Commentary*, ed. G.R. Elton, 2nd ed. (Cambridge: Cambridge Univ. Press, 1982), pp. 106–8; "Star Chamber decree concerning printers, 1586," in *The Tudor Constitution*, ed. Elton, pp. 182–87.

29. "Decree of Starre-Chamber, Concerning Printing, 1637," in *Transcript of the Registers*, ed. Arber, 4:535, 530. According to Siebert, under this decree "the authority of the Company reached its highest point. . . . all printing was placed in its hands. Printing outside the Company was forbidden. The identification of the interests of the Crown with those of the Stationers was complete" (*Freedom of the Press in England*, 134).

30. Alfred W. Pollard, "Some Notes on the History of Copyright in England, 1662–1774," *Library*, 4th series, 3 (1922): 99.

31. See Rappaport, *Worlds within Worlds*, for an extended consideration of the general relationship between the crown and the London companies. On the history and development of the companies, see William F. Kahl, *The Development of London Livery Companies: An Historical Essay and a Select Bibliography* (Boston: Baker Library, 1960); and I.G. Doolittle, *The City of London and Its Livery Companies* (Dorchester: Gavin Press, 1982).

32. "An Ordinance against unlicensed or scandalous Pamphlets, and for the better Regulating of Printing," in *Acts and Ordinances of the Interregnum*,

1642–1660, ed. C.H. Firth and R.S. Rait (London: Wyman and Sons, 1911), 1:1021; "An Act against Unlicensed and Scandalous Books and Pamphlets, and for better regulating of Printing," in *Acts and Ordinances of the Interregnum*, 2:245.

33. "An Ordinance for the Regulating of Printing" (1643), in *Acts and Ordinances of the Interregnum*, ed. Firth and Rait, 1:184; "An Act against Unlicensed and Scandalous Books and Pamphlets, and for better regulating of Printing" (1649) and "An Act for reviving of a former Act" (1653), in *Acts and Ordinances of the Interregnum*, 2:248, 697.

34. Abbe Blum, "The Author's Authority: *Areopagitica* and the Labour of Licensing," in *Re-membering Milton: Essays on the Texts and Traditions*, ed. Mary Nyquist and Margaret W. Ferguson (London: Methuen, 1987), p. 80. For an essay, like Blum's, that goes much futher than previous scholarship in showing how Milton's essay is formed by and directed at the contemporary history of censorship and printing, see Michael Wilding, "Milton's *Areopagitica*: Liberty for the Sects," in *The Literature of Controversy: Polemical Strategy from Milton to Junius*, ed. Thomas N. Corns (London: Frank Cass, 1987), pp. 7–38.

35. John Milton, *Areopagitica*, in *John Milton: Complete Poems and Major Prose*, ed. Merritt Y. Hughes (New York: Odyssey Press, 1957), p. 720. All quotations are from this edition.

36. Stanley Fish, "Driving from the Letter: Truth and Indeterminacy in Milton's *Areopagitica*," in *Re-membering Milton*, ed. Nyquist and Ferguson, p. 243.

37. Barker, *Tremulous Private Body*, p. 47.

38. I take issue here with Barker's insistence that in Milton's essay "an essential relation of the author to [the] text is a property relation" (*Tremulous Private Body*, 50). Earlier legislation, as we have seen, called for a work to bear the name of both author and printer. Milton's hesitation here about which name is more important, and his decision that the printer accept the ultimate responsibility, suggests that Milton has not fully privileged the author as the proprietor of a text. Indeed, the Licensing Order of 1643 stated that books could be licensed and registered with the Stationers' Company only with the consent of the "owner"; as Blum perceptively notes, since seventeenth-century authors often sold their books, the "owner" was often not the author, and in *Areopagitica* "the extent of authorial control" is thus an "ambiguous matter" ("Author's Authority," 76).

39. [Richard Atkyns], *The Original and Growth of Printing* (n.p., n.d.). Both Wing and the British Library catalogue tentatively assign "London, 1660" as the place and date of publication.

40. Richard Atkyns, *The Original and Growth of Printing: Collected Out of History, and the Records of this Kingdome. . . . (London, 1664)*, B^v. All quotations are from this edition.

41. For a discussion of Atkyns's historiography, see Siebert, *Freedom of*

the Press in England, pp. 22–24, 246. See also the *Dictionary of National Biography*; and E.C. Bigmore and C.W.H. Wyman, *A Bibliography of Printing* (1880–1886; rpt. New York: Philip C. Duschnes, 1945).

42. For a discussion of this second decision, see A.F. Havighurst, "The Judiciary and Politics in the Reign of Charles II," part 2, "1676–1685," *Law Quarterly Review* 66 (1950), 236–38.

43. Alfred W. Pollard, "Some Notes on the History of Copyright," p. 100. Cyprian Blagden, "The 'Company' of Printers," *Studies in Bibliography* 13 (1960): 3–17, agrees with Pollard that the Licensing Act of 1662 "put the clock firmly back to 1637" (7).

44. "An act for preventing abuses in printing seditious, treasonable, and unlicensed books and pamphlets, and for regulating of printing and printing-presses," 14 Caroli II. c.33 (1662), in *Statutes at Large*, ed. Pickering, 8:137–38.

45. Ibid., p. 139.

46. On Berkenhead's relationship to the print trade after the Restoration, see P.W. Thomas, *Sir John Berkenhead 1617–1679: A Royalist Career in Politics and Polemics* (Oxford: Clarendon Press, 1969), pp. 210–12, 223–26. For L'Estrange's appointments, see *Calendar of State Papers. Domestic. 1661–62*, 24 Feb. 1662, p. 282; and *Calendar of State Papers. Domestic. 1663–64*, 15 Aug. 1663, p. 240.

47. Sir Roger L'Estrange, *Considerations and Proposals In Order to the Regulation of the Press* . . . (London, 1663), sigs. A3^v–A4. All quotations are from this edition.

48. Thomas Hobbes, *Leviathan*, ed. C.B. Macpherson (London: Penguin, 1968), p. 233.

49. Here L'Estrange refers to the conflict between the printers and the booksellers within the company. This had arisen as early as 1582, when changes in the trade, to some extent caused by the Charter of Incorporation, had shifted power from the printers to the retailers, who were able to amass far more capital than the craftsmen. For a contemporary complaint about the predominance of the booksellers, see *A Brief Discourse Concerning Printing and Printers* (London, 1663). For a scholarly appraisal of the conflicts within the company, see Blagden, "The 'Company' of Printers"; also Graham Pollard, "The Early Constitution of the Stationers' Company," *Library*, 4th series, 18 (1937): 235–60. Kahl suggests that such shifts in power occurred in many companies during the fifteenth and sixteenth centuries: "trade increased and capital grew in importance, with the result that the mercantile and craft functions were increasingly separated in many industries. Trading fell into the hands of a small class of mercantile businessmen while master craftsmen were restricted entirely to manual production" (*Development of London Livery Companies*, 25).

50. John Hetet, "The Wardens' Accounts of the Stationers' Company, 1663–79," in *Economics of the British Booktrade, 1605–1939*, ed. Robin Myers

and Michael Harris, Publishing History Occasional Series I (Cambridge: Chadwyck-Healey, 1985), pp. 32–59.

51. Twyn's trial can be followed in A Complete Collection of State Trials, ed. Howell and Howell, vol. 6, cols. 513–39. For a fascinating examination of this trial, see Joseph F. Loewenstein, "Legal Proofs and Corrected Readings: Press-Agency and the New Bibliography," in The Production of English Renaissance Culture, ed. David Lee Miller, Sharon O'Dair, and Harold Weber (Ithaca: Cornell Univ. Press, 1994), pp. 93–122. Loewenstein demonstrates that one way in which the government struggled to stabilize the field of print was by fixing an "authoritative" text that could function as evidence in legal proceedings. On Twyn's connection to English radicalism, see Greaves, Deliver Us from Evil, pp. 222–25.

52. Serjeant Morton at the trial of Thomas Brewster, A Complete Collection of State Trials, ed. Howell and Howell, vol. 6, col. 549.

53. Bennett, English Books and Readers, p. 51. For a study of minority presses in England, see Rostenberg, Minority Press and the English Crown; for figures on Catholic printing in the first half of the seventeenth century, see Bennett, p. 89.

54. Siebert, Freedom of the Press in England, pp. 243, 1.

55. Hill, "Censorship and English Literature," in Collected Essays, p.52. As one example of the severity of censorship during Charles's reign, Hill notes that the major histories of the Civil War participants had to wait until after 1688 for publication. Ronald Hutton, The Restoration: A Political and Religious History of England and Wales, 1658–1667 (Oxford: Clarendon Press, 1985), p. 157.

56. Greaves, Deliver Us from Evil, p. 8.

57. For the history of the newspaper during the Restoration, see James Sutherland, The Restoration Newspaper and its Development (Cambridge: Cambridge Univ. Press, 1986).

58. For Julian's legal difficulties and biography, see Brice Harris, "Captain Robert Julian, Secretary to the Muses," ELH 10 (1943): 294–309; for Tom Brown's characterization of Julian, see his "From Julian Late Secretary of the Muses, to Will. Pierre of Lincolns-Inn Fields Play-house," in Letters from the Dead to the Living (London, 1702), p. 62; for the poem and its textual history, see "A Familiar Epistle to Mr. Julian, Secretary to the Muses," in Poems on Affairs of State, ed. Lord, 1:387–91, lines 1–4.

59. "News from the Coffee-House" (London, 1667), in The Roxburghe Ballads, ed. W. Chappell and J. Woodfall Ebsworth (1869–1895; rpt. New York: AMS Press, 1966), 5:178.

60. Peter Fraser, The Intelligence of the Secretaries of State and Their Monopoly of Licensed News 1660–1688 (Cambridge: Cambridge Univ. Press, 1956), pp. 116, 127.

61. David Allen, "Political Clubs in Restoration London," Historical

Journal 19 (1976): 562–63. On the leveling tendencies of the coffeehouses, see also Hunter, *Before Novels*, p. 173, and Tim Harris, *London Crowds in the Reign of Charles II*, pp. 28–29, who suggest that they bridged levels of discourse as well as rank and helped blur distinctions between oral and written culture.

62. Roger L'Estrange, *A Word Concerning Libels and Libellers, Humbly Presented to the Right Honorable Sir John Moor, Lord-Mayor of London, and the Right Worshipfull the Aldermen his Brethren* (London, 1681), p. 12; "A New Satirical Ballad of the Licentiousness of the Times" (1679), in *Political Ballads of the Seventeenth and Eighteenth Centuries*, ed. W. Walker Wilkins (London: Longman, 1860), 1:221.

63. Sir Roger North, *Examen: Or, An Enquiry into the Credit and Veracity of a Pretended Complete History . . .*(London, 1740), p. 573.

64. Sir Roger L'Estrange, *The Observator*, No. 40, Saturday, Aug. 6. 1681.

65. Proclamation No. 3570, "To Restrain the Spreading of False News, and Licentious Talking of Matters of State and Government, 12 June 1672. By the King"; and Proclamation No. 3595, "To Restrain the Spreading of False News, and Licentious talking of Matters of State and Government, 2 May 1674. By the King," in *Tudor and Stuart Proclamations 1485–1714*, ed. Robert Steele (Oxford: Clarendon Press, 1910), 1:431, 435.

66. Proclamation No. 3622, "For the Suppression of Coffee-Houses, 29 December 1675. By the King," in *Tudor and Stuart Proclamations*, ed. Steele, 1:439.

67. Proclamation No. 3625, "An Additional Proclamation Concerning Coffee-Houses, 8 January 1675/76. By the King," in *Tudor and Stuart Proclamations*, ed. Steele, 1:439. For the government's considerations regarding the legality of the suppression, see *Calendar of State Papers. Domestic. 1675–76*, entries for 7 and 8 Jan. 1676, pp. 496–500.

68. "An ordinance against unlicensed or scandalous Pamphlets, and for the better Regulating of Printing" (1647), in *Acts and Ordinances of the Interregnum*, ed. Firth and Rait, 1:1022. This punishment is repeated in "An Act against Unlicensed and Scandalous Books and Pamphlets, and for the better regulating of Printing" (1649).

69. Sutherland, *The Restoration Newspaper*, pp. vii–viii.

70. O.W. Furley, "The Whig Exclusionists: Pamphlet Literature in the Exclusion Campaign, 1679–81," *Cambridge Historical Journal* 13 (1957): 19–36. Furley estimates that taken together Tory and Whig pamphlets "form a list of nearly two hundred titles, not as vast a collection as the Civil War produced, but one to compare favorably with the volume of pamphlets occasioned by the Restoration and Revolution" (19).

71. *A Compleat Catalogue of All the Stitch'd Books and Single Sheets Printed since the First Discovery of The Popish Plot . . .* (n.p., 1680); *A Continuation of the Compleat Catalogue of Stitch'd Books and Single Sheets . . .* (London, 1680); *A*

Second Continuation of the Compleat Catalogue of Stitch'd Books and Single Sheets . . . (London, 1680). This final continuation confidently asserts on the title-page that "The Continuation is intended to be publish'd every Term."

72. Timothy Crist, "Government Control of the Press after the Expiration of the Printing Act in 1679," *Publishing History* 5 (1979): 49.

73. Fraser, *Intelligence of the Secretaries of State,* pp. 116-17.

74. *A Letter of Advice to the Petitioning Apprentices* (London, 1681).

75. Narcissus Luttrell, *A Brief Historical Relation of State Affairs from September 1678 to April 1714* (1857; rpt. London: Gregg International, 1969), 1:36.

76. Sir Roger L'Estrange, *A Momento. Treating, Of the Rise, Progress, and Remedies of Seditions: With Some Historical Reflections Upon the Series of Our Late Troubles,* 2nd ed. (Printed in the Year 1642, and now Reprinted for Joanna Brome, 1682), pp. 6–7.

77. Sir Roger L'Estrange, *The Observator,* No. 48, Wednesday, Aug. 31, 1681.

78. *The Character of Those Two Protestants in Masquerade, Heraclitus, and The Observator* (London, 1681), p. 1.

79. "Scandal Proof, Or An Heroick Poem On the Renowned Champions of the Good Old Cause, Impudent Dick Janeway, and the rest of the Factious Tribe" (London, Printed for Don Pedro Valesco, Tasco Rasco Rero, Don John of Austria's Cozens, Uncles, Sisters Son, being his own Nephew, 1681). The bibliographical absurdity continues the attack on Whig printers, who often tried to protect themselves from government sanction by printing false publishing information.

80. J.A. Downie, *Robert Harley and the Press: Propaganda and Public Opinion in the Age of Swift and Defoe* (Cambridge: Cambridge Univ. Press, 1979), p. 1.

81. Luttrell, *Brief Historical Relation,* entries for 20 April 1681, 1:76; 6 Sept. 1681, 1:124.

82. "Whig and Tory, Or the Scribling Duellists" (London, 1681).

83. "A Satyr Against the Pen-men and Speech-men of the Times" (n.p., n.d.). According to the British Library catalog, this was printed in London, 1679.

84. For an account of the formation of the Whigs that touches on the part played by the press, see J.R. Jones, *The First Whigs: The Politics of the Exclusion Crisis, 1678–1683* (London: Oxford Univ. Press, 1961). Jones attends to such questions as well in his essay "Parties and Parliament," in *The Restored Monarchy 1660–1688,* ed. J.R. Jones (London: Macmillan Press, 1979), pp. 48–70. In both he argues that though not political parties in a strictly modern sense, the Whigs and Tories can nonetheless be designated as parties. See also Douglas R. Lacey, *Dissent and Parliamentary Politics in England, 1661–1689: A Study in the Perpetuation and Tempering of Parliamentarianism* (New Brunswick:

Rutgers Univ. Press, 1969). Lacey argues that no "other opposition election activities have such historical import as this press campaign, for this was the first instance in which an intensive and organized effort was made over the country to win the elections by calculated manipulation of public opinion" (115).

85. The relevant entries in the *Journals of the House of Commons* 9 are as follows: 30 Oct. 1680 (p. 643): "*Resolved,* That the Votes of this House be printed, being first perused and signed by Mr. Speaker: And that Mr. Speaker nominate and appoint the Persons to print the same"; 24 March 1680/81 (p. 708): "*Resolved,* That the Votes and Proceedings of this House be printed: And that the Care of the Printing thereof, and the Appointment of the Printers, be committed to Mr. Speaker." For a brief history of Parliament's relations with the press, see Siebert, *Freedom of the Press in England,* pp. 282–88.

86. On the decision to print Commons' votes and proceedings, and the individuals chosen to print and distribute them, see Crist, "Government Control of the Press," p. 67.

87. Luttrell, *Brief Historical Relation,* entry for 10 Dec. 1679, 1:27–28.

88. Proclamation No. 3703, "Against Tumultuous Petitions. 12 Dec. 1679. By the King," in *Tudor and Stuart Proclamations,* ed. Steele, 1:449. The need for this proclamation reveals how quickly events were moving beyond the government's control. Parliament had passed a law in 1661 making such petitions illegal: "An act against tumults and disorders, upon pretence of preparing or presenting publick petitions, or other addresses to his Majesty or the parliament," 13 Caroli II.c.5 (1661), in *Statutes at Large,* ed. Pickering, 8:6.

89. *A Letter of Advice to the Petitioning Apprentices.*

90. For a discussion of judicial involvement in the questions of both printing and petitioning, see Havighurst, "The Judiciary and Politics," part 2, "1676–1685," pp. 235–39.

91. Roger L'Estrange, *The Observator,* No. 31, Thursday, 7 July 1681.

92. J.S. Morrill and J.D. Waller, "Order and Disorder in the English Revolution," in *Order and Disorder,* ed. Fletcher and Stevenson, pp. 151–152.

93. Jones, *The First Whigs,* p. 171. On the question of the addresses, see Lacey, *Dissent and Parliamentary Politics,* pp. 115–16; and M. Dorothy George, "Elections and Electioneering, 1679–81," *English Historical Review* 45 (1930): 552–78. George insists that "the attempt to create a public opinion, and then to represent it as the demand of the nation, voiced at the elections, was new and essentially revolutionary" (575).

94. Tim Harris, *London Crowds in the Reign of Charles II,* provides the most detailed and compelling account of the ways in which the London population succeeded in imposing its presence on the events of 1678–1682; see particularly pp. 96–188.

95. *A Choice Collection of 120 Loyal Songs: All of them written since the Two late Plots . . .* (London, 1684), sigs. a2 and a2^{v}.

96. Luttrell, *Brief Historical Relation*, entries for 17 Dec. 1679, 1:29; 14 April 1681, 75.

5. "The very Oracles of the *Vulgar*"

1. Lord Chief Justice Scroggs, in *A Complete Collection of State Trials*, ed. Howell and Howell, vol. 7, cols. 1127–28.

2. Crist, "Government Control of the Press," p. 67.

3. Proclamation No. 3693, "Ordinance. By-Law for the Stationers Company. 22 August 1679. By the Lord Chancellor," in *Tudor and Stuart Proclamations*, ed. Steele, 1:447.

4. Crist, "Government Control of the Press," p. 62, details Charles's difficulties in securing from his judges the "proper" opinion in this matter. See also Sutherland, *Restoration Newspaper*, p. 15.

5. "The Trial of Henry Care," in *A Complete Collection of State Trials*, ed. Howell and Howell, vol. 7, col. 1114.

6. Siebert, *Freedom of the Press in England*, p. 269.

7. Luttrell, *Brief Historical Relation*, entries for 5–17 Feb. 1680, 1:33–36. Crist, "Government Control of the Press," discusses this trial on pp. 56–57.

8. For the judgment of literary critics on the value of Tory propaganda, see Steven N. Zwicker, *Politics and Language in Dryden's Poetry: The Arts of Disguise* (Princeton: Princeton Univ. Press, 1984), p. 27; and Frank H. Ellis, " 'Legends no Histories' Part the Second: The Ending of *Absalom and Achitophel*," *Modern Philology* 85 (1988): 405–6. Harris, in *London Crowds in the Reign of Charles II*, discusses the issue at length in chap. 6, "The Tory Response," pp. 130–55.

9. Jeremy Black, *The English Press in the Eighteenth Century* (London: Croom Helm, 1987), p. 6.

10. "The Trial of Benjamin Harris," in *A Complete Collection of State Trials*, ed. Howell and Howell, vol. 7, cols. 929–30.

11. Proclamation No. 3699, "For the Suppressing of Seditious and Treasonable Books and Pamphlets. 31 October 1679. By the King," in *Tudor and Stuart Proclamations*, ed. Steele, 1:448.

12. "The Trial of Henry Care," in *A Complete Collection of State Trials*, ed. Howell and Howell, vol. 7, col. 1118.

13. Kamuf, *Signature Pieces*, p. 65.

14. "The Lord Chief-Justice Scroggs's Speech in the King's-Bench, the first Day of this present Michaelmas-Term, 1679, occasioned by many libellous Pamphlets which are published against Law, to the Scandal of the Government, and Public Justice," in *A Complete Collection of State Trials*, ed. Howell and Howell, vol. 7, col. 703. The speech was published, under this same title, in the same year.

15. Pope, *The Dunciad Variorum*, in *The Complete Poems*, 5:336, note to Book III, line 337.

16. "The Lord Chief-Justice Scroggs's Speech," in *A Complete Collection of State Trials*, ed. Howell and Howell, vol. 7, cols. 704–5.

17. Roger L'Estrange, *A Word Concerning Libels and Libellers* . . . (London, 1681), pp. 10–11.

18. Roger L'Estrange, *A Short Answer to a Whole Litter of Libels* (London, 1680), pp. 1, 13.

19. For the emergence of the professional writer in England, see Edwin Haviland Miller, *The Professional Writer in Elizabethan England: A Study of Nondramatic Literature* (Cambridge: Harvard Univ. Press, 1959).

20. Richard Helgerson, *Self-Crowned Laureates: Spenser, Jonson, Milton and the Literary System* (Berkeley: Univ. of California Press, 1983).

21. Loewenstein's "The Script in the Marketplace" provides an excellent account of Jonson's "disruptive career in the literary marketplace," focusing particularly on his "attempts to reshape literary market relations" (103).

22. Sir Roger North, *Examen*, p. 585.

23. Roger L'Estrange, *Notes Upon Stephen College. Grounded Principally upon his own Declarations and Confessions, And freely submitted to Publique Censure*, 2nd ed. (London, 1681), p. 28. All quotations are from this edition.

24. *The Speech and Carriage of Stephen College At Oxford, Before the Castle, on Wednesday August 31. 1681*, "Taken exactly from his own Mouth at the Place of Execution" (London, 1681), p. 3.

25. *A Letter from a Gentleman in London to his Friend in the Countrey, on the Occasion of the Late Tryal of Stephen Colledge* (n.p., n.d.); signed "R.P." Wing tentatively assigns this publication to "London, 1681."

26. "The Trial of Stephen Colledge, at the King's-Bench, for High Treason," in *A Complete Collection of State Trials*, ed. Howell and Howell, vol. 8, col. 571. All quotations from the trial refer to this volume.

27. Pearl, "Change and Stability in Seventeenth-Century London," pp. 15–16.

28. Harris, *London Crowds in the Reign of Charles II*, pp. 11, 164; P.E. Jones and A.V. Judges, "London Population in the Late Seventeenth Century," *Economic History Review* 6 (1935): 54. On the larger urban metropolis that would include Southwark and Westminster as well as the northern and eastern suburbs, see E.A. Wrigley, "A Simple Model of London's Importance in Changing English Society and Economy, 1650–1750," in *Towns in Societies: Essays in Economic History and Historical Sociology*, ed. Philip Abrams and E.A. Wrigley (Cambridge: Cambridge Univ. Press, 1978), 215–43.

29. Pearl, "Change and Stability in Seventeenth-Century London," p. 14.

30. Edward Chamberlayne, *Angliae Notitia, or The Present State of England: Together With Divers Reflections Upon the Antient State Thereof* (London, 1669), pp. 488–89. Cressy emphasises that even during the sixteenth century, "the enfranchised burgesses and yeomen were also constitutionally

significant. They were represented in the House of Commons and participated in elections" ("Describing the Social Order," p. 31). In describing the "citizens and burgesses [who] haue next place to gentlemen," William Harrison explains that they "are to serue the commonwealth in their cities and boroughs, or in corporat townes where they dwell. And in the common assemblie of the realme wherein our lawes are made . . . and giue their consent or dissent vnto such things as passe or staie there in the name of the citie or borow, for which they are appointed" (*Harrison's Description of England*, 130–31).

31. John Crowne, *City Politiques,* ed. John Harold Wilson (London: Edward Arnold, 1967), I.ii.17–18. All quotations are from this edition.

32. Rappaport, *Worlds within Worlds*, p. 291; D.V. Glass, "Socio-economic Status and Occupations in the City of London at the End of the Seventeenth Century," in *The Early Modern Town: A Reader,* ed. Peter Clark (London: Longman, 1976), p. 227. Glass notes that in 1690, of 1,850 freemen listed in the Guildhall, 1,590 had achieved that status through apprenticeship. Rappaport's figure of seven out of eight would predict that figure to be 1,618.

33. Edward Basil Jupp and William Willmer Pocock, *An Historical Account of the Worshipful Company of Carpenters of the City of London Compiled Chiefly From Records in Their Possession,* 2nd ed. (London: Pickering and Chatto, 1887), pp. 202, 294–95.

34. Glass, "Socio-economic Status and Occupations in the City of London," p. 225.

35. M.J. Power, "The Social Topography of Restoration London," in *London 1500–1700: The Making of the Metropolis,* ed. A.L. Beier and Roger Finlay (London: Longman, 1986), p. 213. Power's table concerning the correlation between occupations and dwelling size can be found on pp. 214–15.

36. Chamberlayne, *Angliae Notitia*, p. 492.

37. Glass, "Socio-economic Status and Occupations in the City of London," p. 224; Jeremy Boulton, *Neighbourhood and Society: A London Suburb in the Seventeenth Century* (Cambridge: Cambridge Univ. Press, 1987), p. 290.

38. Henry Laverock Phillips, *Annals of the Worshipful Company of Joiners of the City of London. . . .* (London: Privately printed, 1915), pp. 41, 43. My uncertainty about Phillips's identification has much to do with a paucity of information concerning first names. Phillips maintains that in the 1674–1675 entry that has Philip Colledge taking up his Steward and Livery, "the christain name is a mistake as I find an apprentice taking up his freedom thus 5 March 1688 'Alex Hopkins app Mary Colledge late wife of Philip Colledge late Citizen and Joiner of London doth by Ind dat 7 Feb[y] 1681 was admitted into the freedom of the Comp[y] by consent of the said Mary.' " Though the timing of Hopkins's apprenticeship agrees with the chronology of College's life, the second instance of an incorrect Christian name is worrisome, particularly because L'Estrange reports that College claimed to have a *"Brother, who was a Joyner by Trade,* and dy'd a *Papist, in October,* 1678" (*Notes upon Stephen College,* p. 6). Unfortu-

nately, College's brother is never named. We might still prove Phillips's identification if we could confirm that College's wife was indeed named Mary, but though the material relating to College's trial and execution contains references to his wife, she too is never named. The Edith College who published *A True Copy of the Dying Words of Mr. Stephen Colledge* may be College's wife, but she could also be his sister. As late as 1683, letters from L'Estrange to Secretary Jenkins implicate a sister of College in various plots against the government, but, predictably, this sister is never named (*Calendar of State Papers. Domestic. 1683* [Jan. to June], pp. 336–41). My feeling is that Phillips's identification seems likely, but will have to await further corroborating evidence before it can be confirmed.

39. During College's trial the Attorney General implied that such arms could not have really belonged to "one of his condition, who is by trade a joiner; for if a true estimate were taken of the value of the arms, I believe they were worth twice his whole estate. . . . you will judge whether these be fit tools for a joiner" (col. 589). At work here is not just an attempt to diminish College's economic and social status, but a desire to suggest an elaborate conspiracy involving the Whig leaders. College, according to such a logic, has merely been "set up" by those more highly placed in the party.

40. James Granger, *A Biographical History of England, From Egbert the Great to the Revolution . . .* 3rd ed. (London, 1779), 4:205–6.

41. A.J. Fletcher and J. Stevenson, "Introduction," in *Order and Disorder*, ed. Fletcher and Stevenson, p. 1. David Cressy describes this problem as well in "Describing the Social Order": "Without intensive local research it is rarely possible to assign precise economic and social standing to a man described by a trade. A tanner, for example, could be an artisan or a guildmaster. . . . The tradesmen were an important but heterogeneous group and contemporaries found it difficult in locating them within the traditional hierarchy. What they had in common was the non-agricultural creation of wealth, the production and distribution of goods, and performance of services" (37–39).

42. Luttrell, *Brief Historical Relation*, entry for 11 March 1681, 1:70.

43. *Calendar of State Papers. Domestic. 1680–81*, p. 331.

44. Ibid., Josiah Ricroft, Justice, to the Bishop of London, 11 July 1681, p. 352. A grand jury at this time had two options: either they returned a "true bill," *billa vera*, thus committing the accused to trial, or they could dismiss the charges with the judgment of *ignoramus*.

45. For discussions of the Whig success in packing the London juries during 1680–1681, see Crist, "Government Control of the Press," pp. 63–65; and Harris, *London Crowds in the Reign of Charles II*, pp. 130–31.

46. *Calendar of State Papers. Domestic. 1680–81*, Secretary Jenkins to Lord Norreys, 11 July 1681, p. 353.

47. John Brewer and John Styles, "Introduction" to *An Ungovernable People: The English and Their Law in the Seventeenth and Eighteenth Centuries*, ed.

Brewer and Styles (London: Hutchinson, 1980), pp. 13–14, 19. For a more complete study of the law in seventeenth-century England, see Howard Nenner, *By Colour of Law* (Chicago: Univ. of Chicago Press, 1977).

48. Havighurst, "Judiciary and Politics," part 2, "1676–1685," pp. 250, 249.

49. *A Modest Vindication of the Proceedings of the late Grand-Jury at the Old Baily, who returned the Bill against Stephen Colledge Ignoramus* (London, 1681).

50. L'Estrange, *The Observator*, No. 32, Saturday, July 9, 1681. For other references to the *ignoramus* verdict of the London grand jury, see also Nos. 31, 33, and 34.

51. *A Letter From the Grand-Jury of Oxford To the London-Grand-Jury, Relating to the Case of the Protestant-Joyner* (London, 1681).

52. L'Estrange, *The Observator*, No. 31, Thursday, July 7, 1681. Note the way in which even this relatively simple reference, by associating College with the "Popish Lords," participates in the government campaign to undermine College by questioning the authenticity of his protestantism. In spite of his fanatical reputation, the government consistently implied that College was really a Roman Catholic. When this could no longer be credibly maintained, they made much of his nonconformity.

53. *The Impartial Protestant Mercury*, No. 35, Friday, 19 Aug., to Tuesday, 23 Aug., 1681.

54. Though it is not hard to recognize when opponents adopt College's voice for their own political ends—I indicate these works below—I found it difficult to determine when texts concerning his imprisonment and trial were actually written by College himself. Given the way in which his identity was appropriated by both political allies and enemies, it seemed wisest not to ascribe any of the following works to College: *Modest Vindication of the Proceedings of the late Grand-Jury at the Old Baily, who returned the Bill against Stephen Colledge Ignoramus* (London, 1681); Edward Whitaker, *A Letter from Mr. Edward Whitaker To the Protestant Joyner Upon his Bill being sent to Oxford* (London, 1681); *A Letter From the Grand-Jury of Oxford To the London-Grand-Jury, Relating to the Case of the Protestant-Joyner* (London, 1681); *A Letter From Mr. Stephen Colledge To A Person of Quality, upon his Removal to Oxford, to be Try'd upon an Impeachment of High Treason* (London, 1681); *A Letter concerning the Tryal at Oxford of Stephen College, August 17. 1681* (London, 1681); *An Account of the Tryal of Mr. Stephen Colledge At Oxford, August the 17th 1681. Where he was found Guilty of High-Treason* (n.p., n.d.) [bibliographical data contained in the Catalog of the British Library: "Benjamin Tooke and John Crook: Dublin? 1681"]; *A Letter Written From Oxford By Mr. Stephen Colledge To his Friends in London, &. Written by himself, Immediately after his Condemnation* (London, 1681) [spuriously attributed to College]; *A Letter Written from the Tower by Mr. Stephen Colledge (the Protestant-Joyner) To Dick Janeways Wife* (London, 1681)

[spuriously attributed to College]; "Have You Any Work for a Cooper . . ." (London, 1681); *The Last Speech and Confession of Mr. Stephen Colledge, Who was Executed at Oxford on Wednesday August 31. 1681* (London, Printed for A. Banks, 1681) [spuriously attributed to College]; *The Speech and Carriage of Stephen Colledge At Oxford, Before the Castle, on Wednesday August 31. 1681, Taken exactly from his own Mouth at the Place of Execution* (London, 1681); *A True Copy of the Dying Words of Mr. Stephen Colledge, left in Writing under his own Hand* . . . (London, Printed for Edith Colledge, 1681); Roger L'Estrange, *Notes Upon Stephen College. Grounded Principally upon his own Declarations and Confessions. And freely submitted to Publique Censure* (London, 1681); "A Poem (By way of Elegie) Upon Mr. Stephen Colledge, Vulgarly known by the Name of The Protestant Joyner" (London, 1681); "A Modest Reply To a too Hasty and Malicious Libel, Entituled, An Elegy on Mr. Stephen Colledge, Vulgarly known by the Name of The Protestant Joyner" (London, 1681); "The Whigs Lamentation for the Death of their Dear Brother Colledge, The Protestant Joyner" (London, 1681); *Strange News from Newgate; Or, A Relation how the Ghost of Colledge the Protestant-Joyner, appeared to Hone the Joyner since his Condemnation* . . . (n.p., 1683); "Stephen Colledge's Ghost To The Fanatical Cabal" (n.p., 1681).

55. *A Letter Written from the Tower by Mr. Stephen Colledge (the Protestant-Joyner) To Dick Janeways Wife* (London, 1681). The broadside is spuriously attributed to College and, I suspect, to "R.J."—Richard Janeway—as well.

56. In discussing the trial of Henry Care, Crist notes that he was "the one author during the Exclusion Crisis whose name gained notoriety and prominence equal to that of the leading Whig stationers" ("Government Control of the Press," 61).

57. *Some Modest Reflections upon the Commitment of the Earl of Shaftesbury, Arising from the Late Indictment against Mr. Stephen Colledge,* in *A Collection of Scarce and Valuable Tracts, On the Most Interesting and Entertaining Subjects* . . . (London, 1748), 1:140. The government's desire to implicate Shaftesbury appears in a letter from Secretary Jenkins to the bishop of Oxford concerning a false rumour of College's confession. Jenkins asks that "some proper person be employed to know of him, how letters directed to the Earl of Shaftesbury came to be sent to his house and to ask him from whom they came, by whom they were conveyed and why to his house, for it can be proved that he said that all the Earl's letters or most of them were directed to his house and that he knew whence they came" (*Calendar of State Papers. Domestic. 1680–81,* Secretary Jenkins to the Bishop of Oxford, 29 Aug. 1681, p. 423). For a brief consideration of the relationship between the arrests of College and Shaftesbury, see Hutton, *Charles the Second,* pp. 407–8.

58. John Kenyon, *The Popish Plot* (London: Penguin, 1972), p. 281.

59. *Calendar of State Papers. Domestic. 1680–81,* Capt. Thomas Cheeke to [Sir Leoline Jenkins], 5 Aug., 1681, p. 389.

60. Sir Roger North, *Examen*, pp. 588, 590.

61. *A Letter concerning the Tryal at Oxford of Stephen College, August 17. 1681* (London, 1681); Luttrell, *Brief Historical Relation*, entry for 17 Aug. 1681, 1:117–18.

62. "A declaration which offenses shall be adjudged treason," 25 Edward III. c.2 (1350), in *Statutes at Large*, ed. Pickering, 2:50–51.

63. John Bellamy, *The Tudor Law of Treason: An Introduction* (London: Routledge & Kegan Paul, 1979), pp. 10–11. For considerations of the relationship between treason and printing, see also W.S. Holdsworth, *A History of English Law*, 7th ed. revised. (London: Methuen, 1956–1972) 8:310–17. These issues are discussed in relationship to College's trial by B.J. Rahn, "A *Ra-ree Show*—A Rare Cartoon: Revolutionary Propaganda in the Treason Trial of Stephen College," in *Studies in Change and Revolution: Aspects of English Intellectual History, 1640–1800*, ed. Paul J. Korshin (Menston, Yorkshire: Scolar Press, 1972), pp. 84–86.

64. "An act for safety and preservation of his Majesty's person and government against treasonable and seditious practices and attempts," 13 Caroli II.c.1 (1661), in *Statutes at Large*, ed. Pickering, 8:2; "The Trial of John Twyn," in *A Complete Collection of State Trials*, ed. Howell and Howell, vol. 6, col. 513. For a discussion of the significance of the modifications made by "An act for the safety and preservation" in the treason statute of Edward III, see Havighurst, "Judiciary and Politics in the Reign of Charles II," part 1, "1660–1676," *Law Quarterly Review* 66 (1950): 68–69.

65. *A True Copy of a Letter (intercepted) going for Holland. . . .* (London, Printed for H.B. at his Holinesses Gun in Pouls Church-yard, where they will be Delivered to you Gratis, Feb. 10 1680). This pretended letter is addressed to "Honest Roger" and signed "H.B."

66. For the modern text of the poem, and a discussion of some of its bibliographical history, see *Poems on Affairs of State*, ed. Lord, 2:425–31.

67. One of the most amusing sidelights of College's trial is the way in which it utterly blasted Dugdale's credibility as a witness concerning the Popish Plot. Dugdale had become one of the government's chief witnesses in the Plot trials, College himself having praised his honesty during the trial of Lord Stafford, a fact that L'Estrange used against College in *The Observator*, No. 33, 13 July 1681. During College's trial, however, Dugdale's testimony directly contradicted Oates's, who, defending College, appeared for the first time against the government. To undermine Dugdale, Oates claimed "there was a report given out by Mr. Dugdale's means, that Mr. Dugdale was poisoned; and in truth, my lord, it was but the Pox." Dugdale vehemently denied the charge, claiming that "if any Doctor will come forth, and say he cured me of a clap or any such thing, I will stand guilty of all that is imputed to me" (641). An entry of 15 Oct. 1681 in the *Calendar of State Papers. Domestic. 1680–81* provides the sequel: "At Council yesterday Mr. Dugdale having complained against Dr. Lower and

others for reporting he had been cured of a venereal disease, the doctor appeared and with him the apothecary and chirurgean, to whom, on Mr. Dugdale's application to the doctor, he had directed prescriptions for his distemper, which bills were produced and together with what was affirmed *viva voce* by the doctor and others the Board was satisfied that Dugdale had not been scandalized. The Lord Chancellor gave him a sharp reprimand on hearing the matter, which is the more remarkable in regard that Dugdale put the verity of his whole evidence against College under the falsity of that assertion" (517–18).

68. Sir Roger North, *Examen*, pp. 572–73.

69. *Calendar of State Papers. Domestic. 1680–81*, Secretary Jenkins to the Sheriff of Oxfordshire, 22 Aug. 1681, p. 412.

70. *A Letter Written From Oxford By Mr. Stephen Colledge To his Friends in London, &c.* Written by Himself, Immediately after his Condemnation (London, 1681).

71. *Calendar of State Papers. Domestic. 1680–81*, Secretary Jenkins to the Bishop of Oxford, 22 Aug. 1681, p. 413; Thomas Hyde, Librarian and Archdeacon of Gloucester, to Sir Leoline Jenkins, 27 Aug. 1681, p. 421; Secretary Jenkins to the Bishop of Oxford, 29 Aug. 1681, p. 423.

72. *The Last Speech and Confession of Mr. Stephen Colledge, Who was Executed at Oxford on Wednesday August 31. 1681* (London, Printed for A. Banks, 1681).

73. Jonathan Dollimore and Alan Sinfield, "History and Ideology: The Instance of *Henry V*," in *Alternative Shakespeares*, ed. John Drakakis (London: Routledge, 1985), p. 217. For an examination of the ideological significance of the seventeenth-century genre of the dying confession, see J.A. Sharpe, " 'Last Dying Speeches': Religion, Ideology and Public Execution in Seventeenth-Century England," *Past and Present* 107 (1985): 144–67.

74. *The Impartial Protestant Mercury*, No. 38, Tuesday, 30 Aug. to Friday 2 Sept. 1681.

75. For speculation about the origins of this confession see *Calendar of State Papers. Domestic. 1680–81*, Newsletter to Roger Garstell, Newcastle, 3 Sept. 1681, p. 438: "The paper mentioned in my last printed for one Banks as Mr. College's speech with his name thereto is by all believed a forgery and it is said, was printed by Nathaniel Thomson and that Banks was his servant."

76. *A True Copy of the Dying Words of Mr. Stephen Colledge, left in Writing under his own Hand* . . . (London, Printed for Edith Colledge, 1681).

77. L'Estrange, *Notes Upon Stephen College*, pp. 47–48.

78. "A Modest Reply To a too Hasty and Malicious Libel, Entituled, An Elegy on Mr. Stephen Colledge, Vulgarly known by the Name of the Protestant Joyner" (London, Printed for R. Janeway, 1681). Janeway here responds to a Tory elegy that pretends to celebrate College but really degrades him: "A Poem (By way of Elegie) Upon Mr Stephen Colledge, Vulgarly known by the Name of the Protestant Joyner" (London, 1681).

79. "The Whiggs Lamentation for the Death of their Dear Brother Colledge, The Protestant Joyner" (London, 1681).

80. "Stephen Colledge's Ghost to the Fanatical Cabal" (n.p., 1681).

81. *Strange News from Newgate; Or, A Relation how the Ghost of Colledge the Protestant-Joyner* . . . (n.p., 1683).

82. Michel Foucault, "What Is an Author?" in *Textual Strategies*, ed. Harari, p. 149.

83. The government had attempted from the very beginning to undermine College's credibility by implying that for all his Protestant rhetoric he was in fact a Papist. L'Estrange dismisses the government rumours that allegedly proved this charge, though he then goes on to ridicule College's religion as "a meer *Enthusiastical Whimsie*," insisting that while College flirted with various independent sects, "yet he is neither *one* nor the *other* . . . yet a Friend to *all* but the *Right*" (8).

84. Luttrell, *Brief Historical Relation*, entries for 11 and 18 June 1684, 1:309, 311.

85. Kamuf, *Signature Pieces*, pp. 58–59.

Conclusion

1. For biographical data on Sidney, see John Carswell, *The Porcupine: The Life of Algernon Sidney* (London: John Murray, 1989); Alan Craig Houston, *Algernon Sidney and the Republican Heritage in England and America* (Princeton: Princeton Univ. Press, 1991), pp. 15–67; Jonathan Scott, *Algernon Sidney and the English Republic, 1623–1677* (Cambridge: Cambridge Univ. Press, 1988), and *Algernon Sidney and the Restoration Crisis, 1677–1683* (Cambridge: Cambridge Univ. Press, 1991); Blair Worden, "The Commonwealth Kidney of Algernon Sidney," *Journal of British Studies* 24 (1985): 3–13.

2. "The Trial of Algernon Sidney, at the King's-Bench, for High Treason," in *A Complete Collection of State Trials*, ed. Howell and Howell, vol. 9, col. 818. All references to this trial are to this volume.

3. The question of how many witnesses were needed to prove a defendent guilty of treason was not a simple one: see Bellamy, *Tudor Law of Treason*, pp. 152–62, and Holdsworth, *A History of English Law*, 9:206–7, for the problems created in this regard by the plethora of overlapping statutes legislating the crime of treason. In Sidney's trial the government could produce only one witness, William, third baron Howard of Escrick, who could directly testify to the alleged conspiracy. According to Jeffreys, however, "in case there be but one witness to prove a direct treason, and another witness to a circumstance that contributes to that treason, that will make two witnesses to prove the treason" (892). Because of this question about witnesses, the libel proved crucial to the government's case; as Jeffreys noted about the state's evidence near the end of the trial, "so that it is not upon two, but it is upon greater evidence of

22, if you believe this book was writ by him" (893). In the minds of many contemporaries, the government played fast and loose on this point: Evelyn complained in his diary that Sidney was convicted "upon the single Wittnesse of that monster of a man the L: *Howard* of Eskrick" (*The Diary*, entry for 5 Dec. 1683, 4:353), as did Burnet: "Howard was the only evidence against the prisoners of better rank" (Gilbert Burnet, *Burnet's History of My Own Time*, ed. Osmund Airy [Oxford: Clarendon Press, 1897–1900], 2:400).

4. The unpublished nature of the libel, like the one witness, concerned many of Sidney's contemporaries. According to Doreen J. Milne, "The Results of the Rye House Plot and Their Influence Upon the Revolution of 1688," *Transactions of the Royal Historical Society*, 5th ser. 1 (1951): 91–108, using Sidney's "unprinted manuscripts as direct evidence against him . . . was widely regarded as an unreasonable straining of the law" (97). According to Burnet, "whatever was in those papers, they were his own private thoughts and speculations of government, never communicated to any" (*Burnet's History*, 2:402).

5. Patterson, *Censorship and Interpretation*, p. 7. See pages x–xx for a discussion of how the term "closet" figures in sixteenth- and seventeenth-century attempts to define an author's freedom from state interference.

Bibliography

Primary Sources

(Place of publication for early printed books is London unless otherwise stated.)

An Account of the Tryal of Mr. Stephen Colledge At Oxford, August the 17th 1681. Where he was found Guilty of High-Treason. N.p., n.d. [Dublin? 1681].

Alfred the Great: Asser's Life of King Alfred and Other Contemporary Sources. Translated by Simon Keyes and Michael Lapidge. London: Penguin Books, 1983.

Allen, Thomas. ΧΕΙΡΕΞΟΚΗ *The Excellency or Handy-Work of the Royal Hand*. 1665.

Ames, Richard. *The Folly of Love; Or, An Essay Upon Satyr Against Woman*. In Nussbaum, *Satires on Women*.

————. *Sylvia's Revenge, Or; A Satyr Against Man; in Answer to the Satyr Against Woman*. 1688.

An Answer to a Scoffing and Lying Lybell Put Forth and Privately Dispersed Under the Title of A Wonderful Account of the Curing the Kings-Evil, by Madam Fanshaw the Duke of Monmouth's Sister. 1681.

Aquinas, St. Thomas. *Summa theologica*. Translated by Fathers of the English Dominican Province. 3 vols. New York: Benziger Brothers, 1947.

Arber, Edward, ed. *A Transcript of the Registers of the Company of Stationers of London; 1554–1640 A.D.* 5 vols. 1875–1894. Reprinted, Gloucester, Mass.: Peter Smith, 1967.

[Atkyns, Richard.] *The Original and Growth of Printing*. N.p., n.d. [1660].

Atkyns, Richard. *The Original and Growth of Printing: Collected Out of History, and the Records of this Kingdome. Wherein is also Demonstrated, That Printing appertaineth to the Prerogative Royal; and it is a Flower of the Crown of England*. 1664.

Aubrey, John. *Miscellanies*. 1696.

Baker, Sir Richard. *A Chronicle of the Kings of England From the time of the Romans Government unto the Death of King James. Containing all Passages of State and Church, with all other observations proper for a Chronicle. Faithfully*

Collected out of Authours Ancient and Moderne; and digested into a new Method. Where unto is now added ye reigne of King Charles ye I. And the first thirteen Years of the Reign of King Charles the II. 1670.

Beckett, William. A Free and Impartial Enquiry Into the Antiquity and Efficacy of Touching for the Cure of the King's Evil. Written some time since, in Two Letters: The One to Dr. Steigertahl, Physician to his Majesty, Fellow of the College of Physicians, and of the Royal Society; the Other to Sir Hans Sloane, Bart. President of the College of Physicians, and Vice-President of the Royal Society. Now first published, in order to a compleat Confutation of that supposed supernatural Power, lately justified in a Pamphlet, intituled, A Letter from a Gentleman at Rome, to his Friend in London, &c. To Which is added, A Collection of Records. 1722.

Bigmore, E. C., and C.W.H. Wyman. A Bibliography of Printing. 3 vols. 1880–1886. Reprinted, New York: Philip C. Duschnes, 1945.

Bird, John. Ostenta Carolina: Or The Late Calamities of England With the Authors of Them. The Great Happiness and Happy Government of K. Charles II Ensuing, Miraculously Foreshewn by the Finger of God in Two Wonderful Diseases, the Rekets and Kings-Evil: Wherein is Also Shewn and Proved, I. That the Rekets After a While Shall Seize on No More Children, But Quite Vanish Through the Mercy of God, and By Meanes of K. Charles II. II. That K. Charles II is the Last of Kings Which Shall So Heal the Kings-Evil. 1661.

Blount, Thomas. Boscobel: Or, The History of His Sacred Majesties Most miraculous Preservation After the Battle of Worchester, 3. Sept. 1651. 1660.

Boyle, Robert. The Works of the Honourable Robert Boyle. Edited by Andrew Millar. 5 vols. 1744.

A Brief Discourse Concerning Printing and Printers. 1663.

Broadley, A.M., ed. The Royal Miracle: A Collection of Rare Tracts, Broadsides, Letters, Prints, and Ballads concerning the Wanderings of Charles II after the Battle of Worcester (September 3–October 15, 1651). London: Stanley Paul, 1912.

Brown, Tom. Letters from the Dead to the Living. 1702.

Browne, John. Adenochoiradelogia: Or, An Anatomick-Chirurgical Treatise of Glandules & Strumaes, Or Kings-Evil-Swellings. Together with the Royal Gift of Healing, Or Cure thereof by Contact or Imposition of Hands, Performed for Above 640 Years by Our Kings of England, Continued with Their Admirable Effects, and Miraculous Events; and Concluded with Many Wonderful Examples of Cures by Their Sacred Touch. 1684.

———. Charisma Basilicon, Or, The Royal Gift of Healing Strumaes, Or Kings-Evil Swellings by Contact, or Imposition of the Sacred Hands of Our Kings of England and of France, Given Them at Their Inaugurations. 1684.

Bryant, Arthur, ed. The Letters, Speeches, and Declarations of King Charles II. London: Cassell, 1935.

Bulstrode, Sir Richard. Memoirs And Reflections Upon the Reign and Government of King Charles the Ist. and K. Charles the IId. Containing an Account of several remarkable Facts not mentioned by other Historians of those Times: Wherein the Character of the Royal Martyr, and of King Charles II. are Vindicated from Fanatical Aspersions. 1721.

Burnet, Gilbert. Burnet's History of My Own Time. Edited by Osmund Airy. 2 vols. Oxford: Clarendon Press, 1897–1900.

Calendar of State Papers. Domestic. 1631–1633; 1637; 1661–1662; 1663–1664; 1665–1666; 1675–1676; 1680–1681.

"A Canto on the New Miracle wrought by the D. of M. curing a young Wench of the Kings Evil, as it is related at large by B. Harris in his Prot. Intelligence, publish'd Friday Jan. 7th. 1681. to prevent false Reports." N.p., n.d.

Chamberlayne, Edward. Angliae Notitia, or The Present State of England: Together With Divers Reflections Upon the Antient State Thereof. 1669.

The Character of Those Two Protestants in Masquerade, Heraclitus, and The Observator. 1681.

A Choice Collection of 120 Loyal Songs: All of them written since the Two late Plots, (viz.) The Horrid Salamanca Plot in 1678 And the Fanatical Conspiracy in 1683. Intermixt with some New Love Songs With a Table to find every Song To which is added, An Anagram, and an Accrostic on the Salamanca Doctor. 1684.

A Choice Collection of Wonderful Miracles, Ghosts, and Visions. 1681.

Cleveland, John. The Poems of John Cleveland. Edited by Brian Morris and Eleanor Withington. Oxford: Clarendon Press, 1967.

Clowes, William. A Right Frutefull and Approoved Treatise, for the Artificiall Cure of that Malady called in Latin Struma, and in English, the Evill, Cured by Kinges and Queenes of England. Very Necesssary for All Young Practizers of Chyrurgery. 1602.

Cobbett's Parliamentary History of England From the Earliest Period to the Year 1803. 36 vols. London, 1806–1820.

A Collection of Scarce and Valuable Tracts, On the Most Interesting and Entertaining Subjects: But Chiefly Such as relate to the History and Constitution of these Kingdoms. Selected from an infinite Number in Print and Manuscript, in the Royal, Cotton, Sion, and other Publick, as well as Private Libraries; Particularly that of the Late Lord Sommers. 4 vols. 1748.

A Compleat Catalogue of All the Stitch'd Books and Single Sheets Printed since the First Discovery of The Popish Plot, (September 1678.) to January 1679/80. To which is Added a Catalogue of all His Majesties Proclamations, Speeches, and Declarations, with the Orders of the King and Council, and what Acts of Parliament have been Published since the Plot. 1680.

A Continuation of the Compleat Catalogue of Stitch'd Books and Single Sheets, &. Printed since the First Discovery of the Popish Plot, September 1678. From the 1st of January 1679/80 to the 25th of June. 1680. 1680.

Conway Letters: The Correspondence of Anne, Viscountess Conway, Henry More, and Their Friends, 1642–1684. Edited by Marjorie Hope Nicolson. New Haven: Yale Univ. Press, 1930.

Cowley, Abraham. *Ode, Upon The Blessed Restoration and Returne of His Sacred Majestie, Charls the Second.* 1660.

Crist, Timothy, ed. *Charles II to Lord Taaffe: Letters in Exile.* Cambridge: Rampant Lions Press, 1974.

Crowne, John. *City Politiques.* Edited by John Harold Wilson. London: Edward Arnold, 1967.

Dauncey, John. *An Exact History of the several Changes of Government In England, From the horrid Murther of King Charles I. to the happy Restauration of King Charles II. With The Renowned Actions of General Monck.* 1660.

———. *The History of His Sacred Majesty Charles the II. Third Monarch of Great Britain. Crowned King of Scotland, At Scoone the first of January 1650. Begun from the Death of his Royall Father of Happy Memory, and continued to the present year 1660.* 1660.

"A Dialogue, Between The Dutchess of Portsmouth, and Madam Gwin, at parting." 1682.

Drake, Judith. *An Essay in Defence of the Female Sex.* 1696.

Dryden, John. *The Works of John Dryden.* Edited by H.T. Swedenberg, Jr., *et al.* 20 vols. Berkeley: Univ. of California Press, 1956–.

Egerton, Sarah Fyge. *The Female Advocate: Or, An Answer To a Late Satyr Against the Pride, Lust and Inconstancy of Woman.* 1686.

Eglesfield, Francis. *Monarchy Revived, in The Most Illustrious Charles The Second. Whose Life and Reign Is Exactly Described in the ensuing Discourse.* 1661.

Elton, G.R., ed. *The Tudor Constitution: Documents and Commentary.* 2nd ed. Cambridge: Cambridge Univ. Press, 1982.

Englands Joy or A Relation of The Most Remarkable passages, from his Majesties Arrivall at Dover, to His entrance at White-hall. 1660.

Englands Triumph. A More Exact History of His Majesties Escape After the Battle of Worcester, With A Chronologicall Discourse of His Straits and dangerous Adventures into France, and His Removes from place to place till His return into England, with the most Remarkable Memorials since, to this present September, 1660. 1660.

Evelyn, John. *The Diary of John Evelyn.* Edited by E.S. De Beer. 6 vols. Oxford: Clarendon Press, 1955.

An Exact Narrative and Relation Of His Most Sacred Majesties Escape from Worcester on the third of September, 1651. Till his Arrivall at Paris. 1660.

Female Excellence: or, Woman Displayed, in Several Satyrick Poems. 1679.

Fern, Thomas. *A Perfect Cure for the King's Evil, (Whether Hereditary or Accidental,) By Effectual Alcalious Medicines: Faithfully Approv'd by the Experience of Eighteen Years Practice, and the Testimony of Above Four Hundred Patients Restor'd Beyond Relapse.* N.d. [1709].

Filmer, Sir Robert. *Patriarcha and Other Political Works of Sir Robert Filmer*. Edited by Peter Laslett. Oxford: Basil Blackwell, 1949.

Firth, C.H., and R.S. Rait, eds. *Acts and Ordinances of the Interregnum, 1642–1660*. 3 vols. London: Wyman and Sons, 1911.

Ford, Simon. ΠΑΡΆΛΛΗΛΑ; *Or The Loyall Subjects Exultation For the Royall Exiles Restauration. In The Parallel of K. David and Mephibosheth on the one side; And Our Gracious Sovereign K. Charls, and his loving Subjects, on the Other. Set forth in A Sermon Preached at All-Saints Church in Northhampton, Jun. 28. 1660. Being The Day appointed for Solemn Thanksgiving for his Royal Majesties happy Restitution*. 1660.

Fox, Margaret Askew Fell. *Womens Speaking Justified, Proved and Allowed of by the Scriptures*. 1667.

A full & perfect Relation of the great & bloody fight At Worcester on Wednesday Night Last Being the 3, of Septemb. 1651 between the Parliaments Forces & the King of Scots: With the true particulars thereof, and the manner of the Fight shewing How Charles Stuart (their Captain Gen) & Major Gen Massey charged in the Van, and his Excellency the Lord General Cromwell in person against them. Together with the taking or killing of the said Charles Stuart. 1651. In Broadley, *The Royal Miracle*, pp. 299–301.

Gerbier, Charles. *Elogium Heroinum: Or, The Praise of Worthy Women*. 1651.

Gibbs, Dr. James. *Observations of Various Eminent Cures of Scrophulous Distempers Commonly Call'd the King's Evil; Such as Tumours, Ulcers, Cariosity of Bones, Blindness and Consumptions: With Some New Considerations of the Structure of the Glands, and of Animal Secretion; Of the Influence of the Moon on Human Bodies, Mechanically Explain'd; and Other Phaenomena Relating to the Causes of Scrophulous Diseases. To Which Is Added, An Essay, Concerning the Animal Spirits, and the Cure of Convulsions: Together with a Short Account of the Forms and Qualities of the Essential Particles of Salts and Sulphers*. 1712.

Glanvil, Joseph. *Saducismus Triumphatus: Or, Full and Plain Evidence Concerning Witches and Apparitions. In Two Parts. The First Treating of Their Possibility, The Second of Their Real Existence. With a Letter of Dr. Henry More on the Same Subject. And an Authentick, But Wonderful Story of Certain Swedish Witches; Done Into English by Anth. Horneck. Preacher at the Savoy*. 1681.

Gould, Robert. *Love Given O're: Or, A Satyr Against the Pride, Lust, and Inconstancy, Etc. of Woman*. 1682.

Granger, James. *A Biographical History of England, From Egbert the Great to the Revolution: Consisting of Characters disposed in different Classes, and adapted to a Methodological Catalogue of Engraved British Heads: Intended as An Essay towards reducing our Biography to System, and a Help to the Knowledge of Portraits*. 3rd ed. 4 vols. 1779.

Greatraks, Valentine. *A Brief Account of Mr. Valentine Greatraks, and Divers of* the Strange Cures By Him Lately Performed. Written By Himself in a Letter Addressed to the Honourable Robert Boyle Esq. Whereunto are Annexed the Testimonials of Several Emminent and Worthy Persons of the Chief Matters of Fact Therein Related. 1666.

Gregory, Francis. *David's Returne From His Banishment. Set forth in a Thanks-giving Sermon for the Returne of his Sacred Majesty Charles the II. And Preached at St Maries in Oxon. May 27. 1660.* Oxford, 1660.

Hamilton, Anthony. *The Memoirs of Count De Gramont.* Edited by Allan Fea. London: Bickers and Son, 1906.

The Harleian Miscellany: Or, A Collection of Scarce, Curious, and Entertaining Pamphlets and Tracts, As well in Manuscript as in Print, Found in the late Earl of Oxford's Library. Interspersed With Historical, Political, and Critical Notes. 8 vols. 1744–1746.

Harrison's Description of England In Shakespeare's Youth. Being the Second and Third Books of His Description of Britain and England. Part I. The Second Book. Edited by Frederick J. Furnivall. London: N. Trubner & Co., 1877.

"Have You Any Work for a Cooper: Or, A Comparison Betwixt a Cooper's, and a Joyner's Trade, / Wherein their Qualities are both display'd: / But still the cooper, as you Here may find, / The Joyner does Excell in ev'ry kind." 1681.

Herbert, Sir Percy. *The Princess Cloria: Or, The Royal Romance. In Five Parts. Imbellished with divers Political Notions, and singular Remarks of Modern Transactions. Containing The Story of most part of Europe, for many Years last past.* 1661.

His Grace the Duke of Monmouth Honoured in His Progress In the West of England In An Account Of a most Extraordinary Cure of the Kings Evil: Given in a Letter from Crookhorn in the County of Somerset from the Minister of the Parish and many others. 1680.

Historical Manuscripts Commission Reports: 7th Rept.: App., MSS. of Lord Sackville and Sir H. Verney.

Hobbes, Thomas. *Leviathan.* Edited by C.B. Macpherson. London: Penguin, 1968.

Howell, James. *The Parly of Beasts; or, Morphandra Queen of the Inchanted Iland.* 1660.

Howell, T.B., and T.J. Howell, eds. *A Complete Collection of State Trials and Proceedings for High Treason and Other Crimes and Misdemeanors From the Earliest Period to the Year 1783.* 33 vols. London: 1816–1828.

Hughes, Paul L., and James F. Larkin, eds. *Tudor Royal Proclamations.* 3 vols. New Haven: Yale Univ. Press, 1964–1969.

The Impartial Protestant Mercury. No. 35, Friday, Aug. 19, to Tuesday, Aug. 23, 1681; no. 38, Tuesday, Aug. 30, to Friday, Sept. 2, 1681.

The Intelligencer, 31 Aug. 1663; 13 July 1665; 27 July 1665; 7 Aug. 1665; 21 Aug. 1665.

Jones, Henry. "The Royal Patient Traveller, or, The wonderful Escapes of His Sacred Majesty King Charles the Second from Worcester-Fight; And his making a Hollow Oke his Royall Pallace. The going in a Livery Cloak with Mrs. Lane. And the Discourse between the Kings Majesty, and the Cook-maid imploying the King to wind up the Jack; but being not used to do it, did wind it up the wrong way." N.d. In Broadley, *The Royal Miracle*, pp. 93–97.

Journals of the House of Commons. Vols. 5 and 9.

Jupp, Edward Basil, and William Willmer Pocock. *An Historical Account of the Worshipful Company of Carpenters of the City of London Compiled Chiefly From Records in Their Possession*. 2nd ed. London: Pickering and Chatto, 1887.

Kenyon, J. P., ed. *The Stuart Constitution: Documents and Commentary*. Cambridge: Cambridge Univ. Press, 1986.

La Barre, François Poullain de. *The Woman as Good as the Man: Or, The Equality of Both Sexes*. Translated by A.L. 1677.

La Chambre, Marin Cureau de. *The Art of How to Know Men*. Translated by John Davies. 1665.

Larkin, James F., and Paul L. Hughes, eds. *Royal Proclamations of King James I, 1603–1625*. Vol. 1 of *Stuart Royal Proclamations*. Oxford: Clarendon Press, 1973.

The Last Speech and Confession of Mr. Stephen Colledge, Who was Executed at Oxford on Wednesday August 31. 1681. 1681.

L'Estrange, Sir Roger. *Considerations and Proposals In Order to the Regulation of the Press: Together with Diverse Instances of Treasonous, and Seditious Pamphlets, Proving the Necessity thereof*. 1663.

————. "Minutes of a Project for Preventing Libels." In Lord, *Classical Presences*, p. 115.

————. *A Momento. Treating, Of the Rise, Progress, and Remedies of Seditions: With Some Historical Reflections Upon the Series of Our Late Troubles*. 2nd ed. 1682.

————. *Notes Upon Stephen College. Grounded Principally upon his own Declarations and Confessions, And freely submitted to Publique Censure*. 2nd ed. 1681.

————. *A Short Answer to a Whole Litter of Libels*. 1680.

————. *A Word Concerning Libels and Libellers, Humbly Presented to the Right Honorable Sir John Moor, Lord-Mayor of London, and the Right Worshipfull the Aldermen his Brethren*. 1681.

A Letter concerning the Tryal at Oxford of Stephen College, August 17. 1681. 1681.

A Letter from a Gentleman at Rome, To His Friend in London; Giving An Account of some very surprizing Cures in the King's-Evil by the Touch, lately effected in the Neighborhood of that City. Wherein is contained, The compleatest History of this miraculous Power, formerly practised by the

Kings of England, ever yet made publick; the Certainty of which is confirmed by the most eminent Writers of this Nation, both Catholicks and Protestants, as Malmsbury, Alured, Brompton, Polidore Virgil, Harpsfield, &c. and Tooker, Heylin, Collier, Echard, &c. Translated from the Italian. 1721.

A Letter from a Gentleman in London to his Friend in the Countrey, on the Occasion of the Late Tryal of Stephen Colledge. N.p., n.d. [1681].

A Letter From Mr. Stephen Colledge To A Person of Quality, upon his Removal to Oxford, to be Try'd upon an Impeachment of High Treason. 1681.

A Letter From the Grand-Jury of Oxford To the London-Grand-Jury, Relating to the Case of the Protestant-Joyner. 1681.

A Letter of Advice to the Petitioning Apprentices. 1681.

A Letter Written from Oxford By Mr. Stephen Colledge To his Friends in London, &. 1681.

A Letter Written from the Tower by Mr. Stephen Colledge (the Protestant-Joyner) To Dick Janeways Wife. 1681.

Lloyd, David. *Wonders No Miracles; Or, Mr. Valentine Greatrates Gift of Healing Examined, Upon occasion of a Sad Effect of His Stroaking, March the 7. 1665. at one Mr. Cressets House in Charter-House-Yard. In a Letter to a Reverend Divine, living neer that place.* 1666.

The London Printer his Lamentation; or, The Press oppressed, or overpressed, September, 1660. In *The Harleian Miscellany,* 3:277–82.

Lord, George deForest, et al., ed. *Poems on Affairs of State: Augustan Satirical Verse, 1660–1714.* 7 vols. New Haven: Yale Univ. Press, 1963–1975.

Lower, Sir William. *A Relation in Form of a Journal, of the Voyage and Residence which the most Excellent and most Mighty Prince Charles the II King of Great Britain, &c. Hath Made in Holland, From the 25 of May, to the 2 of June, 1660.* The Hague, 1660.

"The Loyal Subjects Hearty Wishes to King Charles the Second." N.d. [1660?]

Luttrell, Narcissus. *A Brief Historical Relation of State Affairs from September 1678 to April 1714.* 6 vols. 1857. Reprinted, London: Gregg International, 1969.

Makin, Bathsua. *An Essay to Revive the Antient Education of Gentlewomen.* 1673.

Marguetel de Saint-Denis, Charles, seigneur de Saint-Évremond. *Miscellany Essays: By Monsieur de St. Evremont, Upon Philosophy, History, Poetry, Morality, Humanity, Gallantry, &c.* 2 vols. 1692–1694.

Marvell, Andrew. *The Poems and Letters of Andrew Marvell.* Edited by H.M. Margoliouth. 2nd ed. 2 vols. Oxford: Clarendon Press, 1952.

———. *The Rehearsal Transpos'd and The Rehearsal Transpos'd, The Second Part.* Edited by D.I.B. Smith. Oxford: Clarendon Press, 1971.

Matthews, William, ed. *Charles II's Escape from Worcester: A Collection of Narratives Assembled by Samuel Pepys.* Berkeley: Univ. of California Press, 1966.

Milton, John. *John Milton: Complete Poems and Major Prose*. Edited by Merritt Y. Hughes. New York: Odyssey Press, 1957.

"A Modest Reply To a too Hasty and Malicious Libel, Entituled, An Elegy on Mr. Stephen Colledge, Vulgarly known by the Name of The Protestant Joyner." 1681.

A Modest Vindication of the Proceedings of the late Grand-Jury at the Old Baily, who returned the Bill against Stephen Colledge Ignoramus. 1681.

Monck, George, duke of Albemarle. *Observations Upon Military and Political Affairs*. 1796.

Mysogynus: Or, A Satyr Upon Women. 1682.

Neville, Henry. *The Isle of Pines, or, A late Discovery of a fourth Island in Terra Australis, Incognita*. 1668.

North, Sir Roger. *Examen: Or, An Enquiry into the Credit and Veracity of a Pretended Complete History; Showing The Perverse and Wicked Design of it, And the Many Falsities and Abuses of Truth contained in it. Together with some Memoirs Occasionally inserted. All tending to vindicate the Honour of the late King Charles The Second, and his Happy Reign, from the intended Aspersions of that Foul Pen*. 1740.

Nussbaum, Felicity A., ed. *Satires on Women*. Augustan Reprint Society 180. Los Angeles: William Andrews Clark Memorial Library, 1976.

The Observator. No. 31, Thursday, July 7, 1681; no. 32, Saturday, July 9, 1681; no. 33, 13 July 1681; no. 40, Saturday, Aug. 6, 1681; no. 48, Wednesday, Aug. 31, 1681.

Ogilby, John. *The Entertainment of His Most Excellent Majestie Charles II, In His Passage through the City of London To His Coronation: Containing an exact Accompt of the whole Solemnity; the Triumphal Arches, and Cavalcade, delineated in Sculpture; the Speeches and Impresses illustrated from Antiquity*. 1662.

"The Oxford Alderman's Speech to the D. of M. when his Grace made his Entrance into that City about Sept. 1680." N.p., n.d.

The Parliamentary Intelligencer. No. 28. From Monday July 2 to Monday July 9, 1660.

Pepys, Samuel. *The Diary of Samuel Pepys*. Edited by Robert Latham and William Matthews. 11 vols. Berkeley: Univ. of California Press, 1970–1983.

Phillips, Henry Laverock. *Annals of the Worshipful Company of Joiners of the City of London. Extracted From Original Documents, Minute Books, and Renter Warden's Accounts, Etc., From A.D. 1237–1850. Together with a Chronological List of the Feoffees of the Company From A.D. 1497–1885 and An Alphabetical List of the Livery from A.D. 1496–1914, With the Dates of Their Livery*. London: Privately printed, 1915.

Pickering, Danby. *The Statutes at Large. From Magna Charta to the Eleventh Parliament of Gt. Brit., Anno 1761*. 105 vols. Cambridge, 1762–1869.

"A Poem (By way of Elegie) Upon Mr. Stephen Colledge, Vulgarly known by the Name of The Protestant Joyner." 1681.

Political Ballads of the Seventeenth and Eighteenth Centuries. Edited by W. Walker Wilkins. 2 vols. London: Longman, 1860.

Pope, Alexander. *The Complete Poetry of Alexander Pope*. Edited by John Butt, et al. 11 vols. London: Methuen, 1939–1969.

The Protestant (Domestick) Intelligence. Or, News both from City and Country. No. 86, Friday, 7 Jan. 1680 [1681].

The Quenes Maiesties Passage through the Citie of London to Westminster the Day before her Coronacion. 1558. Reprint edited by James M. Osborn. New Haven: Yale Univ. Press, 1960.

The Roxburghe Ballads. Eds. W. Chappell and J. Woodfall Ebsworth. 8 vols. 1869–1895. Reprinted, New York: AMS Press, 1966.

"Rub for Rub: Or, An Answer To A Physicians Pamphlet, Styled, The Stroker stroked." 1666.

"A Satyr Against the Pen-men and Speech-men of the Times." N.p., n.d. [1679].

Savile, George, marquis of Halifax. *A Character of King Charles The Second: And Political, Moral and Miscellaneous Thoughts and Reflections*. 1750.

"Scandal Proof, Or An Heroick Poem On the Renowned Champions of the Good Old Cause, Impudent Dick Janeway, and the rest of the Factious Tribe." 1681.

Scroggs, Sir William. *The Lord Chief-Justice Scroggs's Speech in the King's-Bench, the first Day of this present Michaelmas-Term, 1679, occasioned by many libellous Pamphlets which are published against Law, to the Scandal of the Government, and Public Justice*. 1679.

A Second Continuation of the Compleat Catalogue of Stitch'd Books and Single Sheets Printed since the First Discovery of the Popish Plot, (September 1678.) From the 24th of June to Michaelmas Term 1680. 1680.

Some Modest Reflections upon the Commitment of the Earl of Shaftesbury, Arising from the Late Indictment against Mr. Stephen Colledge. 1681. In *A Collection of Scarce and Valuable Tracts*, 1:134–40.

The Speech and Carriage of Stephen Colledge At Oxford, Before the Castle, on Wednesday August 31. 1681. 1681.

Steele, Robert, ed. *Tudor and Stuart Proclamations, 1485–1714*. 2 vols. Oxford: Clarendon Press, 1910.

"Stephen Colledge's Ghost To The Fanatical Cabal." N.p., 1681.

Strange News from Newgate; Or, A Relation how the Ghost of Colledge the Protestant-Joyner, appeared to Hone the Joyner since his Condemnation: Being an Account of the whole Discourse that past between them. N.p., 1683.

Stubbe, Henry. *The Miraculous Conformist: Or An Account of Severall Marvailous Cures performed by the stroaking of the Hands of Mr. Valentine Greatarick; With a Physicall Discourse thereupon, In a Letter to the Honourable Robert*

Boyle Esq; With a Letter Relating some other of His Miraculous Cures, attested by E. Foxcroft M.A. and Fellow of Kings-Colledge in Cambr: Oxford, 1666.

A Summary of Occurrences, Relating to the Miraculous Preservation Of our late Sovereign Lord King Charles II. After the Defeat of his Army at Worcester in the Year 1651. Faithfully taken from the express Personal Testimony of those two worthy Roman Catholics, Thomas Whitgrave of Moseley, in the County of Stafford Esq; & Mr. John Hudleston Priest, of the holy Order of St. Bennet; the eminent Instruments under God of the same Preservation. 1688.

Tobin, Maurice. A True Account of the Celebrated Secret of Mr Timothy Beaghan, Lately Killed at the Five Bells Tavern in the Strand, Famous for Curing the King's-Evil. In a Letter to Mr. William Cowper, Surgeon. 1697.

To the Kings Most Excellent Majesty. The Humble Petition of Divers Hundreds of the Kings Poore Subjects, Afflicted with that Grievous Infirmitie, Called the Kings Evill. Of which by His Majesties Absence They Have No Possibility of Being Cured, Wanting All Meanes to Gaine Accesse to His Majesty, by Reason of His Abode at Oxford. 1643.

A True and Wonderful Account of a Cure of the Kings-Evil, by Mrs. Fanshaw, Sister to His Grace the Duke of Monmouth. 1681.

A True Copy of a Letter (intercepted) going for Holland. Directed Thus for his (and his Wives) never Failing Friend Roger Le Strange At the Oranges Court with Care and Speed, hast, hast, post hast. 1680.

A True Copy of the Dying Words of Mr. Stephen Colledge, left in Writing under his own Hand, and confirmed by him at the time of Execution, August 31. 1681. at Oxford. Published by his own Relations. 1681.

Vaughan, Henry. The Works of Henry Vaughan. Edited by L.C. Martin. 2nd ed. Oxford: Clarendon Press, 1957.

Vickers, William. An Easie and Safe Method for Curing the King's Evil. With Several Observations Which May be of Use and Service to People Afflicted with that Distemper. To Which Is Added, A Speciman of Success, In a Faithful Relation of Many Extraordinary Cures on Men, Women, and Children. In a Letter to a Friend. 5th ed. 1711.

Von Römer, L.S.A.M., ed. Rochester's Sodom: Herausgegeben nach dem Hamburger Manuscript. Paris: H. Welter, 1904.

[Wade, John.] "The Royall Oak: Or, The wonderful travells, miraculous escapes, strange accidents of his sacred Majesty King Charles the Second." N.d.

Walsh, William. A Dialogue Concerning Women, Being a Defence of the Sex. Written to Eugenia. 1691.

Werenfels, Samuel. A Dissertation Upon Superstition in Natural Things. To which are added, Occasional Thoughts On the Power of Curing the King's-Evil Ascribed to the Kings of England. 1748.

"Whig and Tory, Or the Scribling Duellists." 1681.

"The Whigs Lamentation for the Death of their Dear Brother Colledge, The Protestant Joyner." 1681.

Whitaker, Edward. *A Letter from Mr. Edward Whitaker To the Protestant Joyner Upon his Bill being sent to Oxford*. 1681.

Wilmot, John, earl of Rochester. *The Complete Poems of John Wilmot, Earl of Rochester*. Edited by David M. Vieth. New Haven: Yale Univ. Press, 1968.

Wiseman, Richard. *Severall Chiruricall Treatises*. 1676.

Wonders If Not Miracles Or, A Relation of the Wonderful Performances of Valentine Gertrux Of Affance neer Youghall in Ireland. Who Cureth All Manner of Diseases with a Stroak of His Hand and Prayer, as Is Testified by Many Eare and Eye Witnesses. 1665.

Secondary Sources

Abrams, Philip, and E.A. Wrigley, eds. *Towns in Societies: Essays in Economic History and Historical Sociology*. Cambridge: Cambridge Univ. Press, 1978.

Allen, David. "Political Clubs in Restoration London." *The Historical Journal* 19 (1976): 561–80.

Armstrong, Nancy. *Desire and Domestic Fiction: A Political History of the Novel*. Oxford: Oxford Univ. Press, 1987.

Backscheider, Paula R. *Spectacular Politics: Theatrical Power and Mass Culture in Early Modern England*. Baltimore: Johns Hopkins Univ. Press, 1993.

Barker, Francis. *The Tremulous Private Body: Essays on Subjection*. London: Methuen, 1984.

Barlow, Frank. "The King's Evil." *English Historical Review* 95 (1980): 3–27.

Baudrillard, Jean. "The Structural Law of Value and the Order of Simulacra." In Fekete, *The Structural Allegory*, pp. 54– 73.

Baumann, Gerd, ed. *The Written Word: Literacy in Transition*. Oxford: Clarendon Press, 1986.

Beier, A.L., and Roger Finlay, eds. *London 1500–1700: The Making of the Metropolis*. London: Longman, 1986.

Beier, Lucinda McCray. *Sufferers and Healers: The Experience of Illness in Seventeenth-Century England*. London: Routledge and Kegan Paul, 1987.

Bellamy, John. *The Tudor Law of Treason: An Introduction*. London: Routledge & Kegan Paul, 1979.

Bennett, H.S. *English Books and Readers, 1603 to 1640: Being a Study in the History of the Book Trade in the Reigns of James I and Charles I*. London: Cambridge Univ. Press, 1970.

Bergeron, David M. *English Civic Pageantry, 1558–1642*. Columbia: Univ. of South Carolina Press, 1971.

Berry, Philippa. *Of Chastity and Power: Elizabethan Literature and the Unmarried Queen*. London: Routledge, 1989.

Biersack, Aletta. "Local Knowledge, Local History: Geertz and Beyond." In Hunt, *The New Cultural History*, pp. 72–96.

Black, Jeremy. *The English Press in the Eighteenth Century*. London: Croom Helm, 1987.

Blagden, Cyprian. "The 'Company' of Printers." *Studies in Bibliography* 13 (1960): 3–17.

———. *The Stationers' Company: A History, 1403–1959*. London: Allen & Unwin, 1960.

Bloch, Marc. *The Royal Touch: Sacred Monarchy and Scrofula in England and France*. Translated by J.E. Anderson. London: Routledge and Kegan Paul, 1973.

Blum, Abbe. "The Author's Authority: *Areopagitica* and the Labour of Licensing." In Nyquist and Ferguson, *Re-membering Milton*, pp. 74–96.

Boulton, Jeremy. *Neighbourhood and Society: A London Suburb in the Seventeenth Century*. Cambridge: Cambridge Univ. Press, 1987.

Braverman, Richard. "Capital Relations and *The Way of the World*." *ELH* 52 (1985): 133–58.

Bray, Alan. *Homosexuality in Renaissance England*. London: Gay Men's Press, 1982.

Brewer, John, and John Styles, eds. *An Ungovernable People: The English and Their Law in the Seventeenth and Eighteenth Centuries*. London: Hutchinson, 1980.

Brooks-Davies, Douglas. *The Mercurian Monarch: Magical Politics from Spenser to Pope*. Manchester: Manchester Univ. Press, 1983.

Brown, Laura. *Alexander Pope*. Oxford: Blackwell, 1985.

Burke, Peter. *Popular Culture in Early Modern Europe*. New York: New York Univ. Press, 1978.

———. "Popular Culture in Seventeenth-Century London." In Reay, *Popular Culture in Seventeenth-Century England*, pp. 31–58.

Burke, Peter, and Roy Porter, eds. *The Social History of Language*. Cambridge Studies in Oral and Literate Culture 12. Cambridge: Cambridge Univ. Press, 1987.

Capp, Bernard. "Popular Literature." In Reay, *Popular Culture in Seventeenth-Century England*, pp. 198–243.

Carswell, John. *The Porcupine: The Life of Algernon Sidney*. London: John Murray, 1989.

Carver, Larry. "The Restoration Poets and Their Father King." *Huntington Library Quarterly* 40 (1977): 332–51.

———. "The Texts and the Text of *Sodom*." *The Papers of the Bibliographical Society of America* 73 (1979): 19–40.

Clark, Peter, ed. *The Early Modern Town: A Reader*. London: Longman, 1976.

Clifton, Robin. *The Last Popular Rebellion: The Western Rising of 1685*. London: Maurice Temple Smith, 1984.

Corns, Thomas N., ed. *The Literature of Controversy: Polemical Strategy from Milton to Junius*. London: Frank Cass, 1987.

Crawford, Patricia. "Women's Published Writings, 1660–1700." In Prior, *Women in English Society, 1500–1800*, pp. 211–82.

Crawfurd, Raymond. *The King's Evil*. Oxford: Clarendon Press, 1911.

Cressy, David. "Describing the Social Order of Elizabethan and Stuart England." *Literature and History* 3 (1976): 29–44.

———. *Literacy and the Social Order: Reading and Writing in Tudor and Stuart England*. Cambridge: Cambridge Univ. Press, 1980.

Crist, Timothy. "Government Control of the Press after the Expiration of the Printing Act in 1679." *Publishing History* 5 (1979): 49–77.

Davies, C.S.L. "The Pilgrimage of Grace Reconsidered." In Slack, *Rebellion, Popular Protest and the Social Order in Early Modern England*, pp. 16–38.

———. "Popular Religion and the Pilgrimage of Grace." In Fletcher and Stevenson, *Order and Disorder in Early Modern England*, pp. 58–88.

Dobbs, B. J. T. "Newton as Alchemist and Theologian." In Thrower, *Standing on the Shoulders of Giants*, pp. 128–40.

Dollimore, Jonathan, and Alan Sinfield. "History and Ideology: The Instance of *Henry V*." In Drakakis, *Alternative Shakespeares*, pp. 206–27.

Donnelly, M.L. "Caroline Royalist Panegyric and the Disintegration of a Symbolic Mode." In Summers and Pebworth, *"The Muses Common-Weale,"* pp. 163–76.

Doolittle, I.G. *The City of London and Its Livery Companies*. Dorchester: Gavin Press, 1982.

Downie, J.A. *Robert Harley and the Press: Propaganda and Public Opinion in the Age of Swift and Defoe*. Cambridge: Cambridge Univ. Press, 1979.

Drakakis, John, ed. *Alternative Shakespeares*. London: Routledge, 1985.

Duberman, Martin Bauml, Martha Vicinus, and George Chauncey Jr., eds. *Hidden from History: Reclaiming the Gay and Lesbian Past*. New York: New American Library, 1989.

Duffy, Eamon. "Valentine Greatrakes, the Irish Stroker: Miracle, Science, and Orthodoxy in Restoration England." In Robbins, *Religion and Humanism*, pp. 251–73.

Edie, Carolyn A. "The Popular Idea of Monarchy on the Eve of the Stuart Restoration." *Huntington Library Quarterly* 39 (1976): 343–73.

Eisenstein, Elizabeth L. *The Printing Press as an Agent of Change: Communications and Cultural Transformations in Early-Modern Europe*. 2 vols. Cambridge: Cambridge Univ. Press, 1979.

Elias, Richard. "Political Satire in *Sodom*." *Studies in English Literature* 18 (1978): 423–38.

Ellis, Frank H. " 'Legends no Histories' Part the Second: The Ending of *Absalom and Achitophel*." *Modern Philology* 85 (1988): 393–407.

Elton, G.R. *Policy and Police: The Enforcement of the Reformation in the Age of Thomas Cromwell*. Cambridge: Cambridge Univ. Press, 1972.

Ezell, Margaret J.M. *The Patriarch's Wife: Literary Evidence and the History of the Family*. Chapel Hill: Univ. of North Carolina Press, 1987.

Farquhar, Helen. "Royal Charities" (4 parts). *British Numismatic Journal* 12 (1916): 39–135; 13 (1917): 95–163; 14 (1918): 89–120; 15 (1919–1920): 141–84.

Fekete, John, ed. *The Structual Allegory: Reconstructive Encounters with the New French Thought*. Theory and History of Literature 11. Minneapolis: Univ. of Minnesota Press, 1984.

Ferguson, Moira. *First Feminists*. Bloomington: Indiana Univ. Press, 1985.

Fish, Stanley. "Driving from the Letter: Truth and Indeterminacy in Milton's *Areopagitica*." In Nyquist and Ferguson, *Re-membering Milton*, pp. 234–54.

Fletcher, Anthony, and John Stevenson, eds. *Order and Disorder in Early Modern England*. Cambridge: Cambridge Univ. Press, 1985.

Force, James E. "Newton's 'Sleeping Argument' and the Newtonian Synthesis of Science and Religion." In Thrower, *Standing on the Shoulders of Giants*, pp. 109–27.

Fortescue, G.K., ed. *Catalogue of the Pamphlets, Books, Newspapers, and Manuscripts Relating to the Civil War, the Commonwealth, and Restoration, Collected by George Thomason, 1640–1661*. 2 vols. London: British Museum, 1908.

Foucault, Michel. "What Is an Author?" In Harari, *Textual Strategies*, pp. 141–60.

Frank, Joseph. *The Beginnings of the English Newspaper, 1620–1660*. Cambridge: Harvard Univ. Press, 1961.

Fraser, Antonia. *King Charles II*. London: Macdonald Futura, 1980.

Fraser, Peter. *The Intelligence of the Secretaries of State and Their Monopoly of Licensed News 1660–1688*. Cambridge: Cambridge Univ. Press, 1956.

French, Roger, and Andrew Wear, eds. *The Medical Revolution of the Seventeenth Century*. Cambridge: Cambridge Univ. Press, 1989.

Furley, O.W. "The Whig Exclusionists: Pamphlet Literature in the Exclusion Campaign, 1679–81." *Cambridge Historical Journal* 13 (1957): 19–36.

Gallop, Jane. *Thinking through the Body*. New York: Columbia Univ. Press, 1988.

Gardiner, Anne Barbeau. "John Dryden's Reading of the Ultimate Meaning of History." *Ultimate Reality and Meaning* 12 (1989): 16–29.

———. "The Medal That Provoked a War: Charles II's Lasting Indignation over Adolfzoon's Breda Medal." *The Medal* 17 (1990): 11–15.

George, M. Dorothy. "Elections and Electioneering, 1679–81." *English Historical Review* 45 (1930): 552–78.

———. *English Political Caricature to 1792: A Study of Opinion and Propaganda.* Oxford: Clarendon Press, 1959.

Glass, D.V. "Socio-economic Status and Occupations in the City of London at the End of the Seventeenth Century." In Clark, *The Early Modern Town*, pp. 216–32.

Goldberg, Jonathan. *James I and the Politics of Literature: Jonson, Shakespeare, Donne, and Their Contemporaries.* Baltimore: Johns Hopkins Univ. Press, 1983.

Goody, Jack, ed. *Literacy in Traditional Societies.* Cambridge: Cambridge Univ. Press, 1968.

Greaves, Richard L. *Deliver Us from Evil: The Radical Underground in Britain, 1660–1663.* Oxford: Oxford Univ. Press, 1986.

———. *Enemies under His Feet: Radicals and Nonconformists in Britain, 1664–1677.* Stanford: Stanford Univ. Press, 1990.

Greenberg, David F. *The Construction of Homosexuality.* Chicago: Univ. of Chicago Press, 1988.

Greenblatt, Stephen. *Shakespearean Negotiations: The Circulation of Social Energy in Renaissance England.* Berkeley: Univ. of California Press, 1988.

Greenblatt, Stephen, ed. *The Power of Forms in the English Renaissance.* Norman, Okla.: Pilgrim, 1982.

Guibbory, Achsah. *The Map of Time: Seventeenth-Century English Literature and Ideas of Pattern in History.* Urbana: Univ. of Illinois Press, 1986.

Habermas, Jurgen. *The Structural Transformation of the Public Sphere: An Inquiry into a Category of Bourgeois Society.* Translated by Thomas Burger and Frederick Lawrence. Cambridge: MIT Press, 1989.

Hammond, Brean S. *Pope.* Brighton, Sussex: Harvester Press, 1986.

Harari, Josue V., ed. *Textual Strategies: Perspectives in Post-Structuralist Criticism.* Ithaca: Cornell Univ. Press, 1979.

Harris, Brice. "Captain Robert Julian, Secretary to the Muses." *ELH* 10 (1943): 294–309.

Harris, Tim. *London Crowds in the Reign of Charles II: Propaganda and Politics from the Restoration until the Exclusion Crisis.* Cambridge: Cambridge Univ. Press, 1987.

Havighurst, A.F. "The Judiciary and Politics in the Reign of Charles II." Part 1, "1660–1676." *Law Quarterly Review* 66 (1950): 62–78.

———. "The Judiciary and Politics in the Reign of Charles II." Part 2, "1676–1685." *Law Quarterly Review* 66 (1950): 229–52.

Hayman, Reverend Samuel. "Notes on the Family of Greatrakes" (2 parts). *The Reliquary* 4 (1863): 81–96; 4 (1864):220–36.

Heal, Felicity, and Rosemary O'Day, eds. *Church and Society in England: Henry VIII to James I.* London: Macmillan, 1977.

Helgerson, Richard. "Milton Reads the King's Book: Print, Performance, and the Making of a Bourgeois Idol." *Criticism* 29 (1987): 1–25.

———— Self-Crowned Laureates: Spenser, Jonson, Milton and the Literary System. Berkeley: Univ. of California Press, 1983.

Helm, P.J. Alfred the Great. London: Robert Hale, 1963.

Hetet, John. "The Wardens' Accounts of the Stationers' Company, 1663–79." In Myers and Harris, Economics of the British Booktrade, 1605–1939, pp. 32–59.

Hill, Christopher. "Censorship and English Literature." In Writing and Revolution in 17th Century England. Vol. 1 of The Collected Essays of Christopher Hill. Brighton, Sussex: Harvester Press, 1985, pp. 32–71.

————. Some Intellectual Consequences of the English Revolution. Madison: Univ. of Wisconsin Press, 1980.

Hobby, Elaine. Virtue of Necessity: English Women's Writings, 1649–88. London: Virago, 1988.

Holdsworth, W.S. A History of English Law. 7th ed. revised. 17 vols. London: Methuen, 1956–1972.

Holmes, Geoffrey. Augustan England: Professions, State and Society, 1680–1730. London: Allen & Unwin, 1982.

Horrox, William Arthur. A Bibliography of the Literature Relating to the Escape and Preservation of King Charles II after the Battle of Worcester, 3rd September, 1651. Aberdeen: The Univ. Press, 1924.

Houston, Alan Craig. Algernon Sidney and the Republican Heritage in England and America. Princeton: Princeton Univ. Press, 1991.

Hudson, Anne. Lollards and Their Books. London: Hambledon Press, 1985.

————. The Premature Reformation: Wycliffite Texts and Lollard History. Oxford: Clarendon Press, 1988.

Hughes, Derek. "Providential Justice and English Comedy, 1660–1700: A Review of the External Evidence." Modern Language Review 81 (1986): 273–92.

Hunt, Lynn, ed. The New Cultural History. Berkeley: Univ. of California Press, 1989.

Hunter, J. Paul. Before Novels: The Cultural Contexts of Eighteenth-Century English Fiction. New York: Norton, 1990.

Hutton, Ronald. Charles the Second King of England, Scotland, and Ireland. Oxford: Clarendon Press, 1989.

————. The Restoration: A Political and Religious History of England and Wales, 1658–1667. Oxford: Clarendon Press, 1985.

Irigaray, Luce. Speculum of the Other Woman. Translated by Gillian C. Gill. Ithaca: Cornell Univ. Press, 1985.

Jacob, J.R. Robert Boyle and the English Revolution: A Study in Social and Intellectual Change. New York: Burt Franklin, 1977.

Johnson, J.W. "Did Lord Rochester Write Sodom?" Papers of the Bibliographical Society of America 81 (1987): 119–53.

Jones, J.R. Charles II: Royal Politician. London: Allen and Unwin, 1987.

————. *The First Whigs: The Politics of the Exclusion Crisis 1678–1683*. London: Oxford Univ. Press, 1961.

————. "Parties and Parliament." In Jones, *The Restored Monarchy 1660–1688*, pp. 48–70.

Jones, J.R., ed. *The Restored Monarchy, 1660–1688*. London: Macmillan Press, 1979.

Jones, P.E., and A.V. Judges. "London Population in the Late Seventeenth Century." *Economic History Review* 6 (1935): 45–63.

Jose, Nicholas. *Ideas of the Restoration in English Literature, 1660–71*. Cambridge: Harvard Univ. Press, 1984.

Kahl, William F. *The Development of London Livery Companies: An Historical Essay and a Select Bibliography*. Boston: Baker Library, 1960.

Kamuf, Peggy. *Signature Pieces: On the Institution of Authorship*. Ithaca: Cornell Univ. Press, 1988.

Kantorowicz's, Ernst H. *The King's Two Bodies: A Study in Mediaeval Political Theology*. Princeton: Princeton Univ. Press, 1957.

Kaplan, Barbara Beigun. "Greatrakes the Stroker: The Interpretations of His Contemporaries." *Isis* 73 (1982): 178–85.

Keeble, N.H. *The Literary Culture of Nonconformity in Later Seventeenth-Century England*. Leicester: Leicester Univ. Press, 1987.

Kenyon, John. *The Popish Plot*. London: Penguin, 1972.

Kinnaird, Joan. "Mary Astell and the Conservative Contribution to English Feminism." *Journal of British Studies* 19 (1979): 53–75.

Korshin, Paul J., ed. *Studies in Change and Revolution: Aspects of English Intellectual History, 1640–1800*. Menston, Yorkshire: Scolar Press, 1972.

Kroll, Richard W.F. *The Material Word: Literate Culture in the Restoration and Early Eighteenth Century*. Baltimore: Johns Hopkins Univ. Press, 1991.

Lacey, Douglas R. *Dissent and Parliamentary Politics in England, 1661–1689: A Study in the Perpetuation and Tempering of Parliamentarianism*. New Brunswick: Rutgers Univ. Press, 1969.

Laver, A. Bryan. "Miracles No Wonder! The Mesmeric Phenomena and Organic Cures of Valentine Greatrakes." *Journal of the History of Medicine* 33 (1978): 35–46.

Leinwand, Theodore B. "Negotiation and New Historicism," *PMLA* 105 (1990): 477–90.

Lillywhite, Bryant. *London Coffee Houses: A Reference Book of Coffee Houses of the Seventeenth, Eighteenth, and Nineteenth Centuries*. London: Allen and Unwin, 1963.

Loades, David. *Politics, Censorship and the English Reformation*. London: Pinter, 1991.

Loewenstein, Joseph. "For a History of Literary Property: John Wolfe's Reformation." *English Literary Renaissance* 18 (1988): 389–412.

————. "Legal Proofs and Corrected Readings: Press-Agency and the New

Bibliography." In Miller, O'Dair, and Weber, *The Production of English Renaissance Culture*, pp. 93–122.

———. "The Script in the Marketplace." *Representations* 12 (1985): 101–14.

Logan, Marie-Rose, and Peter L. Rudnytsky, eds. *Contending Kingdoms: Historical, Psychological, and Feminist Approaches to the Literature of Sixteenth-Century England and France*. Detroit: Wayne State Univ. Press, 1991.

Lord, George deForest. *Classical Presences in Seventeenth-Century English Poetry*. New Haven: Yale Univ. Press, 1987.

McKeon, Michael. *The Origins of the English Novel, 1600–1740*. Baltimore: Johns Hopkins Univ. Press, 1987.

———. *Politics and Poetry in Restoration England: The Case of Annus Mirabilis*. Cambridge: Harvard Univ. Press, 1975.

MacLean, Gerald M. *Time's Witness: Historical Representation in English Poetry, 1603–1660*. Madison: Univ. of Wisconsin Press, 1990.

Maguire, Nancy Klein. "The Theatrical Mask/Masque of Politics: The Case of Charles I." *Journal of British Studies* 28 (1989): 1–22.

Marcus, Leah S. "Shakespeare's Comic Heroines, Elizabeth I, and the Political Uses of Androgyny." In Rose, *Women in the Middle Ages and the Renaissance*, pp. 135–54.

Marin, Louis. "The Inscription of the King's Memory: On the Metallic History of Louis XIV." *Yale French Studies* 59 (1980): 17–36.

———. *Portrait of the King*. Translated by Martha M. Houle. Minneapolis: Univ. of Minnesota Press, 1988.

Marotti, Arthur F. *John Donne: Coterie Poet*. Madison: Univ. of Wisconsin Press, 1986.

Mendelson, Sara Heller. *The Mental World of Stuart Women: Three Studies*. Brighton, Sussex: Harvester Press, 1987.

Milhous, Judith, and Robert D. Hume. "Attribution Problems in English Drama, 1660–1700." *Harvard Library Bulletin* 31 (1983): 5–39.

Miller, David Lee. "The Death of the Modern: Gender and Desire in Marlowe's 'Hero and Leander.'" *South Atlantic Quarterly* 88 (1989): 757–87.

———. "Spenser's Poetics: The Poem's Two Bodies." *PMLA* 101 (1986): 170–85.

Miller, David Lee, Sharon O'Dair, and Harold Weber, eds. *The Production of English Renaissance Culture*. Ithaca: Cornell Univ. Press, 1994.

Miller, Edwin Haviland. *The Professionl Writer in Elizabethan England: A Study of Nondramatic Literature*. Cambridge: Harvard Univ. Press, 1959.

Milne, Doreen J. "The Results of the Rye House Plot and Their Influence Upon the Revolution of 1688." *Transactions of the Royal Historical Society*, 5th ser. 1 (1951): 91–108.

Montrose, Louis Adrian. "'Shaping Fantasies': Figurations of Gender and Power in Elizabethan Culture." *Representations* 1 (1983): 61–94.

Moretti, Franco. "'A Huge Eclipse': Tragic Form and the Deconsecration of

Sovereignty." In Greenblatt, *The Power of Forms in the English Renaissance*, pp. 7–40.

Morrill, J.S., and J.D. Waller. "Order and Disorder in the English Revolution." In Fletcher and Stevenson, *Order and Disorder*, pp. 137–65.

Myers, Robin, and Michael Harris, eds. *Economics of the British Booktrade, 1605–1939*. Publishing History Occasional Series I. Cambridge: Chadwyck-Healey, 1985.

Nenner, Howard. *By Colour of Law*. Chicago: Univ. of Chicago Press, 1977.

Nyquist, Mary, and Margaret W. Ferguson, eds. *Re-membering Milton: Essays on the Texts and Traditions*. London: Methuen, 1987.

O'Brien, Patricia. "Michel Foucault's History of Culture." In Hunt, *The New Cultural History*, pp. 25–46.

Ollard, Richard. *The Escape of Charles II after the Battle of Worcester*. London: Hodder and Stoughton, 1966.

————. *The Image of the King: Charles I and Charles II*. New York: Atheneum, 1979.

Palliser, D. M. "Popular Reactions to the Reformation during the Years of Uncertainty 1530–70." In Heal and O'Day, *Church and Society in England*, pp. 35–56.

Patterson, Annabel. *Censorship and Interpretation: The Conditions of Writing and Reading in Early Modern England*. Madison: Univ. of Wisconsin Press, 1984.

Patterson, Lyman Ray. *Copyright in Historical Perspective*. Nashville: Vanderbilt Univ. Press, 1968.

Pearl, Valerie. "Change and Stability in Seventeenth-Century London." *London Journal* 5 (1979): 3–34.

Pelling, Margaret. "Medical Practice in Early Modern England: Trade or Profession?" In Prest, *The Professions in Early Modern England*, pp. 90–128.

Pelling, Margaret, and Charles Webster. "Medical Practitioners." In Webster, *Health, Medicine and Mortality in the Sixteenth Century*, pp. 165–235.

Perry, Ruth. *The Celebrated Mary Astell: An Early English Feminist*. Chicago: Univ. of Chicago Press, 1986.

Plant, Marjorie. *The English Book Trade: An Economic History of the Making and Sale of Books*. 3rd ed. London: Allen & Unwin, 1974.

Pollard, Alfred W. "Some Notes on the History of Copyright in England, 1662–1774." *Library*, 4th series, 3 (1922): 97–114.

Pollard, Graham. "The Early Constitution of the Stationers' Company." *Library*, 4th series, 18 (1937): 235–60.

Porter, Carolyn. "Are We Being Historical Yet?" *South Atlantic Quarterly* 87 (1988): 743–86.

Porter, Roy. *Disease, Medicine and Society in England, 1550–1860*. London: Macmillan, 1987.

————. "The Early Royal Society and the Spread of Medical Information." In

French and Wear, *The Medical Revolution of the Seventeenth Century*, pp. 271–93.

———. "The Language of Quackery in England, 1660–1800." In Burke and Porter, *The Social History of Language*, pp. 73–103.

Potter, Lois. *Secret Rites and Secret Writing: Royalist Literature, 1641–1660*. Cambridge: Cambridge Univ. Press, 1989.

Power, M.J. "The Social Topography of Restoration London." In Beier and Finlay, *London, 1500–1700*, pp. 199–223.

Prest, Wilfrid, ed. *The Professions in Early Modern England*. London: Croom Helm, 1987.

Prior, Mary, ed. *Women in English Society, 1500–1800*. London: Methuen, 1985.

Pye, Christopher. "The Sovereign, the Theater, and the Kingdome of Darknesse: Hobbes and the Spectacle of Power." *Representations* 2 (1984): 85–106.

Rackin, Phyllis. "Genealogical Anxiety and Female Authority: The Return of the Repressed in Shakespeare's Histories." In Logan and Rudnytsky, *Contending Kingdoms*, pp. 323–45.

Rahn, B.J. "A *Ra-ree Show*—A Rare Cartoon: Revolutionary Propaganda in the Treason Trial of Stephen College." In Korshin, *Studies in Change and Revolution*, pp. 77–98.

Rappaport, Steve. *Worlds within Worlds: Structures of Life in Sixteenth-Century London*. Cambridge: Cambridge Univ. Press, 1989.

Reay, Barry. "Popular Culture in Early Modern England." In Reay, *Popular Culture in Seventeenth-Century England*, pp. 1–30.

Reay, Barry, ed. *Popular Culture in Seventeenth-Century England*. London: Croom Helm, 1985.

Reedy, Gerard. "Mystical Politics: The Imagery of Charles II's Coronation." In Korshin, *Studies in Change and Revolution*, pp. 19–42.

Reiter, Rayna R. ed. *Toward an Anthropology of Women*. New York: Monthly Review Press, 1975.

Robbins, Keith, ed. *Religion and Humanism: Papers Read at the Eighteenth Summer Meeting and the Nineteenth Winter Meeting of the Ecclesiastical History Society*. Studies in Church History 17. Oxford: Basil Blackwell, 1981.

Rogers, P.G. *The Dutch in the Medway*. Oxford: Oxford Univ. Press, 1970.

Rose, Mark. "The Author as Proprietor: *Donaldson v. Becket* and the Genealogy of Modern Authorship." *Representations* 23 (1988): 51–85.

Rose, Mary Beth, ed. *Women in the Middle Ages and the Renaissance: Literary and Historical Perspectives*. Syracuse: Syracuse Univ. Press, 1985.

Rostenberg, Leona. *The Minority Press and the English Crown: A Study in Repression, 1558–1625*. Nieuwkoop, Netherlands: B. De Graaf, 1971.

Rousseau, G.S. "The Pursuit of Homosexuality in the Eighteenth Century: 'Utterly Confused Category' and/or Rich Repository?" *Eighteenth-Century Life* 9 (1985): 132–68.

Rubin, Gayle. "The Traffic in Women: Notes on the 'Political Economy' of Sex." In Reiter, *Toward an Anthropology of Women*, pp. 157–210.

Saunders, David, and Ian Hunter. "Lessons from the 'Literary': How to Historicize Authorship." *Critical Inquiry* 17 (1991): 479–509.

Schofield, R.S. "The Measurement of Literacy in Pre-Industrial England." In Goody, *Literacy in Traditional Societies*, pp. 311–25.

Scott, Joan Wallach. *Gender and the Politics of History*. New York: Columbia Univ. Press, 1988.

Scott, Jonathan. *Algernon Sidney and the English Republic, 1623–1677*. Cambridge: Cambridge Univ. Press, 1988.

———. *Algernon Sidney and the Restoration Crisis, 1677–1683*. Cambridge: Cambridge Univ. Press, 1991.

Sedgwick, Eve Kosofsky. *Between Men: English Literature and Male Homosocial Desire*. New York: Columbia Univ. Press, 1985.

Sharp, Buchanan. "Popular Political Opinion in England, 1660–1685." *History of European Ideas* 10 (1989): 13–29.

Sharpe, J.A. " 'Last Dying Speeches': Religion, Ideology and Public Execution in Seventeenth-Century England." *Past and Present* 107 (1985): 144–67.

Sharpe, Kevin, and Steven N. Zwicker, eds. *Politics of Discourse: The Literature and History of Seventeenth-Century England*. Berkeley: Univ. of California Press, 1987.

Siebert, Frederick Seaton. *Freedom of the Press in England, 1476–1776: The Rise and Decline of Government Control*. Urbana: Univ. of Illinois Press, 1952.

Skone James, E.P., Sir John Mummery, J.E. Rayner James, and K.M. Garnett. *Copinger and Skone James on Copyright*. 13th ed. London: Sweet & Maxwell, 1991.

Slack, Paul, ed. *Rebellion, Popular Protest and the Social Order in Early Modern England*. Cambridge: Cambridge Univ. Press, 1984.

Smith, Hilda L. *Reason's Disciples: Seventeenth-Century English Feminists*. Urbana: Univ. of Illinois Press, 1982.

Smuts, R. Malcolm. *Court Culture and the Origins of a Royalist Tradition in Early Stuart England*. Philadelphia: Univ. of Pennsylvania Press, 1987.

Spender, Dale, ed. *Feminist Theorists*. New York: Random House, 1983.

Spufford, Margaret. *Small Books and Pleasant Histories: Popular Fiction and Its Readership in Seventeenth-Century England*. London: Methuen, 1981.

Staves, Susan. *Player's Scepters: Fictions of Authority in the Restoration*. Lincoln: Univ. of Nebraska Press, 1979.

Steneck, Nicholas H. "Greatrakes the Stroker: The Interpretations of Historians." *Isis* 73 (1982): 161–77.

Stone, Lawrence. "Literacy and Education in England, 1640–1900." *Past and Present* 42 (1969): 69–139.

Strong, Roy. *The Cult of Elizabeth: Elizabethan Portraiture and Pageantry*. London: Thames and Hudson, 1977.

Summers, Claude J., and Ted-Larry Pebworth, eds. *"The Muses Common-Weale": Poetry and Politics in the Seventeenth Century*. Columbia: Univ. of Missouri Press, 1988.

Sutherland, James. *The Restoration Newspaper and its Development*. Cambridge: Cambridge Univ. Press, 1986.

Tennenhouse, Leonard. *Power on Display: The Politics of Shakespeare's Genres*. London: Methuen, 1986.

Thomas, Donald. *A Long Time Burning: The History of Literary Censorship in England*. London: Routledge & Kegan Paul, 1969.

Thomas, Keith. "The Meaning of Literacy in Early Modern England." In Baumann, *The Written Word*, pp. 97–131.

———. *Religion and the Decline of Magic: Studies in Popular Beliefs in Sixteenth-and Seventeenth-Century England*. New York: Scribners, 1971.

Thomas, P.W. *Sir John Berkenhead, 1617–1679: A Royalist Career in Politics and Polemics*. Oxford: Clarendon Press, 1969.

Thrower, Norman J.W., ed. *Standing on the Shoulders of Giants: A Longer View of Newton and Halley*. Berkeley: Univ. of California Press, 1990.

Trumbach, Randolph. "Sodomitical Assaults, Gender Role, and Sexual Development in Eighteenth-Century London." *Journal of Homosexuality* 16 (1988): 407–429.

———. "Sodomitical Subcultures, Sodomitical Roles, and the Gender Revolution of the Eighteenth Century: The Recent Historiography." *Eighteenth-Century Life* 9 (1985): 109–21.

Turner, James Grantham. *One Flesh: Paradisal Marriage and Sexual Relations in the Age of Milton*. Oxford: Clarendon Press, 1987.

Underdown, David. *Revel, Riot, and Rebellion: Popular Politics and Culture in England, 1603–1660*. Oxford: Clarendon Press, 1985.

Vieth, David M. *Attribution in Restoration Poetry: A Study of Rochester's Poems of 1680*. New Haven: Yale Univ. Press, 1963.

Walker, J. "The Censorship of the Press during the Reign of Charles II." *History* 35 (1950): 219–38.

Watt, Tessa. *Cheap Print and Popular Piety, 1550–1640*. Cambridge: Cambridge Univ. Press, 1991.

Wear, Andrew. "Medical Practice in Late Seventeenth- and Early Eighteenth-Century England: Continuity and Union." In French and Wear, *The Medical Revolution of the Seventeenth Century*, pp. 294–320.

Weber, Harold. "Charles II, George Pines, and Mr. Dorimant: The Politics of Sexual Power in Restoration England." *Criticism* 32 (1990): 193–221.

Webster, Charles. *The Great Instauration: Science, Medicine and Reform, 1626–1660*. New York: Holmes and Meier, 1976.

Webster, Charles, ed. *Health, Medicine and Mortality in the Sixteenth Century*. Cambridge: Cambridge Univ. Press, 1979.

Whale, R.F., and Jeremy J. Phillips. *Whale on Copyright*. Oxford: ESC, 1983.

White, Hayden. *Metahistory: The Historical Imagination in Nineteenth-Century Europe*. Baltimore: Johns Hopkins Univ. Press, 1973.

Wilding, Michael. "Milton's *Areopagitica*: Liberty for the Sects." In Corns, *The Literature of Controversy*, pp. 7–38.

Williams, Franklin B., Jr. *Index of Dedications and Commendatory Verses in English Books before 1641*. London: Bibliographical Society, 1962.

———. "The Laudian Imprimatur." *Library*, 5th series, 15 (1960): 96–104.

Wood, Gordon. S. "Conspiracy and the Paranoid Style: Causality and Deceit in the Eighteenth Century." *William and Mary Quarterly* 39 (1982): 401–41.

Woodbridge, Linda. *Women and the English Renaissance: Literature and the Nature of Womankind, 1540–1620*. Chicago: Univ. of Chicago Press, 1984.

Woodmansee, Martha. "The Genius and the Copyright: Economic and Legal Conditions of the Emergence of the 'Author.'" *Eighteenth-Century Studies* 17 (1984): 425–48.

Worden, Blair. "The Commonwealth Kidney of Algernon Sidney." *Journal of British Studies* 24 (1985): 1–40.

Wrigley, E.A. "A Simple Model of London's Importance in Changing English Society and Economy 1650–1750." In Abrams and Wrigley, *Towns and Society*, pp. 215–43.

Yates, Frances A. *Astraea: The Imperial Theme in the Sixteenth Century*. London: Routledge & Kegan Paul, 1975.

Zwicker, Steven N. "Lines of Authority: Politics and Literary Culture in the Restoration." In Sharpe and Zwicker, *Politics of Discourse*, pp. 230–70.

———. *Politics and Language in Dryden's Poetry: The Arts of Disguise*. Princeton: Princeton Univ. Press, 1984.

Index